Educational Research and Schooling in Rural Europe

A volume in
Current Research in Rural and Regional Education
Michael Corbett and Karen Eppley, *Series Editors*

Educational Research and Schooling in Rural Europe

An Engagement With Changing Patterns of Education, Space, and Place

edited by

Cath Gristy
University of Plymouth

Linda Hargreaves
University of Cambridge

Silvie R. Kučerová
Jan Evangelista Purkyně University in Ústí nad Labem

INFORMATION AGE PUBLISHING, INC.
Charlotte, NC • www.infoagepub.com

Library of Congress Cataloging-in-Publication Data

A CIP record for this book is available from the Library of Congress
http://www.loc.gov

ISBN: 978-1-64802-163-3 (Paperback)
      978-1-64802-164-0 (Hardcover)
      978-1-64802-165-7 (E-Book)

Front cover artist: Heather Knight
Image: *Dartmoor on a windy day*

Copyright © 2020 Information Age Publishing Inc.

All rights reserved. No part of this publication may be reproduced, stored in a retrieval system, or transmitted, in any form or by any means, electronic, mechanical, photocopying, microfilming, recording or otherwise, without written permission from the publisher.

Printed in the United States of America

CONTENTS

Preface ix
Foreword: Rural Schools in an Iron Cage? Words for the Reader xi
List of Figures xxiii
List of Tables xxvii
Acknowledgments xxix

1 Introduction: European Rural Schools and Their
  Communities: "The Stone in Europe's Shoe?" 1
  Linda Hargreaves

PART I

CONCEPTUALIZING AND MAPPING THE EUROPEAN RURAL SPACE

2 Factors Influencing Elementary Education Systems in Selected
  European Countries 21
  Silvie R. Kučerová, Petr Meyer, and Petr Trahorsch

3 Rural Education in a Globalized World: The Cases of Norway
  and Finland 49
  Karl Jan Solstad and Gunilla Karlberg-Granlund

PART II
ENGAGING WITH CHANGING PATTERNS OF EDUCATION, SPACE, AND PLACE

4 Turbulent Times and Reshaped Rural School Network in Hungary 79
   Katalin Kovács

5 A Consideration of Czech Rural Schools From Different Scales: From Centrally Directed to Autonomous Educational Policies 103
   Silvie R. Kučerová and Kateřina Trnková

6 Rural Schools in Poland in the Period of Post-Socialist Decentralization and Demographic Decline 125
   Artur Bajerski

7 Rural Education in Serbia: Conflict Between Rhetoric and Reality 147
   Ana Pešikan, Slobodanka Antić, and Ivan Ivić

8 Development and Research of the Rural School Situation in Spain 175
   Begoña Vigo-Arrazola and Juana Soriano-Bozalongo

9 Small Rural Primary Schools in Austria: Places of Innovation? 199
   Andrea Raggl

10 Globalizing the Local and Localizing the Global: The Role of the ICT in Isolated Mountain and Island Schools in Italy 217
   Giuseppina Cannella

11 The Role of School Boards and School Leadership in Small Schools in the Netherlands 237
   Marjolein Deunk and Ralf Maslowski

12 Inclusive and Collaborative School Network Planning in Finland: A Critical Process for Rural Schools 259
   Sami Tantarimäki ancd Anni Törhönen

PART III
DEVELOPING AND DEEPENING THEORETICAL ENGAGEMENT

13 The Rural Primary School Head Teacher in the Field 285
    Carl Bagley and Sam Hillyard

14 Putting Lefebvre to Work on "The Rural" 303
    Cath Gristy

PART IV
EDUCATIONAL RESEARCH AND SCHOOLING IN RURAL EUROPE: CHANGE, INNOVATION, AND HOPE

15 Schools and Their Communities in Rural Europe:
    Patterns of Change 323
    Cath Gristy, Linda Hargreaves, and Silvie R. Kučerová

16 Educational Research in Rural Europe: State, Status,
    and the Road Ahead 339
    Linda Hargreaves, Cath Gristy, and Silvie R. Kučerová

    Appendix: The European Migration Crisis and the Status
    of Immigrant Children in Educational Systems 357
    Libor Jelen

    About the Editors 369
    About the Contributors 371
    Index 377

PREFACE

Europe has seen far-reaching political, economic, and societal changes in the past half century. These include the liberation of the Baltic and Eastern European states from Soviet communist domination, the recent "eurozone" economic crises, and the current and future migration of people fleeing war and poverty from the Middle East and Africa. Given the typical emphasis of national educational policies on urban rather than rural schools, authors in this book consider the extent of wider global influences and the degree to which these affect policy and livelihoods in their rural communities and schools.

The authors are from a range of social scientific disciplines including pedagogy, sociology, human geography, psychology, and ethnography and have come together through their involvement with the European Conference on Educational Research (ECER), Network 14. They set out to share knowledge of the contexts and challenges faced by rural schools and their communities across Europe. There is little published knowledge to draw on, so this unrivalled collection provides an important contribution to cognition and understanding of the changes taking place in rural places and spaces across Europe. It was evident that information about education in former Soviet bloc countries in Eastern Europe and their lived realities of rapid, peremptory school closure programs along with rural poverty was particularly scarce in international literature. The work included in this book of the authors from these countries—Czechia, Hungary, Poland, and Serbia—is juxtaposed with chapters about recent educational research, situated in rural contexts, in other European countries—Austria, England, Finland, Italy, the Netherlands, Norway, and Spain.

Individual authors have presented authentic accounts of education and schooling in their countries with details of relevant historical and political contexts. The chapters survey and synthesize the situations in 11 countries, with a focus on education, particularly schooling. They attend to definitions and conceptualizations of "rural" and "schools" in their national contexts and make use of educational and structural statistics in their consideration of wider social, economic, and geographical perspectives.

This book provides a unique collection of valuable work for postgraduate students, researchers, and academic scholars. It offers advances in the field of education by its collection of authors, who speak from particular national contexts whilst engaging with larger socio spatial issues. Although the stories in this book are from Europe, the issues raised and addressed are those of challenges faced contemporaneously by education and schooling in rural places across the world.

—**Cath Gristy**
Plymouth Institute of Education
University of Plymouth, England

FOREWORD

RURAL SCHOOLS IN AN IRON CAGE?

Words for the Reader

People in many European countries are facing threatening changes in local communities and schools, discovering that they gradually are becoming strangers in front of a school system partly created by themselves. The situation clearly needs a research-based reconsideration. The title of the present book is relevant for these changes and directs the spotlight towards educational research and schooling in rural Europe, tracing *changing patterns of education, place, and space* in Eastern and Western European countries.

The book has its grounding in EERA Network 14: *Communities, Families, and Schooling in Educational Research*, and the yearly conference of educational research in Europe, *European Conference on Educational Research* (ECER). This cross-disciplinary network of researchers has been supporting studies of research themes "outside the mainstream" of educational research over a period of 20 years. One of these themes is the relationship between school and community and place-based education. The activity of Network 14 has, since it began in 1995–1996, gradually extended internationally. In 2009, Network 14 researchers completed and published a review of research on communities and their schools in British and Nordic countries in a special issue of the *International Journal of Educational Research* edited by Kvalsund and Hargreaves (2009). Writing and editing articles of this kind as well as chapters in the present book, would have been impossible without a large portion of researchers' voluntary work and a joint interest in developing research to cover knowledge gaps in the field of rural education.

An important step further for researchers of our network has been to get an overview of relevant research in *Eastern European* countries, not least the countries formerly behind the Iron Curtain, following an interest to compare the national situations there with the situation in the West. The present book is a quality contribution to a new balance here. Children growing up in Eastern European countries experience the special effects of a demographic imbalance when their parents migrate to the West to have enough income to live on, leaving grandparents and children alone in many villages for long periods of the year. The principal value of the present book is the invitation to share knowledge of and compare the contextual situations and challenges for rural schools in selected Eastern and Western European countries.

CHILDREN GROW UP IN COMMUNITIES—NOT IN ABSTRACT SOCIETY

Doing comparative research on community, school, and family life implies the inescapable fact that children do not grow up in *abstract societies*, but rather in *real local communities*. This refers to the *everyday socio-materiality of rural living* and points to concrete disparities between urban and rural local communities. The place where a child grows up might thus make a difference and is highly relevant for research. In times when we experience heavy centralization of schools all over Europe, it seems to be a goal to raise its educational quality. Important conceptual dimensions sketching these qualities are crossing each other in this field of research: *local–global, rural–urban, place–space, security, and grounding-freedom*. These dimensions are often formulated *normatively*—what rural places and schools *ought to be*—in the direction of the right rather than of the left point of the dimension. However, the variation in rural is too broad for this way of thinking to be constructive. It is a quality of the present book to treat these concepts and dimensions *empirically and analytically* inviting *comparisons* by specifying the concrete contexts of how they are applied when judging the quality, conditions, and processes of learning in rural schools East and West in Europe.

URBAN NORMALITY—RURAL DEFICIENCY?

Network 14 has for years invited researchers to present and analyze educational research related to selected main themes to which the present book can be connected. One of these themes is to discuss the arguments and research based propositions on the quality of small rural schools and their role in local communities (e.g., the qualification of coming generations for living meaningful local lives in times of globalization). Transition of rural youth to the urban areas of the country has been going on for years—in too many cases, socially draining the local community by exporting the best and brightest recruits to urban areas and cities—or to use Corbett's (2007) term on this process of qualification, these young people are *learning to leave*.

A related theme exemplifying normativity has been the hegemonic and lasting perspective of rural schools as *deficient schools*—deficient versions of larger urban schools in formal as well in informal learning. Keeping rural schools and the long-lasting change of their content in the direction of urban values in classroom teaching and learning, represents a direct challenge to the role schools are supposed to have in local place-based identity building and local community survival. However, if these arguments of deficiency are valid, only cities are acceptable locations for schools. *Normality* in this sense has for years been—and still seems to be—*urban*. The present book challenges this *normative concept of deficient rural schooling* and is a valuable source for comparing Western and Eastern European countries in this respect. However, contemporary tendencies of rural schooling are formed by complementary forces as well.

CENTRALIZATION—DEPOPULATION OR THINNING OUT?

The larger cities in the world, Norway included, have over time experienced huge changes and expansion driven by technological development. This developmental process has led to increased urbanization contrary to earlier predictions. Since 1995, the six largest cities in Norway, for example, have increased their population by 32% compared with 8% for the rest of the country. Centralization and urbanization seem to be a highway to change—but compared with national goals of settlement in all parts of the country—in the wrong direction.

Norwegian patterns of centralization and out-migration have changed over time: from unsubstantiated fear of irreversible *depopulation* of rural and sparsely populated areas in the years before 1980, the understanding has changed to the more nuanced concept of *thinning out communities* describing effects of long lasting population decrease on social cooperation and services offered to the community members (Aasbrenn, 1989; Sørli, 2016)—schools included. A main challenge since 1990, for example in Norway, has been the increasingly *selective out-migration* to the cities by girls, not returning as they used to do to their native rural communities to bear their children and raise their own families. This change is characterized as the *increasing centralization of child settlement* (Sørli, 2016) and explanatory factors have suggested a normative urban direction implying better material living conditions and noneconomic factors related to culture, consumption, and quality of life in urban areas—in other words, preferences that might change in the short run if living costs have a sudden marked increase (Wessel & Barstad, 2016). The resultant decline in the number of children forces rural municipalities to consider closing small schools. However, the later tendency in Norway is that larger schools are being closed as well.

This normative wave of centralization in Norway is clearly *ideological*—demonstrated by the fact that the reorganization of schools into larger units is *without solid grounding in research based knowledge and* is happening *not only with small rural schools*. We have a parallel situation recently initiated by the Norwegian government in the service fields of the welfare-state such as: police, health services and hospitals, courts, municipalities and counties, as well as in the primary production of small scale fishery and farming. All these fields are in a process of structural change towards the creation of larger units and concomitant with the impoverishing of rural communities, threatening their meaning as sources of identity. Smaller units are forced into larger ones framed with new and different borders in each field. This cloud of reforms makes the present situation very unclear.

However, rurality is strongly associated with *small scale*. Small scale—an historically important characteristic of everyday life in Norway—is clearly weakened by this centralization process. Rurality in Norway includes smaller communities, villages, and sparsely populated areas along the entire Norwegian coast, the islands, the Western fjords and valleys as well as the valleys of the Eastern parts of the country and the mountain communities. This is contrary to the misleading proposition that in Norway a key locus of peripherality is spatialized as the "north" (cf. Corbett, 2015, p. 10). The present book sheds light on this variation of rurality—small scale, selective migration, thinning out processes, and multiple locus of spatiality—and invites the reader to judge whether this is the situation in other European countries as well.

SMALL RURAL SCHOOLS—DISTINCTIVE EDUCATIONAL POTENTIAL?

Analyzing schools, and the process and products of learning and teaching more precisely, however, opposes and refutes centralization arguments in several studies (e.g., Corbett, 2015; Kvalsund, 1995; Kvalsund & Hargreaves, 2009; Rogoff, Paradise, Aruz, Correa-Chavez, & Angelillo, 2003; Schafft & Jackson, 2010; Solstad, 1978). We observe that schooling increasingly means forcing children to stay in classrooms, having second hand experiences behind desks as basic qualifications for life. This adult controlled *socialization by deprivation* starts in kindergarten, continues in primary and secondary school, and represents an *entrapment* by adult control of play and learning processes within classroom walls and behind desks, counteracting development of *children's agency and independent judgement through firsthand experiences of meeting nature, production, and culture.*

Having this entrapment in mind, indicators tell us that the temperature on earth is close to reaching the level of irreversible change. In her book *The Sixth Extinction: An Unnatural History,* Elizabeth Kolbert (2014) tells us how and why man has changed life on earth more than any other species. We are enforcing other species into habitats of eradicating living places—the sixth and man-made extinction of species—the reflection of which would possibly lead us to a deeper understanding of our relationship to nature. Yet nothing is said about threatened food production, pollution of the oceans, and energy production. Haraway (2016) poses similar questions and asks how we can learn to live on and with an increasingly damaged planet. *Symbiogenesis* is her metaphor for the potential of coexistence and cooperation between species that is opening constructive possibilities here and now. *Human beings are part of nature* and not positioned outside it as *exploiting consumers* (Vetlesen, 2015).

Seen from this perspective small rural schools have a location and size small enough to be able to help children develop the concrete basic insight and understanding of sustainable ways of living on the planet earth. Place-based local schools might be a part of such a symbiogenesis, combined with participation in production and culture practicing *learning by community participation* rather than *learning by acquisition at classroom desks.* Rural schools contribute to local and regional culture and are carriers of culture (see, e.g., Edvardsen, 1981, 1983, 2004; Jordet, 2010; Kvalsund, 1995; Kvalsund & Hargreaves, 2009; Rogoff et al., 2003; Solstad, 1978). Birkeland (2014), as an example, has conducted a concrete analysis of what it would be possible to learn about climate redirection from one-sided Norwegian industrial communities.

In times of huge climate challenges a central quality of rural schools and education seems to be moved into the background at risk of being forgotten: *the educational potential of small rural schools working closely on nature, production, and culture.* Small rural schools are small enough to be mobile and close to local nature and thereby have an important potential to *meet local and global educational challenges of climate change.* Closing small rural schools is a form of madness considering this important educational potential of breaking out of the non-intended entrapment of institutionalized adult control through the educational regimes at school, threatening the development of children's agency and independent judgement and action, and their relationship to nature. Sociologically informed comparative studies of this phenomenon are needed. Small rural schools by their distinctive closeness to nature could *strongly legitimize their continued existence* inviting researchers to do comparative studies on rural schools from this perspective in Western as well as Eastern European countries.

PLACE BASED GROUNDING—OR URBAN EMANCIPATED MOBILITY AND ESTRANGEMENT?

Early in the 1970s a book by Schumacher (1973) was published with the title *Small is Beautiful: Economics as if People Mattered*. A main point of the book was that small scale decentralized economies and power structures could not only be effective but also ensure that the individuals were taken care of. Researching the rural *size and scale* is still important. Another aspect is that rurality is associated with *remoteness and isolation* as well. Remoteness, however, is bidirectional. Rural places have the potential to be more integrated into challenging nature; cities would be more integrated into mobile and socially crowded culture, living more on the run. Rural living is a choice of *social grounding in a place*, becoming *place competent*, as a primary quality of life compared with *urban freedom to move from place to place* within urban and global space. A paradox might be that rural people who learned to leave and now have an urban freedom to move between places might experience the stronger need to belong to a place—perhaps a romantic dream of their former growing up place relieving their present estrangement?

Places and communities have concrete contextual grounding and borders related to nature and history, and as places they have *inscribed different relations of discipline and power* with profound consequences for social learning (Foucault, 1984). Their *patterns of discipline and power* characterize their schools and local communities as well and must be described, analyzed, and compared in each case for villages, sparsely populated rural areas, or parts of cities—respecting variations of rurality. Chapters in the present book reflect this discussion and impart knowledge of the contexts and challenges faced by rural schools and their communities in former Soviet bloc countries; this gives the reader an opportunity for comparison with what is going on in Western countries on place grounding, discipline, and power in social learning.

URBANIZATION OR "RURBANIZATION"?

Giddens (1984, 1991) presents this kind of theoretical diagnosis of contemporary society. In the period of modernity, industrial society and its organized capitalism, a *sense of security* is ranked over *individual freedom*. The transition to postmodernity means that freedom expels and drives away security when we analyze changes as seen from the position of *the down and out, and the poor*. This would also be the case for marginalized communities and schools. It has become gradually more obvious that *globalization* with its effects of huge social and economic inequalities and poverty (Wilkinson & Pickett, 2009), *sustainable welfare-states* and *democracy* seem to be *incommensurable* and very difficult to realize simultaneously. The nation state with its regions and municipalities is consequently reintroduced in Western countries as *a necessary framing for the existence of (places, local communities, and schools within) a democratic welfare state* (Ghemavat, 2011; Rodrik, 2011). And, place matters, not least in educational processes (cf. Gruenewald & Smith, 2008; Kvalsund, 1995; Kvalsund & Hargreaves, 2009; Schafft & Jackson, 2010; Solstad, 1994; Solstad & Sigsworth, 2005).

Related to the perspective of the nation state alternative concepts might be introduced. Lichter and Brown (2011) speak of the *blurring* of traditional borders analyzing empirical patterns in a rural–urban balance. Themes in the discussion of blurring and change of balance and central questions about the local community are, for example: Backwater society or cultural treasury? Engine of migration or reception of immigration? Food reservoir or energy well? Arena of spectacular experiences and consumption or waste repository? These questions point to tendencies of urban living in rural communities as well as tendencies of rural ways of living in urban communities–a mix of *rurbanization*. These reflections frame a main theme of both EERA-Network 14 and the present book—place based education on a sensible scale positioned between the rural and the urban.

GLOBALIZATION OR "GLOCALIZATION"?

However, in Western European countries, propositions about profound changes related to globalization of society suggest a replacement of the concept of place with the concept of space. The concept of global space, compared with the concept of place, is more abstract and fluid and mirrors a conceptual shift from community and place to faceless space and *globalization* processes. In his book *Understanding Media*, from 1964, Marshall McLuhan states that "we have extended our central nervous system itself in a global embrace, abolishing both space and time as far as our planet is concerned" (p. 3). He expressed this expected globally extended social integration by the phrase "global village." The concept of the village might have the effect of reassuring the continuation of small-scale quality and social integration by using this term. Meyrowitz (1986) analyzed the impact of electronic media on social behavior and concluded that the situation best could be described with *No Sense of Place*—the title of his book. Giddens in his books *The Constitution of Society* (1984) and *Modernity and Self-identity* (1991) analyzes and presents a diagnosis of contemporary society pointing to the disembedding of places into global space and the development of expert systems (e.g., teacher teams in schools) to be trusted by parents and other stakeholders in a community. Urry (2000) speaks of globally non-bounded society and therefore a need for a *sociology beyond society*. The expectation is to disconnect people from place and nation state also in questions of schooling. Bourdieu and Wacquant (2001) present oppositional notes on globalization and New Liberal Speak in what they describe as "the new planetary vulgate" in sociology: *The state* is associated with a series of *negative* qualities (constrained, closed, rigid, immobile, fossilized, past and outdated, stasis, group holism and collectivism, uniformity, and autocratic "totalitarian"). *The market* is on the other hand associated with a series of *positive* qualities (freedom, open, flexible, dynamic, self-transforming, future, novelty, growth, individual, individualism, diversity, authenticity, and democratic). Bourdieu and Wacquant describe this new conceptual flow as strange Newspeak, sprung out of nowhere, but now being on everyone's lips. McGrew (1996) discusses these challenges of modernity and the sociological concept of society answering the question, *A global society?* A message seems to be that the nation state, counties, and communities are under illegitimate conceptual deconstruction from the perspective of capitalist globalization rather than suggesting new concepts of sociology.

However, heavy criticism is formulated by Bauman (1998) pointing to the new liberalist politics unavoidably producing unworthy differences between citizens experienced as losing their sense of security. Bauman criticizes the Polish communist regime's persecution of deviants based on a totalitarian logic of unity, plan, and control (the consequence of which was that he lost his position as professor of sociology). His analysis of changes of society refers to the transition from "modernity" to "postmodernity." The core of the gospel of *postmodernity*, which might be expressed with the signal phrase "anything goes," is not accepted by Bauman; equity for the weaker is a more central value. How globalization processes produce winners and losers is therefore a central proposition and argument in Bauman's books *Postmodernity and Its Discontents* (1997) and *Globalization: The Human Consequences* (1998). Globalization is also associated with what is described as trends of a transition from solid modernity (industrial production, governmental and political management and control, closed groups, discipline, ideas of equality) to structurally grounded fluid modernity (values under continuous discussion, individual freedom, competition, consumption and industrial consumerism—also in friendships, cohabitation, and personal relations—all aspects reinforced by increasing mobility from places not satisfying the person's interests). Bauman (2001), in his book *Seeking Safety in an Unsecure World*, analyzes fluid modernity as decomposing social belonging and security. This difference is also reflected in the content of the concepts of place and space. Bauman, however, represents a *universalism* where nations, local communities, and persons cooperate in universal dependence—what might be described as *glocalization*—a balanced process of individual agency and collective structures quite unlike what happens in competitive economic or capitalist globalization.

BREAKING OUT OF AN IRON CAGE?

Glocalization and rurbanization as potential contextual qualities of place-based education in small rural schools, are still challenged in Western countries—by transnational organizations such as Organisation for Economic Co-operation and Development (OECD). Their Programme for International Student Assessment (PISA) system is critically discussed by Meyer and Benavot (2013) in the book *PISA, Power, and Policy: The Emergence of Global Educational Governance*. Norway is an example here. Without discussion of the founding historical, cultural, and ideological presumptions on which the Norwegian educational system is built, PISA-testing and teaching selected theoretical school subjects now have priority in curriculum planning and daily practice in rural schools, communities, and municipalities. Teaching is practiced as if these measures are covering the content of the national and local curriculum plans—a quality they do not have. Within this educational regime of a place-based content of rural schooling, teachers as knowledgeable agents, are challenged by *standardized teaching programs commercially developed* and based on randomized control trials (RCT) logic. Biased globalized abstract curriculum content contributes substantially to the weakening of place-grounded identity and is in many cases a push factor for out-migration from rural local communities and regions. The emerging centralization and indicators of *global educational governance* illustrate the risk of *system world* power (government, bureaucrats, national, and international capitalism) invading local and regional *life worlds*, draining the meaning of life from local schools and communities. Rural schools are transformed into urban instrumental institutions. A relevant metaphor might be Weber's (1930) Iron Cage: people discovering that they are becoming *strangers in front of a system created by themselves*. People, by rational processes, over time have created a system or "cage" in which they are locked up, losing the meaning of local community life and wider social interaction; such loss of meaning and sense of coherence is what Weber describes as the "iron cage of rationality." In many cases, research is necessary to spot its contours.

Both Eastern and Western European contributions are collected in this book, foregrounding those formerly behind the Iron Curtain. They include Czechia, Hungary, Poland, and Serbia. Little has been published in English on the educational reality of rural schools and communities from these countries. These "new" voices are contrasted and complemented by Western European perspectives from The Netherlands, Spain, Italy, Austria, Finland, Norway, and England. The authors of the present book include several eminent scholars in the field, representing a range of social scientific disciplines. This multidisciplinary approach is an additional strength and quality of the present book helping a broader range of readers to compare and better understand the rural population group struggle to handle "rurbanized" and "glocalized" meaningful lives. The research presented in this book will hopefully help readers escaping the urban educational iron cages of rural education, global educational governance included.

—Rune Kvalsund
Volda University College, Norway

REFERENCES

Aasbrenn, K. (1989). Uttynningssamfunnet: Det demografiske uttynnede— men ikke avfolkede utkantsamfunn [The thinning out society: Demographically thinned out, but not depopulated communities in the periphery]. *Tidsskrift for samfunnsforsking,* (5–6), 509–519.
Bauman, Z. (1997). *Postmodernity and its discontents.* London, England: Polity Press.
Bauman, Z. (1998). *Globalization: The human consequences.* New York, NY: Columbia University Press.
Bauman, Z. (2001). *Seeking safety in an unsecure world.* Cambridge, England: Polity Press.
Birkeland, I. (2014). *Kulturelle hjønesteiner. Hva kan vi lære av ensidige industristeder for klima-omstilling* [Cultural cornerstones: What can we learn about climate redirection from one-sided industrial communities]? Oslo, Norway: Cappelen Damm.
Bourdieu, P., & Wacquant, L. (2001, January/February). Neoliberal newspeak: Notes on the new planetary vulgate. *Radical Philsophy, 105*(2–5).
Corbett, M. (2007). *Learning to leave: The irony of schooling in coastal community.* Halifax, Canada: Fernwood.
Corbett, M. (2015). Rural education: Some sociological provocations for the 'field'. *Australian & International Journal of Rural Education, 25*(3), 9–25.
Edvardsen, E. (1981). Skolen som parentes i samfunnet [School as a parent in the community]. *Norsk Pedagogisk Tidsskrift,* (7), 283–291.
Edvardsen, E. (1983). Kateteret og det anonyme levebrød [The position of teacher's desk and the anonymous livelihood]. In K. Skagen, & T. Tiller (Eds.), *Perspektiv på lærerarbeid* [Teacher work in perspective] (pp. 104–119). Oslo, Norway: Aschehoug.
Edvardsen, E. (2004). *Samfunnsaktiv skole. En skole rik på handling* [Socially active school: A school rich in action]. Tromsø, Norway: Oplandske Bokforlag.
Foucault, M. (1984). Space, knowledge and power. In P. Rabinov (Ed.), *The Foucault reader* (pp. 239–256). Harmondsworth, England: Penguin.
Giddens, A. (1984). *The constitution of society.* London, England: SAGE.
Giddens, A. (1991). *Modernity and self-identity: Self and society in the late modern age.* London, England: Stanford University Press.
Ghemawat, P. (2011). *World 3.0 global prosperity and how to achieve it.* New York, NY: Harvard Business Review Press.
Gruenewald, D. A., & Smith, G. A. (Eds.). (2008). *Place-based education in the global age: Local diversity.* New York, NY: Routledge.

Haraway, D. (2016). *Staying with the trouble*. Durham, NC: Duke University Press.
Jordet, A. N. (2010). *Klasserommet utenfor. Tilpasset opplæring i et utvidet læringsrom* [The outdoor classroom: Adapted training in an extended room of learning]. Oslo, Norway: Cappelen Akademisk.
Kolbert, E. (2014). *The sixth extinction: An unnatural history*. New York, NY: Henry Holt and Company.
Kvalsund, R. (1995). *Elevrelasjonar og uformell læring. Samanliknande kasusstudiar avfådelte og fulldelte bygdeskular* [Pupil relations and informal learning: Comparative case studies of multi-grade and single-grade schools]. (Doctoral dissertation). University of Trondheim, Trondheim, Norway.
Kvalsund, R., & Hargreaves, L. (Guest Eds.). (2009). Reviews of research on rural schools and their communities in British and Nordic countries. *International review of Educational Research, 48*(2), 80–88.
Lichter, D. T., & Brown, D. L. (2011). Rural America in an urban society: Changing special and social boundaries. *Annual Review of Sociology, 37*(1), 565–592.
McGrew, A. (1996). A global society? In S. Hall, D. Held, D. Hubert, & K. Thompson (Eds.), *Modernity: An introduction to modern societies* (pp. 436–465). Oxford, England: Blackwell.
McLuhan, M. (1964). *Understanding media: The extensions of man*. New York, NY: McGraw-Hill.
Meyer, H. D., & Benavot, A. (Eds.). (2013). *PISA, Power and Policy: The emergence of global educational governance*. Oxford, England: Symposium Books.
Meyrowitz, J. (1986). *No sense of place: The impact of the electronic media on social behavior*. New York, NY: Oxford University Press.
Rodrik, D. (2011). *The globalisation paradox*. London, England: W. W. Norton.
Rogoff, B., Paradise, R., Aruz, R. M., Correa-Chavez, M., & Angelillo, C. (2003). First hand learning through intent participation. *Annual Review of Psychology, 54*, 175–203.
Schafft, K. A., & Jackson, A. Y. (Eds.). (2010). *Rural education for the twenty-first century: Identity, place and community in a globalizing world*. University Park: Pennsylvania State University Press.
Schumacher, E. F. (1973). *Small is beautiful: Economics as if people mattered*. London, England: Harper & Row.
Solstad, K. J. (1978). *Riksskole i utkantstrøk* [National school in peripheral and sparsely populated areas]. Oslo, Norway: Universitetsforlaget.
Solstad, K. J. (1994). *Equity at risk. Schooling and change in Norway* (Doctoral thesis). Oslo, Norway: University of Oslo.
Solstad, K. J., & Sigsworth, A. (2005). *Small rural schools: A small inquiry*. Report 64. Nesna, Norway: Nesna University College.
Sørli, K. (2016). Bosetting, flytting og regional utvikling [Settling down, migration and regional development]. In I. Frønes, & L. Kjølsrød (Eds.), *Det norske samfunnet* [The Norwegian Society] (Vol. 1; 7th ed., pp. 36–60). Oslo, Norway: Gyldendal akademisk.
Urry, J. (2000). *Sociology beyond societies*. London, England: Routledge.
Vetlesen, A. J. (2015). *The denial of nature: Environmental philosophy in the era of global capitalism*. London, England: Routledge.

Weber, M. (1930). *The protestant ethic and the spirit of capitalism.* London, England: Allen & Unwin.
Wessel, T., & Barstad, A. (2016). Urbanisering go urbanisme [Urbanisation and urbanism]. In I. Frønes & L. Kjølsrød (Eds.), *Det norske samfunnet* [The Norwegian Society] (Vol. 1; pp. 61–86). Oslo, Norway: Gyldendal akademisk.
Wilkinson, R., & Pickett, K. (2009). *The spirit level: Why equality is better for everyone.* Harmondsworth, England: Penguin.

LIST OF FIGURES

Figure 1.1	To show the European countries whose rural educational conditions are represented in this book.	2
Figure 2.1	Structure of schools according to categories of number of pupils at schools, average of years 2012–2016.	30
Figure 2.2	Percentage proportion of types of elementary schools operators in four selected countries in the 2010s.	34
Figure 2.3	Population density on the LAU2 level in four selected countries as of 2011.	35
Figure 2.4	Population estimates for four selected countries as of July 1, 2015	37
Figure 2.5	Road network density on LAU2 level in four selected countries as of 2016	40
Figure 2.6	Development types of numbers of elementary schools in selected countries	42
Figure 3.1	Number of school closures in 110 Norwegian SPA-municipalities from 1980–2015 and expected closures from 2016–2020	57
Figure 3.2	School closures, by year of closure, and number of pupils in the year before closure	58
Figure 3.3	Percentage of municipalities reporting too few pupils, school quality, municipal economy, and parents' wish to be *very important* for the closure of each school by periods: 2005 or earlier, 2006 or later (the other alternatives were *of no importance* and *somewhat important*)	59

List of Figures

Figure 3.4	(a) Local resistance to school closures; (b) degree of delays in decision-making	60
Figure 3.5	The intersection of pedagogy, structure, and culture in school.	70
Figure 4.1	Decrease of the average number of students per rural school site by NUTS-2 regions 2010/2001 (%)	89
Figure 4.2	The average number of students per rural school site by NUTS-2 regions in 2010 ($N = 1,199$)	90
Figure 4.3	Changing importance of alternative school maintenance by churches and NGOs in rural and urban contexts 2010–2015	92
Figure 4.4	Attendance of Roma students of segregated neighborhoods and non-Roma students of the vicinity in basic and secondary education in 2011	97
Figure 4.5	Rate of socially disadvantaged students in rural and urban schools in 2005–2015	99
Figure 5.1	Typology of municipalities according to presence of elementary schools, Czechia, 1961	109
Figure 5.2	Typology of municipalities according to presence of elementary schools, Czechia, 2004	109
Figure 5.3	Territory belonging to incomplete elementary schools (IES) in Turnov region in 1961	112
Figure 5.4	Incomplete elementary school (IES) districts in Turnov region in 2014	113
Figure 5.5	Numbers and directions of pupils commuting daily to elementary schools over the borders of their municipalities in Turnov region in 2001	114
Figure 6.1	Number of primary schools in Poland in the years 1998–2012	129
Figure 6.2	Number of closures of primary schools in Poland in the years 1990–2012	129
Figure 6.3	Intensity of school closure in rural areas of Poland in the years 2003–2008	130
Figure 6.4	Intensity of school closure in rural areas of Poland in the years 2008–2013	130
Figure 6.5	Distribution of rural primary schools with combined classes in Poland in 2012	138
Figure 6.6	Share of primary schools with combined classes (%) in Poland in total number of rural schools in Poland's municipalities in 2012	138
Figure 7.1	Structure of the education system of Serbia.	157

Figure 12.1	Changes to the Finnish school network from 2001(a) to 2013(b)	262
Figure 12.2	Typical phases in the school discussion and the school network planning process. It is described here as a circle because of its (partly self-fulfilling) repetitiveness	267
Figure 12.3	"Closure spikes" of the comprehensive schools between years 2001–2014	271
Figure 12.4	The proportion of municipalities of the Provinces of Finland that have/have not had school network discussions during the years 2013–2017	274
Figure 12.6	Matters considered important to future school network planning. The most important ones are shown in the upper corner with the less important ones in the lower corner	276
Figure 12.7	A suggestion for the collaborative school network planning model with its central steps and stages	277
Figure A.1	Foreign born population in the EU member states in 2015	359
Figure A.2	First-time asylum applicants according to citizenship in 2015	360
Figure A.3	MIPEX Index: The migrant integration policy index (2015)	364

LIST OF TABLES

Table 1.1	How Do Urban Schools in European OECD or Partner Countries Differ From Non-Urban Schools?	6
Table 2.1	Selected Analyzed Factors Underlying Spatial Organization of Elementary Education	26
Table 2.2	Selected Characteristics of Organization of Compulsory Education Levels	28
Table 2.3	Average Number of Pupils in a Class as of 2013	31
Table 2.4	Selected Indicators for Observed European Countries as of 2011	33
Table 3.1	Norway and Finland Compared (Selected Geographical, Demographical, and Administrative Characteristics)	51
Table 3.2	Selected Characteristics of Globalization and Their Possible Consequences for Rural Life	53
Table 4.1	Directions of Change in Rural School Network 2001–2015 (%)	88
Table 4.2	Changes of Rural School Maintenance 2001–2015	91
Table 4.3	Changing Numbers of Schools Between 2005–2015 Where Ethnic Segregation is Likely to be at an Advanced Stage	98
Table 6.1	Size Structure of Rural Schools in Poland in 2012	132
Table 6.2	Size Structure of Rural Schools With Combined Classes Teaching Systems in 2012	137

Table 7.1	The Economic Status of Children and Youth in Rural Areas of Serbia	155
Table 7.2	Pre-School Education Coverage of Children in Serbia	156
Table 8.1	Percentage of Primary Schools Based on the Number of Pupils in the 2016–2017 School Year	178
Table 8.2	Percentage Distribution of Primary Schools Based on the Number of Classrooms in the Academic Year 2016–2017	179
Table 8.3	Forecast for the 2016–2017 Academic Year	179
Table 8.4	Milestones and Arguments in the Development Rural School	185
Table 9.1	Case Studies of Small Rural Schools With a Montessori Approach	203
Table 12.1	Waves of School Closure From 1960s to 2000s	261
Table 12.2	Prompt Phrases Used in the Survey	270
Table 12.3	The Change in the Size of the Schools in Finland Between 2005–2016 (Statistics Finland 2017)	272
Table 12.4	Members of the School Network Planning Teams Named at Least Three Times in the Reports 2013–2017	275
Table 15.1	Definitions and Percentage of All Schools Considered "Small" or "Very Small" (Continued)	
Table 15.1	Definitions and Percentage of All Schools Considered "Small" or "Very Small"	332
Table 16.1	Research Designs Set at One Point in Time but Several Points in Space	342
Table 16.2	Research Designs Focused on One Point in Space but Several Points in Time	343
Table 16.3	Research Designs Using Several Points in Time and Several Points in Space	343
Table A.1	Number of First Time Asylum Applicants	363

ACKNOWLEDGMENTS

The editors, Cath Gristy, Linda Hargreaves and Silvie Rita Kučerová would like to thank:

- The researchers who have contributed the chapters that constitute this book;
- All the communities, families and schools that have contributed to the research included here;
- EERA for its annual European Conferences on Educational Research (ECER) that have enabled researchers from all over Europe to meet and share their research in Network 14 (Communities, Families and Schooling in Educational Research), and for Network 14 funding to support an invited seminar at Charles University in Prague, and the academic writing of authors for whom English is a second language;
- Our series editors, Mike Corbett and Karen Eppley, and the external reviewers for constructive advice and encouragement at various stages of writing;
- University technical staff for advice and support;
- Our own families for patience, listening (or appearing to) and all-round care;
- George, Lisa and the team at IAP for their support;
- And most importantly, Liz Sprowson-Lea for linguistic support, editing, proof-reading, and manuscript collation, without whom the book would not yet have appeared in print.

CHAPTER 1

INTRODUCTION: EUROPEAN RURAL SCHOOLS AND THEIR COMMUNITIES

"The Stone in Europe's Shoe?"

Linda Hargreaves
University of Cambridge

This book focuses on educational provision in rural schools and their communities in Europe, and the effects, real or suspected, of national, global, and local forces, upon it. It includes the writing of educational researchers from four former socialist European countries, whose research rarely appears in English. It has been made possible by the improved flow of information around the globe, and the opportunities presented by the European Educational Research Association's (EERA) annual European Conference on Educational Research (ECER). Locations including Ljubliana, Istanbul, Budapest, and Lisbon have made the conference accessible and affordable for European researchers from low domestic product (GDP) countries. Unusually, too, the book focuses largely on elementary/primary schools; the

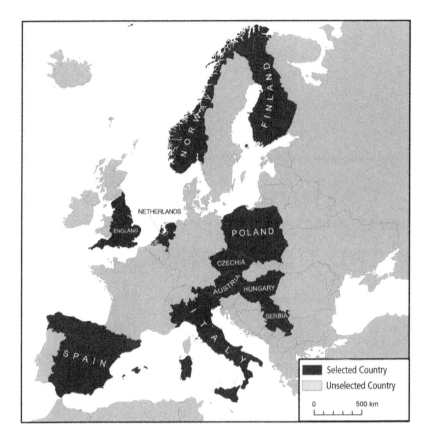

Figure 1.1 To show the European countries whose rural educational conditions are represented in this book.

concentration on primary schooling allows exploration of aspects of educational quality other than performance statistics (see Figure 1.1).

Our aim is to present authoritative European rural research voices to show the changing patterns of education in the ever-changing contexts of space and place: to make visible the interplay between global and local forces and their influence on rural educational provision in Europe.

OBJECTIVES, PRINCIPLES, AND QUESTIONS

This book has four main objectives:

1. to describe the contexts and challenges faced by rural schools and their communities in Europe;

2. to include recent research in European rural schools that can contribute to the processes of comparing, contrasting, and discussing these national situations;
3. to present authentic accounts of national, historical, and political contexts by authors who are citizens of the nation states that they describe;
4. to be open to a variety of social science disciplines concerned with rural issues and educational provision, including sociology, psychology, philosophy, politics, and geography.

The book is not concerned with international achievement tables, nor comparing the academic performance of the nations represented here. Some authors present national statistics comparing urban and rural performance figures, but this is not our main focus as there remain more fundamental issues concerning small and rural schools: such as their survival.

This opening chapter presents the objectives of the book, and introduces key features of its conceptual and literature-based landscapes such as the question of why rural matters in Europe and recent calls for improvements in the quality of rural educational research. We also begin an exploration of complex key concepts such as "rural" and "globalization." More detailed engagements with some of these matters and other themes that emerge from the chapters will be found in Chapters 15 and 16. This introductory chapter closes with an introduction to each of the book chapters.

The contributing authors were asked to consider the following questions, as a guide but not a template, and respond to them with respect to their national contexts, and their own research.

In your country:
- What are the contexts of rural education, and how significant are they?
- How is rural defined, if at all?
- What have been the principal drivers of educational change in rural areas, and what impact have these had on children, families, and communities?
- What is the nature and status of research on rural educational provision?

We have not proposed an *a priori* set of themes and issues of rural schools determined from other literatures, such as strategies for centralization/decentralization, effects of economic change, rural depopulation, or rural–urban achievement differences. We argue that this would constrain authors' freedom to identify their national issues. Rather, we have looked for themes to emerge and these are discussed in Chapters 15 and 16.

Given Europe's glorious linguistic diversity (see European Commission/EACEA/Eurydice, 2019), we have tried to retain the flavor or "sound" of each author's first language but not, we hope, at the expense of readability.

The reader will note variation in the terminology used across different countries and even within individual countries. For example, the words used to identify schools and classrooms where children of different ages are taught together are referred to in many different ways; the reader will find the terms used here include pluriclasse, multi-age, mixed age, incomplete, and multigrade. Again, rather than impose a common set of terms, we respect each author's and each country's own terminology to preempt the transfer of assumptions associated with a concept in one country being associated with a similar, but different concept in another.

The book's subtitle refers to changing patterns of education, space, and place. It recognizes the ways the past 40 years have seen schools and their communities adapting, spontaneously or obligatorily, to major political, economic, and demographic shifts. The research reported here exposes the rural consequences of national and local responses to these changes. We turn now to some key features in rural schools' conceptual and literature landscapes.

WHY DOES RURAL EDUCATIONAL PROVISION IN EUROPE MATTER?

Rural educational provision in Europe matters because, in 2015, 92% of the European Union (EU 28) land cover was wetland, woodland, shrubland, grassland, and cropland; (Eurostat 2020, April) and home to 143,800,000 people: 28% of the EU 28's 513.5 million population (Eurostat, 2020, April). Early school leaving rates among 20–24 year-olds in rural areas were 12.2% of the total EU population, compared with 9.8% in cities. 17.9% of rural 18–24 year-olds were not in employment, education, or training; compared with 14.2% in cities. Only 27.9% of rural 30–34 year olds achieved tertiary level education (International Standard Classification of Education [ISCED] 2011 levels 5–8) compared with 48.1% in cities (Eurostat, 2018, June). Despite national variations, these educational gaps between rural and city populations are consistent and widening. These statistics show why education in rural Europe matters.

In the United States, "Why rural matters" (WRM) is the title of a biennial publication of the U.S. Rural School and Community Trust, first published in 1999–2000. In the eighth edition of "Why rural matters 2015–2016" (Showalter, Klein, Johnson, & Hartman, 2017) the authors address aspects of rural education through five "gauges" including the *importance* (% rural schools, % small rural school districts, % rural students, etc.), the *diversity, educational policy, educational outcomes*, and, in 2013–2014, *socioeconomic challenges* in each state. These gauges facilitate comparison over time, and within and between states. Through this book, we ask whether a similar set of indicators could improve the visibility of rural contexts in Europe.

Status of the "Urban Advantage"

Education in rural areas has for decades been almost invisible: unseen, underfunded, under-researched, underestimated, and overgeneralized: an irritant for governments—"the stone in Europe's shoe," according to Ana Pešikan. The Organization for Economic Cooperation and Development's (OECD, 2013) rural–urban analysis of the 2009 Program for International Students Assessment (PISA) reading scores identified a so-called urban advantage:

> On average across OECD countries, students who attend schools in cities of more than 100,000 people perform better in PISA than students who attend schools in villages, rural areas, or towns with up to 100,000 inhabitants. This difference in performance translates to about 20 PISA score points—the equivalent of half-a-year of schooling. (OECD, 2013, p. 1)

The OECD attributed this rural–urban difference to the higher socioeconomic status of children living in large cities, and urban schools being typically "larger, [with] greater responsibility for resource allocation... less likely to experience staff shortages, more likely to have [more] qualified teachers, and... higher student–teacher ratios than schools in rural areas and towns" (OECD, 2013, p. 2).

On closer examination of the PISA data, Table 1.1, shows the significant urban–rural differences in teacher perceptions in the PISA 2009 questionnaire (OECD, 2013, p. 3). In the European countries included here, there is no significant difference in 70% of the cells, which suggests the so-called urban advantage arises beyond Europe. In fact, in his commentary on this feature of the PISA data, Schleicher (2013) gives an example from rural China, rather than any location in Europe, to illustrate an education system that valorizes "urban" schools. A new town school (Qiao Tou Lian He, near Tengchong, 3,000 km southwest of Shanghai) houses 29 teachers and 714 children, most of whom are weekly boarders, and replaced four isolated mountain schools to provide access to "high quality education." Schleicher extols the children's independence, resilience, and enthusiasm for their new school, but notes that they have several hours' walk to reach their homes. Zhang Fang (2013) also describes children "struggling against the high mountain in their four-hour-long walks to a township school after their own four village schools were shut down permanently" (p. 2) in rural Sichuan, where the proportion of rural schools has fallen from 30% to 10% in 10 years. Whilst the Chinese authorities have subsequently reopened

TABLE 1.1 How Do Urban Schools in European OECD or Partner Countries Differ From Non-Urban Schools?

	Austria	Czechia	Finland	Hungary	Italy	Netherlands	Norway	Poland	Serbia	Spain	UK
Socio-economic status		X	X	X	X		X	X	X	X	
Disciplinary climate											
School size	X	X	X		X		X	X	X	X	
Responsibility for curriculum and assessment						X					
Responsibility for resource allocation			X		X					X	
Material educational resources			X	X			X				
Teacher shortage							–				
Extra-curricular activities									X		
Student–teacher ratio					X				–	X	–
Proportion of qualified teachers											
Student–teacher relations											X

Note: X/− signs indicate a positive/negative and statistically significant difference between urban and non-urban schools. No sign indicates that differences between urban and non-urban schools are not statistically significant.

Source: Extracted from OECD, 2013, p. 3. (The source of the full table is given as OECD 2009 database.)

some village learning centres for the younger children, the human costs of "high quality education" must be taken into account.

Organization for Economic Cooperation and Development's argument for an urban advantage undermines the achievements of rural children in Europe including Belgium, Denmark, Germany, and the United Kingdom who performed as well or better than their urban counterparts. It also focuses on school characteristics but omits the effects of, say, creating amalgamated schools on children's lives. School closures and amalgamations into larger, theoretically more "efficient" units can be seen as rural representations of "globalization." The urban advantage argument could also be seen to legitimize the imposition of urban models on rural education, rather than stimulating rural investment.

Instead of focusing on urban advantage, we argue for focusing on the examples of *rural advantage* which could justify investment to ensure adequate provision of qualified teachers, better material resources, and teacher education for smaller, multiage classes (Galton & Patrick, 1990; Harfitt, 2013; OECD, 2013).

Defining Rural

The search for a standard definition of rural remains a challenging, and possibly futile, task. Most chapters here offer either a different culturally meaningful definition, though often framed in statistical or geospatial terms. Sometimes, however, the national definitions are distinctly unsatisfactory, determined largely in terms of what is not classified as urban: In other words, the rural has no identity of its own—implying that it does *not* matter. Chapter 2 provides a more detailed discussion of the definition of rural and there is an extended engagement with the issue in Chapter 15. In this brief introduction we present two formal, official European definitions: the European Union's Eurostat definition and the OECD definition, the latter being the most widely used in the chapters to follow.

The European Union's (EU) on-line glossary (Eurostat, 2018, December 6) provides the following series of linked definitions. A "rural area" is one "where more than 50% of its population lives in rural grid cells, as used in the degree of urbanisation." Rural grid cells are "grid cells that are not identified as urban centres or urban clusters." An urban centre is "a cluster of contiguous grid cells of 1 km^2 (excluding diagonals) with a population density of at least 1,500 inhabitants per km^2 and collectively a minimum population of 50,000 inhabitants after gap-filling. "Degree of urbanisation" classifies local administrative units (LAUs) as cities, towns and suburbs, and rural areas based on a combination of geographical contiguity and population density, measured by minimum population thresholds applied to 1 km^2

population grid cells: each LAU belongs exclusively to one of these three classes.' Cities are defined as 'densely populated areas; towns and suburbs as intermediate density areas; and rural areas as thinly populated areas. The link to further information on 'degree of urbanisation' reveals a map of the degree of urbanisation of European LAUs (e.g., communes, municipalities) (Eurostat, 2018). It is overwhelmingly green, the colour signifying "rural areas." Paradoxically, then, although "rural areas" are defined by their absence from urban areas, they are essentially the color of Europe.

Another classification of territory referred to by authors and countries in this book is that of the OECD (2011). This has three descriptors:

- predominantly urban (PU), if the share of population living in rural local units is below 15%;
- intermediate (IN), if the share of population living in rural local units is between 15% and 50%; and
- predominantly rural (PR), if the share of population living in rural local units is higher than 50%.

The descriptors for PR are adjusted in 3 steps:

1. A territory is declared as rural if the population density is below 150 inhabitants per square kilometre.
2. A territory is "predominantly rural" if the share of population living in rural local units is higher than 50%.
3. A region classified as predominantly rural by Steps 1 and 2 becomes "intermediate" if it contains an urban centre of more than 200,000 inhabitants representing at least 25% of the regional population.

The question must be raised as to whether the idea of a European education area, mentioned above and being developed by the European Commission (2017) with inclusion and social mobility at its heart will make rural Europe visible. Discussion of the European "rurals" visible or not, is provided by Kučerová, Meyer, and Trahorsch in Chapter 2, and revisited in Chapter 15.

"Globalization"

Although globalization is not the principal focus of this book, its influence can be detected frequently in its contents. Kvalsund's Foreword lays out the territorial ground work in this regard. Held, McGrew, Goldblatt, and Perraton (1999), who see the vigorous resurrection of globalization in controversies concerning "the evidence for, as well as the explanatory significance of, contemporary globalisation" discuss globalization's existence, rise, and putative demise colorfully (p. 1). They argue

> Globalization denotes the intensification of world-wide social relations such that distant events acquire very localized impacts and vice versa. It involves a rescaling of social relations from the economic sphere to the security sphere, beyond the national, to the transnational, transcontinental and transworld. (p. 1)

Globalization's relevance here, and particularly the localized impacts of distant events, concerns its influence and implications for education in rural contexts. Notions of the establishment of a policy-convergent "European Educational Space" (Novoa, 2002) can be tested through the book's chapters. Ozga (2012), for example, suggests that globalization in the European context, where "enlightenment ideas of education are being displaced by utilitarian concepts of learning, [is] a consequence of contemporary problems in governing across the European Union" (p. 440).

Scholte's (2008) discussion of the meaning of globalization rejects terms such as universalism, internationalization, liberalization and Westernization as offering no new insights, but reminds us that "relations between people always occur somewhere; in a place, a location, a domain, a site. No description of social circumstance is without a spatial component" (p. 1479). This is a particularly useful and important contribution in the rural context because, as Tikly (2001) observed, rural locations are apt to be overlooked in globalization research, apparently dispensable in the quest for economic growth. In addition to Kvalsund in his Foreword to this book, Solstad and Karlberg-Granlund, in Chapter 3 also critique the rhetoric of globalization, but go on to derive a set of potential influences on rural educational provision, and present evidence of policy-divergence between Finland and Norway.

Tikly (2001, p. 156) draws attention to another feature of contemporary globalization, that of "a massive increase in migrations of populations." Given worldwide awareness of the huge migrations into Europe we expected reference to it from the contributing authors. To our surprise, the migrant movement into Europe is rarely mentioned, apart from by the authors of the chapters from Spain and Serbia. We therefore devote part of Chapter 15 to an overview and discussion of the effects of this crisis in rural areas, and include an Appendix, which provides more detail.

EUROPE IN THE POST-SOVIET CONTEXT

Since the fall of the Iron Curtain in 1989, many Eastern European countries have experienced conflict and challenging economic circumstances.

Recently, however, their educational research has begun to appear in English and this book aims to further that process. These countries are often enveloped, undifferentiated, under the label "eastern bloc."

Following the seismic changes of 1989, many East and Central European countries were liberated from the oppressive authority of Soviet communism. During the Cold War between the United States and Union of Soviet Socialist Republics (USSR), also referred to as the "bipolar world" (Fukuyama, 1992), the *post-soviet* countries Estonia, Latvia, Lithuania, Ukraine, and Belarus were members of the Soviet Union and under its direct rule. Czechia, Poland, Hungary, Bulgaria, Slovakia, and Romania are known as *post-socialist* countries (Hirt, 2013) and although under the political and economic authority of the Soviet Union, were not part of it. They were internationally independent, autonomous states which adopted the communist model. They are known as the *post-socialist* states. The countries of the former Yugoslavia, including Serbia, are also sometimes referred to as post-socialist, but they had a different relationship with the Soviet Union.

These post-socialist and post-soviet countries now differ economically, socially, and demographically, despite years of homogeneity during the Soviet era. They have gone through phases of really severe political persecutions and stages of greater freedom. The main common feature of their communist regimes was state control of the economy, public life, population, and territory. Education (curriculum, textbooks, etc.) was under strict state supervision and "schools and teachers were to become tools for advancing socialist ideology" (Zounek, Šimáně, & Knotová, 2017, p. 2). Some of the educational policies were similar to Western policies of the time, for example, preference for urban schools and central delimitation of school districts. However, the rigid hierarchically controlled regimes used a climate of fear and sanctions to promote universal implementation of decisions and reforms. Other concepts and policies from Western European countries, such as the marketization of education from the 1980s passed over these countries.

After the fall of the Iron Curtain, complex societal, political, and economic transformations took place; some of these happened very quickly. Governance and organization of public sector systems moved from totalitarian regimes, towards large-scale decentralization, with high levels of autonomy awarded to localities (Knieling & Othengrafen, 2016). In education, this included implementation of free market principles, and free parental choice of schools.

Each country has sought its own way in educational policy and practices, which are developing differently and are often incomplete. It is evident that some decisions and policies were premature and inadequately conceptualized and these complex societal, political, and economic transformations are reported in relevant chapters in this book.

RURAL RESEARCH: A NEW AGENDA, A NEW ATTITUDE, AND A PLACE FOR PLACE

If rural matters in education, then rural educational research has a key role to play in promoting its visibility. At present, rural research is a marginalized, minority interest. Recent calls for researchers to rethink their practices could, arguably, improve its impact in national policy development.

In 2009, Kvalsund and Hargreaves published an agenda for rural educational research in Britain and the Nordic countries in the *International Journal of Educational Research*. This agenda called for: (a) more theory-based and less policy-driven research; (b) more sophisticated research designs, including multiple case studies, longitudinal studies and more comparative rural–urban research; and (iii) more research evidence from children themselves, and people in rural communities whose schools have been closed. Inspirational papers by Coladarci (2007), Corbett (2015), and Shucksmith (2016), have also exhorted rural researchers to raise their game. Coladarci, reflecting on 15 years as editor of the *Journal of Research in Rural Education*, asks researchers to be more critical, rigorous, and more attentive to validity in distinguishing between research and advocacy in their reports on small schools in rural communities. Corbett and Shucksmith, in different ways, urge rural researchers to be more imaginative. Both call for those who live in rural areas to assume agency, and have this recognized, in envisioning, constructing, and managing policies that affect their lives.

Shucksmith (2016) highlights the irony that so many rural developments in the United Kingdom are authored exogenously, "by environmentalists, big business or the government's chief scientist" despite government encouragement for local "people to engage in place-shaping, parish planning... [and building]... a shared vision of how collectively they would like their place to be in the future" (p. 2). Ironically, he does not include rural schools or educational researchers in this vision. Corbett (2015), however, speaks directly to rural researchers, in "Towards a Rural Sociological Imagination." He invites researchers to move on from a repetitive discourse of rural disillusion and disadvantage to the kind of "sociological imagination" envisaged by Wright Mills (1959). Corbett entreats rural researchers to "exploit" better the conceptual space they inhabit, and to enable rural people to see their lives as a set of choices and decisions rather than "a series of traps."

Both Shucksmith and Corbett reiterate the case for regional and central educational policy-makers to take more notice of the concepts of place and space, as the physical reality of distance/proximity and location have been compressed by advances in transport and communication. For people in small and/or isolated rural settlements anxiety about loss of the uniqueness, the customs and idiosyncrasies of small rural settlements, as their shops, pubs, chapels, post offices and schools close, and internet shopping and international retail chains take over urban high streets is never far away. Such fear need not be a longing for some mythical rural idyll, as Massey (1994) shows us.

Massey (1994) rejects the idea that such place attachment is necessarily reactionary. Although her arguments are exemplified in her local urban high street, her vision is of a progressive "global sense of place," conceptualized in terms of social interaction, without the boundaries that create tension between insiders and "incomers." Instead, it acknowledges not only the uniqueness of a place, but also the continual process of reproduction of its uniqueness, as new connections are made, forming new layers of local experience upon the underlying history, itself a continual process of change. Massey cautions that different groups may experience the same location very differently, encompassing inequalities of access and opportunity. Her conceptualization of place merits consideration in the context of this book. That said, Massey too leaves school out of the picture, despite its potential to encourage a progressive and inclusive sense of place. Yet, as we shall see in the chapters to follow, such potential is not always realized.

Introduction to the Chapters

The book has 16 chapters. After this introductory one, Chapters 2 and 3 present comparative overviews of education in Rural Europe, helping us to conceptualize and map the rural space. The focal countries of Chapters 5 to 12 form Part II of the book, and go roughly geographically from eastern and central to western Europe. A principal aim of these chapters has been to inform English speakers internationally about past and present situations concerning small and/or rural schools in the former socialist countries. In many cases this information has been available only in minority languages. As we move west, however, there is a greater emphasis on underlying theory, and in the third part of the book Chapters 13 and 14 are detailed case studies, framed round the theories of Bourdieu and Lefebvre respectively. They show how working through a theoretical analysis of ethnographic data can provide new insights into rural schools and their communities.

In Chapter 2, Kučerová, Meyer, and Trahorsch analyze the various national situations to identify the principal influences on the spatial organization of rural elementary education in Europe. These include physical, geographical, historical, and sociocultural influences, such as population density, ethnicity, and political and economic factors. They note that educational factors such as optimal school size, and composition of classes typically have the least impact.

After a critical discussion of the concept of "globalization" Karl Jan Solstad and Gunilla Karlberg-Granlund, in Chapter 3, focus directly on the putative effects of globalization in rural communities and schools in Norway and Finland. They compare the Norwegian and Finnish policy responses to these global forces. Their detailed analysis has two aspects of international relevance: firstly, Solstad and Solstad's (2015) research showing the negative effects of ever longer school journeys on children's physical and psychological health; secondly, the progress made in both countries towards local community consultation on the future of small schools.

Chapters 4, 5, 6, and 7 are set in the postcommunist countries of Hungary, Czechia, Poland, and Serbia, respectively. Here we see a common determination to decentralize policy-making, after the fall of communism, but this was a process conducted in different ways, and with differing consequences for rural schools and communities.

Katalin Kovács' discussion in Chapter 4 of the recent history of rural schools in Hungary reveals several radical reforms that have, ironically, gone "full circle" from communist centralized control, to rapid, extreme decentralization, and back through a process of associations of small rural schools, and teacher resistance, to reimposition of central control in 2017. Kovács also reports the incipient process of ethnic segregation in rural Hungary as schools experience "White flight" in the face of Roma children attending small village schools, but also identifies positive cases of social cohesion and inclusive rural communities, where teachers are more interactive, and rolls subsequently rising.

In contrast to Hungary, Czechia has experienced a long process of decentralization since the fall of communism. In Chapter 5, Silvie Rita Kučerová and Kateřina Trnková report that in 2017, some 2,000 elementary schools (60% of all elementary schools) serve the rural municipalities (defined as having fewer than 3,000 inhabitants). They draw on Trnková's (2012) meta-analysis of elementary school research, and on Kučerová and colleagues' (e.g., Kučerová & Kučera, 2012) studies of the change in spatial distribution of schools between 1961 and 2004, and its effects on everyday life, such as commuting patterns.

In Chapter 6, Artur Bajerski relates the history of Poland's rural schools from the rapid decentralization after 1989 to local authority supervision, still with central funding. This "too rapid" transformation in Poland's rush towards a market economy, has led to lasting conflicts between local and central government, and local authorities and their communities. Nevertheless, Bajerski, also reports positive developments where communities have been allowed to reopen closed schools, up to a roll of 70 children. There are now 3,700 such schools. He argues for greater interdisciplinarity in rural research in Poland.

Ana Pešikan, Slobodanka Antić, and Ivan Ivić report that in Serbia (Chapter 7), 25% of rural, primary age children are not enrolled in school, compared with only 5% of urban children. Early school dropout rates are also a bigger problem in the rural areas, which accommodate some 46% of the national population. The authors detail a constructive policy designed to counter negative assumptions by focusing on the actual qualities of the rural schools. "Rural educational tourism" includes the whole community in active, out-of-school learning, and is a meaningful positive initiative in relation to the local rural economy.

In Chapter 8, Begoña Vigo Arrazola and Juana Soriano Bozalongo present the checkered history of rural "one-room" and "incomplete" rural primary schools in Spain since the 1960s. School clusters were established decades ago aiming to improve educational provision in isolated communities by bringing children together to experience activities requiring larger numbers for short periods of time. The end of the totalitarian Franco regime in 1975 has engendered emphases on autonomy and democracy in regions and institutions. These authors build on the pedagogical theories of Freinet and Freire, whose influence can be seen in the rise of partnerships between rural teachers and local universities to study inclusive practices with families and community. Vigo and Soriano call for more research on the internal processes of small and rural schools.

Next, in Chapter 9, Andrea Raggl writes about the small schools situation in Austria. Many small rural schools in Austria are close to larger settlements and under threat of closure or amalgamation. A global development here has been the Montessori "rescue" of small village schools from closure, which, as Raggl (2015) shows, is attracting new pupils from nearby urban areas, but, ironically, driving some local families to send their children to more traditional schools. Raggl invokes Bourdieu's concept of social capital to explain these developments.

In Chapter 10, Guiseppina Cannella presents strategies using digital media to overcome the inaccessibility and isolation of Italy's 1,400 schools situated in mountainous and island regions. They accommodate 900,000 students. Small school closures have been occurring rapidly since 2011, despite a stable student population. Cannella refers to Bronfenbrenner's (1979) bioecological systems theory and Lefebvre's (1974/1991) three-part spatial theory (see Gristy, Chapter 14) as ways to conceptualize education in very isolated rural settings. Her Italian research is investigating the use of two innovative models of teaching using digital technology to enable classes to work together.

Marjolein Deunk and Ralf Maslowski (Chapter 11) present the situation in the Netherlands where small (under 100 on roll) and very small (under 50 on roll) schools are numerous, but not necessarily rural. They identify global forces in recent policy moves to amalgamate groups of 20 to 30 small schools, under single "multi-school boards," supervised by people with no authentic connection with the schools. Parallel moves to raise the minimum rolls in "rural" areas to 100 have been resisted in the light of academic results which defy assumptions of poor educational provision in very small schools. Deunk and Maslowski present their own research on the critical nature of the relationship between small schools' principals and the multi-school boards.

Chapter 12 focuses on the process of developing community consultation in school network planning in Finland, from the planners' perspective. Sami Tantarimäki and Anni Törhönen present an historical timeline, showing periods of rapid reduction and relative stability in the number of village schools. Recent policy, however, represents positive developments in public consultation, expecting each municipality to conduct a local discussion of the future of education in its area. Their 5-year research examines the arguments for, and the progress in, the development of these discussions. This chapter offers a democratic and realistic vision that values the power of local decision-making in the face of global pressure.

As noted above, Part III of the book includes two chapters set in England. Carl Bagley and Sam Hillyard, in Chapter 13, provide an in-depth Bourdieusian analysis of the critical part played by the enterprising headteacher of one small rural school and its community in North East England. Their 3-year ethnographic study depicts the centrality of the school in the established community despite the school's physical separation from the village. Bagley and Hillyard use Bourdieu's theory to show how this headteacher exploits her educational and cultural *capital* and *habitus* to play a strategic game, keeping the pressures of the global economic *field* (prevalent threat of closure, for example) at bay in order to sustain her richer vision of education and its role in the local community.

Cath Gristy, in Chapter 14, applies Lefebvre's (1974/1991) trialectric theory of the social construction of space, normally used in urban settings, to a rural context. Through interviews with local people, including school students, Gristy graphically undermines the "rural idyll" myth. Her use of theory shows how theory can strengthen case study research, and be valuable in national and international comparative studies. While Lefebvre's three spatial perspectives coincide in Gristy's case study, this approach could also demonstrate Massey's (1994) observation that different groups (e.g., children, women, vulnerable adults) can have diverse experiences of the same place.

Finally, in Part IV, the book's editors Gristy, Hargreaves, and Kučerova, survey and discuss the emergent themes, in response to the four general questions posed earlier. In Chapter 15 they briefly review the preceding chapters, and highlight the patterns of change reported in the book. They include a discussion of the "migrant crisis in Europe," a theme that was anticipated but failed to materialize. The problems of definition of the relative concepts of "small" and "rural" are discussed. In the final chapter, Chapter 16, the editors look forward and consider the status of rural educational research in relation to mainstream educational research, and conclude with an overview of the innovative strategies and stories of hope for rural schools and communities identified by the contributing authors.

CONCLUSION

The chapters here represent a cross-section of rural educational conditions and research in Europe. An important contribution to the field is the inclusion of research from four previously socialist European countries. Accompanying chapters from western Europe reveal many different responses to the imposed, global pressures for economic efficiency and marketization, regardless of their rural consequences. While presenting the case for more engagement and investment in rural schooling, the chapters to follow are authentic, realistic, and research-based.

REFERENCES

Bronfenbrenner, U. (1979). *The ecology of human development*. Cambridge, MA: Harvard University Press.

Coladarci, T. (2007). Improving the yield of rural education research: An editor's swansong. *Journal of Research in Rural Education, 3*(22), 1–9.

Corbett, M. (2015). Towards a rural sociological imagination: Ethnography and schooling in mobile modernity. *Ethnography and Education, 10*(3), 263–277. https://doi.org/10.1080/17457823.2015.1050685

European Commission. (2017, November). *Strengthening European identity through education and culture*. The European Commission's contribution to the leaders' meeting in Gothenburg, Sweden. Report no. 673.

Eurostat. (2018, June). Statistics on rural areas in the EU para: 1.5, Statistical Office of the European Union, https://ec.europa.eu/eurostat/statistics-explained/index.php/Statistics_on_rural_areas_in_the_EU Para: 1.5

Eurostat. (2018, December). *Further information: Degree of urbanisation: Background.* https://ec.europa.eu/eurostat/web/degree-of-urbanisation/background

Eurostat. (2018, December). *Glossary: Degree of urbanisation.* Statistical Office of the European Union, https://ec.europa.eu/eurostat/statistics-explained/index.php?title=Glossary:Degree_of_urbanisation

Eurostat. (2018, December). *Glossary: Rural area.* https://ec.europa.eu/eurostat/statistics-explained/index.php?title=Glossary:Rural_area

Eurostat. (2018, December). *Glossary: Urban centre.* https://ec.europa.eu/eurostat/statistics-explained/index.php?title=Glossary:Urban_centre

Eurostat. (2020, April). *Land cover statistics.* Statistical Office of the European Union. https://ec.europa.eu/eurostat/statistics-explained/index.php/Land_cover_statistics#Land_cover_in_the_EU

European Commission/EACEA/Eurydice. (2019). *The teaching of regional or minority languages in schools in Europe. Eurydice Report.* Luxembourg: Publications Office of the European Union.

Fukuyama, F. (1992). *The end of history and the last man.* New York, NY: Free Press.

Galton, M., & Patrick, H. (Eds.). (1990). *Curriculum provision in the small primary school.* London, England: Routledge.

Harfitt, G. (2013). Why 'small' can be better: An exploration of the relationships between class size and pedagogical practices. *Research Papers in Education, 28*(3), 330–345. https://doi.org/10.1080/02671522.2011.653389

Held, D., McGrew, A., Goldblatt, D., & Perraton, J. (1999). *Global transformations: Politics, economics, culture.* Cambridge, MA: Polity Press.

Hirt, S. (2013). Whatever happened to the (post)socialist city? *Cities, 32*(S1), S29–S38.

Kučerová, S., & Kučera, Z. (2012). Changes in the spatial distribution of elementary schools and their impact on rural communities in Czechia in the second half of the 20th century. *Journal of Research in Rural Education, 27*(11), 1–17.

Kvalsund, R., & Hargreaves, L. (2009). Reviews of research on rural schools and their communities: Analytical perspectives and a new agenda. *International Journal of Educational Research, 48*(2), 140–149.

Knieling, J., & Othengrafen, F. (2016). En route to a theoretical model for comparative research on planning cultures. In J. Knieling, & F. Othengrafen (Eds.), *Planning cultures in Europe* (pp. 39–62). New York, NY: Routledge.

Lefebvre, H. (1991). *The production of space* (D. Nicolson-Smith, Trans). Oxford, England: Blackwell. (Originally published in 1974)

Massey, D. (1994). A global sense of place. In D. Massey (Ed.), *Space, place and gender.* (pp. 146–156). Cambridge, MA: Polity Press.

Nóvoa, A. (2002) Ways of thinking about education in Europe. In A. Nóvoa & M. Lawn (Eds), *Fabricating Europe* (pp. 131–155). Springer, Dordrecht.

OECD. (2011). *Regional typology: Directorate for public governance and territorial development.* Paris, France: Author.

OECD. (2013). *PISA in focus 28: What makes urban schools different?* http://dx.doi.org/10.1787/5k46l8w342jc-en

Ozga, J. (2012). Governing knowledge: Data, inspection and education policy in Europe. *Globalisation, Societies and Education, 10*(4), 439–455. https://doi.org/10.1080/14767724.2012.735148

Raggl, A. (2015). Teaching and learning practices in small rural schools in Austria and Switzerland: Opportunities and challenges from teachers' and students' perspectives. *International Journal of Educational Research, 74,* 127–135.

Schleicher, A. (2013). *Learning in rural China: The challenges for students.* [Blog post]. Retrieved from http://oecdeducationtoday.blogspot.co.uk/2013/10/learning-in-rural-china-challenges-for.html

Scholte, J. A. (2008). Defining globalisation. *The World Economy, 31*(11), 1471–1502. https://doi.org/10.1111/j.1467-9701.2007.01019.x

Showalter, D., Klein, R., Johnson, J., & Hartman, S. (2017). *Why rural matters 2015–2016: Understanding the changing landscape.* A Report by The Rural School and Community Trust. Washington, DC: Rural School and Community Trust.

Shucksmith, M. (2016). Re-imagining the rural: From rural idyll to good countryside. *Journal of Rural Studies, 59,* 163–172. http://dx.doi.org/10.1016/j.jrurstud.2016.07.019

Solstad, K. J., & Solstad, M. (2015). Meir skyss—Mindre helse? [More shuttle—Less health?] *NF-rapport 07/2015.* Bodø, Norway: Nordlandsforskning.

Tikly, L. (2001). Globalisation and education in the postcolonial world: Towards a conceptual framework. *Comparative Education, 37*(2), 151–171.

Trnková, K. (2012, September). *Educational research of rural elementary schools.* Paper presented at European Conference on Educational Research (ECER) 2012. Cádiz.

Wright Mills, C. (1959). *The sociological imagination.* New York, NY: Oxford University Press.

Zhang, F. (2013). *China's rural education at risk.* Retrieved from http://www.china.org.cn/china/2013-01/08/content_27618239.htm

Zounek, J., Šimáně, M., & Knotová, D. (2017). Primary school teachers as a tool of secularisation of society in communist Czechoslovakia. *History of Education, 46*(4), 480–497.

PART I

CONCEPTUALIZING AND MAPPING
THE EUROPEAN RURAL SPACE

CHAPTER 2

FACTORS INFLUENCING ELEMENTARY EDUCATION SYSTEMS IN SELECTED EUROPEAN COUNTRIES

Silvie R. Kučerová
J. E. Purkyně University in Ústí nad Labem, Czechia

Petr Meyer
Charles University, Czechia and
J. E. Purkyně University in Ústí nad Labem, Czechia

Petr Trahorsch
J. E. Purkyně University in Ústí nad Labem, Czechia

Education is a sociocultural process whose form depends on a number of aspects. Průcha (2005), for example, says that the educational process is immediately influenced by *entry determinants*, which are the characteristics of individual *elements* within the educational process: characteristics of pupils, teachers, schools, educational documents, and instruments (cf.

Fraser, Walberg, Welch, & Hattie, 1987). According to Průcha (2005), these elements of the educational process appear in the *educational environment* (place) where education occurs, and also include the internal psychosocial environment of the participants. From an even broader perspective, the process of education takes place in *interactive space-time*, created by the geographic, social, economic, and political environment. However, there is the question of whether *space* can be considered directly as one of the entry determinants, rather than the milieu in which a process takes place. In fact, the characteristics of a space considerably influence the nature of education, its forms, and, above all, its spatial distribution and external relations within an educational system. For example, the fact that a school is located in rural space has an influence on its form: its size, teaching, and pedagogical-didactic organization and general culture (Bell & Sigsworth, 1987; Cuervo, 2016).

Parts of each chapter of this book deal with the existing conditions for (rural) schooling and the determinants operating in individual European countries. This chapter pursues the objective of comparing the conditions in the individual countries. On the general level, the goal is to classify the factors that influence elementary education. In addition, on the empirical level, several key factors will be analyzed in detail, across the various European countries, and will aim to classify the countries into several typological groups. A differentiation between the conditions for the number and spatial organization of schools will be presented, including cartographically.

FACTORS INFLUENCING SPATIAL ORGANIZATION OF ELEMENTARY EDUCATION WITH RESPECT TO A EUROPEAN CONTEXT

Based on the knowledge gained through studies by the authors in this book, we have tried to identify groups of factors that influence the spatial organization of elementary education in Europe. We examine those relevant to the countries in the publication. In other natural conditions and other sociocultural areas, one could certainly identify other factors, too. With the term *spatial organization of education* (Hampl, 2000), we understand not only how schools are distributed in space, but also what their vertical and horizontal links are: For example, which school fulfills the function of the central school in a region, how schools cooperate with or compete for pupils' enrollment, and from where home–school commuting occurs, and so on.

Physical geographic factors are the primary group with an influence on the number and distribution of schools. Seemingly, it is possible to eliminate or even overcome their influence in modern society (Hampl, 2000). Nevertheless, basic physical geographic factors are expressed in the very extent and structure of a settled area (the *ecumene*). Settlement patterns depend largely on altitude and climatic conditions. Once a population is sufficiently concentrated, there is a need for the provision of an education service (Green & Letts, 2007). At the meso and micro regional levels, the distribution of schools in spaces is primarily given by *orography*, the topography of mountains (e.g., Kučerová, Bláha, & Kučera, 2015). According to some localization rules of spaces (Roberts, 1996), one can expect, for example, schools to be primarily concentrated in a valley network, and that their concentration will be higher near the junction of a valley with a neighboring valley. Within the framework of Europe, this can be a vital aspect—for example, in the Alpine countries such as Austria and the mountain areas of Italy).

The second group influencing spatial organization of a school network is created by the factors that can be summarily denoted as *historical*. The existing form of a school network arises from its past development in a given area at a given time, from specific historical decisions and events (e.g., as a result of a war conflict, such as the situation in Serbia) and also as a result of long-standing tendencies, established customs, and traditions (e.g., Bell & Sigsworth, 1987; Dvořák, Starý, & Urbánek, 2015; Šimáně, 2010).

The third, broad group of *sociocultural* factors includes the characteristics of population (including cultural values), settlement, and economic activities. As already mentioned in connection with physical geographic factors, the form of a school network depends on population distribution (population density). This population distribution might be classified along a core–periphery continuum. On the other hand, distribution is associated with territorial concentrations of populations where the size and structure of settlements are considered, such as the extent of urbanization (e.g., Bajerski, 2015; Hampl, 2004). This is the rural–urban continuum.

The demand for education in an area or a locality is determined by its population size, the age structure (especially of its child component), and possibly also by the demographic and migration conditions that indicate its future population development (Barakat, 2015; Hulík & Tesárková, 2009). The spatial organization of education is also influenced considerably by ethnic and social structure; for example, the presence of several ethnic groups in an area often demands establishment of minority schools (Šimáně, 2010). There are a number of studies that explore the different accessibility or social inequality of various schools for individual ethnic, cultural, and socioeconomic population groups, which are translated into the character of school catchment areas (Burgess, Greaves, Vignoles, & Wilson, 2011; Kovács, 2012; Nekorjak, Souralová, & Vomastková, 2011).

Other sociocultural factors include transportation from home to school, and this group of factors impact strongly on the distribution of schools (Masoumi et al., 2017). The transport accessibility to schools is influenced mainly by the density and form of the road network, the offer of the means of transport, its quality and efficiency (Farrington & Farrington, 2005; Kučerová, Mattern, Štych, & Kučera, 2011).

There is another group of sociocultural factors affecting spatial distribution of education, which include the issue of attitudes to education; for example, the tasks and aims that should be fulfilled by basic education, according to the expectations of whole societies and particular social groups (van de Werfhorst, 2014). In connection with this, attention is paid to the manner in which an education system is organized, the mechanism of its funding and how it is governed; these aspects can be summarized into four groups of *political and economic factors*. One of the fundamental dilemmas in managing educational systems is regulation of the degree of centralization and decentralization (Kvalsund, 2009; Ribchester & Edwards, 1999). By this we mean the degree to which the managing and controlling powers are concentrated and executed by state authorities and the degree of financial autonomy that lower administrative units, particularly schools, have. These aspects primarily arise from the political doctrine of a given country, such as the form of the state regime, the ruling ideology, and so on (Gyuris, 2014; Halsey, Lauder, Brown, & Wells, 1997), the economic situation of that country and its broader frameworks and rules for financing public services like education. However, the resources that end up allocated to education services also depend on the method of distribution of financial and other supplies, and the size of the budgets of the lower-level administrative units responsible for the provision of education within their areas (Trnková, 2009).

The physical spatial organization of schools then arises from forces such as regional development policies, from national policies (or even supranational ones like the EU, as in the majority of countries in this publication) down to the coordination of activities and services at the local departmental level of communities and specific spaces (e.g., Basu, 2007; Holloway & Pimlott-Wilson, 2012). The influence of the territorial size of state administrative units responsible for education will also influence the spatial distribution of schools, through, for example, the size and organization of school catchments. Each territorial unit will have a limited number of institutions providing education. Some administrative units operate fewer larger schools with extensive commuting districts. Other similar territories may be divided into many fragmented administrative units where each needs to operate their own school (Kučerová et al., 2015).

There are two other interconnected political and economic factors associated with educational policy that influence school distribution: Who has the power to make decisions concerning the enrolment of pupils, and which organizations are involved in the operation of schools? More specifically what proportions of schools in a national education system are run by the state and what proportions are run by other organizations, such as religious groups, charities, businesses and nongovernment institutions?

Here it is necessary to consider the concept of directive school catchment districts, where children living in a school's hinterland are enrolled based on their place of residence (Bajerski, 2015), and the system of parental school choice that has evolved under the influence of liberal economic, market oriented approaches to education and a wider supply of types of educational provision (Maroy & van Zanten, 2009). For many, the diversity of schooling in an educational system and the possibility of choice can be seen as an advantage on an individual level.

The prevailing educational-methodological principles of how teaching, classes, and forms of knowledge transmission are organized (Bertrand, 1998) are other *educational policy factors* that influence the spatial organization of education. This group of factors includes the topics of preferred or minimum school size, the ways in which classes are organized and the segregation or inclusion of pupils with special educational needs within "standard" classes and schools, and so on. In the development of modern compulsory education systems there tends to be a dominance of large urban schools with classes each composed by one age cohort (Åberg-Bengtsson, 2009), although as seen in this book, there have also been trends in favor of small schools, in connection with support for the diversity of the educational system and development at a local level (Bell & Sigsworth, 1987; Tantarimäki & Törhönen, Chapter 12, this volume). Small schools are, in some places, a feature of rural areas but are also found in cities. There are, of course, debates about the changing nature of education systems, including whether they might be informed by (or perhaps transformed by) consideration of different, alternative forms of education systems (Kraftl, 2012; OECD, 2011).

There is a wide package of factors that appear to influence the resulting character of educational systems with various degrees of complexity, from partial and locally specific to general and complex. Some of these factors appear to influence the system primarily and explicitly, whereas, some of them only implicitly within a wider contextual framework. Examples of the most important key factors that we will analyze in more detail are presented in Table 2.1.

RESEARCH APPROACH AND METHODOLOGY

The authors of this chapter used data offered by the authors from the 11 European countries represented in this book (see Figure 1.1, p. 2): Austria, Czechia, Finland, Hungary, Italy, the Netherlands, Norway, Poland, Serbia, Spain, and the United Kingdom. The conditions of spatial organization and the provision of elementary schooling differ between these countries in many respects, although the effects of the key factors also show similarities between some regions. We selected several groups of key factors that

TABLE 2.1 Selected Analyzed Factors Underlying Spatial Organization of Elementary Education

Group of Factors	Factor	Indicator/Information	Source
Educational Policy Factors	Organization of stages of compulsory education	• Duration of compulsory education (years) • Education organization model	• EURYDICE (2012). *Key Data on Education in Europe 2012*. Brussels: Education, Audiovisual and Culture Executive Agency.
	Size structure of schools	• Average number of pupils in a class • Structure of schools according to number of pupils (in %)	• *Education at a Glance 2015: OECD Indicators*. Paris: OECD publishing • National Educational Statistics
Political and Economic Factors	Administrative division	• Number and area (in km²) of administrative units LAU2	• LAU2 polygon layer from Eurostat
	Structure of school operators	• Proportion of types of elementary school operators (in %)	• National Educational Statistics
Physical Geographic + Sociocultural Factors	Population distribution	• Population density (population number per 1 km² of area)	• Number of inhabitants in particular municipalities from national statistics • LAU2 polygon layer from Eurostat
	Age structure of the population	• Population structure in 5-year age groups (in %)	• United Nations Population Division, the 2015 Revision of World Population Prospects
	Transport servicing	• Road network density (kilometres of roads per km² of area)	• Line layer of roads network from Open Street Map • LAU2 polygon layer from Eurostat

Source: authors

seem to be crucial for the number of elementary schools and for the resulting spatial organization of education (see Table 2.1). The nature of the data available to the authors from the different countries limited the scope and scale of the analysis. There was a good deal of variation in the kinds of both quantitative statistical data and qualitative descriptive data available.

In the first part of the chapter, we describe general factors ranging from natural ones (those relatively independent of humans) to the characteristics of populations and onto the impact of human activities, institutions, and societies. Our comparisons of the countries using empirical data were made in the following sequence: from the setting of organizational stages of compulsory education and the characteristics of schools, up to the features of the geographical space of an educational system.

Different kinds of data were available and were gained in several ways. Of particular value was information sent by representatives of individual countries or authors of individual chapters. Along with quantitative data and direct references to national statistics, the authors provided explanations of some specific features of particular countries (but see above for discussion of the variation in kinds of data and the limits this placed on analysis). Further data were searched for both in the national and international statistical databases (United Nations and OECD databases, Eurydice Network data on education). Last but not least, it was necessary to find complementary information in professional publications in the fields of educational policy, geography of education, sociology of education, or demography.

For the needs of cartographic visualization, vector data were gained in the form of a polygon layer representing the LAU2 (Local Administrative Unit, Level 2) from the Eurostat database. In most cases, the number of LAU2s corresponds with the number of municipalities in the selected countries, while exceptions were found separately. The statistical data for municipalities were added to this LAU2 layer by means of the Geographic Information System (GIS). Statistical data that were not collected automatically by the software were collected manually and added. The data for a visualization of the road network were gained from the project Open Street Map. From this web map, a line layer of a complete road network was downloaded for the individual countries. Only the lines representing roads were preserved in it. With the utilization of the program ArcGIS for Desktop, the population density and road network densities were calculated.

The data were visualized to make clear the spatial patterns of the observed indicators in particular. This is why one has to take into account that the presented maps, for example, do not have a uniform interval scale. However, most data were compared by their relative values (including graphs of age structures).

In the concluding section of the chapter, the studied countries were categorized on the basis of the development of the total number of elementary schools. Owing to the inaccessibility of the relevant data from all the countries, at this stage of the research we were unable to analyze the transformations of the spatial pattern of schools (Kučerová & Kučera, 2012), although this knowledge would also have very practical value.

ANALYSIS PART 1—EDUCATIONAL POLICY FACTORS IN ELEMENTARY EDUCATION

Although elementary education is generally compulsory in all the observed countries, the duration and organization of school attendance levels differ (see Table 2.2). Pupils start compulsory education at ages ranging from aged five (as in the Netherlands or Hungary) to seven (in Finland). In addition, some countries (such as the Netherlands) have a compulsory last year of preprimary education. The duration of compulsory education ranges between 8 to 13 years. The shortest compulsory education is in Serbia, the longest in the Netherlands and Hungary (however, in the latter two countries, the last few years are only "partially" compulsory—as part time; compulsory education ends in the year when age 16 is reached).

School Organization Models

The model of education organization and the connections and movement between individual types of schools influences educational pathways for individual students and social segregation. It also has an influence

TABLE 2.2 Selected Characteristics of Organization of Compulsory Education Levels

Country	Start of Compulsory Education (age)	Duration of Compulsory Education (years)	Model of Primary and Lower Secondary Education
Austria	6	9	Differentiated branches
Czechia	6	9	Combination common core curriculum and single structure
Finland	7	9	Single structure
United Kingdom	5	11	Common core curriculum
Hungary	5	13	Combination common core curriculum and single structure
Italy	6	10	Common core curriculum
Netherlands	5	13	Differentiated branches
Norway	6	10	Single structure
Poland	6	10	Common core curriculum
Serbia	6(7)	8	Common core curriculum
Spain	6	10	Common core curriculum

Source: authors, according to Eurydice (2012).

on the number and distribution of schools and commuting relationships (Altrichter, Heinrich, & Soukup-Altrichter, 2014). According to Eurydice (2012), three different organizational models for compulsory education can be distinguished across Europe. These can be defined as:

1. "Common core" provision of the curriculum. Here after primary education (ISCED 1) is completed, all students follow the same integrated common core curriculum within lower secondary education (ISCED 2) over a period of time. This is how most of the observed countries function (see UNESCO, 2012).
2. Single structure education. Primary and lower secondary education is combined, without a need for transition from primary to lower secondary levels. Norway and Finland, for example, can be included in this category.
3. Differentiated branches model. Primary education is followed by differentiated secondary education delivered through distinct educational pathways. At the beginning of lower secondary education parents must choose (or schools decide on) an educational pathway or a specific type of schooling for students. These singled out educational pathways are mutually barely permeable. In addition, since their differentiation occurs at the very early age of pupils, they are considerably segregatory (Geppert, Knapp, Kilian, & Katsching, 2015). Out of the observed countries, this group includes Austria and the Netherlands.

In Czechia and Hungary, compulsory education is organized in a single structure up to the age of 14/15, but from the age of 10/11 pupils can be enrolled in separate establishments at certain stages, providing both lower and upper secondary education (Dvořák & Straková, 2016).

School Size

The observed countries also differ with regard to the size of schools, according to the number of enrolled pupils. The comparison of the schools has been rather complicated by national statistics that use different size categories of schools. For the sake of clarity, it has been necessary to break down the gap between 100 and 500 graphically by means of a raster (see Figure 2.1). There are countries with a prevalence of large schools with several hundreds of pupils, such as the Netherlands or Norway. There are other countries with predominantly smaller schools, such as Poland or Austria, where, for example, Raggl (Chapter 9, this volume) mentions that "40% of the Austrian primary schools have fewer than 50 pupils" (p. 200). In Spain,

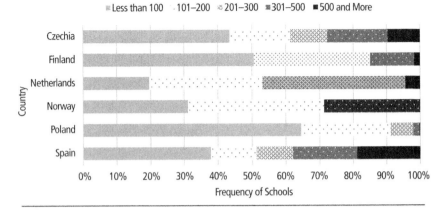

Country	Categories of Number of Pupils at Schools				
	Fewer Than 100	100–500			501 and More
		100–200	201–300	301–500	
Czechia	43.5	17.9	10.9	18.1	9.6
Finland	50.6	34.5	13.1		1.8
Netherlands	19.6	33.5	42.5		4.4
Norway	31.1	40.2		28.7	
Poland	64.5	26.7	6.7	1.9	0.2
Spain	37.9	13.4	10.7	19.1	18.9

Figure 2.1 Structure of schools according to categories of number of pupils at schools, average of years 2012–2016. *Source*: Ministry of Education, Youth and Sports (2016). Cited 2017-01-18. Available from: http://toiler.uiv.cz/rocenka/rocenka.asp; CBS Statline (2016). Cited 2017-01-18. Available from: https://1url.cz/FzRCN; Statistics Norway (2015). Facts about education in Norway 2015. Oslo: Ministry of Education and Research and Directorate for Education and Training.; and information of authors of the monograph.

there is a relatively even representation of schools categorized by size. It is clear that each type of school experience has particular challenges, such as pupil anonymity in large schools or the enormous financial costs of maintenance of networks of small schools (Åberg-Bengtsson, 2009; Cuervo, 2016; Ribchester & Edwards, 1999). The data also show that the distribution of types of schools leads to other socio-spatial patterns and so, for example, areas with many small schools have different challenges from those areas with fewer larger schools.

As a rule, the size of a school also influences the average number of pupils in a class (Table 2.3). However, this can depend on pedagogical and

TABLE 2.3 Average Number of Pupils in a Class as of 2013

Country	Primary School	Lower Secondary School
Austria	18	21
Czechia	20	22
Finland	19	22
Hungary	21	21
Italy	19	22
Netherlands	23	N
Norway	*)	*)
Poland	18	22
Serbia	23	26
Spain	22	25
United Kingdom	25	19
Mean	**21**	**22**

Note: *) = Pupils are organized in groups whose size varies during the school day.
N = data unavailable.

Source: Authors according to Education at a Glance 2015: OECD Indicators.

organizational factors. What matters is whether emphasis is put on direct instruction with a teacher at the front of a class, or research-oriented teaching in class, or the levels of individual tuition and other alternative forms of education.

However, there is also the second aspect to the spatial distribution of schools categorized by size. It is impossible to say merely from the absolute number whether a particular type of school is concentrated in certain areas. It can be presumed, for example, that large schools tend to be localized in urban agglomerations. By contrast, in the areas with a lower population density (remote and rural areas), a larger number of schools for fewer students, including those with composite classes/multigrade classrooms (Trnková, 2009), are established in order to provide for accessibility to compulsory education.

For the sake of an international comparison, it seems to be significant to look at the definitions of the "small school" and the "rural school" for the purposes of this book. Similar to the definition of rural space, definitions are not standardized in Europe and in the chapters in this book, the definitions tend to be derived from the context presented by each author. Rural schools are frequently associated with small schools, which is misleading, because in urban space one can also see very small schools (Kučerová & Kučera, 2012). For instance in the Netherlands, where the urbanization rate is over 90%, schools with fewer than 50 pupils are denoted as "very small" and those with 50–100 pupils as "small schools" (Deunk & Maslowski, Chapter 11, this volume). In Norway, schools with fewer than 90 pupils (typically 12–55 pupils) are regarded as "small" (Kvalsund, 2009). Finland and Poland define small and, at the same time, rural schools as having limits of 50 pupils (Bajerski, Chapter 6, this volume; Tantarimäki & Törhönen, Chapter 12, this volume). Based on an analysis of the works by various authors, Hargreaves (2009) says that internationally the upper limit for a small school is 70 pupils for a primary school and 400 for a secondary school (cf. Harber, 1996). However, this is not a generally accepted definition.

In order to define rural schools other criteria are added in some countries. For example, in Spain and Austria the definition of rural applies to the school with composite classes (Arrazola & Bozalongo, Chapter 8, this volume; Raggl, Chapter 9, this volume). A majority of authors define rural schools according to the location in the area which could be denoted as rural in a particular country (Bibby & Brindley, 2013; Arrazola & Bozalongo, Chapter 8, this volume) or is defined as rural on the basis of legislation or state strategic documents (Cannella, Chapter 10, this volume; Kučerová & Kučera, 2012).

ANALYSIS PART 2—POLITICAL AND ECONOMIC FACTORS IN ELEMENTARY EDUCATION

The observed countries differ considerably in their administrative divisions, differences that were examined on the LAU2 level. The biggest differences were recorded in the number and size of these administrative units. One could expect that along with a country's growing area the number of LAU2s would increase as well. However, it is apparent from Table 2.4 that this is not so. This can be exemplified by countries of similar sizes, such as Serbia and Czechia, where the number of LAU2s in Czechia is 35 times higher than in Serbia. Neither can a similar correlation be found in the relationship between the population number and the number of LAU2s. In this respect, Scandinavian countries (Finland and Norway), along with Serbia, differ most. In the case of Scandinavian countries with large uninhabited areas, the median size of LAU2s may be up to 10 times higher compared with other countries (see Table 2.4). In other countries where the distribution of the population is more evenly spread, smaller administrative units that still have a sufficient number of inhabitants can be defined. In some postcommunist countries (Hungary, Czechia, Poland) there is a high frequency of small administrative units and this is the result of historically specific disintegration of local authorities after the fall of centralized political power (Kovács, 2012; Kučerová, Dvořák, Meyer, & Bartůněk, 2020).

Administrative units determine school distribution, as local governments are usually responsible for the provision of elementary education within their areas. The number and organization of these units then underpins the

TABLE 2.4 Selected Indicators for Observed European Countries as of 2011

Country	Whole Country			Median Values per LAU2	
	Area (km²)	Number of Inhabitants	Number of LAU2s	Area (km²)	Number of Inhabitants
Czechia	78,862	10,490,406	6,253	8	419
Finland *)	337,476	5,287,607	320	609	5,934
Italy	301,299	59,423,965	8,092	22	2,437
Hungary	93,012	9,966,206	3,154	19	826
Netherlands	37,371	16,628,181	408	68	25,715
Norway	323,801	4,919,829	428	470	4,571
Poland	311,737	38,511,897	2,479	112	7,518
Austria	83,899	8,403,007	2,354	24	1,579
United Kingdom	252,804	65,987,442	9,499	5	5,394
Serbia	77,669	7,186,862	165	385	26,022
Spain	506,482	46,816,010	8,200	35	558

Note: *) Data from 2010.
Source: Authors according to Eurostat and national statistics.

distribution and organization of schools. As a public service, elementary education in all the observed countries is also primarily financed from public budgets, including co-financing for the other administrators who take part in the provision of elementary education. These can be private institutions, churches, and others that establish schools on the basis of some religious, ideological, or educational views (Deunk & Maslowski, Chapter 11, this volume). The lowest proportion of private schools, where parents contribute to the financing of schools by paying for tuition, is in Serbia (roughly 0.5%), Finland, Czechia, and Austria (less than 5%). By contrast, the highest proportion of private schools is in the United Kingdom (over 20%; cf. Koinzer, Nikolai, & Waldow, 2017). A differing representation of non-state/nonpublic school operators (see Figure 2.2) is most frequently influenced by the previous historical development of a country. The representation of privately funded education is still very low in countries where oppressive regimes were in power during the 20th century and where other than state-run education was inadmissible (such as Czechia and Serbia). The dominant public sector in education in Scandinavian countries is associated with their general policy of public social services. The situation is different in the Netherlands, for example, where the nonpublic sector is responsible for the operation of most elementary schools—but even these schools are financed by the state (Deunk & Maslowski, Chapter 11, this volume).

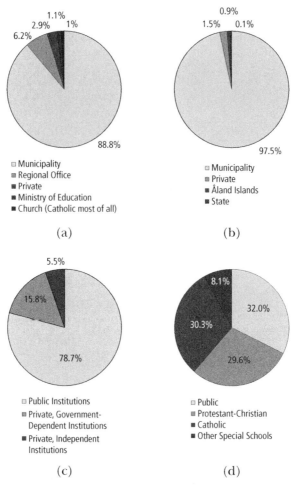

Figure 2.2 (a) Czechia, (b) Finland, (c) United Kingdom, (d) Netherlands. Percentage proportion of types of elementary schools operators in four selected countries in the 2010s. *Source*: Authors according to the Ministry of Education, Youth and Sports (2016). Cited 2017-01-18. Available from: http://toiler.uiv.cz/rocenka/rocenka.asp; Eurydice (2012); and information of the authors of the monograph.

ANALYSIS PART 3—PHYSICAL GEOGRAPHIC AND SOCIOCULTURAL FACTORS IN ELEMENTARY EDUCATION

The spatial distribution of the people who are being educated is the basic condition of school organization. Although Europe is relatively densely inhabited, there are considerable differences on both regional levels (between individual countries) and local levels (lower administrative units of the given

Factors Influencing Elementary Education Systems ▪ 35

countries). In general the rural, peripheral, and remote areas, including the mountain areas, have the lowest population density. The highest values of population density are recorded in the most populous cities and their hinterlands, as well as in lowland and coastal areas. Out of the observed countries, the Netherlands (Figure 2.3) can be denoted as the most densely inhabited.

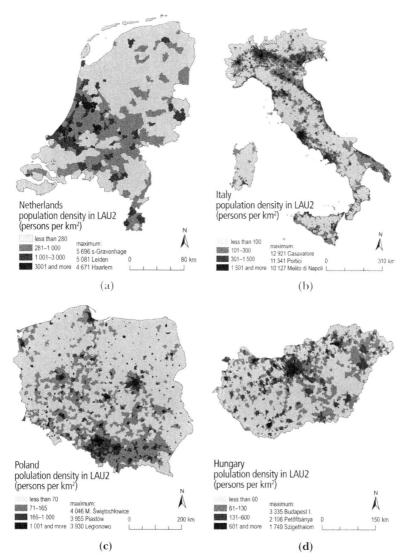

Figure 2.3 Population density on the LAU2 level in four selected countries as of 2011. *Source:* Authors according to Eurostat (2017a). Cited 2017-01-20. Available from: https://1url.cz/UzRUZ and Eurostat (2017b). Cited 2017-01-20. Available from: https://1url.cz/7zRUI.

Physical Geographic Factors and Population Distribution

Primary physical geographic factors (orography in particular) have the biggest effect on the population distribution in Austria, Spain, and Italy. It is obvious, for example, that in Italy (Figure 2.3) the lowest population density appears in the Apennine Mountains. By contrast, in coastal and lowland areas (such as the Po Valley), the population density is over 1,000 inhabitants/km^2. In the case of Norway and Finland, the population distribution is also considerably influenced by latitude. This results in the densely populated Scandinavian south and very sparsely inhabited areas in the north (Autti & Hyry-Beihammer, 2014). In the countries with less broken relief (such as the Netherlands, Poland, Hungary), secondary socioeconomic factors play the dominant role in the distribution of population on the macro regional scale. In Poland (Figure 2.3) there are obvious higher population densities in the south, with its concentration of main centres of industrial production. The population distribution in Poland is also influenced by historical factors, such as the mass migration of people when the Polish borders were changed after World War II, or as a result of the conflict in Serbia in the 1990s (Nikitović, Bajat, & Blagojević, 2016).

Each type of area faces its own specific problems. In the case of very densely populated areas and the rapidly expanding (suburban) hinterlands of large cities, there can be an insufficient capacity of schools (Hulík & Tesárková, 2009), a competition struggle, or a segregation of some population groups when it comes to their access to quality education (Jennings, 2010). By contrast, peripheral areas generally face a shortage of pupils, the question of the long-standing non-profitability of schools and their closures in these areas (Kučerová & Trnková, Chapter 5, this volume; Tantarimäki & Törhönen, Chapter 12, this volume). The sparsely populated areas in Nordic countries have, for example, particular EU regional policy objectives (as identified by the EU) to maintain public services and settlements in the region (Solstad & Karlberg-Granlund, Chapter 3, this volume).

Population Age Structure

Along with the distribution and absolute numbers of a population, the age structure of countries tends to influence the general conditions of educational policies. For example, the numbers of school-aged children in a given micro regional/local level are linked to the form of the spatial distribution of schools.

The age structure of the population in the countries being studied shows a number of differences (see Figure 2.4) that are subsequently translated into

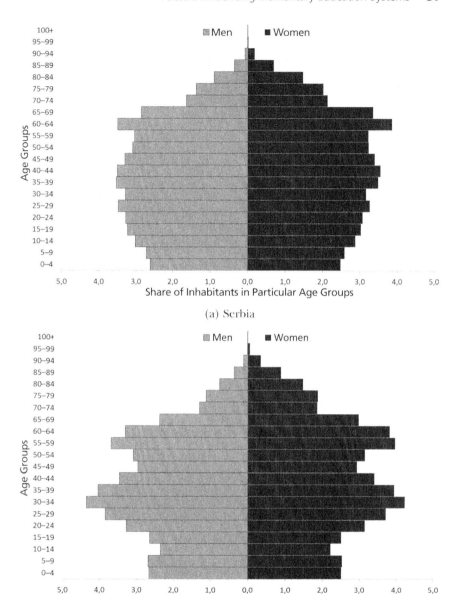

Figure 2.4 Population estimates for four selected countries as of July 1, 2015.
(continued)
Source: K. Hulíková for S. R. Kučerová according to the United Nations (2017). Cited 2017-01-02. Available from https://population.un.org/wpp/

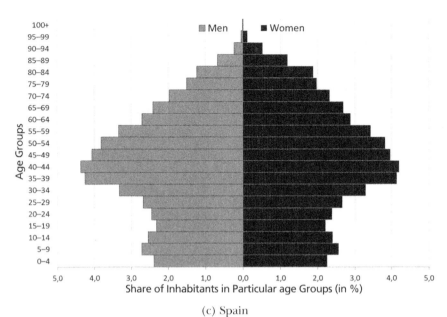

(c) Spain

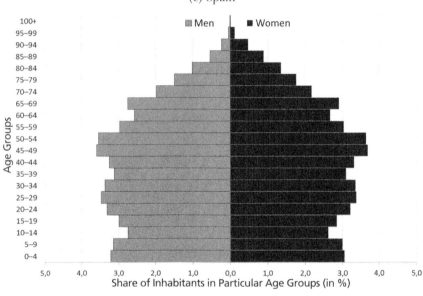

(d) United Kingdom

Figure 2.4 (cont.) Population estimates for four selected countries as of July 1, 2015. *Source*: K. Hulíková for S. R. Kučerová according to the United Nations (2017). Cited 2017-01-02. Available from https://population.un.org/wpp/

the provision of elementary education (for more see, e.g., Barakat, 2015). Based on age structure, the observed countries can be divided into four basic groups (cf. Monnier, 2006). Serbia has the youngest age structure, although there is a continual decline in its number of births. A considerable transformation of demographic behavior occurred after the fall of the Iron Curtain in postcommunist European countries (e.g., see Poland in Figure 2.4). At first, these countries saw a steep fall in the number of births, now compensated by a higher age of mothers at the birth of their first child. European countries (such as Spain) have been facing a similar issue for decades—that of population ageing. By contrast, the Scandinavian countries, Britain and the Netherlands have more stable birth rates. Austria is rather closer to the latter countries. In the case of the United Kingdom and the Netherlands in particular, demographic behavior varies between different ethnic population groups.

Transport

Transport servicing in an area is another factor with an impact primarily on the physical accessibility of schools. In some countries, the tradition of transporting children to school by public transport (e.g., in the United Kingdom) is well established, while elsewhere, individual automobile transport by parents is more often provided (Faulkner, Buliung, Flora, & Fusco, 2009; Kučerová et al., 2011; Masoumi et al., 2017). Although the transport accessibility is primarily of major importance on the micro regional scale level, we tried to depict the total road network density in the observed countries (see examples in Figure 2.5). From the spatial viewpoint, this naturally correlates with population distribution. Again, Austria and Spain show evidence of the influence of orography on the distribution of population and economic activities involving their road networks. In Austria, the Tauern Mountains clearly delineate the areas with a high/low road density network. In Spain, one can identify the densest in its coastal areas, with the exception of the transport links of its capital Madrid in the center of the country. The very high road density in the large area of north west Spain is caused by a fragmented settlement structure, with numerous small villages many kilometres apart that need to be connected (see Arrazola & Bozalongo, Chapter 8, this volume). In Finland too, one can see in the spatial distribution of road network density, primarily influenced by latitude, notably in the sparsely inhabited north. Unlike other observed countries, Serbia has a relatively low road network density, reflecting the basic spatial distribution of core urbanized and rural areas. On the micro regional level, transport accessibility has a very strong impact on the form of the

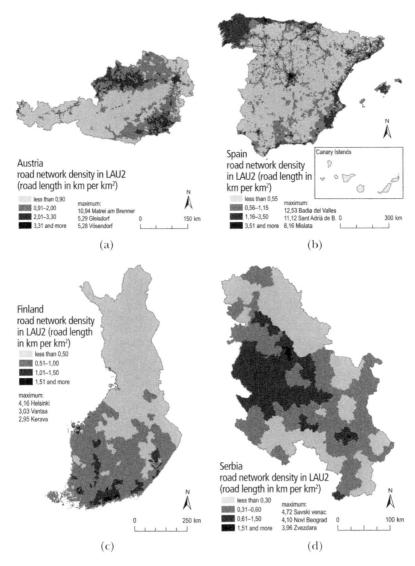

Figure 2.5 Road network density on LAU2 level in four selected countries as of 2016. *Source:* Authors according to Eurostat (2017a). Cited 2017-01-20. Available from https://1url.cz/UzRUZ and Open Street Map (2017). Cited 2017-01-23. Available from https://1url.cz/KzRfW.

catchment areas of individual schools and on competition between them. In a number of studies parents cite proximity and transport accessibility as key factors when choosing schools (Meyer & Kučerová, 2018; cf. Holloway & Pimlott-Wilson, 2012).

CONCLUSION—A TYPOLOGY OF THE DEVELOPMENT OF NUMBERS OF ELEMENTARY SCHOOLS

The previous text has shown the diversity of conditions in elementary education and its spatial distribution in the observed European countries. To create any typology of countries according to their characteristics and organization of their educational systems classification needs to be multidimensional. The principal dimensions seem to be the political–historical factors (main dichotomy: former liberal versus post-socialist states) on the one hand, and the physical geographic factors (main dichotomy: mountain and remote areas of territory versus predominantly lowland states). Nevertheless, this is a rather crude division and overlooks the other conditions such as the size structure of schools or territorial administration.

To conclude, we tried to analyze the development of the number of elementary schools in these countries over the broadest possible period for which the necessary statistical data were at our disposal. Because of data limitations, we could not observe the development of the number of small or rural schools separately, but only of elementary schools in their total. Nevertheless, referring to other studies (Autti & Hyry-Beihammer, 2014; Bell & Sigsworth, 1987; Kučerová & Kučera, 2012), it can be stated that small and rural schools are those whose numbers change most frequently as a result of school closures. The numbers of elementary schools were measured both by the basic index (the number of schools in the n-year is referenced to the same original, basic year) and the chain index of development (the number of schools in the n-year is referenced to the previous $n-1$ year). This was due to the uneven time series, which often involved very different years for the individual countries (such as the year 1961 for Hungary and 1991 for Finland).

In the development of the number of elementary schools over time there are two clearly different patterns in the observed countries. The first group displays a dynamic fall in numbers of elementary schools, especially in the course of the 1960s and the 1970s. In this period, the chain index reached values of around 95%, meaning a 5% annual loss of schools. After 2000, as a rule, the number of schools diminishes only slightly. The described developmental trend is seen for example in Czechia (Figure 2.6). Other countries with a similar development trend include Poland, Spain, and also, to some extent, Hungary. All the countries in question seem to have the common denominator of having been under the rule of authoritarian regimes during the 20th century, which enabled directive central planning during the period of the biggest closure of schools.

By contrast, the other group is made up of economically strong countries of western and northern Europe, in which no authoritative regimes ruled in the latter half of the 20th century. In the case of this group there

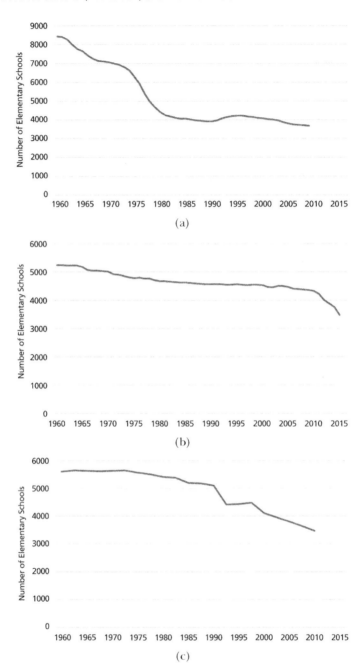

Figure 2.6 (a) Type 1, Example Czechia; (b) Type 2, Example Austria; (c) Serbia. Development types of numbers of elementary schools in selected countries. *Source:* Kučerová (2012), Statistics Austria (2016). Cited 2016-11-29. Available from: https://www.statistik.at/, Bogojević et al. (2002), and Mujanović (2014).

was a gradual, slight decline through those years in the number of elementary schools, when the chain development index ranged between 98% and 101%. In some areas and in some periods, due to the reduced birth rate or to immigration from the countryside, a large number of schools were closed (for Finland see Kalaoja & Pietarinen, 2009), followed by a period of stability and support for (rural) schools as community centres (for Norway see Kvalsund, 2009). However, in the past 10 to 20 years there has been an accelerated process of closure of schools and the chain index acquires higher values—again up to 95%. The trend is exemplified by Austria (Figure 2.6). This group also includes Finland, Norway (Autti & Hyry-Beihammer, 2014; Solstad & Karlberg-Granlund, Chapter 3, this volume), and to some extent the Netherlands, as well as England (the data for the United Kingdom as a whole cannot be found, as in the case of Italy).

The case in Serbia is somewhat different. In the late 1970s, a fall in the number of elementary schools began as it did in the first group. However the war conflict in the former Yugoslavia played a crucial role in the country and school numbers stabilized through the 1990s. Since 2000, the decline in the number of primary schools in Serbia has continued to decrease (Bogojević, Ivić, & Karapandža, 2002; Mujanović, 2014).

The concepts of regionalization of Europe in terms of administration and spatial planning have been carried out (see Knieling & Othengrafen, 2016) and several cultures constituted on different political and administrative structures have been described. In this chapter we have looked just at education and particularly the provision of schools. The typology of school network changes we have constructed is tentative. Our evaluations of the conditions underlying the organization of the educational systems and their development is incomplete but is an initial step towards an international project with participants across countries, to search for joint indicators and provide vital knowledge for educational policy, planning and development.

ACKNOWLEDGMENT

Silvie R. Kučerová would like to thank the European Union, European Social Fund and the Ministry of Education, Youth and Sports of the Czech Republic for the financial support of this paper (Project Smart City—Smart Region—Smart Community—CZ.02.1.01/0.0/0.0/17_048/0007435).

REFERENCES

Åberg-Bengtsson, L. (2009). The smaller the better? A review of research on small rural schools in Sweden. *International Journal of Educational Research, 48*(2), 100–108. https://doi.org/10.1016/j.ijer.2009.02.007

Altrichter, H., Heinrich, M., & Soukup-Altrichter, K. (2014). School decentralization as a process of differentiation, hierarchization and selection. *Journal of Education Policy, 29*(5), 375–699. https://doi.org/10.1080/02680939.2013.873954

Autti, O., & Hyry-Beihammer, E. K. (2014). School closures in rural Finnish communities. *Journal of Research in Rural Education, 29*(1), 1–17.

Bajerski, A. (2015). Erosion of the school catchment system as local policy: The case of Poznań, Poland. *KEDI Journal of Education Policy, 12*(1), 41–60.

Barakat, B. (2015). A 'recipe for depopulation'? School closures and local population decline in Saxony. *Population, Space and Place, 21*(8), 735–753. https://doi.org/10.1002/psp.1853

Basu, R. (2007). Negotiating acts of citizenship in an era of neoliberal reform: The game of school closures. *International Journal of Urban a Regional Research, 31*(1), 109–127. https://doi.org/10.1111/j.1468-2427.2007.00709.x

Bell, A., & Sigsworth, A. (1987). *The small rural primary school: A matter of quality.* London, England: Routledge.

Bertrand, Y. (1998). *Théories contemporaines de l'éducation* [Contemporary theories of education], (4th ed.). Lyon, France: Chronique Sociale.

Bibby, P., & Brindley P. (2013). *Urban and rural area definitions for policy purposes in England and Wales: Methodology.* Newport, England: Office for National Statistics.

Bogojević, A., Ivić, I., & Karapandža, R. (2002). *Optimization of the network of schools in Serbia.* Education Forum.

Burgess, S., Greaves, E., Vignoles, A., & Wilson, D. (2011). Parental choice of primary school in England: What types of school do different types of family really have available to them? *Policy Studies, 32*(5), 531–547. https://doi.org/10.1080/01442872.2011.601215

CBS Statline. (2016). Cited 2017-01-18. Available from https://1url.cz/FzRCN

Cuervo, H. (2016). *Understanding social justice in rural education.* New York, NY: Palgrave Macmillan.

Dvořák, D., Starý, K., & Urbánek, P. (2015). *Škola v globální době. Proměny pěti českých základních škol* [School in the global age. Transformation of five Czech elementary schools]. Prague, Czech Republic: Karolinum.

Dvořák, D., & Straková, J. (2016). Konkurence mezi školami a výsledky žáků v České republice: Pohled zblízka na šetření PISA 2012 [School competition and pupil achievement in the Czech Republic: A close look at the PISA 2012 study]. *Pedagogika, 66*(2), 206–229. https://doi.org/10.14712/23362189.2015.740

Eurostat. (2017a). Cited 2017-01-20. Available from https://1url.cz/UzRUZ

Eurostat. (2017b). Cited 2017-01-20. Available from https://1url.cz/7zRUI

Eurydice. (2012). *Key data on education in Europe 2012.* Brussels, Belgium: Education, Audiovisual and Culture Executive Agency.

Farrington, J., & Farrington, C. (2005). Rural accessibility, social inclusion and social justice: Towards conceptualisation. *Journal of Transport Geography, 13*(1), 1–12. https://doi.org/10.1016/j.jtrangeo.2004.10.002

Faulkner, G., Buliung, R., Flora, P., & Fusco, C. (2009). Active school transport, physical activity and body weight of children and youth: A systematic review. *Preventative Medicine, 48*(1), 3–8. https://doi.org/10.1016/j.ypmed.2008.10.017

Fraser, B. J., Walberg, H. J., Welch, W. W., & Hattie, J. A. (1987). Syntheses of educational productivity research. *International Journal of Educational Research, 11*(2), 147–252.

Geppert, C., Knapp, M., Kilian, M., & Katsching, T. (2015). Volba školy pod tlakem reformních snah [School choice under the pressure of reform efforts]. *Studia Paedagogica, 20*, 10–28. https://doi.org/10.5817/SP2015-1-2

Green, B., & Letts, W. (2007). Space, equity, and rural education: A 'trialectical' account. In K. N. Gulson, & C. Symes (Eds.), *Spatial theories of education. Policy and geography matters* (pp. 57–76). New York, NY: Routledge.

Gyuris, F. (2014). *The political discourse of spatial disparities*. Cham, Germany: Springer.

Halsey, A. H., Lauder, H., Brown, P., & Wells, A. S. (Eds.). (1997). *Education. Culture, economy, and society*. Oxford, England: Oxford University Press.

Hampl, M. (2000). *Reality, society and geographical/environmental organization: Searching for an integrated order*. Prague, Czech Republic: Charles University.

Hampl, M. (2004). Současný vývoj geografické organizace a změny v dojížďce za prací a do škol v Česku [Current development of geographical organisation and changes in commuting to work and schools in Czechia]. *Geografie, 109*(3), 205–222.

Harber, C. (1996). *Small schools and democratic practice*. Nottingham, England: Educational Heretics Press.

Hargreaves, L. M. (2009). Respect and responsibility: Review of research on small rural schools in England. *International Journal of Educational Research, 48*(2), 117–128. https://doi.org/10.1016/j.ijer.2009.02.006

Holloway, S. L., & Pimlott-Wilson, H. (2012). Neoliberalism, policy localisation and idealised subjects: A case study on educational restructuring in England. *Transactions of the Institute of British Geographers, 37*(4), 639–654.

Hulík, V., & Tesárková, K. (2009). Dopady demografického vývoje na vzdělávací soustavu v České republice [Influence of demographic development on the education system in the Czech Republic]. *Orbis Scholae, 3*(3), 7–23.

Jennings, J. L. (2010). School choice or schools' choice? Managing in an era of accountability. *Sociology of Education, 83*(3), 227–247. https://doi.org/10.1177/0038040710375688

Kalaoja, E., & Pietarinen, J. (2009). Small rural primary schools in Finland: A pedagogically valuable part of the school network. *International Journal of Educational Research, 48*(2), 109–116. https://doi.org/10.1016/j.ijer.2009.02.003

Knieling, J., & Othengrafen, F. (2016). En route to a theoretical model for comparative research on planning cultures. In J. Knieling & F. Othengrafen (Eds.), *Planning cultures in Europe* (pp. 39–62). New York, NY: Routledge.

Koinzer, T., Nikolai, R., & Waldow, F. (Eds.). (2017). *Private schools and school choice in compulsory education*. Wiesbaden, Germany: Springer.

Kovács, K. (2012). Rescuing a small village school in the context of rural change in Hungary. *Journal of Rural Studies, 28*(2), 108–117. https://doi.org/10.1016/j.jrurstud.2012.01.020

Kraftl, P. (2012). Towards geographies of 'alternative' education: A case study of UK home schooling families. *Transactions of the Institute of British Geographers, 38*(3), 436–450. https://doi.org/10.1111/j.1475-5661.2012.00536.x

Kučerová, S. (2012). *Proměny územní struktury základního školství v Česku* [Changes in the territorial structure of primary education in Czechia]. Prague, Czech Republic: ČGS.

Kučerová, S. R., Bláha, J. D., & Kučera, Z. (2015). Transformations of spatial relationships within elementary education provision: A case study of changes in two Czech rural areas since the second half of the 20th century. *Moravian Geographical Reports, 23*(1), 34–44. https://doi.org/10.1515/mgr-2015-0004

Kučerová, S. R., Dvořák, D., Meyer, P., & Bartůněk, M. (2020). Dimensions of centralization and decentralization in the rural educational landscape of post-socialist Czechia. *Journal of Rural Studies, 74*, 280–293.

Kučerová, S., & Kučera, Z. (2012). Changes in the spatial distribution of elementary schools and their impact on rural communities in Czechia in the second half of the 20th century. *Journal of Research in Rural Education, 27*(11), 1–17.

Kučerová, S., Mattern, T., Štych, P., & Kučera, Z. (2011). Změny dostupnosti základních škol v Česku jako faktor znevýhodnění regionů a lokalit [Changes in the accessibility of elementary schools in Czechia as a factor of disadvantage impacting regions and localities]. *Geografie, 116*(3), 300–316.

Kvalsund, R. (2009). Centralized decentralization or decentralized centralization? A review of newer Norwegian research on schools and their communities. *International Journal of Educational Research, 48*(2), 89–99. https://doi.org/10.1016/j.ijer.2009.02.006

Maroy, C., & van Zanten, A. (2009). Regulation and competition among schools in six European localities. *Sociologie du Travail, 51*(S1), e67–e79. https://doi.org/10.1016/j.soctra.2009.01.005

Masoumi, H. E., Zanoli, G., Papageorgiou, A., Smaga, S., Miloš, A., van Rooijen, M.,... Çağan, B. (2017). Patterns of children's travel to school, their body weight, spatial factors, and perceptions: A survey on nine European cities. *GeoScape, 11*(2), 52–75.

Meyer, P., & Kučerová, S. R. (2018). Do pupils attend the nearest elementary school to their homes? Factors in school choice in the urban environment of Liberec, Czechia. *Acta Universitatis Carolinae Geographica, 53*(1), 70–82.

Ministry of Education, Youth and Sports. (2016). Cited 2017-01-18. Available from http://toiler.uiv.cz/rocenka/rocenka.asp

Monnier, A. (2006). *Démographie contemporaine de l'Europe. Évolutions, tendances, defies* [Demography of contemporary Europe. Development, trends, challenges]. Paris, France: Armand Colin.

Mujanović, M. (2014). *Školství v tranzici: Srovnání vzdělávací soustavy v Česku, Bosně a Hercegovině, Chorvatsku a Srbsku na počátku 21. Století. Diplomová práce* [Education in transition: Comparison of the educational system in the Czech Republic, Bosnia and Herzegovina, Croatia and Serbia at the beginning of the 21st century. Diploma thesis]. Prague, Czech Republic: Charles University.

Nekorjak, M., Souralová, A., & Vomastková, K. (2011). Uvíznutí v marginalitě: Vzdělávací trh, 'romské školy' a reprodukce sociálně prostorových nerovností [Stuck in marginality: The education market, 'Roma schools' and the reproduction of social and spatial inequalities]. *Sociologický časopis, 47*(4), 657–680.

Nikitović, V., Bajat, B., & Blagojević, D. (2016): Spatial patterns of recent demographic trends in Serbia (1961–2010). *Geografie, 121*(4), 521–543.

OECD. (2011). *What schools for the future?* Paris, France: Author.

Open Street Map. (2017). Cited 2017-01-23. Available from https://1url.cz/KzRfW

Průcha, J. (2005). *Moderní pedagogika* [Modern pedagogy]. Prague, Czech Republic: Portál.

Ribchester, C., & Edwards, B. (1999). The centre and the local: Policy and practice in rural education provision. *Journal of Rural Studies, 15*(1), 49–63.

Roberts, B. K. (1996). *Landscapes of settlement: Prehistory to the present.* London, England: Routledge.

Šimáně, M. (2010). K problematice zřizování českých menšinových obecných škol na Ústecku v letech 1867–1918 [To the problems of the foundation of the Czech minority elementary schools in Ústí nad Labem and its surroundings during 1867–1918 period]. *E-Pedagogium, 10*(4), 83–92.

Statistics Austria. (2016). Cited 2016-11-29. Available from https://www.statistik.at/

Statistics Norway. (2015). *Facts about education in Norway 2015.* Oslo: Ministry of Education and Research and Directorate for Education and Training.

Trnková, K. (2009). Village schools: Wrinkles for mayors? *European Countryside, 1,* 105–112. https://doi.org/10.2478/v10091/009-0009-1

UNESCO. (2012). *International standard classification of education, ISCED 2011.* Montreal, Canada: UNESCO Institute for Statistics.

United Nations. (2017). *Revision of world population prospects 2015.* Cited 2017-01-02. Available from https://population.un.org/wpp/

van de Werfhorst, H. G. (2014). Changing societies and four tasks of schooling: Challenges for strongly differentiated educational systems. *International Review of Education, 60,* 123–144. https://doi.org/10.1007/s11159-014-9410-8

CHAPTER 3

RURAL EDUCATION IN A GLOBALIZED WORLD

The Cases of Norway and Finland

Karl Jan Solstad
Nordland Research Institute, Norway

Gunilla Karlberg-Granlund
Åbo Akademi University, Finland

In this chapter our aim is to identify, exemplify, and discuss how and to what extent various aspects of globalization have an impact on, and also possibly threaten, rural communities, rural life and culture, and, in particular, rural schools. Although we will draw mainly on Norwegian and Finnish research and examples, the overall picture will be very similar to that of many other Western and Northern European countries. Based on a brief account of the concept of globalization, the authors identify aspects of globalization of particular importance in a rural context: the neoliberal downgrading of national or regional authorities, deregulation and privatization of public services, the introduction of New Public Management (NPM) applying business models for governance to the public sector, the international testing regimes, and the global flow of information and ideas. To focus on Finland and Norway as cases and analyze the long term development of rural education in these countries may be particularly interesting. Although both countries are similar in terms of geography, size of population and culture, there are also striking differences. Economically, the last international recession has hit Finland much harder than it has Norway. In educational performance, Finland stands out as a winner in the global testing game, whereas Norway, in spite of being among the countries spending the most per capita on compulsory education, is just mediocre in its performance. In our study we try to explore how, and possibly why, aspects of globalization result in different manifestations of rural educational development in the two countries.

AN OVERVIEW

To understand how external, supranational forces or trends impact on the running of, and the developments within, educational provision in rural communities, and especially how they might manifest themselves differently in different countries, we need to consider the frames within which this education has to operate (Lundgren, 1985). Following a brief overview of some structural features in our two countries, we will identify aspects of globalization of particular importance in a rural context, before embarking on the actual analyses of how rural education and small schools have fared in Norway and Finland.

Structural Features of Importance for Rural Education

The geographical, demographical, and administrative structures of Norway and Finland within which the rural schools have to operate have many similarities. As Table 3.1 shows, the two countries are fairly similar in terms of total area, size of population, and regional and municipal structures. Even the shapes of the countries have common features (see the two bottom rows of Table 3.1) although Norway with its coastline, fjords, valleys, and mountain areas also makes a contrast to the Finnish lowland features, lakes, and vast woodlands. Both countries have a huge number of islands, Finland almost 800 in one square kilometer (km^2) or more and Norway around 700. Most of these islands are inhabited and many are without road connections to the mainland or to other neighboring islands.

In both countries the proportion of the population living in sparsely populated rural areas has decreased tremendously during the last half century. Actually, whereas in the mid-1900s a clear majority of the population in both countries lived in sparsely populated rural areas, this situation now

TABLE 3.1 Norway and Finland Compared (Selected Geographical, Demographical, and Administrative Characteristics)

Geographical Characteristic	Norway	Finland
Area (square kilometers)	386,209 km²	336,851 km²
Population (2018)	5,295,600	5,503,300
Percentage living in sparsely populated areas (< 200 inhabitants; 1960 and 2017)	69% and 19%	55% and 20%
Levels of politically elected governing bodies (national, regional, municipal)	3 (national, county, municipal)	2 (national, municipal)
Number of regions/counties	19	19
Number of municipalities (2018)	422	311
Average population size of municipalities (2018)	12,550	17,000
Largest population size of municipalities (2018)	658,400	604,000
Smallest population size of municipalities (2018)	208 (next two: 454; 474)	98 (next two: 246; 441)
Average area size of municipalities (square km)	902 km²	1,040 km²
Vertical (north–south) length of country	1,748 km	1,110 km
Horizontal (east–west) width of country	432 km (max) – 10 km (min.)	444 km (max) – ca.140 km (min.)

applies to barely 20 %. Today, 8 out of 10 people are to be found in built-up areas with more than 200 inhabitants, or in towns or cities.

Compulsory education—that is primary and lower secondary schooling—is in both countries run by the municipalities. The size of the municipalities varies enormously, from having fewer than 200 inhabitants to 500,000 or more in the capitals of Oslo and Helsinki. The very smallest municipalities may take care of a single island or a cluster of small neighboring islands.

The number of municipalities has decreased dramatically over the years; in Norway from 744 in the 1930s down to 422 after a recent restructuring; in Finland from 518 up to the 1970s to the present 311.

The structure of required schooling is similar in Norway and Finland with 10 years of compulsory education starting at the age of six. Private schools cater for fewer than 3% of the primary and lower secondary school populations in both Finland and Norway, although the establishment of small private schools to replace closed municipality schools is increasingly common in the latter. In both our countries, rural schools have been axed in large numbers since around 1990, reflecting a similar trend in other European countries (Sigsworth & Solstad, 2005; Karlberg-Granlund, 2009).

We see this massive closure of rural schools as related to processes associated with globalization. So what is globalization?

GLOBALIZATION: PROGRESS OR THREAT? AND FOR WHOM?

In his exegesis of the concept of globalization, Ampuja (2015, p. 17) underlines "inclusiveness" as typical, and further notes that globalization is not only being used to *describe* changes in social life, but actually to *explain* such changes. This is what we are aiming at. We want to show that certain aspects of globalization have impacted on the educational provision in sparsely populated areas of developed countries, using Norway and Finland as the empirical base. A first challenge is to identify those features of globalization that are of particular relevance in the context of rural education.

The American economist and writer Robert J. Samuelson (2000) provides a similar broad description of globalization as, on the one hand, "a powerful vehicle that raises economic growth, spreads new technology, and increases living standards" (n.p.), but, on the other hand, makes up "an immensely controversial process that assaults national sovereignty, erodes local culture and tradition, and threatens economic and social stability" (n.p.).

Despite this composite and somewhat elusive nature of globalization, most writers on the theme underline the close relationship between globalization and a neoliberal ideology, an ideology that embraces a strong belief in capitalism as the only system that may stimulate development and secure prosperity. Within the critical literature of globalization, it is seen as primarily driven by a neoliberal doctrine (Ampuja, 2015; Colás, 2005). Litonjua (2008) goes a step further and simply states, "Globalisation is the global spread of the economic system of capitalism. Promoted by the ideology of neoliberalism, the goal is a wholly deregulated global market society" (p. 254).

By drawing, in particular, on the close relationship between globalization and neoliberal capitalism, we identify in Table 3.2 four broad and partly overlapping aspects included in most recent volumes on globalization theory, and how it relates to rural education and rural communities (Boston, Martin, Pallot, & Walch, 1996; Rizvi & Lingard, 2010; Smith, 2008; Zajda, 2015).

In the following we will first look into how rural communities and sparsely populated areas in countries like Norway and Finland have fared under the influence of globalization and neoliberal policies. The main part of the chapter will focus on how certain aspects of globalization have impacted, directly or indirectly, on the education provision in such areas.

TABLE 3.2 Selected Characteristics of Globalization and Their Possible Consequences for Rural Life

Aspects of Globalization	Potential Negative Impacts on Rural Education and Rural Communities
Neo-liberalism: Competition as the driving force for progress, free choice, stressing the individual rather than the collective good.	Minimizing the public sector, privatization, deregulation, decentralization of power → small, peripheral organizations, institutions, and communities unable to compete successfully.
New public management (NPM): The introduction of business models for governance and management in the public sector; accountability in terms of spending and output down to the individual unit.	Pupils, parents, and teachers as consumers; a stress on cost cutting, efficiency, and cutback management → small rural municipalities, small school units particularly at risk.
Supra-national institutions: The emergence of institutions like EU, EES, WB, OECD, Efta, PISA, etc.	Formal regulations or requests (e.g., EU) or powerful recommendations (e.g., OECD) → limit the freedom of national authorities to tailor measures to protect or stimulate, for instance, small remote communities and areas being exposed to harsh climate, costly transport, etc.
ICT-driven compression of space and time: Globalized, mainly urban based, cultural values, and expressions reach out immediately and unfiltered to everyone and everywhere.	Communal ties and identities may be weakened and the sustainability and renewal of local rural livelihoods undermined.

RURAL ECONOMY, RURAL COMMUNITIES, AND RURAL LIFE IN A GLOBALIZING WORLD

The traditional population distribution of Northern European countries, like Norway and Finland, mirrors the natural resources of land and sea available for human survival. In Norway the concentration of settlements was to be found in the south east and along the coastline and the fjords up to the very north. Similarly, in Finland the highest concentration of villages and rural settlements was to be found in the southwest and the more sparsely populated areas in the northern and eastern parts. The mechanisation and rationalization of fishing, farming, and forestry after World War II substantially reduced the demand for a labor force in the primary sector of the economy, thus forcing or tempting young people in particular to leave the countryside.

With neoliberal ideas gaining ground throughout the 1980s, state level interventions to stimulate economic activities in remote and sparsely populated areas—such as subsidized transport and differentiated labor taxation—became less popular and were made partly impossible by international agreements through the World Trade Organization or EU/EEC. The Norwegian economist Paul Olav Berg (2004) demonstrates how the peripheral and sparsely populated areas become the losers when state-run services are privatized or floated on the stock market, subject to demands for profit just like private industries. Unprofitable railway lines are terminated, electrical power lines serving few consumers are not maintained, and provision of high-speed broadband is seriously delayed or even denied for small peripheral places. This more aggressive way of running basic services puts established companies at risk and makes the creation of new businesses less likely. Successful local firms are at risk of being taken over by big chains, thus losing their local ownership and concomitant sense of loyalty and responsibility for the local workforce and community. Furthermore, when production is managed from a distant big city, local subcontractors are less likely to be hired. Again, the small rural communities tend to be the losers (Lindkvist, 2004).

Overall, demographic changes in both Norway and Finland since 1990 have been very significant: the typically rural areas have suffered out-migration to the cities and suburbs, which have enjoyed a substantial rise in their share of the population (NOU, 2004, p. 2; Tantarimäki & Törhönen, Chapter 12, this volume). However, perhaps such demographic changes exceed what might be explained by economic and free market mechanisms. In both Norway and Finland, young people leave rural places, even those places with ample employment opportunities. Thus, we may ask, do young people want to live in small rural places without the kind of facilities that the cities may offer? This leads us to the final aspect of globalization as listed in Table 3.2.

The compression of time and space due to modern ICT, television, video films, and the availability of advanced smartphones and computers and so on, even amongst preschool children, makes young people everywhere in the industrialized world exposed to, and stimulated by, the same fantasy figures and perspectives of life as presented from a few influential and wealthy urban milieus, especially the United States. This new flow of impressions, impulses, and information reaches out to the children directly, no longer filtered through family, playmates, or teachers. Such phenomena have led Anthony Giddens (1990) to his theory of *modernity*, of the modern individual being dis-embedded from family, social grouping, or local community. Giddens and other theorists (e.g., Ziehe, 1995) provide explanations that chime well with the impression of a present day globalized world dominated by individualistic rather than collectivist codes for behavior. It is the free choice and the many options for each individual that count.

Over time, these processes, combined with fewer local arenas for cooperation and interaction, have changed rural life. Typically, working life within the primary sector of the economy has become a one-person/family enterprise: the local shop, the post office, the bank, and the school may be gone. The result may be a cultural homogenization of rural areas, to the extent that there is no longer such a thing as a local rural *community*.

We have addressed several developments likely to reduce the viability of rural life and communities in our countries: rural population loss during after the World War II years due to mechanization and rationalization within the primary sector of the economy; various globalization related developments disfavoring rural areas, (e.g., by weakening important infrastructure), reducing the willingness and/or political power of national authorities to support rural economies and communities; and successful rural businesses being moved to more central locations to make them even more profitable. One combined effect of these developments is the loss of natural arenas for rural people to meet, interact, and cooperate. Typically, as working life within the primary sector of the economy has become a one-person/family enterprise (the local shop, the post office, the bank, and the school may be gone) rural people neither have the natural meeting places nor the obvious need to interact and cooperate. Furthermore, on the cultural side, we have the massive urban-based bodies of information and options for entertainment through the various mass media to which everyone is individually exposed.

To the extent that the above picture of the rural situation in the present globalized world is true, we may question whether there is such a thing as a *local* community, a *local* culture, or a *local* identity. Are we witnessing a cultural homogenization within our countries making the whole concept of *rural communities* superfluous? Is it no longer the case that people living in certain places or local areas have distinct feelings of identity, belongingness, shared values, and perspectives, and so on?

Yet, despite the weakening effects of globalization, people living in rural settlements still have a lot in common, such as nature and climate, culture and history, family relations, leisure time experiences, and so on. We will argue that the concept of rural *communities* is still meaningful, even if the feeling of being integrated, of local identity and of place-attachment may be weaker than before the globalization era. Three Norwegian studies of identity formation among young people in the rural north challenge the concept of modernity and "setting free" (Bæck, 2004; Paulgaard, 2001; Wiborg, 2001). Interviews with rural youth from six European countries, including Finland, showed considerable variation in urbanization and setting free between and within countries (Dax & Machold, 2002). The example of Finnish youth from the central eastern municipality of Suomussalmi supports the Norwegian studies; local identity and attachment are far from lost (Muilu & Onkalo, 2002).

One common incident that brings people to manifest their belongingness and commitment to a *local community* is when their local school is under threat of closure. This brings us to the more direct effects of globalization on the educational provision in rural areas.

SMALL RURAL SCHOOLS AND THE GLOBALIZING POLICIES: GENERAL CONSIDERATIONS

Several aspects of globalization are likely to interfere in the provision of education in rural areas. Let us look first at the processes of decentralization and deregulation.

An improved infrastructure for school transportation combined with a strong belief that the way of improving rural education was to make the schools larger, led to extensive school centralization in many countries during the 1950s–1960s. This massive closure of schools—in Finland 300 a year, in Norway 150—gradually came to a halt for two reasons: firstly, educational research in many countries gave no support to the view that the pupils' learning was at risk in small schools, and secondly, long school journeys were found to have negative effects on pupils' physical development and general well-being (Käppi, 1971; Solstad, 1978). During the period 1970–1990, the rate of school closures was dramatically reduced both in Finland (Laukkanen & Muhonen, 1981) and Norway (Solstad, 2009).

When the neoliberal inspired legislation became established in the 1980s–1990s, the official national policies of both Norway and Finland were still to keep up a decentralized school structure. The Norwegian Minister for Education declared that small schools should not be closed for financial reasons (O.tid. 1984–1985, pp. 616–633). As we will see, this promise was not kept.

Around the turn of the millennium, several legislative changes with potentially significant consequences for rural communities and rural schools were introduced both in Norway and Finland. Firstly, the municipalities were granted more freedom to handle their matters across the various sectors of municipal services, in Norway in 1988 and 1992, in Finland in 1989. Secondly, a system of earmarked grants (for running compulsory schooling) from state to municipal level was abandoned, in Norway in 1986, in Finland in 1993. Thirdly, in Finland a special state level allowance targeting small schools was terminated in 2006, whereas in Norway various measures to secure teacher coverage in small and outlying schools were gradually discontinued.

Thus, in both Norway and Finland, education was no longer specially protected from the competition with the health sector, technical services, and so on, for municipal funds. As these changes coincided with recession in the public economy, although less so in Norway than in Finland, the rural school structure came under considerable pressure. The legislative changes made school closures more tempting for the municipalities struggling to balance their budgets, and they were now also freer to do so.

Traditionally, in both our countries, the rural community had a strong standing. The rural school was often seen as a cornerstone, a place for parents to meet, a place to arrange adult education, for various local associations to have their meetings, and so on. In short, the school was an integral part of the local community (Kalaoja, 1988; Kalaoja & Pietarinen, 2009; Solstad, 1978). However, with the global stress on the individual rather than the collective, such as the local community, concern for the fate of the communities in cases of school closure is less obvious.

RURAL SCHOOLS UNDER NEW FINANCIAL AND ADMINISTRATIVE ORDERS

The available statistics and research in our two countries do not allow for readily comparable data. In Norway, surveys of 110 *sparsely populated area* (SPA) municipalities, conducted in 2005 (Solstad, 2009) and 2015 (Solstad & Solstad, 2015), are available. (The surveys included 142 SPA municipalities altogether, of which 110 responded to both. Most of the results in Figure 3.1 refer to these 110 municipalities.) In addition to statistical data on school closures between 1980 and 2015, the surveys also cover the reasons for school closure decisions, local reactions to the process of closure, and, in 2005 only, how the threat of being closed is experienced by school staff.

School Closures and Their Reasons

Figure 3.1 demonstrates a dramatic increase in the numbers of school closures in Norwegian SPA-municipalities following the transfer of financial

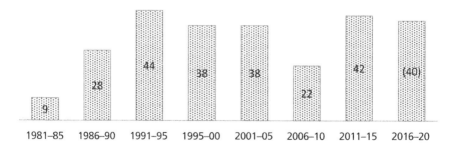

Figure 3.1 Number of school closures in 110 Norwegian SPA-municipalities from 1980–2015 and expected closures from 2016–2020. *Source:* Solstad & Solstad, 2015, pp. 38–39.

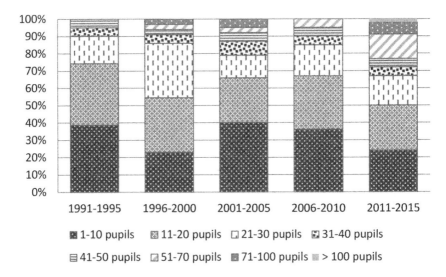

Figure 3.2 School closures, by year of closure, and number of pupils in the year before closure. *Source:* Solstad & Solstad, 2015, p. 45.

responsibility from national to municipal level. The irregularity in the period from 2006–2010 may be related to a change of government in 2005, with the promise of more money for the municipalities. According to some 2005 respondents this resulted in a temporary halt in the planning of new school closures. The 2015 survey also provides data on expected school closures over the next 5 years, assuming that the closure rate will remain the same as in most previous 5-year periods. In 1990, there were 470 schools in these 110 SPA-municipalities. By 2020, this number will have almost halved.

Very small schools with under 10 pupils make up a large fraction of the schools being closed (Figure 3.2), but in 2011–2015, schools with 50+ pupils make up almost one in four of them, compared with none of this size in 1991–1995. There was also a tendency over those 25 years to close schools more often even if the pupils had to endure quite lengthy school journeys (Solstad & Solstad, 2015, p. 46). As we shall see later, this tendency to close not so small rural schools, and to accept closures despite lengthy school journeys may be seen as related to the globalization driven concern for accountability and quality, narrowly interpreted as achievement on international and national tests in a few academic subjects (Smith, 2016).

Figure 3.3 presents data on the main reasons why a municipality, as perceived by the education officer, made the decision to close each individual school. Budgetary concerns were the most important factor for local politicians both before and after 2005, followed by considerations related to low

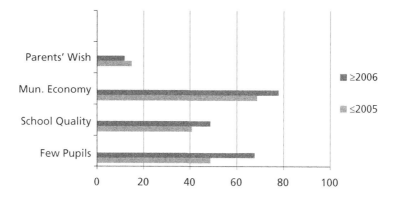

Figure 3.3 Percentage of municipalities reporting too few pupils, school quality, municipal economy, and parents' wish to be *very important* for the closure of each school by periods: 2005 or earlier, 2006 or later (the other alternatives were *of no importance* and *somewhat important*). Source: Derived from Solstad & Solstad, 2015, p. 51, Table 6.

and sinking pupil enrollment, which revealed a change from under 50% before to almost 70% after 2005. These findings also indicate that the local politicians' conceptions of "too small to be viable" have changed during the period. On the other hand, the low proportion (12%) of parents' wishes, considering it *very important* to close the school, suggests that parents were not worried about the quality of education in a small local school. On the contrary, most were fighting against closure. We shall return to this shortly.

In Finland also, the number of small schools (of fewer than 50 pupils) has been reduced drastically since the global recession of the 1990s and the legislative changes referred to above. Between 1991 and 2012 almost 2,100 schools were reduced to 660 (Autti & Hyry-Beihammer, 2014). During 2000–2010 an average of about 100 schools were closed annually (for further details, see Tantarimäki & Törhönen, Chapter 12, this volume). As in Norway, the decision to take a school away was often met with anger and protests from local people. This kind of conflict was clearly demonstrated through an analysis of debates in local newspapers when a municipality consisting of a town surrounded by a number of smaller rural communities planned to close several schools. The small village schools were seen to have the double function of mediating education and of representing community life (i.e., pedagogy and culture). The struggle for the local school was also a defence of the local quality of life and of educational quality for each individual child. There seemed to be an inbuilt conflict in the political ambition to simultaneously achieve equality, economic efficiency, and quality (Karlberg-Granlund, 2009, p. 289ff.).

The Process of Closing Schools

Whereas the neoliberal inspired measures from national level to decentralize and deregulate the running of compulsory schooling has provided municipal bodies with both good reasons and the formal power to rationalize its school structure, there is, in most cases, substantial local mobilization to prevent such decisions.

Returning to the Norwegian survey, according to Figure 3.4a, 85% of the closures are met with typically strong organized protests from local people, parents, and others. Although this survey cannot show those cases where protests were helpful in saving schools, Figure 3.4b suggests that such local resistance often delayed the decision-making processes. In over half the cases, the municipal proposal to close a school had been voted on several times.

Nearly half of the still existing schools in the 142 SPA-municipalities covered in the 2005 survey had been threatened with closure between 1990 and 2005. Perhaps the more effective mobilizations occurred in communities rich in "social capital" (Coleman, 1988) or "rural literacy" (Corbett & Donehower, 2017) and, hence, were in the best position to save their schools. That said, there are many examples in Norway of extremely well-organized and competent local action groups with the full backing of their whole local communities who failed to save their public schools, but then succeeded in organizing private schools to replace the closed municipality ones (Solstad, 2016). A national survey covering 2002–2012 shows that of around 90 private schools established in Norway, 60% were substitutes for slaughtered municipal schools (Udir, 2013).

Schooling Under Threat of Closure

As we have seen, since around 1990, it is quite common in rural Norway to live with, to run, to teach, or be taught in schools that are under threat of

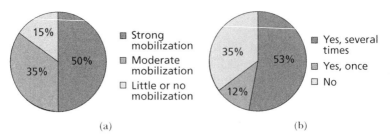

Figure 3.4 (a) Local resistance to school closures; (b) degree of delays in decision-making. *Source:* Based on 74 school closures during 2006–2015; see Solstad & Solstad, 2015, pp. 48–49.

closure. Except in a few cases where head teachers saw a short-term benefit for school, home, and community relations in having the school as a common cause, the overwhelming majority reported on the negative experiences associated with the fear of being wiped out. Head teachers and teachers felt squeezed between their employer's policy of school closure and the struggle on behalf of parents and community to save the school. Sapping of energy, frustration, and dispiritedness were felt to interfere negatively with the quality of the education provided. Head teachers reported other specific negative effects of the threat of closure on long term planning, staff energy and creativity to promote learning, and adoption of a strategy of minimum demands for resources with consequent deterioration of equipment, school buildings, and school sites, and, most seriously, teachers' job insecurity, making it difficult to retain or recruit teaching staff (Solstad, 2009, pp. 127–149).

In Finland, Karlberg-Granlund (2011) analyzed the coping strategies of a teacher in a one-teacher school that had been continually under threat of closure for several years. The story of this teacher strongly points to the need for formal and informal support networks and for confidential dialogue about the challenges to be met in times of uncertainty about the future of a school. Such backup helps a teacher to find the necessary strength to cope and manage in times of increasing demands.

RURAL EDUCATION FACING THE INTERNATIONAL TESTING REGIMES

We have seen that at national levels the neoliberal inspired global trend of decentralization and deregulation has changed the school structures of the rural areas of our countries. This *decentralization of power* has resulted in a massive *geographical centralization* of rural schools, at least to some extent contrary to the proclaimed national policies (Kvalsund, 2009). But states are also giving up power by subjugating themselves to international agencies. For the last 10–15 years, especially due to the OECD-run PISA (Programme for International Student Assessment), "nation states are ceding power over what used to be considered a 'sacred' part of their jurisdiction," their education (Meyer & Benavot, 2013, p. 16). Ulf Lundgren (2014), also known as the father of PISA, talks about making PISA an important premise for a country's educational priorities, a view strongly supported by Svein Sjøberg (2014), who has also been involved in developing the PISA testing program.

As explained by Kamens (2013, pp. 117ff), this development is related to central elements of globalization; namely, the demand for accountability and the view that competition is the driving force for development and prosperity at all levels, from the individual person to the global society.

Furthermore, it is taken for granted that *human* capital (Becker, 1964), too narrowly interpreted as *economic* capital (Bourdieu, 1997), can be raised through education, and that achievement testing, perceived as objective, neutral, and reliable, is a necessary tool for practicing accountability and competition. Activities related to the international testing programs PISA, TIMMS (Trends in International Mathematics and Science Study), and PIRLS (Progress in International Reading Literacy Study), as well as annual national testing schemes, can take up a very substantial amount of time—in the United States up to 40 school days a year (Sherer, 2009). Further, the following description of the weight and standing of international and national testing arrangements may apply, at least in a Norwegian context:

> The assumed, taken-for-granted, nature of testing can be described as the global testing culture and permeates all aspects of education... The reinforcing nature of the global testing culture leads to an environment where testing becomes synonymous with accountability, which becomes synonymous with education quality. (Smith, 2016, p. 7)

As Sjøberg (2014) points out, some Norwegian local authorities, notably Oslo city, carry out all the international tests, a national testing scheme, and its own Oslo-tests. Furthermore, Norway has, as part of the NPM principles for school governance, also implemented a series of other time consuming control routines, all detracting from the teachers' main task: to promote learning (Blossing, Imsen, & Moos, 2014).

Since PISA began in 2000, Finland has consistently performed well amongst a few top countries worldwide, often enthroned at the very top (Aurén & Joshi, 2013) in the international league tables of reading, mathematics, and science. This has been the case although Finland's educational policies and practices in many respects have been running counter to the dominating international doctrines of accountability (Varjo, Simola, & Rinne, 2013, p. 53). Norway, on the other hand, has performed consistently in the middle of participating European countries. As Norway is often number one in other international rankings (e.g., "the best country to live in"), politicians and business sector groups have demanded a better performance in education in order to compete successfully in a globalized economy. Added to this demand is also the fact that Norway spends more money per pupil on education than most other nations (ECON, 2002).

The Case of Norway

When education does not deliver according to expectations, it is common to target the teachers. Questions as to the quality of recruitment and training of teachers follow, although a positive correlation between a teacher's formal subject knowledge and the pupils' learning progress on that subject has never been established (Hattie, 2009, p. 111; Wragg, 1989). Nevertheless, Norwegian politicians have imposed structural changes on teacher education in the last 10–20 years to strengthen teachers' subject knowledge in PISA-relevant subjects. The changes, and their apparent consequences include: raising the entry threshold in mathematics in 2015, with a subsequent reduction in applications for teacher education; increasing training time devoted to Norwegian, English, and mathematics, leading to a narrowing of student teachers' subject choices, at the cost of aesthetic and practical subjects; a break with the long-standing tradition of the *general* teacher (class teachers) to teach primary level pupils (Grades 1–6/7) across the curriculum, now replaced by *subject* teachers; a division of training courses in 2010 into two tracks, for Grades 1–7 and 5–10, resulting in more recruits, especially men opting for the 5–10 track.

These PISA-driven changes are likely to increase primary staffing problems in general, but especially for small two to three teacher schools in sparsely populated areas (Østerud et al., 2015). Head teachers of small combined primary and lower secondary schools in island communities have already expressed such concerns (Solstad et al., 2016). In Norway, it is the sparsely populated, peripheral and northernmost areas that suffer the most in times of teacher shortage (Eikeland & Lie, 1994; Solstad, 1997). Altogether, these developments are likely to add to the existing financial pressure to close small rural schools.

Furthermore, influential circles (e.g., the National Directorate for Education) have promulgated new doubts as to the quality of small schools, notably referring to Hattie (2009) whose meta-analyses identified a moderate, but statistically significant, relationship between school size and pupils' academic performance. His conclusion (Hattie, 2009, p. 79f) was based on American High School studies. Although of no relevance to Scandinavian primary and lower secondary education, such information may be highly convenient for politicians and bureaucrats with budgetary concerns. Decisions to close small schools can be based on idealistic rather than financial reasoning.

The Case of Finland

The international testing regimes have also influenced Finland, but quite differently from Norway. Toom et al. (2010, p. 331) conclude that the Finnish pupils' success in international comparisons has endorsed the Finnish approach to teacher education as the right way to go.

Teacher education in Finland has been a research-based master's level program placed in universities since 1971 (Laukkanen, Muhonen, Ruuhijärvi, Similä, & Toivonen, 1986). It gives teachers thorough scientific knowledge of pedagogy and didactics, as well as competence to analyze and develop their own work (Hansén & Eklund, 2014; Tirri, 2014; Toom et al., 2010). Primary teachers of 6–12 year olds (preschool to Grade 6) have a master's level exam with pedagogy as the main subject, and a thesis in the field of education. They are general teachers (class teachers) who also specialize in the didactics of one or two subjects. Lower secondary (ages 13–15 years, Grades 7–9) and upper secondary teachers, on the other hand, are specialist subject teachers, whose theses are subject-based (Hansén & Eklund, 2014; Tirri, 2014). Subsequently, Finnish teachers' academic professionalism and pedagogical thinking have been seen as one of the success factors behind the "Finnish miracle" (Sahlberg, 2010).

A further important factor in Finnish teacher education has been recognition of the prevalence of small rural schools in Finland, and the special context of teaching in them. Karlberg-Granlund (2009) suggests that the small school may be considered to have its own pedagogy. Student teachers, therefore, may complete a practical placement with multigrade classes in some of the universities' practice schools (cf. Laukkanen et al., 1986). It would be important for student teachers to engage in the pedagogical thinking appropriate to the small rural school context, which includes not only the pedagogy, but also a unique culture dependent on the collaboration between the teachers, pupils, parents, and the local community (Karlberg-Granlund, 2019). This traditional, even symbiotic, relationship can surprise new teachers who are unaware of the teacher's very important role in a small community. Known in the 19th century as "the light of the people" (in Finnish, "Kansan kynttilä"), something of this ideal is still prominent in the Finnish countryside.

According to the Finnish Basic Education Act of 1998, a child should normally be assigned to a "neighbourhood school" (Section 6) to ensure adequate equity in education across the country (Section 2). This ideal, however, is now under pressure as the economic situation has led municipalities to different strategies in planning school networks (see Tantarimäki & Törhönen, Chapter 12, this volume). Kalaoja and Pietarinen (2009) concluded that "the continuing process of centralisation endangers the basic Finnish right to equal basic education in rural areas" (p. 109). Ironically, as Sahlberg (2011) has warned, even good test results can be used as an excuse for the downgrading of economic resources. Sahlberg (2011) also points out that many teachers are worried that reducing "quality of [an] education system" to the pupil's achievements in a few academic subjects may be at "the expense of social studies, arts, sports, music, and the development of the whole person" (p. 131).

Furthermore, the international tests might also promote education policies that are neither transferrable nor acknowledging of local and cultural characteristics. According to the Finnish PISA team, the results should be analyzed in connection with many interrelated factors, such as students' own interests and leisure activities, the learning opportunities, parental support and involvement, as well as the social and cultural contexts of learning and the education system as a whole (Välijärvi, Linnakylä, Kupari, Reinikainen, & Arffman, 2007).

RURAL PUPILS AND RURAL COMMUNITIES WITHOUT RURAL SCHOOLS

In rural areas, school closures make it difficult to achieve many of the fundamental aims of education, including children's health and well-being, good partnerships between home and school, and pupils' identity formation and place attachment.

In general, school closures necessitate school transportation. Formal regulations in Norway entitle 6-year-old pupils to free school transport if the distance from home to school exceeds 2 km; for older pupils the limit is 4 km. There is no absolute regulation for journey time, but in 1985 the (Norwegian) Ministry of Transport issued guidance on the upper limits for "acceptable time consumed" (walking, plus waiting, plus the bus journey) on home to school travels: up to 45 minutes one way for Grade Level 1–3 pupils, 60 minutes for Grade 4–6 pupils, and 75 minutes for Grade 7–9 pupils (Samferdselsdepartementet, 1985). The increased demand for school transportation, due to school closures, is illustrated by data from the rural study already referred to. Whereas, on average, slightly fewer than half of the children were entitled to school transportation before the 1990 closures; afterwards, all pupils had to be transported by school bus. Before the closures during 1990–2015, the average bus journey was 8 km; afterwards the average school journey for all pupils was 15 km (Solstad & Solstad, 2015, p. 73). Following the 2005 closures, this distance was over 30 km in almost 1 of 10 cases, indicating even longer bus journeys for those already travelling to their former school by bus (p. 46).

In Finland, the 1998 Finnish Basic Education Act entitles pupils to free transportation if the home to school distance exceeds 5 km, or less if the travel conditions are difficult when considering the child's age. Daily school travel, however, can be very time-consuming; for under 13s it can be two and a half hours including waiting time, while pupils aged 13+ face as much as 3 hours.

Health and Well-Being

The most negative direct consequences of lengthy school transportation are the inconveniences of having to get up early, come home late, lose free time, and be restricted in after school activities. Lower secondary pupils in an island municipality, facing the prospect of school journeys of over 1 hour each way, were clear about the negative effects on their daily life (Solstad et al., 2016). There are also health risks that often seem to be overlooked. Finnish and Norwegian studies from the 1970s (Käppi, 1971; Solstad, 1973) and the 1980s (Nilsson & Raundalen, 1985) found a negative relationship between school transportation and physical fitness. A more recent Danish study (Cooper et al., 2006) identified the value of pupils' cycling to and from school as particularly beneficial for the pupils' fitness. Missing the natural exercise inherent in walking or cycling to school causes a reduction in balance and flexibility in the back and hip areas and a propensity for back problems (Haselgrove et al., 2008; Sjølie, 2002; Szpalski, Gunzburg, Balague, Nordin, & Melot, 2002). The severity of these problems increases with distance or time spent on transportation. Moreover, a proportion of the children—some 25% if the journeys exceed about 10 km—suffer from various types of psychological uneasiness during, and for some also after, the bus ride (Amundsveen & Øines, 2003; Nilsson & Raundalen, 1985; Solstad, 1975).

Growing concern internationally about increased numbers of overweight and obese in the school age population of urban areas is matched by the marked shrinkage in the proportion of pupils reaching school by their own means (McDonald, 2007; Mendoza & Liu, 2014; Rosenberg, Sallis, Conway, Cain, & McKenzie, 2006). Therefore, in several countries programs have been launched to deter parents in *urban* and *suburban* areas from driving their kids to school (e.g., Crawford & Garrard 2013; McDonald, 2007; McMinn, Rowe, Murtagh, & Nelson, 2011). In rural areas, school bussing cannot be avoided. Norwegian analyses of national health data have demonstrated a significantly higher occurrence of overweight pupils in rural areas (Grøholt, Stigum, & Nordhagen, 2008; Heyerdahl, Aamodt, Nordhagen, & Hovengen, 2012). Heyerdahl et al. (2012) suggest that this may be related to rural pupils' common exemption from the compulsory daily exercise of walking or cycling to school.

Overweight, reduced fitness, and restricted flexibility in the hip area are disadvantageous for the children and adolescents affected, but such physical problems at a young age tend to prevail in adult life (Raitakari et al., 1994; Stucky-Ropp & DiLorenzo, 1993). Overweight people are also more susceptible to developing diabetes, cardiovascular diseases and trouble with knees and hips, all health problems that reduce individual quality of life, and increase the need for sick leave and early retirement, amounting to large expenses on public health budgets (Brage, Ihlebæk, Natvig, & Brusgaard, 2010). We might question whether the globalization driven extensive school closures we are witnessing in countries like Finland and Norway really pay, even in strict economic terms, if a cross sectorial and long-range perspective is applied.

School–Home Relations

The importance of close cooperation between schools and parents, and between schools and local communities, is stressed in the basic education acts and national curricula of both Norway and Finland.

It may be almost axiomatic that the kind of close school–home liaison envisaged is more difficult to establish the greater the distance between home and school. A Norwegian study compared the amount and quality of home and school relationships between small rural schools with geographically narrow catchment areas and relatively large rural schools serving several villages or settlements. Whereas most parents from both types of schools met for the few statutory meetings, the parents of the small rural school pupils were far more likely to participate actively in parents' councils, in joint school–home enterprises, and in informal and varied school contacts (Kvalsund, Løvik, & Myklebust, 1991).

Identity Formation

The introduction to the Norwegian national curriculum also underlines the importance of the pupils' home environment for "developing a sense of local roots and identity," and to achieve this "the pupil's knowledge about and bonds with their local community and its natural environment, industries, traditions, and way of life must be strengthened and emphasized" (Ministry of Education [MOE], 1999, p. 58). With the massive closures of schools, implying the removal of the school from vast numbers of local communities, meeting these demands is increasingly difficult. In an evaluation of the 1998 Norwegian national curriculum, it was especially the teachers and head teachers of small rural schools who saw these tasks of the school as important (Solstad, 2004). Even for those local communities still having their schools, the present focus on pupil performance in a few academic subjects makes time spent on locally based learning more risky. In general, rural education is now in a poorer position to support the development of a local and rural identity among its pupils. Over time this may aggravate the difficulties of recruiting people to live in school-less and rural communities, as Corbett (2007) demonstrates in his study of the functioning of a centralized school system in a remote, small coastal settlement in Canada. Such observations are relevant also for our next topic.

Communities Without Schools

Elsewhere, we described three levels of school to local community relations (Solstad, 1997, pp. 151–152). The *community ignorant* school behaves in the same way regardless of its context. Such a school will easily become an isolated island in the community, and will, in its pure form, not be accepted. The *community passive school* takes advantage of the local community as a learning resource, but limits its cooperation with the community accordingly. The *community active school* not only adjusts its learning activities to the local context, but also plays a more active role in the community. According to the current Norwegian national curriculum, primary and lower secondary schools indeed have a role at this highest level of school to local community relationship (MOE, 1999, p. 50). The degree to which Norwegian schools actually function in this way varies a lot, but such schools are most frequently found among small schools serving tiny communities (Solstad, 2004). Rønning, Solstad, and Øines (2003, pp. 107–116) identify four broad functions of community active schools: (a) having extended functions within education and care (e.g., adult education), (b) as *local service centres* (e.g., making school facilities available for local people), (c) as a *social resource* (e.g., by running a Saturday café as a pupils' enterprise), and (d) being a *cultural bearer* (e.g., documentation of place names as a result of pupils' project work).

A local community that has lost its school is unlikely to see such benefits from the public school system. With the school gone, several job opportunities, particularly those demanding higher education, are also lost. Thus, centralization of rural schools implies draining rural areas of graduates. Arguably, the place or the local community is left in a poorer state. The pupils from such communities have been deprived of several opportunities for meaningful learning, for establishing a sense of identity or roots important for sustainable communities, and for individuals to decide where to spend their futures.

A common argument for maintaining a decentralized school structure is that with the school gone the people will also leave. Although no longitudinal Norwegian or Finnish, or indeed international, studies establishing such a relationship have been identified, this view is frequently voiced when talking with parents of outlying communities at risk of losing their local school (e.g., Solstad et al., 2016). One father left little room for doubt: "When we married and got kids, we moved out of the city, Tromsø, and came to this place. Unless a school here, we would not have come" (Solstad et al., 2016, p. 37). This statement illustrates the point that, although people do not leave with the school, the lack of a school reduces that community's chances to recruit new families, thus making it less sustainable (Hagen, 1992).

CONCLUDING REMARKS AND DISCUSSION

Referring to an abundant literature on globalization we have subsumed under this heading some important trends in ideological and political priorities, public management, and communication structures that impact on the provision of basic education in rural areas of developed countries like Norway and Finland. Although these two countries are similar in terms of geographical, cultural, political, and economic dimensions, we have demonstrated how some aspects of globalization have affected developments within rural education quite differently. Before trying to grasp the complexities of education as concretized in a rural school context, we will, in these concluding remarks, first give a summary of our main findings.

Since the 1980s we have seen changes in both countries to the rural landscape, due to large-scale rural to urban migration. These changes are seen as related to neoliberal ideas, such as reducing state level interventions, introducing business models (NPM) for the public sector, including the notion that every production unit (such as a school) should be efficient in terms of per unit produced (e.g., pupil), and so on.

Legislative changes in both countries have transferred power and responsibility from a national to a municipal level. The introduction, around 1990, of a block grant system for transferring money between these levels, has, in both countries, contributed to school closures far beyond what could be explained by population changes alone.

The international recession hit Finland more severely than it did Norway, thus also increasing the pressure to reduce costs in running public education. Altogether, school closures have hit even harder in Finland than in Norway.

Generally, the rural village or the local community fights hard, often over several years, to keep their school. We identify a number of mechanisms, which, during the periods of unrest and conflict, endanger the routines, the long term and day-to-day planning, and the enthusiasm and creativity of staff, who may also be difficult to keep or replace as a result of these very uncertainties.

The introduction of international testing regimes has affected Finnish and Norwegian education policies very differently. Finland being on or near the top in international comparisons, has had a more relaxed attitude to the tests, whereas Norway, at a more mediocre level, despite high spending on education, has implemented various measures to try to improve its standing. One such measure relates to teacher education in ways incompatible with the needs of small rural schools.

The massive closures of rural schools since the era of globalization have left large and increasing numbers of pupils depending on daily school transportation. We have explored the loss of welfare and the various health risks incurred. Physical problems developed at a young age tend to follow into adulthood, thus reducing the quality of life for individuals and increasing the risks of sick leaves, early retirement, and hospitalization, all at great expense and pressure on public budgets.

According to the general duties assigned by school acts and national curricula, the basic school has, in both countries, a legitimate role as an active community partner beyond that of teaching children and youngsters. Communities, having lost their schools, can no longer count on this resource for enriching their environment and its attractiveness. School centralization on the scale we are witnessing in countries like Norway and Finland definitely leaves the countryside in poorer shape.

The comparisons between developments in Norway and Finland give rise to some conclusions, which we illustrate in a model, Figure 3.5. Through the model we try to illustrate some of *the complexities of education*, and how these are concretized in the rural school context (cf. Karlberg-Granlund, 2009). We will also argue that the meaning of the small rural schools needs interdisciplinary analysis, as the school in its smallness is a mirror for larger issues in society.

In the model (Figure 3.5) the school is shown in the middle. The work, teaching and learning in school is affected by pedagogy, culture, and structure (see also Karlberg-Granlund, 2009). By *pedagogy* we mean the educational foundations and pedagogical competences that enable equitable teaching and learning for all pupils in the country. By *culture* we mean the social, cultural, and physical aspects of life and existence. The cultural meaning of a school might often not be realized until the school

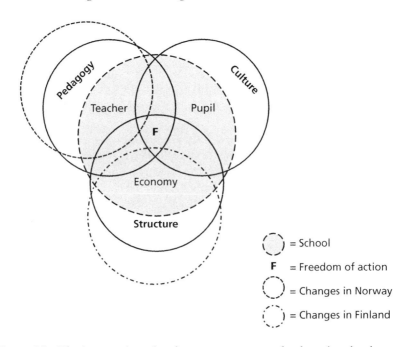

Figure 3.5 The intersection of pedagogy, structure, and culture in school.

is under threat of closure. By *structure* we mean the economical, legislative, and structural frames, which enable or constrain the work and learning of teachers and pupils in small rural schools.

In an ideal situation there is harmony in the interplay between pedagogy, culture, and structure realized in the school; the three circles, symbolizing pedagogy, culture, and structure of the school system, are in balance in Figure 3.5. If there are tensions or conflicts within one of the dimensions affecting the school it may have wider and more long-term effects than would be acknowledged at first. The changes affect the teachers, the pupils, the families, and the villagers as well as the local authorities. The changes also affect what is possible for them to accomplish. Thus, in the very center of the model is a free space, which is affected if one of the foundations for and dimensions of the school is weakened. We call this space *the freedom of action (F)*, which is framed in the interplay between pedagogy, culture, and structure. Issues and questions about educational quality, pedagogical relations and aims, as well as resources are also at stake.

In both Norway and Finland, we have documented the local protests against school closures. We have concluded that the bond or connection between the school and the community is close in a small context. The teachers in these contexts have a broad and responsible role in promoting education that also implies cooperation between the school, the families, and the local community.

If we analyze these national developments more deeply we notice that (as a consequence of globalization?) there are different views about what good and effective education is; which school is a good and effective school, and what teacher qualification might be the best. These discussions have affected the development of the rural schools and the school networks in our countries, as well as the development of teacher education. In Figure 3.5 different dotted circles for Norway and Finland illustrate the main tendencies of the different developments in our countries. As we have discussed earlier, there have been changes in the Norwegian teacher education to strengthen teachers' subject knowledge, which, however, may threaten the equal access to high quality comprehensive education all over the country. In Finland, the structural changes and school closures endangers the pupils' basic rights to education.

To ensure a high quality education as well as of local life in small and rural communities the teachers need to be supported in their work. In preservice teacher education there is a need to better recognize the preparation for teaching in all parts of our countries. The continual professional development of rural and small-school teachers is also important. Establishing teachers' learning communities and networks might be one way to strengthen and even broaden the teaching competences. Distance education for pupils in small and remote schools now has better possibilities than ever.

In spite of the qualities of small rural schools as learning arenas, as important institutions in the communities and as working places, and in spite of the unquestionable disadvantages that school journeys have for the children's health and welfare both in childhood and later life, both individually and collectively, the closure of rural schools is likely to go on. Only a shift in the legislative and financial running of rural education may save the future of rural schools—and of many rural communities.

REFERENCES

Ampuja, M. (2015). Globalisation and neoliberalism: A new theory for new times? In J. Zajda (Ed.), *Second international handbook on globalisation, education and policy research* (pp. 17–31). Dordrecht, The Netherlands: Springer.

Amundsveen, R., & Øines, T. (2003). Lisa gikk til skolen... Hvilke konsekvenser har skolenedleggelser for skoleskyssen? *NF-rapport 14/2003*. Bodø, Norway: Nordlandsforskning.

Aurén, H., & Joshi, D. (2013). Teaching the world that less is more: Global education testing and the Finnish national brand. In H. D. Meyer, & A. Benavot (Eds.), *PISA, power, and policy: The emergence of global educational governance* (pp. 63–83). Oxford, England: Symposium Books.

Autti, O., & Hyry-Beihammer, E. K. (2014). School closures in rural Finnish communities. *Journal of Research in Rural Education, 29*(1), 1–17.

Bæck, U. D. (2004). The urban ethos. Locality and youth in north Norway. *Young, 12*(2), 99–115.

Becker, G. S. (1964). *Human capital*. New York, NY: Colombia University Press.

Berg, P. O. (2004). Staten som distriktspolitisk aktør. In K. B. Lindkvist (Ed.), *Ressurser og omstilling – et geografisk perspektiv på regional omstilling* (pp. 237–265). Bergen, Norway: Fagbokforlaget.

Blossing, U., Imsen, G., & Moos, L. (Eds.). (2014). *The nordic education model – 'A school for all' encounters neo-liberal policy*. Dordrecht, The Netherlands: Springer.

Boston, J., Martin, K., Pallot, J., & Walch, P. (1996). *Public management: The New Zealand model*. Auckland, New Zealand: Oxford University Press.

Bourdieu, P. (1997). The forms of capital. In A. H. Halsey, H. Lauder, P. Brown, & A. S. Wells (Eds.), *Education – culture, economy, and society* (pp. 46–58). Oxford, England: Oxford University Press.

Brage, S., Ihlebæk, C., Natvig, B., & Brusgaard, D. (2010). Muskel-og skjelettlidelser som årsak til sykefravær og uførelidelser. *Tidsskrift for Den norske legeforening, 130*, 2369–2370.

Colás, A. (2005). Neoliberalism, globalisation and international relations. In A. Saad-Filho, & D. Johnston (Eds.), *Neoliberalism: A critical reader* (pp. 70–80). London, England: Pluto Press.

Coleman, J. S. (1988). Social capital in the creation of human capital. *American Journal of Sociology, 94*(1998), S99–S120.

Cooper, A. R., Wedderkopp, N., Wang, H., Andersen, L. B., Froberg, K., & Page, A. S. (2006). Active travel to school and cardiovascular fitness in Danish children and adolescents. *Medicine and Science in Sports and Exercise, 38*(10), 1724–1731.
Corbett, M. (2007). *Learning to leave: The irony of schooling in a coastal community.* Black Point, Canada: Fernwood.
Corbett, M., & Donehower, K. (2017). Rural literacies: Toward social cartography. *Journal of Research in Rural Education, 32*(5), 1–13.
Crawford, S., & Garrard, J. (2013). A combined impact-process evaluation of a program promoting active transport to school: Understanding the factors that shaped program effectiveness. *Journal of Environmental and Public Health, 2013*(3), 1–14.
Dax, T., & Machold, I. (2002). *Voices of rural youth: A break with traditional patterns?* Vienna, Austria: Bundesanstalt für Bergbaueren Fragen.
ECON. (2002). Ressursbruk i skolen—statistiske analyser. *Rapport 86/02.* Oslo, Norway: ECON senter for økonomisk analyse.
Eikeland, S., & Lie, I. (1994). Ein betre finnmarksskole? *NIBR-rapport 1994:14.* Oslo: Norsk institutt for by- og regionforskning.
Giddens, A. (1990). *The consequences of modernity.* Stanford, CA: Stanford University Press.
Grøholt, E. K., Stigum, H., & Nordhagen, R. (2008). Overweight and obesity among adolescents in Norway: Cultural and socio-economic differences. *Journal of Public Health, 30*(3), 258–265.
Hagen, T. (1992). Skulen og busetjinga. *Rapport 9212.* Volda, Norway: Møreforsking.
Hansén, S-E., & Eklund, G. (2014). Finnish teacher education—Challenges and possibilities. *Journal of International Forum of Educational Research, 1*(2), 1–12.
Haselgrove, C., Straker, L., Smith, A., O' Sullivan, P. M., Perry, M., & Sloan, N. (2008). Perceived school bag load, duration of carriage and method of transport to school are associated with spinal pain in adolescents: An observational study. *Australian Journal of Physiotherapy, 54*(3), 193–200.
Hattie, J. (2009). *Visible learning: A synthesis of over 800 meta-analyses relating to achievement.* London, England: Routledge.
Heyerdahl, N., Aamodt, G., Nordhagen, R., & Hovengen, R. (2012). Overvekt hos barn—hvilken betydning har bosted? *Tidsskrift for Den norske legeforening, 132,* 1080–1083.
Kalaoja, E. (1988). *Maaseudun pienten koulujen kehittämistutkimus. Osa I. Koulu kyläyhteisössä.* Faculty of education 52. Oulu, Finland: University of Oulu.
Kalaoja, E., & Pietarinen, J. (2009). Small rural primary schools in Finland: A pedagogically valuable part of the school network. *International Journal of Educational Research, 48*(2), 109–116.
Kamens, D. H. (2013). Globalization and the emergence of an audit culture: PISA and the search for 'best practices' and magic bullets. In H. D. Meyer, & A. Benavot (Eds.), *PISA, power, and policy: The emergence of global educational governance* (pp. 117–139). Oxford, England: Symposium Books.
Käppi, P. (1971). *Kouluhallituksen kokeiluja tutkimustoimiston.* Jyväskyla, Finland: Jyväskyla University.

Karlberg-Granlund, G. (2009). *Att förstå det stora i det lilla: Byskolan som pedagogik, kultur och struktur* (Doctoral dissertation). Åbo, Finland: Åbo Akademi University Press.

Karlberg-Granlund, G. (2011). Coping with the threat of closure in a small Finnish village school. *Australian Journal of Education, 55*(1), 62–71.

Karlberg-Granlund, G. (2019). Exploring the challenge of working in a small school and community: Uncovering hidden tensions. *Journal of Rural Studies, 72,* 293–305.

Kvalsund, R. (2009). Centralized decentralization or decentralized centralization? A review of newer Norwegian research on schools and their communities. *International Journal of Educational Research, 48*(2), 89–99.

Kvalsund, R., Løvik, P., & Myklebust, J. O. (1991). *Relasjonar som raknar. Rapport nr. 9107.* Volda, Norway: Møreforsking.

Laukkanen, R., & Muhonen, L. (1981). Finland's small schools and combined grades: An overview with special reference to the Kuusamo District. In J. Sher (Ed.), *Rural education in urbanized nations: Issues and innovations* (pp. 255–276). Boulder, CO: Westview Press.

Laukkanen, R., Muhonen, L., Ruuhijärvi, P., Similä, K., & Toivonen, E. (1986). *Pieni koulu. Kunnallisen koulutoimen kehitys. Opetus pienissä kouluissa.* Vantaa, Finland: Kunnallispaino.

Lindkvist, K. B. (Ed.). (2004). *Ressurser og omstilling—et gografisk perspektiv på regional omstilling.* Bergen, Norway: Fagbokforlaget.

Litonjua, M. D. (2008). The socio-political construction of globalization. *International Review of Modern Sociology, 34*(2), 253–278.

Lundgren, U. P. (1985). Educational research and educational change: The case of Sweden. In J. Nisbet, J. Megarry, & S. Nisbet (Eds.), *World yearbook of education 1985: Research, policy and practice* (pp. 218–230). London, England: Kogan Page.

Lundgren, U. P. (2014). Advarer Mot PISA Hysteri. *Klassenkampen.* https://arkiv.klassekampen.no/article/20140306/ARTICLE/140309976

McDonald, N. C. (2007). Active transportation to school: Trends among US schoolchildren, 1969–2001. *American Journal of Preventive Medicine, 32*(6), 509–516.

McMinn, D., Rowe, D. A., Murtagh, S., & Nelson, N. M. (2011). The Strathclyde evaluation of children's active travel (SE-CAT): Study rationale and methods. *Public Health, 11,* 958–970.

Mendoza, J. A., & Liu, Y. (2014). Active commuting to elementary school and adiposity: An observational study. *Childhood Obesity, 10*(1), 34–41.

Meyer, H. D., & Benavot, A. (2013). PISA and the globalization of education governance: Some puzzles and problems. In H. D. Meyer, & A. Benavot (Eds.), *PISA, power, and policy – the emergence of global educational governance* (pp. 9–26). Oxford, England: Symposium Books.

Ministry of Education. (1999). *The curriculum for the 10-year compulsory school in Norway.* (The English version of the 1998 national curriculum. The general part was kept unchanged in a new national curriculum 2006.)

Muilu, T., & Onkalo, P. (2002). Rural young people and unemployment: The case of Suomussalmi, Finland. In T. Dax, & I. Machold (Eds.), (2002). *Voices of rural* youth: A break with traditional patterns? (pp. 59–78). Vienna, Austria: Bundesanstalt für Bergbaueren Fragen.

Nilsson, D., & Raundalen, M. (1985). *Barns opplevelse av skoleskyssen.* Kongsvinger, Norway: Kongsvinger sykehus.

NOU, 2004: 2. [Official Norwegian Reports]. *Effekter og effektivitet.* [New Immigration Act].

O.tid., 1984-85. [Accounts of parliamentary discussions].

Østerud, P., Sunnanå, S., & Frøysnes, Ä. (2015). *Norsk lærarutdanning i etterkrigstida: Ei utvikling i spenning mellom tradisjon og fornying.* Oslo, Norway: AMB-media.

Paulgaard, G. (2001). Sted og tilhørighet. In K. Heggen, J. O. Myklebust, & T. Øia (Eds.), *Ungdom. I spenning mellom det lokale og det globale* (pp. 18–36). Oslo, Norway: Samlaget.

Raitakari, O. T., Porkka, K. V. K., Taimela, S., Telam, R., Rasanen, L., & Vikari, J. S. A. (1994). Effects of persistent physical activity and inactivity on coronary risk factors in children and young adults. *American Journal of Epidemiology, 140*(3), 195–206.

Rizvi, F., & Lingard, B. (2010). *Globalizing education policy.* New York, NY: Routledge.

Rønning, W., Solstad, K. J., & Øines, T. (2003). Det trengs ei hel bygd for å oppdra et barn. *NF-Report 3/2003.* Bodø, Norway: Nordlandsforskning.

Rosenberg, D. E., Sallis, J. F., Conway, T. L., Cain. K. L., & McKenzie, T. L. (2006). Active transportation to school over 2 years in relation to weight status and physical activity. *Obesity, 14*(10), 1771–1776.

Sahlberg, P. (2010). *The secret to Finland's success: Educating teachers.* Scope: Research brief. Stanford, CA: Stanford Center for Opportunity Policy in Education. Retrieved from https://edpolicy.stanford.edu/sites/default/files/publications/secret-finland's-success-educating-teachers.pdf

Sahlberg, P. (2011). PISA in Finland: An education miracle or an obstacle to change? *CEPS Journal, 1*(3), 119–140.

Samferdselsdepartementet. [Norwegian Ministry of Transport] *Rundskriv N-4/85.*

Samuelson, R. J. (2000, January 4). Growing market offers huge potential—But also peril: Globalization's double edge. Looking ahead to century 21. Second of eight essays. International Herald Tribune. *The New New York Times.* https://www.nytimes.com/2000/01/04/news/growing-market-offers-huge-potential-but-also-peril-globalizations.html

Sherer, M. (2009). The tests that won't go away. *Educational Leadership, 67*(3), 5.

Sigsworth, A., & Solstad, K. J. (Eds.). (2005). *Small rural schools: A small inquiry.* Nesna, Norway: Høgskolen i Nesna.

Sjøberg, S. (2014). PISA-syndromet. Hvordan norsk skolepolitikk blir styrt av OECD. *Nytt norsk tidsskrift, 31*(1), 30–43.

Sjølie, A. N. (2002). *Lifestyle and health in a cohort of Norwegian adolescents: With special emphasis on school journeys and low back pain* (Doctoral dissertation). Bergen, Norway: Universitetet i Bergen.

Smith, M. K. (2008). *Globalization and the incorporation of education. The Encyclopedia of Informal Education.* Retrieved from http://infed.org/mobi/globalization-and-the-incorporation-of-education/

Smith, W. C. (Ed.). (2016). *The global testing culture: Shaping education policy, perceptions, and practice.* Oxford, England: Symposium Books.

Solstad, K. J. (1973). School transportation and physical development. *Scandinavian Journal of Educational Research, 19*(1), 117–126.
Solstad, K. J. (1975). Pupils' views on school transportation. *Scandinavian Journal of Educational Research, 19*(1), 27–43.
Solstad, K. J. (1997). *Equity at risk.* Oslo, Norway: Scandinavian University Press.
Solstad, K. J. (1978). *Riksskole i utkantstrok.* Oslo, Norway: Universitetsforlaget.
Solstad, K. J. (2004). Generell kunnskap gjennom lokal læring. In K. J. Solstad, & T. O. Engen (Eds.), *En likeverdig skole for alle? Om enhet og mangfold i grunnskolen* (pp. 60–88). Oslo, Norway: Universitetsforlaget.
Solstad, K. J. (2009). *Bygdeskolen i velstands-Noreg.* Vallset, Norway: Opplandske Bokforlag.
Solstad, K. J. (2016). Nedlegging av skular—grunnar og konsekvensar. *Betre skole, 3,* 28–32.
Solstad, K. J., & Solstad, M. (2015). Meir skyss—mindre helse? *NF-rapport 07/2015.* Bodø, Norway: Nordlandsforskning.
Solstad, K. J., Andrews, T., & Løvland, J. (2016). Spredt eller samla? Utredning av ungdomsskolestrukturen i Vågan kommune. *NF-rapport 03/2016.* Bodø, Norway: Nordlandsforskning.
Stucky-Ropp, R. C., & DiLorenzo, T. M. (1993). Determinants of exercise in children. *Preventive Medicine, 22*(6), 880–889.
Szpalski, M., Gunzburg, R., Balague, F., Nordin, M., & Melot, C. (2002). A 2-year longitudinal study on low back pain in primary school children. *European Spine Journal, 11,* 459–464.
Tirri, K. (2014). The last 40 years in Finnish teacher education. *Journal of Education for Teaching, 40*(5), 600–609.
Toom, A., Kynäslahti, H., Krokfors, L., Jyrhämä, R., Byman, K., Stenberg, K., . . . Kansanen, P. (2010). Experiences of a research-based approach to teacher education: Suggestions for future policies. *European Journal of Education, 45*(2), 333–344.
Udir. (2013). *Endringer i landskapet de siste ti årene: Statistikknotat 02/2013.* Oslo, Norway: Utdanningsdirektoratet.
Välijärvi, J., Linnakylä, P., Kupari, P., Reinikainen, P., & Arffman, I. (2007). *The Finnish success in PISA—And some reasons behind it.* Jyväskylä, Finland: Koulutuksen tutkimuslaitos. Retrieved from https://jyx.jyu.fi/bitstream/handle/123456789/37478/978-951-39-3038-7.pdf?sequence=1&isAllowed=y
Varjo, J., Simola, H., & Rinne, R. (2013). Finland's PISA results: An analysis of dynamics in education politics. In H. D. Meyer, & A. Benavot (Eds.), *PISA, power, and policy—The emergence of global educational governance* (pp. 51–76). Oxford, England: Symposium Books.
Wiborg, A. (2001). Utdannelse, mobilitet og identitet. In K. Heggen, J. O. Myklebust, & T. Oia (Eds.), *Ungdom. I spenning mellom det lokale og det glokale* (pp.136–151). Oslo, Norway: Samlaget
Wragg, T. (1989, December). *Evaluating the effectiveness of schools and teachers* (Lecture). British Council Course. Improving the Effectiveness of Schools. London, England.
Zajda, J. (Ed.). (2015). *Second international handbook on globalisation, education and policy research.* Dordrecht, The Netherlands: Springer.
Ziehe, T. (1995). *Kulturanalyser, ungdom, utbildning, modernitet.* Stockholm, Sweden: Symposium Library.

PART II

ENGAGING WITH CHANGING PATTERNS OF EDUCATION, SPACE, AND PLACE

CHAPTER 4

TURBULENT TIMES AND RESHAPED RURAL SCHOOL NETWORK IN HUNGARY

Katalin Kovács
Hungarian Academy of Sciences

The main goal of this chapter is to provide an overview of the most important changes that have been shaping the Hungarian rural school network during the last decade and a half. The 15 years in question covered an unprecedentedly turbulent period in the Hungarian educational system with deep structural changes governed by policy arrangements of a different nature. Between 2002 and 2010, when left-wing and liberal coalition governments led the country, two main policy goals were to be realized: the "rationalization" of the school system towards enhanced cost-effectiveness on the one hand, and the increase of its fairness towards children starting primary education from disadvantaged social and economic backgrounds on the other. Neoliberal views were thus accompanied with equity considerations and demands for fairness in an extremely decentralized system where primary schools were maintained by local governments.

Rationalization was meant to be achieved through specific incentives that aimed at decreasing the size of school networks, urban and rural alike. Incentives were also the main tools of enhancing equity of education: In other words, indirect measures were applied when implementation of policy goals was at stake. In contrast, the new right-wing regime that came to power with a two-thirds majority of votes in 2010, and which has kept its popularity ever since, chose a straightforward way of pushing its concepts through. The rural end of the school network was fully renationalized when, from January 2013, the maintenance of schools was taken over by the central state from local governments in all settlements of fewer than 3,000 inhabitants (85% of settlements) and the entire network has become directed by one single central government agency, the Klebelsberg Intézményfenntartó Központ (Klebelsberg Institution Maintenance Centre) and its inspectorates set up at the district level of the equally reformed public administration. Moreover, from January 2017, all (general) primary schools were drawn under state maintenance independent of size of their municipality.

The extreme centralization and concentration of the direction followed by schools has been somewhat softened since January 2017, when leadership was deconcentrated to 58 larger school districts, through which the Centre (called the Klebelsberg Centre) itself operates and exercises coordination and control. The set of "softening measures" was introduced as a reflection mainly of ineffectiveness and the pressing, huge amount of financial deficit that the central agency had accumulated during the 3 years of operation. However, a civic movement, called "Tanítanék" (Would like to teach) that emerged in larger cities in January 2016, also influenced events and decisions. The movement rebelled with street demonstrations against the ill-working institutional setup, the autocratic leadership, the complete loss of teachers' autonomy, obviously reducing the chances of students to access quality education verified by the Programme for International Student Achievement (PISA) results of 2012 and 2015, according to which Hungarian students' performance has been steadily declining even as compared to the weak achievements of the former rounds of assessment.

This chapter does not deal with the achievements of primary education of rural Hungary; rather, it provides the reader with some background information of structural importance. In the first part indirect policy tools, aiming to increase the cost-effectiveness of the rural school network and their impact, are introduced. In the second part, the most important structural changes of the renationalized education system are discussed, followed by a short conclusion.

COPING WITH SERVICE PROVISION IN SMALL VILLAGES THROUGH ASSOCIATIONS

Traditionally, a village school was regarded as constitutive of its community. It symbolized the strength and the vividness of the community that children were born into, through sufficient numbers and showing that the village was wealthy enough to take care of the proper education of their offspring. The village school used to link generations where fathers and grandfathers went as schoolboys, thus representing at the same time roots, present stability, and the community's self-confidence. These aspects explain most village communities' insistence on attendance at the local school, as much as through practical aspects like easy and quick access. These general patterns still prevailed in rural Hungary in the wake of the millennium, but have strongly deteriorated since then.

SOME CHARACTERISTICS OF LOCAL ADMINISTRATION IN RURAL HUNGARY

After the fall of socialism, the local government system became fragmented to an extreme degree in Hungary, due to the disintegration of the previously forcibly amalgamated rural municipalities. In consequence, the number of local authorities increased, to such an extent that even the smallest villages could, and did, reestablish their own local governments. To illustrate the challenge deriving from fragmentation, according to the last census of 2011, 55% of municipalities in rural Hungary have fewer than 1,000 inhabitants where as few as 8% of the population lived. The spatial structure is only part of the problem. In the years following the millennium, limitations in relation to sustainability occurred and deepened for two main reasons: the overly broad definition of the scope of municipalities' tasks, on the one hand, and the reluctance of the self-governing bodies to cooperate on the other. Moreover, as Vigvári (2008) pointed out, the conversion of local council entitlements during state socialism into property owned by local self-governments in the wake of the political shift, brought obvious rigidity into the system and impeded the creation of sustainable cooperation in the delivery of services.

OPERATING SCHOOLS JOINTLY: THE STATE AND VOLUNTARY ASSOCIATIONS

During the first half of the 1990s, co-operation aimed at the joint maintenance of education and health services between municipalities was only sporadic. When the first relevant legal framework on municipal associations, Act CXXXV of 1997, on the Associations and Co-operation of Local Self-Governments (hereinafter: the "Act on Associations") came into force, the number of formal cooperation agreements increased significantly. According to Imre's (2004) research findings, in 2000/2001, 70% to 77% of villages with fewer than 2,000 inhabitants participated in one or more associations, whilst 60% of the smallest villages with fewer than 500 inhabitants operated joint mayors' offices, and 56% provided educational services (kindergartens, primary schools) within the framework of so-called "institutional maintenance associations." The rate of voluntary cooperation was similarly high in villages having 500–1,000 inhabitants. Of these, 42% were cooperating in the field of municipal administration and 53% in education.

Voluntary associations, particularly those aimed at the joint maintenance of kindergartens and primary schools, were promoted by special state subsidies, particularly targeting small villages schools. However, despite generous central government support at the time, the operating costs of small rural schools became less and less affordable for municipalities. The smaller the village (and its school), the larger was the gap between the costs of maintenance and the state subsidies (budgetary entitlements called "normative" in Hungarian contexts supplemented with additional subsidies); they reached more than 50% in villages with fewer than 1,100 inhabitants (Horn, 2005). Despite these difficulties, the number of closures remained relatively low until 2004 when the financial viability of small rural schools came under an increasing threat, which called for a policy response. The problems resulting in an accelerated shrinkage of enrollment were as follows:

1. seepage to nearby urban schools;
2. seepage to non-Roma schools in those rural areas where a process of ghettoisation was on the rise;
3. attempts by central government to rationalize the delivery of public services, most importantly that of primary education.

This increasing threat was related to a demographic decline that progressed further nationwide, resulting in growing competition for children in the schools. Estimates suggest that in towns and cities 34% of primary school children were enrolled from outside the schools' catchment areas in 2005 (Lannert, 2008). Growing excess capacities in towns and cities motivated urban schools to increase the pool from which they drew their students at the expense of rural schools, particularly within their commuting fringes and in the upper grades. Parents had always been ready to enroll their children for better schools outside catchment areas ever since free choice was provided as a major democratic achievement during the erosion phase of State Socialism in 1985.

Oppressive Legislation: Semi-Voluntary Associations for Enforcing Joint Operation of Schools

Under the pressure of growing public expenditure and an increasing budgetary deficit in the wake of Hungary's accession to the European Union, the government decided to rationalize financing of local governments and delivery of public services in 2004. Act CVII of 2004 on the Multi-Functional Micro-Regional Associations (hereinafter: the "Multifunctional LG Associations") built upon the 1997 regulation (Act on Associations). But since the coalition government could not command the two-thirds majority necessary to amend the 1990 Act LXV on Local Governments, the suggested assembling into multifunctional associations at the level of the LAU-1 (Local Administrative Unit) statistical micro-regions remained on paper voluntary rather than compulsory. The voluntary aspect was an illusion, however, in most cases, given the strong pressure exerted on local authorities to join.

The 2004 Act on Multifunctional LG Associations was much less liberal than the Act of Associations that was passed 7 years earlier. Its oppressive nature can be identified from the following provisions:

- It stipulated mandatory spatial and organizational structures (exclusive membership of mayors of the LAU-1 area) as well as mandatory tasks (coordinating territorial development goals and activities, organizing certain aspects of education, social services, and health care).
- It partially rescaled the provision of state incentives (targeted subsidies): Some incentives, including additional state subsidies supporting schools, were passed to the beneficiaries (municipalities) via the Multifunctional LG Associations from 2005, only if strict eligibility criteria were met.
- As far as the additional subsidies for the maintenance costs of small schools were concerned, two major criteria of eligibility were introduced: firstly, the joint operation, or amalgamation, of schools; and secondly, meeting a minimum number of students per school within 3 years (123 students in an eight-grade school).

In the course of only 3 years, all local authorities joined multifunctional associations. They had no other option. Most were trapped by severe financial shortages that hindered delivery of public services as well as the upkeep of their assets. They badly needed targeted subsidies that could be accessed exclusively via Multifunctional LG Associations.

The trap, however, was prepared carefully. As a first step, budgetary entitlements to primary education were cut by an average of 10% in 2007. Then additional earmarked funds were made available via municipal associations for those municipalities that united for the joint provision of services. Those municipalities that did not associate with others in keeping up their educational services were deprived of additional entitlements. As targeted research pointed out, due to this scheme, the number of villages capable of maintaining primary schools on their own dropped to one half between 2004 and 2008 (Balázs & Kovács, 2012). Many of the closed schools were small, segregated (Roma-only) village schools, thus closure was apparently in line with national and EU anti-segregation policies at that time. However, a closer view reveals that most schools were closed without any careful preparation for the desegregation of pupils at the host school, and furthermore, that the majority of representatives in the local councils simply did not want to run a school for the Roma, as long as non-Roma parents were educating their children elsewhere—generally at the schools of the local rural centres (Kovács, 2012b; Kovács & Váradi, 2012; Nikitscher & Velkey, 2012; Vidra, 2012; Virág, 2012).

The closures of the segregated Roma-only schools coincided with an accelerating increase in the Hungarian population declared of Roma ethnicity (self-declared Roma), which doubled to 3.2% between 2001 and 2011. The representation of Roma was higher in rural areas (5.9%) compared to urban areas, reflecting a rural–urban bias (Somogyi & Tellér, 2011); this was accompanied with geographical bias in the north, northeast, and the southwest NUTS-2 (Nomenclature of Territorial Units for Statistics) regions of Hungary. The proportion of self-declared Roma population was ranging from 1.4% in Central Hungary to 7.7% in Northern Hungary, according to the same Census figures. However, estimates suggest that the real number of Romany people in Hungary is about twice as many as the census data indicate. In rural areas, especially in peripheral communities of the three above mentioned NUTS-2 regions hit by extreme poverty, the high fertility rate as a coping strategy of Roma women has reoccurred. Thus, the number and proportion of Roma children in kindergartens and schools has been growing faster than that of the rural population at large. Wherever the rate of Roma students reached a certain percentage, and research suggests around 20%–25% (Havas, 1999; Messing & Molnár, 2008), "White flight" accelerated and soon resulted in an advanced degree of segregation.

Three examples of village schools facing closure and/or ethnic segregation illustrate the challenges and their solutions. More examples, and a detailed theoretical analysis of such cases can be found in Kovács (2015) and Váradi (2012). Kovács (2015) argues that Wacquant's (2008) concepts of "advanced marginality" and the process of ghettoization, are even more intensely demonstrable in rural Hungary and Slovakia after "the fall of state socialism because of the collapse of industries that employed masses of unskilled Roma wage labourers...in mining, construction, and large scale agriculture" (p. 787) than in Wacquant's examples in the U.S. metropolitan context.

The village school of Village-1, in North Hungary, a village of 1,777 inhabitants of whom approximately 5% were Roma, was closed down in 2007 when the amalgamation of the school districts with the nearby town was initiated by the local self-government. The non-Roma students had already abandoned the school, as parents were exercising their right to free choice of schooling. Within 5 years, the enrollment rate had dropped by half, and full segregation happened extremely quickly. Some council members called into question running a Roma-only school with 70 children. Subsequently, the short distance between the two settlements (5 kilometers) made bussing pupils relatively cheap, while strong cooperation between the leaders of the two local governments also facilitated the closure process. The third very important condition of the absorption of Roma pupils in the neighboring town was the relatively large sizes of the two receiving schools, with 300–400 students on roll. When divided between the two schools, the 10–15% Roma children did not pose a direct threat causing an exodus of non-Roma students (Kovács, 2015).

The small primary school of Village-2 (North Hungary) with its 100 children was fully segregated by 2013. The village population of 1,207 in 2011 was 50% Roma. The non-Roma children went to schools in neighboring villages. School maintenance had been transferred to the National Minority Roma Self-Government, based in Budapest, in 2012, and after the Catholic Church had refused to take over the school, the National Roma Minority Self-Government did so with the help of the local Roma Minority Self-Government. Using government subsidies, new teaching methods (such as project-based learning, differentiated teaching, all-day education) were introduced to motivate and protect children. Further support was provided through the so-called Pedagogical Program for Integration (PPI) to obtain schoolbooks and equipment free of charge for every student. Mentoring was widely practiced, and a preparatory secondary (vocational) school was launched jointly by the village and school leaders in order to keep the children in education for as long as possible (see Kovács, Schwarcz, & Tagai, 2014).

In a third example, the primary school of Village-3 (West Hungary, 263 inhabitants in 2001) was closed in 2005, without a legal successor. Ethnic and social segregation had not been a problem here, but the low number of students (just 45 in its last year), decreasing budgetary support, and a history of conflicts with the other village schools in their schools' maintainers' association led to the inevitable closure. Furthermore, Village-3 had lost its position as a micro-regional centre, along with its decreasing economic capacities and the necessary outflow of its active, mobile and young inhabitants. The parents tried but were unable to mobilize support in the decreasing, ageing, and impoverished population. When organization of the multifunctional LG Association started at district level in 2005, both the local government of Village-3 and the parents wished to retain the school as a site belonging to one of the neighboring school centres, but the accelerating erosion made even this scenario impossible. In this case, free parental choice of schools during an earlier stage, parallel outmigration of the young and skilled population, and the stemming vulnerable demographic context, overturned the maintainer's and the remaining parents' intents.

Some of the Village-3 children, however, moved to the nearby village school of Village-4, which had benefited from the consolidation and closure of small village schools of the vicinity. The school roll was increasing annually, due, not to any intentional "hunt for children," but rather due to its good reputation, founded on its children-centered, innovative, integrated educational work conducted in small classes and focused equally on grooming talents and helping lagging students to catch up, in a balanced way. In addition, this village of 648 inhabitants (in 2011) was characterized by a strong demand for autonomy in both administration and economic activities, a powerful sense of local identity and an active social life, and registered only moderate population loss compared to the neighboring villages. There had not been a single instance of a Village-4 parent enrolling his/her child at another school. Village-4 is an example of how relatively small settlements, surrounded by even smaller villages, can profit from free parental choice of schools (Váradi, 2012).

During the Fall of 2012, the government of Hungary issued the 2012/CLXXXVIII Act to regulate dramatic changes that targeted primary schools: As a reflection of the spreading and deepening financial difficulties of indebted self-governments, the primary (general) schools in settlements of fewer than 3,000 inhabitants were renationalized. According to recent research, the level of centralization of Hungarian primary education as well as its rigidity was unprecedented in Europe (Györgyi, 2016). Since then (January, 2013), teachers' salaries, as well as the operational costs of these schools, were paid by a centralized maintaining authority—at the time it was "Klebelsberg Institution Maintenance Centre" (abbreviated in Hungarian as "KLIK")—whilst municipalities of larger settlements (typically towns and cities) were allowed to decide whether they were willing to keep their primary schools and cover the operational costs, or pass them over to the state. (School buildings have continued to be owned by municipalities.) The distinction between maintenance costs (covering teachers' salaries) carried by the State, and operational costs (covering the running costs of the buildings and related personnel) brought about a dual system in the larger towns and cities until 2017, when the state took over primary schools fully (see below). Syllabi as well as teaching materials and schoolbooks became centrally determined. Policy instructions were mediated via school districts originally tailored to the 174 LAU-1 level administrative units (districts).

Resistance and Reorganization

In 2016, a group of teachers, secondary school leaders of one of the regional centres, Miskolc, and those of the capital city, Budapest, rebelled against the extreme rigidity of management of the centrally governed school system. The movement, named *Tanítanék* (Would like to teach), called for and succeeded in organizing street demonstrations and made the inacceptable mechanisms of centrally managed schools explicit to the public. Under the pressure of demonstrations and frustrated by the huge deficits accumulated by KLIK, the government launched roundtable discussions (although representatives of the *Tanítanék* movement did not participate at these meetings) with civic movements and professional organizations, that concluded in an amendment of the Act on Education (134/2016 [VI.10.] Government decree on maintaining institutions of public education and that of the Klebelsberg Centre; CXXXVI/2016 Act on amendment education-related legislation).

Centralization of maintenance had become general by January 2017, when the duality of the maintenance and operation of schools had also ceased to exist in larger municipalities. The central maintenance authority (KLIK) was reorganized along with its territorial offices: a smaller central unit (Klebelsberg Centre) and a network of 58 school districts were established. Some of the former entitlements of school principals have been re-assigned; others, like the authority controlling the appointment of teachers have been shared between the directors of school districts and principals in a way that enables principals to recommend teachers for appointment and directors of districts to approve (or refuse) their suggestions. Due to the amendment of the Act, the operation of schools has become smoother since school districts execute centrally determined policy measures; however, nothing has changed with regard to the (centralized) nature of the system, only the level of its territorial concentration has diminished.

Ironically, the dramatically transformed, nationalized and still highly centralized education system has provoked less open discontent against top–down policy interventions within the ranks of municipal leaders than before, particularly in rural areas. Obviously, most leaders of local authorities have been relieved of the burden of school maintenance, which—in the context of the financial crisis—had become more and more difficult, due to diminishing state funds and the scarcity of their own source revenues. The frustration of the leaders of the so-called single school (rural) municipalities was understandably the greatest before 2010, because small schools were openly and increasingly threatened with enforced closure or, at the very least, amalgamation with other schools to meet the requirements of semi-voluntary municipal associations.

Following the period from 2005 to 2010, the decline of the rural school network stopped, remained intact, and even grew to some extent; most village schools kept on running. At worst, the upper grades were merged with larger schools; operational school sites remained available for villagers.

DYNAMICS OF THE RURAL SCHOOL NETWORK FROM 2001–2015: SCHOOLS, SCHOOL SITES, AND STUDENTS OF PRIMARY (GENERAL) SCHOOLS

Facts and Figures on Changes in the School Network from 2001–2015

Whenever the category of rural schools is mentioned in this section of the chapter, it refers to schools run by villages and rural towns of fewer than 10,000 inhabitants. The rest are categorized as urban schools. Data collected and provided by the Statistical section of the State Secretariat in Charge of Education of the Ministry of Human Capacities (KIR-STAT in Hungarian) and arranged by the Data Bank of the Centre for Economic and Regional Studies, Hungarian Academy of Sciences facilitated the analysis of the changes to the rural school network between 2001 and 2015. (See Table 4.1.)

The general rule unfolding from Table 4.1 suggests that rural schools did worse than their urban counterparts in all three periods between 2001 and 2015. Student enrollment has been diminishing continuously throughout this timespan in rural schools, unlike schools operating in larger towns and cities, where there was a 2% increase in the number of students between 2010 and 2015. The total number of rural schools (institutions) was 2,030 in 2001, reduced to 1,190 in 2015; the decline represents a 41% drop

TABLE 4.1 Directions of Change in Rural School Network 2001–2015 (%)

Period Examined	Type of Schools	Basis of Comparison	Changes Related to the		
			Number of Students	Number of Schools	Number of School Sites
2005/2001	urban	100% = figures for 2001	87%	94%	98%
	rural		88%	90%	93%
2010/2005	urban	100% = figures for 2005	84%	85%	101%
	rural		76%	65%	85%
2015/2010	urban	100% = figures for 2010	102%	100%	112%
	rural		90%	101%	111%

Source: KIR-STAT, panel of primary education data 2001–2015.

Note: The author is grateful to Melinda Tir and Bálint Koós for providing the data-files.

at the rural end of the school network, twice that of urban schools, which only dropped by 20% between 2001 and 2015.

The number of school sites (operating units of schools independent of their institutional status) dropped comparatively less in rural areas (87% between 2001 and 2015), whilst the number of school sites in urban areas grew from 1,575 to 1,759 during the same period (10% growth). These data clearly indicate that closure did not threaten urban schools as much as it did rural ones, rather, they were reorganized through amalgamations in a way that most school sites continued to operate under the umbrella of a school center. New schools were also built in towns and cities rather than in villages.

Regional differences in the degree of shrinkage of the rural school network also deserve attention. The map (Figure 4.1) shows that the drop in the average size of schools (by the number of enrolled students) was the highest in two regions of Transdanubia (Southern and Central), followed by regions of the Great Hungarian Plain. Smaller drop rates express less dramatic change but do not indicate the size of the schools concerned that might have been small even before the 2005 turn brought about by Multifunctional LG Associations.

The deterministic impact of the settlement structure on the size of rural school sites expressed in average enrollment numbers is indicated in

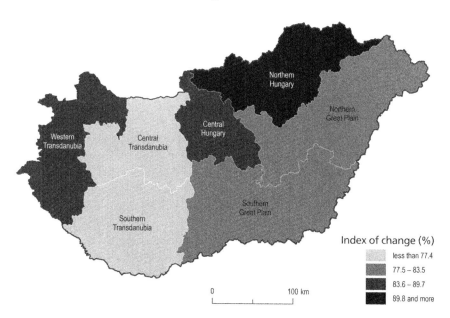

Figure 4.1 Decrease of the average number of students per rural school site by NUTS-2 regions 2010/2001 (%). *Source:* KIR-STAT, panel of primary education data 2001–2015. *Note:* The author is grateful to Bálint Koós for drawing the map.

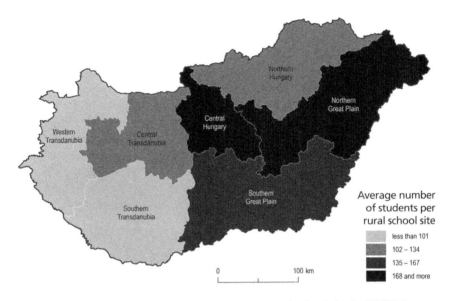

Figure 4.2 The average number of students per rural school site by NUTS-2 regions in 2010 ($N = 1,199$). *Source:* KIR-STAT, panel of primary education data 2001–2015. *Note:* The author is grateful to Bálint Koós for drawing the map.

Figure 4.2. The average number of students per school site in regions where most of the towns are small themselves (Southern and Western Transdanubia with an average settlement size of 1,424 and 1,502 respectively) is significantly smaller than in regions where small towns and larger villages dominate the landscape (Central Hungary, the Southern Great Plain region, and the Northern Great Plain region where the average settlement size is 15,673, 5,109, 3,837, respectively).

The dramatic change in the maintenance of schools from January 2013 appeared as illustrated by Table 4.2.

From 2001 to 2005 more than 10% of rural schools closed down and the number run by voluntary municipal associations also diminished by 4% despite a gradual and voluntary cooperation by municipalities for the delivery of educational services. Such a pace of closure/amalgamation was in line with the shrinkage of the network before and after the years of the turmoil during the political shift from State Socialism to Capitalism (1989–1990). (Similar processes were taking place during and after the State Socialist era in the Czech Republic exhaustively analyzed by Kučerová, Bláha, & Kučera, 2015.) The most salient change in Hungary, however, as indicated by Table 4.2, shows almost a full shift from municipal to State maintenance of rural schools by 2015. The difference between rural and urban school networks from the point of view of a maintenance structure is that the share

TABLE 4.2 Changes of Rural School Maintenance 2001–2015

Maintainers	2001	2005	2010	2015	2001	2005	2010	2015
	Numbers				%			
Municipalities	1,540	1383	657	25	76%	75%	55%	2%
Associations	376	361	439	0	19%	20%	37%	0%
State	35	1	1	1,026	2%	0%	0%	86%
Churches	26	33	50	124	1%	2%	4%	10%
Higher Education Institutes, Counties, Budapest	40	34	18	1	2%	2%	2%	0%
NGOs	11	22	19	16	1%	1%	2%	1%
Other Institutions	2	0	4	7	0%	0%	0%	1%
Total Number	2,030	1,834	1,188	1,199	100%	100%	100%	100%

Source: KIR-STAT, panel of primary education data 2001–2015.

Note: The author is grateful to Melinda Tir and Bálint Koós for providing the data-files.

of State-owned urban primary schools was considerably less, only 70% in 2015, than in rural areas—86%. The gap between urban and rural schools concerning their maintainers is explained by discrepancies regarding the availability and strength of NGOs (civic organizations) and churches as alternative maintainers.

Paths of escape from closure were already observed during the first period of 2001–2005 with a shift towards church and NGO maintenance, although their rate was, and remained, relatively low (together 2–6% between 2001–2010 and 11% in 2015), though significant by 2015 (see Figure 4.3). Schools have been mostly taken over by the Catholic Church, followed by the Reformed (Protestant) Church.

Selectivity and Separation: Two Mechanisms of Continuity

Churches and NGOs (usually foundations) have often been blamed for increasing selectivity through "creaming off" middle-class students in the already highly selective operation of Hungary's primary education system. Selectivity that hit disadvantaged children of Roma ethnicity the most, via multiplying the segregation of schools, derives mainly from the statutory free parental enrollment choice, which was neither touched upon by the radical changes in 1989–1990, nor in 2012–2013.

However, free choice of schools cannot be held solely responsible for massive and increasing selectivity. Structural reasons within the system of education, like the intertwined phenomena of early tracking (towards six

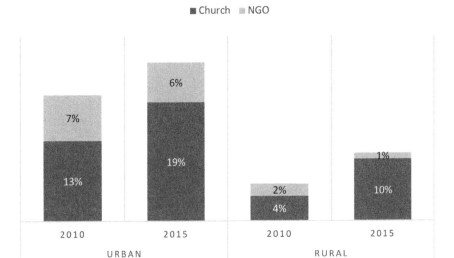

Figure 4.3 Changing importance of alternative school maintenance by churches and NGOs in rural and urban contexts 2010–2015. *Source:* KIR-STAT, edited from panel of primary education data 2001–2015 (provided by Databank CERS HAS).

and eight grade secondary schools) and the declining prestige of comprehensive schools have also played major roles, independent of the shift from decentralized to centralized maintenance of primary education (Kozma, 2014; Sáska, 2011; Szolár, 2015). Castejón and Zancajo (2015) also point to the importance of building such educational systems. They cite Mons' (2004) classification and have adapted it to subsume OECD countries into four groups classified by their integration mechanisms as (a) separation, (b) uniform, (c) á-la-cart, and (d) individualized models. According to their analysis of disadvantaged students' data from the 2009 PISA assessment, Hungarian children accounted for the highest degree (50%) of low achievers, whilst the rate of high achievers among them was last but one (7.2%). In the authors' classification system, Hungary belongs to the first group of countries where separation is the dominant integration model "characterised by the existence of a short common core curriculum, in addition to presenting a generalised use of grade retention in managing students' progress [and] grouping students according to ability (in different schools and in different classes)" (Castejón & Zancajo, 2015, p. 230).

In the last decades Kertesi and Kézdi (2005, 2009, 2014) have conducted several quantitative studies aiming to reveal the scale, causes, and consequences of Roma segregation in primary education. Their most important results from this chapter's perspective are

- their analysis of individual data highlighting that 23% of residents of "one-school villages" and small rural towns went to non-catchment schools in 2001; the scale of children's commuting was significantly related to their parents' level of education:
  - 20% of children of the least educated parents (maximum vocational school)
  - the rate redoubled in the case of children of highly educated parents;
- in their 2006 study they found that achievements of Roma children at segregated schools were 20% less at 4th grade and 40% four years later; according to their regression models, 10% of the lagging behind of these children can be explained as a direct impact of separated teaching (Kertesi & Kézdi, 2009);
- according to their 2013 research in 100 Hungarian towns (Kertesi & Kézdi, 2014), scale of segregation correlated with
  - number and rate of children of higher social status enrolled in a non-catchment school,
  - number and rate of Roma children in the town, and
  - was influenced by local politics in relation to school segregation.

Two further observations in relation to the increased ethnicity-based selection of children at primary education need to be added here, stemming from qualitative research.

Increased selectivity can also occur in ordinary schools maintained by municipalities or the State, both prior to, and after, 2013 in rural contexts. Geographical discontinuities of residential segregation, reinforced by the defence practices of village communities, explain the parallel appearance of spaces with both a high degree and (almost) a zero degree of ethnic segregation at nearby schools or neighborhoods/settlements. An example is provided by a case study of a small school of around 60 students run by a minor municipality of approximately 600 inhabitants; this was the school where White flight was directed to from the neighboring village school. As a result, the small school, targeted by the flow of non-Roma students, escaped closure in 2007–2010, whilst the neighboring school had become an almost Roma-only institution within a decade (Kovács, 2012a). This example conveys much about the nature of selectivity driven by mainly (lower) middle class—in this case even working class—parental aspirations aimed at securing good education for their children that cannot be achieved in a ghetto school. Such aspirations can be lifted to a community level, where, as in the concerned village, a strong and well-organized community managed to bias parental choice in the neighboring village by providing transport on the village bus to overcome financial burden and inconvenience to the parents.

The process is triggered by parents' fears of a quick decline in the level of teaching at schools impacted by ghettoization. Messing and Molnár (2008) pointed out that in classes of eighth graders where the rate of Roma students exceeds 40%, the number of students who intend to continue education at a gymnasium drops sharply. The results confirm the outcomes of an earlier study on negative impacts of social and ethnic segregation on secondary education (Kertesi & Kézdi, 2005). Moreover, segregated schools are generally disadvantaged themselves, restricted to poor teaching endowments, including scarce availability of regular and complementary services, equipment and facilities, as well as a less qualified and/or overloaded, underpaid teaching staff, that makes low teaching quality understandable (Havas, 2008). Opting for alternative maintainers is more common in urban than in rural contexts. In rural areas, NGOs are usually weak or do not exist at all, and churches are not eager to accept small schools. There are many more alternative paths offered in larger towns and cities as the graph illustrates (Figure 4.3). The tendency of an increasing influence of churches on primary education both in urban and rural contexts, however, is clearly seen from the figures.

When closing this subsection, the structural, societal causes being influential behind selectivity must be emphasized. The degree of marginalization of roughly one third of the Hungarian Roma population (estimated by Havas, 2008) as a cumulative effect of exclusions from access to open labor markets and all kinds of amenities of the society (out of which access to good education is only one, but one of major importance), inevitably increases the gap between marginalized Roma people and that of the majority population. The need for addressing structural causes of marginalization is obviously called for by Mowat (2015) too.

The Aspect of Equity as Reflected by PISA Assessment

As noted at the beginning of this chapter, according to the PISA assessment, the performance of 15-year-old Hungarian children has steadily worsened since 2006. In terms of reading, the percentage of low achievers (students performing below proficiency Level 2) was 17.6% in 2006; it grew to 19.7% by 2012 and continued to increase to as high as 27.5% by 2015, whilst the rate of top performers (students performing proficiency Level 5 or above) dropped from 6.1% through 5.6% to 4.3%, respectively (OECD, 2016). Science results indicated a similar decline: the rate of low achievers increased from 15% in 2006 to 18% in 2012 and 26% in 2015. At the same time, the top performers' achievements drew an opposing curve from 6.9%, 5.9%, and 4.6%, respectively (OECD, 2016). The high level of centralization, rigidity, and teachers' low level of autonomy prevailing since 2013 has certainly contributed to declining achievements.

However, there are a number of other factors impacting students' poor performance at the PISA assessment, such as budgetary cuts to spending on education, down from 5.6% of the GDP in 2010 to 4.6% in 2013. By 2015 the rate was readjusted to 5.2% (Eurostat, general government expenditure by function (COFOG) [gov_10a_exp]), and budgetary support of primary and lower secondary education was particularly meager: Hungary sacrificed the second lowest proportion of public expenditure to these grades of education in Europe (after Romania)—1.52% in 2012 and 1.17% in 2014 (Eurostat, Public expenditure on education by the education level and program orientation—as percentage of GDP [educ_uoe_fine06]).

The third factor that influences students' achievements is the meagre emphasis of primary education on equity despite targeted policy measures, the so-called "Pedagogical Programme for Integration" (PPI), developed by the left-wing-liberal government in 2004. These measures were unable to achieve any breakthrough during their decade-long operation. The PPI made incentives available for primary schools threatened with social and ethnic segregation to make sure that teaching is pursued in an integrated manner, with special attention to children arriving from disadvantaged socioeconomic and cultural backgrounds. (Later on vocational schools and kindergartens had become eligible for PPI funding as well.) The majority of targeted children in the framework of PPI were Roma. In its classical form, PPI provided extra income for the teachers in exchange for their efforts aimed at developing and using a locally adapted methodology of inclusive teaching. Participating students were also eligible for program-related entitlements. In the best cases—in addition to food, books, and toolkits available for disadvantaged children for free—students received individually provided mentoring, especially if they considered continuing their studies in secondary education. (See the good example of the Roma only school of Village-2.)

Though state support was diminishing, more and more schools applied for funding within PPI illustrated below; many of them without sincere commitment towards inclusive teaching.

During the school-year 2012/2013, HUF 3.3 billion (approx. EUR 12.2 million) was available for funding the program in 174 eligible schools; during the following year, HUF 2.8 billion HUF (approximately EUR 10.4 million; Varga, 2016); in 2014, much less than 0.9 billion HUF (approximately EUR 3.5 million) were made available between 718 institutions. (Source for 2014 data: http://www.emet.gov.hu/hatter_1/integracios_pedagogiai_rendszer/)

Disturbances, however, had already occurred in PPI implementation in 2012–2013 in the delivery of additional payments. The extra payment for teachers then disappeared, in parallel with the new remuneration policies at nationalized schools. By the year of 2015, PPI, the emblematic policy tool, considered a leading innovation targeting disadvantaged students a decade ago, ceased to exist amongst influential governance policies. It was shifted to project level funded by the Human Resources Operational Programs from 2015 (TÁMOP-3.3.19-15/1).

It must be added that inner inconsistencies of PPI also contributed to its final failure, such as its controversial attitude towards segregated schools. (Being undesired, segregated schools were excluded from PPI funding during the first phase of the program.) Policy makers also underestimated the impacts of residential segregation and family background: in the context of the unfolding financial crisis from 2006–2007, and the deepening poverty of the marginalized Roma people, the chances of PPI to compensate for acute disadvantages were significantly constrained. In many cases, spreading extreme poverty imposed serious limitations on the abilities of poor Roma parents to cooperate with teachers. Without strong family support PPI could not fulfill its goal. (For an analysis of intertwining residential and school segregation in Hungary and Slovakia see Kovács, 2015.)

Evidence related to the diminishing availability of integrated teaching in Hungary appeared in the literature and was reflected in the results of the 2015 PISA assessment as well. As a publication issued in the final year of the Decade of the Roma Inclusion points out, 19% fewer Roma than others had completed primary school in 2015, showing a significant worsening of the situation since 2005. The same was found regarding the dissociated teaching of Roma children, 20% of whom received segregated education (Roma Inclusion Index, 2015). According to a recent European Commission publication, "The impact of pupils' socioeconomic background on education outcomes [in Hungary] is the strongest in the EU. These statements seem to be in line with two relevant pieces of data from the latest PISA assessment, indicating that firstly, Hungary scores are second highest (after Luxemburg) according to the Index that measured between-school variations in science performance (80.1%), and secondly, Hungary was ranked sixth considering the likelihood of low performance among disadvantaged students, after Dominica, Argentina, Peru, Singapore, and France (OECD, 2016, p. 205 and p. 222, respectively).

The so-called Roma Regional Survey of the UNDP in 2011 provides relevant information from rural contexts concerning the participation of Roma students in both compulsory and upper secondary education. Interviews were carried out face-to-face in the homes of Roma and non-Roma respondents living within close proximity of each other. (The survey was conducted in collaboration with the World Bank and FRA. http://www.eurasia.undp.org/content/rbec/en/home/ourwork/sustainable-development/

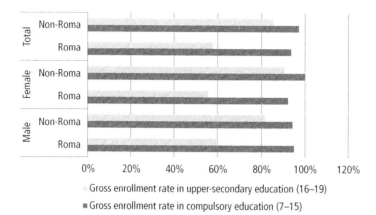

Figure 4.4 Attendance of Roma students of segregated neighborhoods and non-Roma students of the vicinity in basic and secondary education in 2011. *Source:* Roma-data UNDP/WB/EC Regional survey 2011.

development-planning-and-inclusive-sustainable-growth/roma-in-central-and-southeast-europe/roma-data.html)

Hungarian data suggest that after a balanced participation of Roma and non-Roma children in preschooling, the gap starts to grow in the case of female students already at lower secondary level and gets much wider at the upper secondary level. (See Figure 4.4.)

Our KIR-STAT dataset used in the section on "Facts and Figures on changes in School Network 2001–2015" is not appropriate for confirming the statements in relation to the increase of segregated teaching, although this does not threaten the validity of the indications. To resolve this paradox, the reader must see its cause: lacking data broken down by ethnicity, the only proxy indicator of the socioeconomic character of schools is that of the number (proportion) of disadvantaged and multiply disadvantaged students. Sticking with disadvantaged children (the term includes multiple disadvantaged children, too); their number and rate do not show any increased accumulation, rather, data indicate a significant decrease from 2010 to 2015 as a consequence of four factors:

- The classification of the category of "disadvantaged children" changed in 2013 (Act XXVII of 2013 on the amendment of legislation related to social issues, child protection, and others) along with the process of registration (the agency that pursues registration) meaning that data are not comparable before and after 2013.
- Public work programs that targeted the rural poor significantly reduced long-term unemployment between 2011 and 2015, which

influenced one of the three criteria of eligibility for the category of "disadvantaged students" (parents' long-term unemployment).
- There is no need to register the disadvantaged status of children any more, since income poverty in any family provides enough evidence for students to be eligible for free meals and study books—therefore, parents tend not to register their children.
- After 2014–2015, when the financial crisis had passed, the labor market was revitalized and absorbed many of the unemployed; therefore, the rate of extreme poverty indeed diminished, which did not mean, however, that segregated teaching diminished as well.

Table 4.3 indicates the changing numbers of schools where ethnic segregation is likely at an advanced stage. This group of schools was selected according to the numbers of disadvantaged students, showing those where the rate was above 50%. The significant reduction in the numbers between 2010 and 2015 indicates decreasing poverty, but allows only projections about ethnic relations.

Using the same indicators from another aspect, Figure 4.5a. shows that socially disadvantaged students tend increasingly to attend rural schools (68% of the disadvantaged students were thought in rural schools in 2015, reflecting a 10% increase from 2010). Figure 4.5b indicates the same tendency from another angle: whilst the share of students learning at rural schools is dwindling, the proportion of multiple disadvantaged children learning in them is on the increase.

What these tendencies project for the future is that rural schools will have to face prolonged social pressures that are likely to be accompanied by ethnic tensions.

TABLE 4.3 Changing Numbers of Schools Between 2005–2015 Where Ethnic Segregation is Likely to be at an Advanced Stage

Rate of Disadvantaged Students at School	2005		2010		2015	
	The Number of Schools					
	Urban	Rural	Urban	Rural	Urban	Rural
51–60%	53	184	67	140	14	106
61–75%	30	203	55	177	20	92
76–90%	17	108	27	154	17	74
More Than 90%	25	61	19	84	7	49
Total	125	556	168	555	58	321

Source: KIR-STAT, panel of primary education data 2001–2015.

Note: The author is grateful to Melinda Tir and Bálint Koós for providing the data-files.

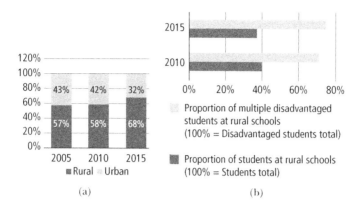

Figure 4.5 Rate of socially disadvantaged students in rural and urban schools in 2005–2015. *Source:* KIR-STAT, edited from panel of primary education data 2001–2015 (provided by Databank Centre for Economic and Regional Studies).

CONCLUSIONS

The Hungarian system of primary education, particularly its rural end, has had to endure fundamental and opposing government interventions during recent decades as part of initially moderate and then radical centralization policies. In retrospect, major sustainability issues were addressed but neither of these interventions handled the most important structural weaknesses of the rural school network adequately, notwithstanding the structural weaknesses of the educational system at large.

Beyond targeted policies, broader circumstances also influenced the present unfavorable state of the art. Hungary in general and rural areas in particular had to face huge challenges between 2006 and (approximately) 2014 both inside and outside education, triggered mainly by the global financial crisis that hit economically an already weakened country. Economic and social consequences of the intertwined internal and external crises induced or accelerated existing selective migration and, consequently, polarization in rural areas, within and across local communities and institutions. These macro-processes, exacerbated by mistaken or just weak policies addressing education and its equity aspects, contributed to the negative spiral of social and spatial processes, ending up—amongst other consequences—in worsening segregation rates of the most vulnerable social layers in residential neighborhoods and schools. The poor achievements of the 15-year-old students at the PISA 2015 assessment were obviously impacted by these macro- and micro-scale challenges.

However, recently some positive developments have begun to occur in the wider economic context (since about 2014), such as the revitalization of the labor market and a decrease of poverty rates, and, in the field of education, since 2016, the relaxation of the rigidity of the architecture of the educational governance of the 2013 setup. Budgetary spending has also been increasing since 2014, which might result in a positive turn concerning rural communities and their schools, with more stability, smarter governance and more effective education, with enhanced emphasis on inclusion.

ACKNOWLEDGMENT

The chapter was written as background study to the research project numbered K120400, titled: *The school is not an island. Education and social resilience in multi-ethnic environments.* The project was supported by the National Research, Development, and Innovation Office, Hungary, Europe.

REFERENCES

Balázs, É., & Kovács, K. (Eds.). (2012). *Többcélú küzdelem. Helyzetképek a kistérségi közoktatásról* [Multi-purpose struggle. Status of education at the districts.]. Budapest, Hungary: Institute for Educational Research and Development.

Castejón, A., & Zancajo, A. (2015). Educational differentiation policies and the performance of disadvantaged students across the OECD countries. *European Educational Research Journal, 14*(3–4), 222–239.

European Union. (2017). *Education and training monitor.* Luxembourg: Publications Office of the European Union.

Györgyi, Z. (2016). Közoktatás-irányítási változások. Új Pedagógiai Szemle [Changes in leadership of education]. *New Pedagogical Review,* 5–6. Retrieved from http://folyoiratok.ofi.hu/uj-pedagogiai-szemle/kozoktatas-iranyitasi-valtozatok

Havas, G. (1999). A kistelepülések és a romák [Small-scale settlements and Roma people]. In F. Glatz (Ed.), *A cigányok Magyarországon* [Roma people in Hungary] (pp. 163–204). MTA Társadalomtudományi Kutatóközpont. Budapest, Hungary: Research Institute of Social Sciences.

Havas, G. (2008). Equality of opportunity, desegregation. In K. Fazekas, J. Köllő, & J. Varga (Eds.), *Green book for the renewal of public education in Hungary* (pp. 131–150). Budapest, Hungary: ECOSTAT.

Horn, D. (2005). Mennyibe kerül egy gyerek? [How much does a child take?]. In Z. Hermann (Ed.), *Hatékonysági problémák a közoktatásban* [Problems of effectiveness of public education] (pp. 35–46). Budapest, Hungary: Országos Közoktatási Intézet.

Imre, A. (2004). *A kistelepülési iskolák szerepe a települések népességmegtartó képességében* [The role of schools in population-retaining abilities of small settlements]. Budapest, Hungary: Országos Közoktatási Intézet.

Kertesi, G., & Kézdi, G. (2005, April). Általános iskolai szegregáció. Okok és következmények [Segregation at primary school. Causes and consequences]. *Közgazdasági Szemle, 52*(4), 317–355.

Kertesi, G., & Kézdi, G. (2009, November). Általános iskolai szegregáció Magyarországon az ezredforduló után [Primary school segregation in Hungary at the turn of the century]. *Közgazdasági Szemle, 56*(11), 959–1000.

Kertesi, G., & Kézdi, G. (2014). *Iskolai szegregáció, szabad iskolaválasztás és helyi oktatáspolitika 100 magyar városban* [School segregation, free choice of school and local educational policy in 100 Hungarian towns]. Budapesti Munkagazdaságtani Füzetek 2014/6. Budapesti Corvinus Egyetem – MTA KRTK.

KIR-STAT. (Statistics on Public Education). Ministry of Human Capacities. Panel data on primary education provided by DATABANK of Centre for Economic and Regional Studies.

Kovács, K. (2012a). Rescuing a small village school in the context of rural change. *Journal of Rural Studies, 28*(2), 108–117.

Kovács, K. (2012b). Teaching and promoting Roma integration in a small rural school in Hungary. In J. Nikula & L. Granberd (Eds.), *Traces of peasantry and post-socialism* (pp. 73–92). Tampere, Finland: Juvenes Print.

Kovács, K. (2015). Advancing marginalisation of Roma and forms of segregation in East Central Europe. *Local Economy, 30*(7), 1–17.

Kovács, K., Schwarcz, G., & Tagai, G. (2014). *The territorial dimension of poverty and social exclusion in Europe. Applied Research*. Nógrád County, Hungary: TiPSE. Retrieved from https://www.espon.eu/sites/default/files/attachments/Annex_2_Appendix_6_Case_Study_Report_Nograd_HU.pdf

Kovács, K., & Váradi, M. M. (2012). Már mindenki együttműködik, aki földrajzilag, fizikailag együtt tud működni [Everybody is cooperating who is able to co-operate physically and geographically]. In É. Balázs & K. Kovács (Eds.), *Többcélú küzdelem. Helyzetképek a kistérségi közoktatásról* [Multi-purpose struggle. Status of education at the districts] (pp. 159–206). Budapest, Hungary: OFI.

Kozma, T. (2014). A központosítás haszna és ára [The use and price of centralization]. *Educatio, 23*(1), 3–12.

Kučerová, S., Bláha, J. D., & Kučera, Z. (2015). Transformations in spatial relationships in elementary education: A case study of changes in two rural areas since the second half of the 20th century. *Moravian Geographical Reports, 23*(1), 34–43.

Lannert, J. (2008). *Szabad iskolaválasztás. Az oktatási jogok biztosa által megrendelt vizsgálat* ["More attention should have needed." Barriers of Success at School]. Retrieved from http://koloknet.blog.hu/2008/04/28/szabad_iskolavalasztas

Messing, V., & Molnár, E. (2008). 'Több odafigyelés kellett volna' A roma gyerekek iskolai sikerességének korlátairól. *Esély, 19*(4), 77–93.

Mons, N. (2004). *De l'école unifiée aux écoles plurielles: Évaluation internationale des politiques de différenciation et de diversification de l'offre éducative* [From uniform to pluralistic school: international evaluation of differentiation and diversification policies of education's offer] (Doctoral thesis). Bourgogne, France: Université de Bourgogne.

Mowat, J. G. (2015). Towards a new conceptualisation of marginalisation. *European Educational Research Journal, 14*(5), 454–476.

Nikitscher, P., & Velkey, G. (2012). 'Mert az iskolának maradnia kell' Közoktatási feladatellátás a Pásztói kistérségben ["The school must be maintained." Education in the Pásztó District]. In É. Balázs & K. Kovács (Eds.), *Többcélú küzdelem. Helyzetképek a kistérségi közoktatásról* [Multi-purpose struggle. Status of education at the districts] (pp. 207–242). Budapest, Hungary: OFI.

OECD. (2016). *PISA 2015 results (Volume I): Excellence and equity in education*. Paris, France: Author. http://dx.doi.org/10.1787/9789264266490-en

Roma-data. UNDP/WB/EC regional Roma survey 2011 data. https://www.eurasia .undp.org/content/rbec/en/home/ourwork/sustainable-development/ development-planning-and-inclusive-sustainable-growth/roma-in-central -and-southeast-europe/roma-data.html

Roma Inclusion Index 2015. (2015). *Demonstrating progress and measuring outcomes within the decade*. Budapest, Hungary: Decade of Roma Inclusion Secretariat Foundation.

Sáska, G. (2011). Ideológiák és az oktatás [Ideologies and Education]. *Educatio, 20*(1), 3–17.

Somogyi, E., & Tellér, N. (2011). *Supplementary background document to the VADEMECUM: Improving housing conditions for marginalized communities, including Roma*. Retrieved from https://www.opensocietyfoundations.org/sites/default/files/ housing-vademecum-supplementary.pdf

Szolár, É. (2015). Change, continuity and path dependency in the Hungarian public education. *European Educational Research Journal, 14*(3–4), 331–346.

Váradi, M. M. (2012). A bizonytalanság bizonyossága: Változások és konfliktusok zalai kisiskolák világában [Certainness of insecurity. Changes and conflicts in small schools in Zala County]. In É. Balázs & K. Kovács (Eds.), *Többcélú küzdelem. Helyzetképek a kistérségi közoktatásról* [Multi-purpose struggle. Status of education at the districts] (pp. 65–112). Budapest, Hungary: OFI.

Varga, A. (2016). A hazai oktatási integráció—Tapasztalatok és lehetőségek [Integration in education. Experiences and possibilities]. *Neveléstudomány, 4*(1), 71–91.

Vidra, Z. (2012). Kistérségi közoktatás szervezés a Nagykállói kistérségben [Educational service provision in the Nagykálló District]. In É. Balázs & K. Kovács (Eds.), *Többcélú küzdelem. Helyzetképek a kistérségi közoktatásról* [Multi-purpose struggle. Status of education at the districts] (pp. 275–306). Budapest, Hungary: OFI.

Vígvári, A. (2008). Szubszidiaritás nélküli decentralizáció [Decentralisation without subsidiarity]. *Tér és Társadalom, 22*(1), 141–167.

Virág, T. (2012). "A sötét Abaújból—most leghátrányosabb—ennyi az előrelépésünk" [From the dark Abaúj—now the most disadvantaged—this is our progress]. In É. Balázs & K. Kovács (Eds.), *Többcélú küzdelem. Helyzetképek a kistérségi közoktatásról* [Multi-purpose struggle. Status of education at the districts.] (pp. 243–274). Budapest, Hungary: OFI.

Wacquant, L. (2008). *Urban outcast: A comparative sociology of advanced marginality*. Cambridge, MA: Polity Press.

CHAPTER 5

A CONSIDERATION OF CZECH RURAL SCHOOLS FROM DIFFERENT SCALES

From Centrally Directed to Autonomous Educational Policies

Silvie R. Kučerová
J. E. Purkyně University in Ústí nad Labem, Czechia

Kateřina Trnková
Masaryk University, Czechia

The main goal of this chapter is to present the current situation regarding research into rural education and schooling in Czechia. By the term *rural schooling*, as applied to the Czech context, we mean researching external rather than internal school relationships (their spatial pattern and availability) while *rural education* addresses directly the operation of individual schools, educational processes, and policies. The first aim of the chapter is to conduct a meta-analysis of elementary schools research within main

Czech scientific journals and present an overview of pertinent literature compiled by the authors. Secondly, we aim to present our research into the geography of education as a synthesis of knowledge about the development of the network of Czech rural elementary schools during the last 50 years. This synthesis includes reference to general as well as region-specific and historical-specific processes. In addition, a case study of a peripherally located rural region in Czechia will be used to illustrate problems of small rural schools in these kinds of regions, and the roles of particular actors in the process of their failure or success.

Czechia is a country that has, over the past decades, progressed from having a centralized economy run by the communist regime in the second half of the 20th century, to a renewal of democratic society with a free market economy in the 21st century. The economic, political, and social transitions are reflected in the organization of elementary schooling. According to the principles of centrality of power and governance in the field of education (Brock, 2016) these transitions could be described as a shift from a strong and strictly hierarchically directed educational policy to a decentralized and rather vague autonomous organization of schooling (for further details see, e.g., Kučerová, Dvořák, Meyer, & Bartůněk, 2020). Under the rules of the communist party, a policy of elementary school catchment was applied, as in a number of other European countries (see Bajerski, 2015; Echols, McPherson, & Williams, 1990). This is a system in which each school is strictly allocated a catchment area from which all pupils with permanent addresses within that area are obliged to attend that particular school. In Czechia, in addition, the state managed the school distribution pattern and all school closures. Features of the neoliberal free market economy, which emerged in educational systems in Western Europe in the 1980s (Holloway & Pimlott-Wilson, 2012), were naturally not implemented in this communist country. However, after the political turnover of 1989, even in Czechia free school choice by parents and the decentralization of schools' management began to be adopted simultaneously, with delegation being passed from the state to municipalities for the competent establishment of elementary schools (Nekorjak, Souralová, & Vomastková, 2011).

The changes in school life and school governance in Czechia since 1989 can be analyzed from different perspectives: personal (individual), community (societal), school (institutional), regional (territorial). An example of a research study looking at the personal level is that of Zounek, Šimáně, and Knotová (2017). Here the individual perceptions of the realities of education and schooling and the impacts on their biographies and behaviors are the main focus. Other researchers such as Sedláček (2008) deal with community, the relations within as well as between groups, and community behavior towards school and its personnel. The institutional perspective focuses on school culture, relationships between schools, and other institutions; legislative and political environment is also a subject of research (see, e.g., Dvořák, Starý, Urbánek, Chvál, & Walterová, 2010). On the regional scale, researchers are looking at the organization of educational process in space, the spatial distribution, and the physicality and materiality of educational environments and places (see, e.g., Hampl, 2004). The authors argue that to gain a full understanding of the complexity of educational realities, a synthesis at all levels is required. For example, the multi-level work of Kučerová, Kučera, and Chromý (2010) examines how individuals are linked into collective behavior and into institutional planning within spatial relations.

RECENT RESEARCH IN RURAL EDUCATION AND SCHOOLING IN CZECHIA

Czech research in rural schooling reaches relatively far back but until recently has been unsystematic. Czechia has an important advantage within its rich statistical databases on formal education, which are rooted in their detailed, long-term statistical record keeping. Thanks to the need for auditing in the educational system, lists of numbers of schools from the beginning of the 20th century have been available, including school descriptions and rich cartographic detail. As Czechia has undergone a number of territorial administrative reforms, the numbers of schools for particular municipalities have had to be manually recounted retrospectively. For an example of how this kind of database has been used see Kučerová (2012) who mapped changes in the numbers of schools in all municipalities of Czechia during the 4 years of 1961, 1976, 1990, and 2004.

Isolated studies dealing with rural education in Czechia appeared during the 20th century (e.g., Hitnaus, 1969) but more research has emerged in different disciplines in the 21st. The most attention to rural education and rural schooling in Czechia is given by pedagogical studies. A consistent line of investigation emerged in 2000 about education in rural spaces with emphasis on small schools with composite (mixed age) classes (Emmerová, 2000; Trnková, 2006), from the educational policies of rural municipalities (Trnková, 2008; 2009) and school management (Sedláček, 2008) to relationships between the schools and local communities (Trnková, Knotová, & Chaloupková, 2010). Another area of research compares the operation of different types of elementary schools in similar contexts (Dvořák, Starý, & Urbánek, 2015; cf. Taylor, 2001), or as case studies (cf. Berg, 2007; Dvořák et al., 2010). There is a third area of educational research that considers competition in the educational quasi-market (Dvořák & Straková, 2016) and parental school choice (Straková & Simonová, 2015), an issue for both urban and rural contexts (Kučerová, Bláha, & Pavlasová, 2015; Meyer &

Kučerová, 2018; Nekorjak et al., 2011). The last area to which attention is paid is historical pedagogy, focusing on different aspects of education in the past (Zounek et al., 2017), including, specifically, the issue of Czech minority schools in border areas with the German-speaking population before World War II (Šimáně, 2014).

Another discipline where rural schooling has been a consistent focus of research is in geography. Wahla (1988) defined the principles of geography of education as a discipline (cf. Johnston, 2009) to consider education's spatial aspects. Geography of education is a suitable partner for educational sciences, which have been experiencing the so-called spatial turn (Holloway & Jöns, 2012), that is, paying increased attention to the spatiality of phenomena and processes. For example, the geography of education has explored the familiar geography research focus of commuting and the delimitation of catchment areas for various institutions, including schools (see Hampl, 2004). This has been done using time-spatial frameworks of the movement of people within areas (Ouředníček, Špačková, & Feřtová, 2011), and computer modeling of school availability using geographic information systems (GIS; Kučerová, Mattern, Štych, & Kučera, 2011). Secondly, aspects of education in regional and local development studies have focused research on human and social capital and regional identity (e.g., Dostál & Markusse, 1989; Jančák, Havlíček, Chromý, & Marada, 2008). An attempt to connect these two lines of research in the context of rural schooling can be seen in works by Kučerová (2012); Kučerová and Kučera (2012); and Kučerová, Bláha, and Pavlasová (2015). The use of demographic estimates and projections of future pupils in particular regions (Hulík & Tesárková, 2009) has also been applied to studies on rural schools in Czechia.

Despite the relatively extensive list of works dealing with rural education and schooling in Czechia, neither the research nor the researchers are very prominent. This can be seen in the meta-analysis of elementary schools' research done by Trnková (2012), in seven Czech peer-reviewed journals of education between 1990 (after the breakdown of the communist regime) and 2016,[1] which has been updated for this chapter. The meta-analysis included a total of 343 empirical studies, nearly 90% of which were published after 2000. An overwhelming majority of texts (93%) were not concerned with spatial aspects of education; studies focusing directly on elementary education in urban/rural space, or comparing them, were rare (only 24 studies). Comparisons of rural and urban locations were the most frequent (22%), followed by research undertaken in cities (17%). Only 3.5% of all studies were drawn from elementary schools exclusively from rural areas. The conclusions of this meta-analysis do not significantly differ from the findings of others, which positions research about rural education generally outside the mainstream of educational research and publication (see White & Corbett, 2014).

When summing up rural education research in Czechia, we see that there is none published on the following issues that appear in research on rural education in other countries:

1. Specifics of education and didactics in rural schools (see, e.g., Karlberg-Granlund, 2009; Smit, Hyry-Beihammer, & Raggl, 2015). The neglect of this subject by researchers in Czechia is a concern.
2. Competition, cooperation, and influence in a variety of subjects (including private or church schools, etc.) on the educational market in rural areas. Until very recently 95% of schools were governed by the municipality, so there has been no diversity or "choice" in schooling in this sense.
3. A multicultural perspective on transformations of rural education in the context of migration and changes in functions played by rural areas (Hruška, 2014). The international dimension of migration has not been visible in Czech rural areas until very recently.

The authors argue that the biggest problem is the general "ungroundedness" of rural school research and the lack of interdisciplinary research. We argue the goal of research should be the interconnection of the individual, the community, and the national (see, e.g., Sherman & Sage, 2011).

This section has attempted an overview to summarize the scope and scale of research on schools in rural areas of Czechia. Research work continues to be published, including that of the authors of this chapter, who are focusing their work on the missing themes from their analysis of the published literature.

A Case Study of Changes in the Network of Czech Rural Elementary Schools From the Turnov Region

The research presented here is a synthesis of knowledge about the geography of education in Czechia acquired collectively by the authors over several years. It is based on partial studies, some of which have already been published (Kučerová, 2012; Kučerová & Kučera, 2012; Kučerová et al., 2015; Kučerová et al., 2015). The focus is the Turnov region of Czechia, a rural interior area, and will be presented here to illustrate the consequences of the historical development of the rural elementary schools network in Czechia.

Czech Educational System and Brief Framing of Rural Schooling

Firstly, it is necessary to point out some important specific features of the Czech education and settlement system that influence communities and the development of elementary education.

Primary school attendance, according to the Act No. 561/2004 Coll. on Education, is compulsory for 9 years and is provided through either large, *complete* elementary schools (CES), which have all nine grade levels, or by smaller, *incomplete* elementary schools (IES), where fewer primary classes are taught (Grades 1 to 5 or perhaps fewer) from where students must subsequently commute to a larger 9-year school to complete their basic education. In addition, the incomplete schools often have *composite classes*; where pupils of two or more grades are taught together in a class (Trnková, 2008).

The territory of Czechia (78,000 km^2) has approximately 15,000 settlements (towns, villages, hamlets), governed by 6,250 local self-governing units (municipalities). That means the settlement pattern is extremely fragmented, and, for this reason, rural municipalities in Czechia are defined as those with fewer than 3,000 inhabitants (90% of all municipalities in Czechia are defined as "rural"). In this rural space approximately 2,000 elementary schools operate (60% of the country's total; Kučerová & Kučera, 2012).

The origins of the dense elementary school patterns in Czechia date back to 1869 when compulsory schooling began (Váňová, Rýdl, & Valenta, 1992). The development of Czech rural schools continues to this day and can be divided into five key stages (for more details see Kučerová & Kučera, 2012):

1. An increase in school numbers in parallel with building up a system of available local education, until World War II;
2. A decrease of redundant schools in areas with a population decrease in the 1960s;
3. An extreme nationwide decrease in rural schools due to settlement system regulation and centralization of educational (especially curricular) policies in the 1960s and 1970s;
4. A revitalization of the school network associated with local democratic self-governance renewal in early 1990s;
5. At the beginning of the 21st century, a continuing slight decrease in school numbers and significant spatial differentiation in education provision, due to demographic and internal-migration changes, decentralization and liberalization of the educational market.

The elementary school network continues to decrease and concentrate into central municipalities, as a consequence of population decline in rural areas and the transformation of transport and commuting possibilities. However, it must be pointed out that the primary phase of this process occurred during the 1970s as a result of the implementation of a unique totalitarian policy of centrally directed settlement development. The extent of elementary school reduction during this period is visible from the comparison of Figures 5.1 and 5.2. The massive centralization and concentration processes seen in Czechia are important and distinctively different

A Consideration of Czech Rural Schools From Different Scales ▪ **109**

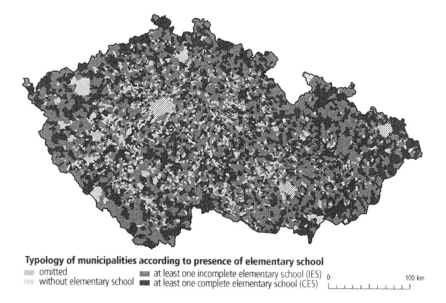

Figure 5.1 Typology of municipalities according to presence of elementary schools, Czechia, 1961. *Source:* Petr Meyer based on the data published in the *Statistical Lexicon of Municipalities of Czechoslovakia* (1965).

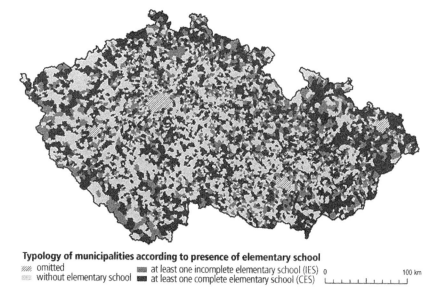

Figure 5.2 Typology of municipalities according to presence of elementary schools, Czechia, 2004. *Source:* Petr Meyer based on the *Database of Statistical Data on Towns and Municipalities* (2004).

from the patterns seen in western (democratic) European countries in the 1970s, which saw a relatively stable period for rural schools and support for disadvantaged rural areas (see Figure 2.7a in Chapter 2, this volume).

Case Study Methodology and Research Procedure

Both quantitative and qualitative approaches were used in analysis of the case study in the Turnov region. First, the quantitative data were analyzed to investigate general trends and conditions of schooling in the region. Secondly, two schools in the region were selected as examples of typical small rural schools. School A was closed down in the 1970s while School B is still in operation. The aim of studying the stories of these two schools was to illustrate the challenges faced in these kinds of regions, and the roles of particular actors in the process of school closure or survival.

The quantitative approaches included analysis of the changes in number and spatial distribution of schools, commuting flows, and changes in school catchment areas. Schools in the Turnov region still in operation were located on the map by their addresses. Buildings of previously closed down schools were identified in a field survey or through online application of Street View within Google Maps. Paradoxically, we have not managed to get enough information on the strictly defined school districts of the era of the communist regime. It was therefore necessary to use data regarding the closest school for each municipality as stated in the *Statistical Lexicon of Municipalities of Czechoslovakia, 1965*. The current catchment areas were identified based on the questionnaire survey among municipality mayors. Data on pupils commuting to school beyond the border of their municipality are provided by the population census that is done every 10 years. Our study, however, had to rely on older data from 2001, as the item covering commuting in the most recent census of 2011 was not filled in by over one third of the population (since many people, reacting to the experiences of recent history, mistrust the authorities and prefer to keep personal information private). The spatial data were cartographically processed with ArcGIS software using our own and public data layers, and the outcomes were finalized in Corel DRAW software. Some characteristics were, moreover, ascertained through a questionnaire survey among school and municipality representatives.

Purely qualitative research methods included so-called "school stories." We carried out and analyzed in-depth interviews with people we called "period witnesses" who were people representing municipalities and schools, and parents of pupils, undertaken in three phases in 2009, 2011, and 2013. In order to preserve the anonymity of respondents, model schools, just like individual respondents were referred to by pseudonyms. The key informants regarding School A were Mrs. A, a formal local authority member, and current Local Authority Member A. School B was covered by Headmaster B,

Local Authority Member B, and Parent B. Each interview was recorded and supplemented with written notes. The interviews were then fully transcribed and subjected to qualitative analysis by open coding using the pencil-and-paper method; subsequently, Atlas.ti software was used.

We also carried out nonparticipant observation in the field, and studied local newspapers and key schools' documents to understand the causes and consequences of the change processes.

Transformations of Servicing Turnov Region by Elementary Schools in the Second Half of the 20th Century

The Turnov region may be regarded as an economic peripheral area within Czechia, while the development of the spatial distribution of schools shows features common to the whole country. The characteristics of the school network are primarily influenced by natural conditions and the nature of the settlement pattern. There is a cluster of sandstone rocks in the eastern part of the region, presenting a transport limitation and predetermining some commuting routes. The settlement pattern can be characterized by a high degree of fragmentation with many small settlements having fewer than 100 inhabitants. This is making the provision of schools in particular localities rather difficult, due to the low numbers of pupils and public transport organization.

The biggest centre dominating the region is the town of Turnov (with approximately 14,000 inhabitants); other smaller centres are important only locally. There have been seven complete elementary schools (CES) in the region since the 1950s, all located in the major centres. The network of incomplete elementary schools (IES) has undergone dynamic changes. Although this network was relatively dense in mid-20th century (with 35 IES in 1961), many small settlements did not have a school of their own and pupils attended schools in neighboring villages. In the following decades the IES pattern was changed dramatically by a number of general factors: for example, a decreasing number of pupils in rural areas, a system of central settlement units, and developments in transport. Currently less than one third of the schools that were in operation in the 1960s (only 11 schools) remain open.

As the distribution of schools was changing, the shape and size of the catchment areas were changing as well (Kučerová et al., 2015). Figures 5.3 and 5.4 illustrate the transformation in IES catchment areas. At the beginning of the period under examination, territories belonging to particular IESs were highly fragmented. Each IES provided school services for a small catchment area within which the distance to the nearest school was rarely longer than 3 km as the crow flies. As for CESs, schools in Turnov catered for the largest part of the region; the rest of the region was allocated to CESs in smaller micro-regional central settlements. In the mid-20th century, Turnov was performing the role of a hub connected to various destinations by

Figure 5.3 Territory belonging to incomplete elementary schools (IES) in Turnov region in 1961. *Source:* Kučerová, Bláha, & Kučera (2015, p. 39).

bus lines suitable for commuting, even from the peripheries of the region (Kučerová, 2012). The dominance of Turnov became even more prominent following mass IES closures in the 1960s and 1970s. Firstly, the size of districts of those IESs that survived the reduction grew dramatically (see Figure 5.4); hence, the commuting distances grew by several times (see Figure 5.5). Many catchment districts of the former IESs are now serviced by CESs in Turnov from the very first grades of elementary school, although the commuting pupils could attend a school in a local rural centre situated at the same distance, if not closer. Commuting data do not allow us to find out how many pupils from the 1st stage commute to a CES beyond their municipality, in spite of the fact that they can attend primary school in their own place of residence. This fact, just like the reasons for this behavior, may

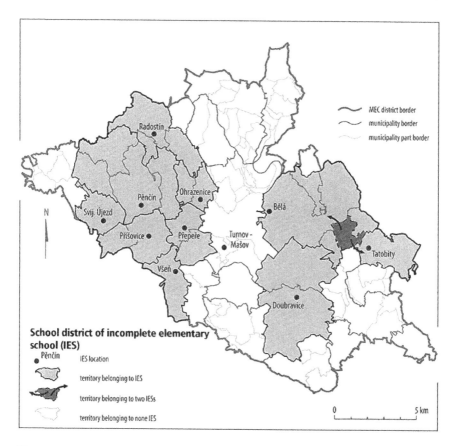

Figure 5.4 Incomplete elementary school (IES) districts in Turnov region in 2014. *Source:* Kučerová, Bláha, & Pavlasová (2015, p. 618).

be studied only by direct questioning of people living in the region or of representatives of their schools.

Facing the Threat of School Closure, Twice

Within the Turnov region, in villages with several hundreds of inhabitants, two typical rural schools were selected. School A was closed down in the 1970s; School B is still in operation. Both were incomplete elementary schools with fewer than 30 pupils.

When School A was closing down, it was by no means a decision made by local inhabitants.

> It was the times that these small schools with composite classes were not preferred, that they were fused with those in town. [...] And those calculations

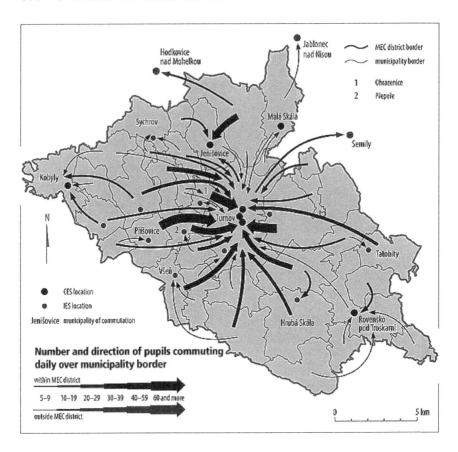

Figure 5.5 Numbers and directions of pupils commuting daily to elementary schools over the borders of their municipalities in Turnov region in 2001. *Source:* Kučerová, Bláha, & Pavlasová (2015, p. 621).

> all the time, they had calculations till year... 1982 I guess, how many children there would be here. Something like six it was. (Mrs. A)

Local people viewed the school as a kind of symbol of independence, prestige, and cultural heritage similar to the way Karlberg-Granlund (2009) and Bell and Sigsworth (1987) describe rural schools.

> We wanted our school preserved because the church, the parsonage and the school, they used to be three basic... simply buildings and personalities, you know, the parson, the headmaster and... the innkeeper, what was happening around the village. (Mrs. A)

There were a number of rational reasons for preserving the school in the same place:

The children were few, it was a one-class school in fact, five grades and they were around 10 [...]. But there was the headmaster and the background and another teacher who had just finished her studies, so even the teachers were available. And in those times school was divided into shifts in towns, not enough classrooms. So what is better, twelve or thirteen children going to school in Turnov by bus when there were not enough buses and not every family had a car, or one teacher coming here to teach the children in our place? (Mrs. A)

Mrs. A also argued at meetings with local authority representatives for preserving the school by pointing out the risk of future population decline in the village if the school were to close down: "I was trying to assemble all mothers, even younger women, to come to the public meeting [...], to speak their opinion, to make us more visible." A similar process is reported in Ribchester and Edwards (1999). In School A there was, however, no right of appeal against the official decision:

It was all staged, that was just a play being acted out, then representatives of district authorities came and told us the decision and... I was aware, but I simply wanted the resolution to contain the statement that we do not agree, that we are against. (Mrs. A)

The closure was a huge disappointment to the people in the village, a sad finale to a period of bloom. The school closure was also associated with the elimination of other key institutions in the village, and made even more painful by the tragic death of the local headmaster. "He had to commute then to teach in Turnov [...] and this is how the tragedy happened, because he was swept off the curb by a car" (Mrs. A).

Although a sense of uncertainty persisted in the village for several years after the closure of the school, most people adjusted to the situation without changing their place of domicile. "People when you ask them cannot see the difference between the times we had a school and now because they have been living here continuously and perceive the differences as they occur, so they aren't conscious of this" (Local Authority Member A). However, the time-spatial patterns of the movement of people in the area changed radically; children did not walk to school anymore, having to use buses or be taken to school by car (see Ouředníček et al., 2011). Although commuting is very costly, Local Authority Member A also admits a general trend of development encouraging commuting to complete schools in towns: "It's kind of a matter of prestige nowadays to send your kids to school in town; the school there has a better image. There is an offer of various leisure-time activities and parents also usually work there."

The situation in Municipality A has thus stabilized over the span of more than 3 decades and people have adapted the time-spatial patterns of their activities to the new environment of a village within the catchment area of a strong center, adjusting their values accordingly.

School B was also facing a threat of a closure several years ago. After School A closed down, and especially after the change towards free parental choice of schools in the 1990s, School B was playing the role of a natural catchment school for pupils from Municipality A. The situation of School B seemed even more dismal. The agent who caused the school closure was not a person in a superior position outside the region: the phenomenon that happened in School B has been described by Bell and Sigsworth (1987) as the "death of school by voting by feet." This happens when parents enroll their children either immediately or gradually at other schools in the area, even though they can choose a school in their own municipality, causing a situation where the local school lacks pupils.

The unstable situation of School B was reported even by Mrs. A during our collection of data in Spring 2009:

> And now they may also be facing a closure. [...] There were some problems, with the teaching staff; they had one headmaster after another. I counted seven headmasters in 14 years there! [...] That school there... they needed new windows and everything. [...] Well but investing half a million crowns into renovating [...] when you have no idea how it's going to... Now eight children are going to leave because it's not known yet who will be leading the school or whether at all the school is going to open in September.

And indeed, regional media published the news in September 2009 that School B has become the smallest school in the region overnight. "The school had four pupils in 1st September 2009, all first-graders. Yet 24 pupils got their school report here in June" (Turnovsko v akci, 2009, para. 1). During the summer holiday parents transferred the majority of enrolled pupils to schools in town. How this could have happened, despite the fact that the municipality had enough pupils to run its own incomplete school, has been described by Local Authority Member B:

> And then the generation of old teachers left and... the new teachers... they did not do so much for the kids, unfortunately. And what happened in one period was that two ladies teachers came who—I don't know why—officially telling us to keep calm because they were doing all they could for the school while telling parents "Transfer your children to Turnov, there's not going to be school here." They were cancelling our school without our agreement! And then we learned when a photographer came to take a picture of the kids, that "They told me last year not to come again because the school would be cancelled...!"

The local authority had only the 2 summer months to stabilize the school and to take the necessary measures to open it in September. "Well we didn't agree to close the school down and we had to find a teacher, a headmaster and at least three pupils" (Local Authority Member B). A headmaster and teacher (one person) was found—Headmaster B characterized his role as "a great challenge; I basically desired to have a village elementary school, built up on greenfield, where I could try to work with children the way I have always wanted to." In the limited time, he attempted to launch a marketing campaign to win over pupils:

> I was trying to avert the threat, I was putting up posters, talking to people, I launched a big campaign on the internet [...]. But... it basically came to nothing. By July we only had four first-graders whose parents wanted their children to go to our school from the beginning anyway.

Municipality B was not giving up; they started the school year and sustained their efforts to get more pupils. The school year, however, brought a new challenge:

> Fears were expressed that we were a Waldorf school, but it's my fault because it was me who said that—to explain things and give the school some... face, so I said I'd be working using Waldorf pedagogy principles. Now the parents... they have fears that something will be different, that we would be praying... (Headmaster B)

Although School B cannot be regarded as an institution following this particular pedagogical concept, the education it provides is in many respects different from that of a standard school. A majority of parents thus feel School B does not meet their expectations of an ideal educational institution:

> I somehow expected that in rural Czechia there are normal schools, because they should serve the village and its immediate surroundings. And things being different or alternative, that's something I'd rather expect somewhere in town. [...] I mean the school is extremely alternative! [...] The kids are given total freedom, even in what they can do in class... if they do the tasks or they don't. They have no textbooks... (Parent B)

Local Authority Member B as well as Headmaster B views the mission of the school primarily in terms of values, attitudes, and community identity development:

> Performance, what this means to me is that the child can learn something, can create something, can resolve a situation. And secondly, that he or she is bringing some culture or is contributing to the culture of the village. [...] So

the school in fact organises the out-of-school activities or event attended also by children going to other schools, and by their parents too [...]. And besides that I think that the school is also giving people joy that the kids can greet them nicely for instance... (Headmaster B)

Although School B is striving to win local people, it is presenting itself as an educational alternative for a specific group of clients, shaped by their cultural and higher socioeconomic status rather than spatial proximity (the commuting distance of pupils to school B is up to 40 km). This marketing strategy has given the school some stability and may postpone or even avert its closure. There is, however, the problem that the school does not play the role of a standard elementary school servicing the rural region, although there is no doubt that it does play a very important part in providing an alternative educational offer within the regional school network and beyond. It is a sensitive question as to whether it is justifiable to fund an institution of super regional significance from the local municipality budget. The operation and existence of the school are determined by the headmaster and local authority members who support him, although the situation may change significantly in the future. It is also hard to predict the inhabitants' interest in their local school, considering they have now become adapted to daily commuting to schools in other places.

CONCLUSIONS

Although rural schools have not received much consistent attention in Czech research, the second part of the 20th century has seen a number of events and processes that have shaped elementary education provision. The case study from the Turnov region provides an illustration of the ways the behavior of individual inhabitants and actors in the municipality have marked the key processes within the structure of elementary schools. It also illustrates the changing relationships between the actors, the institutional frameworks, and spatial physical structures. Giddens' (1984) Theory of Structuration might be usefully applied here. This theory ascribes autonomous elements (actors) with the role of forming and changing the social systems (structures) in their spatial dimension, wherein they act on a daily basis. Application and adaptation of this theory into the rural education setting might help to analyze the changes of schools´ spatial patterns as a result of the distribution of pupils according to parents' preferences and the actions of municipal communities and schools within legislative and institutional frameworks.

Under the communist regime, implementation of various economic, regional-developmental, and settlement plans and educational concepts led either immediately, or within a very short span of time, to a mass reduction of schools, especially in rural areas, and a concentration of them in towns. Most problems and conflicts were caused by the state directly managing education, which dictated the number of schools and the placement of pupils. For example the communist regime forced inhabitants of communities to commute to schools; there was no choice about which school. Larger urban schools were favored over small rural schools as the authorities were sceptical of the quality of the smaller schools, which in turn influenced public opinion and larger more urban schools were seen as more favorable. In the case study reported here, Mrs. A narrates a situation, when the hierarchically higher office closed down a school in the municipality even though the capacity of the urban school, to which pupils had to commute, was insufficient, and the municipality had the conditions and the will to operate their local one.

Since the fall of the regime, there is a tendency for municipalities to manage their resources alone, without support (Kučerová, 2012). With the renewal of democracy, the school network in Czechia has changed qualitatively. This has involved changes in school governance, in parental activity in the educational market, and the associated change in commuting patterns (Kučerová, 2012; Kučerová et al., 2015). The responsibility for the development of the school system has been increasingly influenced by the development of greater autonomy for municipalities in their role as school operators, which may further shape the school network and potentially lead to a new wave of rural school closures. These influences include those of the abovementioned rural inhabitants who might consider a rural school to be a local heritage, but not "for my child" (Sherman & Sage, 2011). Here, the preference for the perceived higher quality of urban schools and improved resources for commuting, leads to students choosing urban schools over rural ones. At the same time, however, the power of municipality leaders may remain and be regarded as those who keep local independent municipality schools despite the high costs and effort required (Trnková, 2009).

It can be concluded that the common conditions of existence of small rural schools in Czechia depend on three groups of key actors. The first is the behavior of the political body empowered to make decisions regarding the existence of the school. If the political bodies view rural schools favorably and are willing to subsidize them the spatial structure of the schooling network can have a lasting character despite unfavorable broader situations. In the role as political body there could be a higher authority beyond the region itself (such as a regional public authority body, as it was under the communist regime, which ordered school closures); or a plan by the national or regional government (such as a decision to reduce the school network); or a local governing body (such as the local authority responsible for funding schools).

Secondly, the existence of schools depends on the preferences of pupils' parents; existing or potential. Parents can influence the number of pupils and the "profitability" of the education provision by their decision to enroll or not enroll their child at a given school. This is affected (especially during periods when educational policies allow free parental school choice) by the activities of people who support the maintenance of a school within a municipality, or by competition between schools, even during periods when the national institutional system does not promote these modes of regulation (Maroy & van Zanten, 2009).

Thirdly, the shape of education and schools' existence also strongly depends on the human factor within schools. Drawing on their qualities of character, their skills, and experience, these key persons are managing schools and providing for their operation and for the education of individuals. In small rural schools it is often a single teacher/headmaster or a very small team. The key person is at the same time influenced by the two previous factors, that is, he/she acts within the legal and political context with only meager opportunities to influence it, and his/her position is dependent of the favor of pupils' parents.

This chapter aims to make a partial contribution to understanding the complex issues of rural education in Czechia as an addition to international comparisons of the development of rural schools in other countries. However, some issues, which were mentioned only slightly, merit deeper attention from rural school researchers. The main necessity is to properly understand the specificity of the post-socialist school quasi-market, of preferences for school choice and parents' decision-making, not only in urban space (Maroy & van Zanten, 2009), but in rural space as well.

NOTE

1. The original text by Trnková (2012) also analysed research monographs. Considering the fact that defining their basic list was close to impossible, due to the system of library item cataloguing practised in Czech libraries, this study only includes the series of pedagogical journals.

REFERENCES

Bajerski, A. (2015). Erosion of the school catchment system as local policy: The case of Poznań, Poland. *KEDI Journal of Education Policy, 12*(1), 41–60.

Bell, A., & Sigsworth, A. (1987). *The small rural primary school: A matter of quality.* London, England: Falmer Press.

Berg, G. (2007). From structural dilemmas to institutional imperatives: A descriptive theory of the school as an institution and of school organizations. *Journal of Curriculum Studies, 39*(5), 577–596.

Brock, C. (2016). *Geography of education: Scale, space and location in the study of education.* London, England: Bloomsbury Academic.

Dostál, P., & Markusse, J. (1989). Rural settlements networks and elementary service provision: Two scenarios for the matching of demand and supply. In G. Clark, P. Huigen, & F. Thissen (Eds.), *Planning and the future of the countryside: Great Britain and the Netherlands* (pp. 62–78). Utrecht, The Netherlands: Royal Dutch Geographical Studies.

Dvořák, D., Starý, K., & Urbánek, P. (2015). *Škola v globální době. Proměny pěti českých základních škol* [School in the global age: Transformations of five elementary schools]. Prague, Czech Republic: Karolinum.

Dvořák, D., Starý, K., Urbánek, P., Chvál, M., & Walterová, E. (2010). *Česká základní škola: Vícepřípadová studie* [Czech elementary school: Multiple case study]. Prague, Czech Republic: Karolinum.

Dvořák, D., & Straková, J. (2016). Konkurence mezi školami a výsledky žáků v České republice: Pohled zblízka na šetření PISA 2012 [School competition and pupil achievement in the Czech Republic: A close look at the PISA 2012 study]. *Pedagogika, 66*(2), 206–229.

Echols, F., McPherson, A., & Williams, J. D. (1990). Parental choice in Scotland. *Journal of Education Policy, 5*(3), 207–222.

Emmerová, K. (2000). Malotřídky v současném prostředí českého venkova [Small schools in the current milieu of the country in Czech Republic]. *Sborník prací Filosofické fakulty Brněnské univerzity*, U 3–4. Masaryk University in Brno, 81–96.

Giddens, A. (1984). *The constitution of society: Outline of the theory of structuration.* Cambridge, MA: Polity Press.

Hampl, M. (2004). Současný vývoj geografické organizace a změny v dojížďce za prací a do škol v Česku [Current development of geographical organisation and changes in commuting to work and schools in the Czech Republic]. *Geografie, 109*(3), 205–222.

Hitnaus, L. (Ed.). (1969). *Problémy výchovy a vzdělávání venkovské mládeže* [Problems of upbringing and education of rural youth]. *Sborník příspěvků z konference* [Conference Proceedings]. České Budějovice, Czech Republic: Pedagogická fakulta Jihočeské Univerzity.

Holloway, S. L., & Jöns, H. (2012). Geographies of education and learning. *Transactions of the Institute of British Geographers, 37*(4), 482–488.

Holloway, S. L., & Pimlott-Wilson, H. (2012). Neoliberalism, policy localisation and idealised subjects: A case study on educational restructuring in England. *Transactions of the Institute of British Geographers, 37*(4), 639–654.

Hruška, V. (2014). Proměny přístupů ke konceptualizaci venkovského prostoru v rurálních studiích [Changing approaches to the conceptualisation of rural space in rural studies]. *Sociologický časopis, 50*(4), 581–601.

Hulík, V., & Tesárková, K. (2009). Dopady demografického vývoje na vzdělávací soustavu v České republice [Impacts of the demographic development on the education system in the Czech Republic]. *Orbis Scholae, 3*(3), 7–23.

Jančák, V., Havlíček, T., Chromý, P., & Marada, M. (2008). Regional differentiation of selected conditions for the development of human and social capital in Czechia. *Geografie, 113*(3), 269–284.

Johnston, R. J. (2009). Education. In D. Gregory, R. Johnston, G. Pratt, M. Watts, & S. Whatmore (Eds.), *The dictionary of human geography* (5th ed.; pp. 186–187). Chichester, England: Blackwell.

Karlberg-Granlund, G. (2009). *Att förstå det stora i det lilla. Byskolan som pedagogik, kultur och struktur* [Understanding the great in the small: Pedagogy, culture and structure of the village school]. (Dissertation thesis.). Vaasa, Finland: Pedagogiska fakulteten, Åbo Akademi in Vasa.

Kučerová, S. (2012). *Proměny územní struktury základního školství v Česku* [Changes in the territorial structure of primary education in Czechia]. Prague, Czech Republic: ČGS.

Kučerová, S. R., Bláha, J. D., & Kučera, Z. (2015). Transformations of spatial relationships within elementary education provision: A case study of changes in two Czech rural areas since the second half of the 20th century. *Moravian Geographical Reports, 23*(1), 34–44.

Kučerová, S. R., Bláha, J. D., & Pavlasová, Z. (2015). Malé venkovské školy na trhu se základním vzděláváním: Jejich působnost a marketing na příkladu Turnovska [Small rural schools in the primary education market: The example of Turnov region]. *Sociologický časopis, 51*(4), 607–636.

Kučerová, S. R., Dvořák, D., Meyer, P., & Bartůněk, M. (2020). Dimensions of centralization and decentralization in the rural educational landscape of postsocialist Czechia. *Journal of Rural Studies, 74*, 280–293.

Kučerová, S., & Kučera, Z. (2012). Changes in the spatial distribution of elementary schools and their impact on rural communities in Czechia in the second half of the 20th century. *Journal of Research in Rural Education, 27*(11), 1–17.

Kučerová, S., Kučera, Z., & Chromý, P. (2010). An elementary school in networks: Contribution to geography of education. *Europa XXI, 21*, 47–61.

Kučerová, S., Mattern, T., Štych, P., & Kučera, Z. (2011). Změny dostupnosti základních škol v Česku jako faktor znevýhodnění regionů a lokalit [Changes in the accessibility of elementary schools in Czechia as a factor of disadvantage impacting regions and localities]. *Geografie, 116*(3), 300–316.

Maroy, C., & van Zanten, A. (2009). Regulation and competition among schools in six European localities. *Sociologie du Travail, 51*(S1), 67–79.

Městská a obecní statistika. (2004). *Database of statistical data on towns and municipalities*. Prague, Czech Republic: ČSÚ. Retrieved from http://vdb.czso.cz/xml/mos.html

Meyer, P., & Kučerová, S. R. (2018). Do pupils attend the nearest elementary school to their homes? Factors in school choice in the urban environment of Liberec, Czechia. *Acta Universitatis Carolinae Geographica, 53*(1), 70–82.

Nekorjak, M., Souralová, A., & Vomastková, K. (2011). Uvíznutí v marginalitě: Vzdělávací trh, 'romské školy' a reprodukce sociálně prostorových nerovností [Stuck in marginality: The education market, 'roma schools' and the reproduction of social and spatial inequalities]. *Sociologický časopis, 47*(4), 657–680.

Ouředníček, M., Špačková, P., & Feřtová, M. (2011). Změny sociálního prostředí a kvality života v depopulačních regionech České republiky [Changes in social milieu and quality of life in depopulating areas of the Czech Republic]. *Sociologický časopis, 47*(4), 777–803.

Ribchester, C., & Edwards, B. (1999). The centre and the local: Policy and practice in rural education provision. *Journal of Rural Studies, 15*(1), 49–63.

Sedláček, M. (2008). Řízení školy na vesnici (případová studie) [Village school management: A case study]. *Studia Paedagogica, 13*, 85–99.

Sherman J., & Sage, R. (2011). Sending off all your good treasures: Rural schools, brain-drain, and community survival in the wake of economic collapse. *Journal of Research in Rural Education, 26*(11), 1–14.

Šimáně, M. (2014). Učitelé českých menšinových škol pohledem dějin každodennosti [Teachers of Czech volksschule from the perspective of the history of everyday life]. *Studia Paedagogica, 19*(3), 89–122.

Smit, R., Hyry-Beihammer, E. K., & Raggl, A. (2015). Teaching and learning in small, rural schools in four European countries: Introduction and sythesis of mixed-/multi-age approaches. *International Journal of Educational Research, 74*, 97–103.

Statistický lexikon obcí ČSSR 1965. (1966). *Statistical lexicon of municipalities of Czechoslovakia 1965*. Prague, Czech Republic: Central Committee of People's Control and Statistics and Ministry of the Interior.

Straková, J., & Simonová, J. (2015). Výběr základní školy v ČR a faktory, které jej ovlivňují [Primary school choice in the Czech Republic and related factors]. *Sociologický časopis, 51*(4), 587–606.

Taylor, C. (2001). Hierarchies and "local" markets: The geography of the "lived" market place in secondary education provision. *Journal of Education Policy, 16*(3), 197–214.

Trnková, K. (2006). Vývoj málotřídních škol v druhé polovině 20. století [Development of the small schools with composite classes in the 2nd half of the 20th century]. *Sborník prací FFBU U11*, LIV.Brno: MU, 133–144.

Trnková, K. (2008). Obce s malotřídkou [Municipalities with small schools with composite classes]. *Studia Paedagogica. Sborník prací FFBU* U13, LVI. Brno: MU 53–64.

Trnková, K. (2009). Village schools: Wrinkles for mayors? *European Countryside, 1*(2), 105–112.

Trnková, K. (2012, September). *Educational research of rural elementary schools*. Paper presented at ECER 2012. Cádiz, Spain.

Trnková, K., Knotová, D., & Chaloupková, L. (2010). *Málotřídní školy v České republice* [Small schools with composite classes in Czech Republic]. Brno, Czech Republic: Paido.

Turnovsko v akci. (2009). *Jak se žije v nejmenší základní škole v Libereckém kraji?* [What is the smallest school in Liberec region like?]. Retrieved from http://www.turnovskovakci.cz

Váňová, R., Rýdl, K., & Valenta, J. (1992). *Výchova a vzdělání v českých dějinách* [The upbringing and education in Czech history] (Part IV; 1st vol.). Prague, Czech Republic: Karolinum.

Wahla, A. (1988). *Geografie vzdělání obyvatelstva* [The geography of education of population]. Prague, Czech Republic: SPN.

White, S., & Corbett, M. (Eds.). (2014). *Doing educational research in rural settings*. London England: Routledge.

Zounek, J., Šimáně, M., & Knotová, D. (2017). Primary school teachers as a tool of secularisation of society in communist Czechoslovakia. *History of Education, 46*(4), 480–497.

CHAPTER 6

RURAL SCHOOLS IN POLAND IN THE PERIOD OF POST-SOCIALIST DECENTRALIZATION AND DEMOGRAPHIC DECLINE

Artur Bajerski
Adam Mickiewicz University in Poznan, Poland

In 1989, Poland's Soviet dominated socialist regime changed to a democratic one with an ensuing progressive decentralization of the state. This, in addition to the implementation of a market economy, led to substantial changes in almost every area of life in the country. Education was one of the spheres that experienced the most profound changes. The consequences of these changes were most visible in rural Poland (Bajerski & Błaszczyk, 2015; Herbst, 2012). This was, on the one hand, owing to the specific nature of rural areas and rural education, which are more affected by alterations to organization and funding of educational activities. On the other hand, upheavals also resulted from the various social, demographic, and economic transformations taking place in a changing Poland, the negative consequences of which were felt most strongly in rural areas. It was all connected to the "shock therapy" program implemented for the Polish economy that forced the laws of market economics upon the country in a very short time period. Consequentially, the first years of post socialist state transformations led to the closure of many large operations that provided employment (including state-owned farms). This caused a rapid and considerable rise in unemployment, and a social and economic crisis in Poland's rural areas ensued (Bański, 2003, 2005; Bański, Pantylej, Janicki, & Wesołowska, 2014).

This chapter seeks to define the impact of post-socialist decentralization on the operation of rural schools and present the general characteristics and context of rural primary education in Poland to an international readership. It deals with (a) the nature of the post-socialist decentralization of education and its demographic, social, and economic context; (b) the transformation of the rural schools' network; (c) a review of research on rural schools; and (d) selected issues related to the functioning of these.

POST-SOCIALIST DECENTRALIZATION OF EDUCATION IN POLAND

Before 1989, schools in Poland were under national government control: the curriculum, the buildings, and the staff. At the very beginning of the political transformation process education was denationalized and the handover of the supervision of schools to local governments was the main priority set out by the national authorities. Proposals adhered strictly to the belief of the independent self-governing trade union "Solidarity" (NSZZ Solidarność) which was that the country's governance must be decentralized. Denationalization of schools was one of the approaches that aimed to end the reign of the communist authorities (Levitas & Herczyński, 2012). However, the significance of other problems, such as the economy and unemployment, meant that the restructuring of education was of low priority in the process that changed Poland's regime from communist to capitalist. As Levitas and Herczyński (2012) suggested, the responsibility for education was passed on to the local self-governments "not because they were treated as an important partner of the educational reform, but because Solidarity saw decentralization as the fastest means to disassemble the communist state" (p. 62). They added that

> on the one hand, the legislators wanted to grant ownership rights and the financial responsibility for the schools to local governments in order to eliminate the remnants of the old political system. On the other, though, they

attempted to maintain centralised supervision over the education system as a whole in order to implement reforms and amend the curricula and the schooling methods. (Levitas & Herczyński, 2012, p. 62)

So the first few years of changes in education saw little transformation of the learning program.

Little attention was paid to the potential administrative and financial consequences of the changes in the rules governing education. This is clear when considering the amended Local Governments Act and the Education System Act of 1990 and 1991, which set out that issues directly connected to education—primary schools, kindergartens, as well as other educational facilities—were to be managed and supervised by the representatives of the municipalities. However, the national government continued to finance education centrally. The situation started changing in the mid-1990s, and in 1998 there were significant education reforms. Replacing eight-grade primary schools with six-grade schools and creating three-grade lower-secondary schools changed the school system. Education is compulsory from the age of 7 to 18. In addition a legal obligation was imposed on local authorities to finance education in their regions (Bajerski, 2014b; Herbst, 2012).

The national government determined the core curriculum and the rules for the recruitment of teachers, and regulated teachers' salaries. Regional superintendents of schools that were appointed by the government monitored the quality of education. Local governments financed both the development and renovation of school infrastructure and paid salaries to teachers (for which they received an education subsidy).

Levitas and Herczyński (2012) suggest there were three reasons why this division caused an increasing number of problems, especially for the rural municipalities. First and foremost, there was a significant demographic decline of numbers in the 1990s and at the beginning of the 2000s. Rural municipalities experienced an additional decrease in population linked to migration to urban areas and abroad. As a result, the number of children attending schools dropped, the network of schools, particularly in rural areas, fragmented, and there was a dramatic increase in the cost of education per student, particularly in small rural schools.

Secondly, in the period after 1989, the government increased the salaries of the teachers. This, however, was not provided for by a higher subsidy granted to the local authorities.

Thirdly, local governments were under heavy political pressure from voters, who demanded that school networks be restructured and the infrastructure modernized. Special opportunities in this respect presented themselves after 2004, when Poland joined the European Union and was able to take advantage of European funding. Between 2007 and 2013 it was common to obtain funding to invest in new school buildings, establish new kindergartens, construct playgrounds, sports grounds, extracurricular activities for students and teacher training courses (Gabryelak & Psyk-Piotrowska, 2015). Cofinancing was required to use European funds and as this period saw a global financial crisis, local governments quickly exhausted possibilities to access European funds for education because of a drop in their own revenues.

CHANGES TO THE SCHOOL NETWORK IN RURAL AREAS—MASS SCHOOL CLOSURES AFTER 1998

The requirement to create lower-secondary schools in municipalities went hand in hand with the reorganization of the primary school network, as some primary schools were transformed into lower-secondary schools and others were closed. Pawlak (2004) suggests that the most significant problem that the authorities of small rural municipalities experienced was the lack of sufficient funding to implement the provisions of the reforms. In addition to constructing new secondary schools and adapting primary school buildings, school buses, essential computers, and teaching aids for the schools had to be purchased. Under these conditions, the decision was often taken to profoundly reorganize a school network, closing the smallest primary schools and developing a network of "collective schools," which meant bringing students in from many villages (including from where schools had been closed).

The change in the number of rural primary schools between 1990 and 2012 in Poland is clearly illustrated in Figures 6.1 and 6.2. In the period prior to the education reforms, between 1990 and 1998, the number of these schools dropped from 14.8 thousand to 13.2 thousand (i.e., by 10%). During the implementation of the reforms and the change of the educational system between 1998 and 2004, there was a further drop in the number of rural schools by another 21% compared to 1990 (see Figure 6.1). Between 1990 and 2012, the number of rural schools dropped by nearly 40%, which corresponded to the closure of nearly 6,000 schools. It is noteworthy to compare this situation to that of urban schools, whose numbers only dropped by 14% (from 4.6 to 4.0 thousand) within the same period. Of all the primary schools closed between 1998 and 2012, as many as 80% were rural schools. Therefore, the rate at which the number of schools changes is de facto dependent on the rural school closures (Figure 6.2).

The process of closing schools in rural areas changed over time and by geographical region. There was a considerable difference in the scale and rate of school closures carried out in the western and eastern parts of the country. In Western Poland, school closures were carried out in only a small number of municipalities; however, school closures were widespread

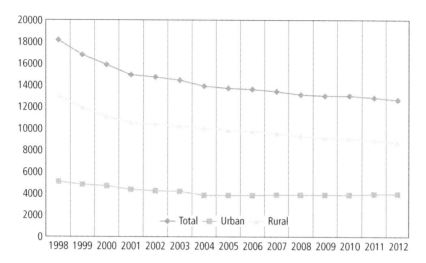

Figure 6.1 Number of primary schools in Poland in the years 1998–2012. *Source:* Own collaboration on the basis of Polish Statistical Office data.

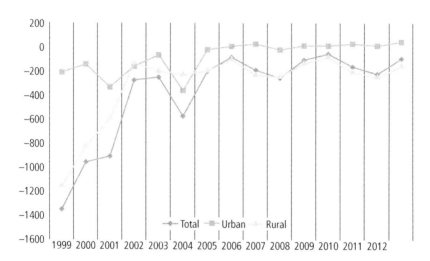

Figure 6.2 Number of closures of primary schools in Poland in the years 1990–2012. *Source:* Own collaboration on the basis of Polish Statistical Office data.

in Eastern Poland, leading to a substantial transformation of the school network. This difference is linked to different histories of the expansion of settlements and school networks; Western Poland mainly comprises lands annexed after 1945 that were formerly a part of Prussia. At the end of World War II relatively large settlements were built from scratch on these lands and a school network was based on large schools. In Eastern Poland the majority of settlements are scattered, small villages. A network of many small schools was established here, and this network, with some modifications, persisted until 1989.

The differences in the process of school closures are presented in Figures 6.3 and 6.4. It should be noted that despite the widespread closure of schools in Eastern Poland, there are areas where no closures occurred. This is linked to the diverse structure of settlements in this part of the country,

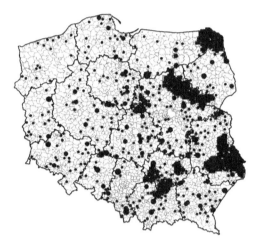

Figure 6.3 Intensity of school closure in rural areas of Poland in the years 2003–2008. *Source:* Own collaboration on the basis of Polish Statistical Office data.

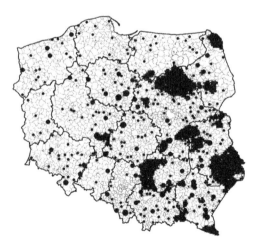

Figure 6.4 Intensity of school closure in rural areas of Poland in the years 2008–2013. *Source:* Own collaboration on the basis of Polish Statistical Office data.

resulting in differently structured school networks (Bajerski, 2014a). It can also be seen that some areas, which experienced school closures in 2003 and 2008, did not see the same scale of the process between 2008 and 2013. This phenomenon linked periods during which local authorities experienced problems funding schools, which often led to closures.

The process of mass school closures in rural areas, especially in Eastern Poland, has led to multiple local community conflicts in recent years (Bajerski, 2014c; Bajerski & Błaszczyk, 2015; Kloc, 2012; Pawlak, 2004; Pilch, 2009; Sobotka, 2016; Uryga, 2013). The background of this tension was similar to circumstances in other countries and connected to a sense of loss for the institutions that had been deeply rooted in local communities, offering education in an almost family-like atmosphere, and perceived as integral to the local social identity (Åberg-Bengtsson, 2009; Autti & Hyry-Beihammer, 2014; Bauch, 2001; Bell & Sigsworth, 1987; 1992; Kvalsund & Hargreaves, 2009; Kučerová & Kučera, 2012; Lyson, 2002; Oncescu & Giles, 2012; Piwowarski, 2000; Trnková, 2009). It became a part of a wider international story of rural people finding themselves in battles for the maintenance of public and social institutions (Åberg-Bengtsson, 2009).

There are specifically Polish elements in these conflicts: (a) a widespread "culture of distrust," distrust of authorities on various levels, including local governments (CBOS, 2012; Swianiewicz, Herbst, Lackowska, & Mielczarek, 2008; Sztompka, 1996) and (b) the "Polish specificity" of the plans for reorganization of school networks in rural areas. These plans were based on the principle of financial efficiency requiring school networks to be as cheap to run as possible, to minimize the risk of further school closures in the future. One of the widespread practices was to transfer students from the catchment areas of the closed schools to ones at risk of closure and in need of students, even if they were located in a distant part of the municipality. As a result, school catchment areas became inconsistent and students were transported to schools far from home, sometimes even passing schools more closely located. These actions undertaken by the local authorities, although economically valid, provoked opposition from the community that considered them socially unreasonable or simply incomprehensible (Bajerski, 2014c). The dissatisfaction of local residents when their schools were closed was additionally aggravated by the fact that school buildings were sold to private investors rather than being dedicated to community projects (Pawlak, 2004).

The mass school closures that occurred after 1989 and affected, primarily, the smallest schools, have not substantially changed the size structure of rural schools. Table 6.1 shows that in 2012, 10% of schools still taught fewer than 30 pupils and over 42% taught fewer than 70 students per school (now adopted in Poland as the minimum number of students for a school).

The depopulation of the rural areas (Bański, 2002; Gawryszewski & Potrykowska, 1988), particularly in the eastern part of the country (Wilkin,

TABLE 6.1 Size Structure of Rural Schools in Poland in 2012

No. of Pupils in School	No. of Schools	% of Schools
500 and More	18	0.2
300–499	163	1.9
200–299	591	6.7
150–199	730	8.3
100–149	1,615	18.4
70–99	1,961	22.3
50–69	1,548	17.6
30–49	1,272	14.5
10–29	761	8.7
9 and Fewer	124	1.4

Source: Own collaboration based on Polish System of Educational Information.

2007), still plays a dominant role, leading to a continuing reduction in the number of students, especially in peripheral areas (Bajerski, 2014a).

RURAL EDUCATION IN POLAND—A REVIEW OF RESEARCH UNDERTAKEN BY PEDAGOGUES, SOCIOLOGISTS, GEOGRAPHERS, AND ECONOMISTS

The issue of rural education in Poland has been investigated recently by pedagogues, but also by sociologists, geographers, and economists. The discourse concerning rural education in pedagogical sciences in Poland is focused around stereotypes. There has been a prevailing conviction that "rural education is an education of inferior quality. Some of the issues include the following: (limited) infrastructure, (poor) teaching facilities, (problematic) organisation of the school's operations, (difficult) staffing situations, (relatively low) levels of education" (Stańczak, 2015, p. 133). This was the image of rural education in successive studies and publications prepared during the era of socialism and resonating with the educational policies of the time, demonstrating a gap in standards between rural and urban schools (Kwieciński, 1970; Ozga, 1960, 1974; Szymański, 1978).

Nowadays, the image of a rural school as one that is "bad and poor" is increasingly being called into question. Contemporary studies of rural schools show that they are not worse than and can compete with urban schools (Marzec-Holka & Rutkowska, 2010; Uryga, 2013; Stańczak, 2015). It should, however, be noted that there remains a stereotypical picture of rural schools by Polish pedagogues who portray them as places where children are noticed (are less anonymous), where school environments integrate more easily, where the participation of parents requires less effort and where there are greater opportunities to establish closer teacher–student relationships. This kind of school then recognizes and supports children with "special educational needs," adapting education to individual requirements and abilities (Marzec-Holka & Rutkowska, 2010; Uryga, 2013; Stańczak, 2015). The stereotyping nature of this work has been suggested by Stańczak (2015), who, for example, argues that the relationship with parents is not a result of a school's size or context but of the focus on its educational impact (Waloszek, 2005).

Educational inequalities between rural and urban schools are most frequently explored in sociological research. This is partially a result of the depth and permanence of the socioeconomic and regional divisions of the Polish provinces (Hryniewicz, 2015; Jezierski & Leszczyńska, 1994; Jezierski & Leszczyńska, 2003; Rutkowski, 1946; Zarycki, 2008) and partially the major differences in educational infrastructure, quality and levels of education in urban and rural areas and between various rural regions—in particular between central and peripheral areas (Domalewski, 2010; Domalewski, 2015; Kwieciński, 1973; Szymański, 1973). As recently as the 1970s, primary schools in rural areas were deemed less effective than urban schools and as a result their curriculum was reduced by 25%, which made their students less likely to continue their studies in secondary schools (Długosz, 2012; Długosz & Niezgoda, 2010). In the long term these differences affected the structure of the rural social strata, only yielding to changes during periods of rapid urbanization or industrialization—for example, during the period of socialism (Niezgoda, 1993). Consequently, in Poland, as well as in many other countries, rural education, although certainly a channel to social advancement, actually strengthened the processes of social and cultural marginalization in rural regions, because of an inferior quality of education and lower educational aspirations (Domalewski, 2010).

The results of studies on educational inequalities after the 1998 reforms indicate that deep differences in the educational achievements of students from rural and urban schools have been eliminated (Domalewski, 2010). Other authors, however, point to the fact that the system became more selective, emphasizing the significance of the financial and cultural capital of families (e.g., being able to pay for tutors) in educational achievements of students (Niezgoda, 2011; Sawiński, 2008; Szczucka & Jelonek, 2011). We should then replace the traditional division of rural–urban educational inequalities with a more appropriate one of peripheral and central areas (major urban agglomerations) that not only differ because of the availability of social, cultural, and financial capital resources, but also of actual accessible opportunities to select schools and extracurricular activities (Bajerski, 2011; Dolata, 2008; Domalewski, 2015).

Geographical research studies on rural education focus on the problem of accessibility and availability of education, a concept linked to educational inequalities. The research includes studies on spatial proximity and physical accessibility of schools as well as school choice and quality. Geographical studies lead to similar conclusions of the pedagogical and sociological studies, pointing to a considerable gap between rural and urban school facilities, infrastructure, equipment, and teacher qualifications (Duś, 2002; Flaga & Wesołowska, 2002; Grykień & Tomczak, 2002). Research also confirms that rural students get lower results in national exams, completed at various stages of education (Bański, Kowalski, & Śleszyński, 2002; Czapiewski & Janc, 2012, 2013; Herbst, 2004; Śleszyński, 2003). However, both the rural–urban division and spatial differentiation of rural schools' exam results were, in fact, a derivative of differences in the level of people's education, as well as the socioeconomic situation of individual municipalities (lower results in the areas with a high level of unemployment), which point to a conclusion that lower education results for students in Poland are principally a consequence of their social environment and not the quality of rural school education (Herbst, 2004; Śleszyński, 2003).

For the past few years, researchers have frequently studied the transformation of school networks in rural areas in relation to mass school closures. On the one hand, the results of this research pointed to some quite obvious consequences of the examined process, such as (a) transforming local school networks from multi-facility networks with varied levels of organization into networks based on one or two large schools bringing students together from nearby towns and villages; and (b) longer home to school commuting distances and their increased frequency. Other factors (environmental, social, economic) impact differently in various geographical locations in Poland's rural areas, increasing the diversification of school networks (Bajerski, 2014a; Gil & Semczuk, 2015a,b). Sobotka (2016) shows that specific features and strengths of the social capital within local communities affected the scale and rate of the school network transformation, so municipalities with similar settlement circumstances could have completely different scales and rates of reorganization. However, as a result of school closures and limited opportunities to be educated near home, as well as the opportunity for parents and students to select the school of their choice (Dolata, 2008), student migrations from one catchment area to another have intensified. This results in school zones overlapping (Bajerski, 2014c; Gil & Semczuk, 2015a,b), making it difficult for local authorities to manage their school networks.

The main question tackled in economic research concerning rural schools' networks was the issue of education funding, which plays a key role in understanding the post 1998 transformations. Economists studied the relation between the amount of educational subsidy paid to local authorities, and expenses incurred for education. As research shows (Herbst, Levitas, & Herczyński, 2009), the size of the subsidy is increasingly disproportionate to the costs of running schools, which, in addition to a decreasing number of students in many rural areas, forces authorities to look for savings and make decisions on school closures. The structure of the subsidy itself is considered defective, as local authorities have to cover all the costs of local education, including teachers' salaries, even though the central government authorities determine their amount and components (Herbst et al., 2009). There is also the issue of the controversial "rural scale" which gives a greater amount of educational subsidy per student in schools in rural areas and small towns of up to 5,000 residents. Research (Herbst et al., 2009; Herczyński & Siwińska-Gorzelak, 2011; Swianiewicz et al., 2008) suggests the rural scale does not serve its intended purpose; municipalities with scattered rural settlements find it difficult to establish large schools with amounts that are sufficient to fulfill their needs. At the same time, in cases of municipalities with concentrated settlements, including suburban municipalities, the amounts are, in fact, too large (much larger than their actual needs). Economists have been advocating for many years that the educational subsidy algorithm should combine with the settlement structure, to direct funding to actual rural areas, in particular those with a scattered settlement structure.

A common denominator in pedagogical, geographical, and economic research on rural schools in Poland is the attempt to develop a definition and typology of rural schools. This typology would help analysis and explanation in future research on the diversification of school networks and factors that impact on the quality, availability, and costs of education (Bajerski, 2014a; Domalewski, 2002; Flaga & Wesołowska, 2002; Piwowarski, 1992).

SELECTED ISSUES RELATED TO THE OPERATION OF RURAL SCHOOLS IN POLAND

What is a Small Rural School?—The Definition Problem

Problems relating to small schools have never been at the center of educational discourse in Poland. Although small schools have dominated the Polish education system for decades (Falski, 1925; Ozga, 1960, 1974; Piwowarski, 1992, 2000) they have been regarded as a short-term necessity to be eliminated in the future. The purpose of the school network development programs during the socialism period (1945–1989) was to base education on a collective school system, educating large numbers of students, transported from nearby towns, in good technical conditions. The objective was to offer equal access to quality education for rural and urban students

(Kwieciński, 1970; Ozga, 1974). These ambitious plans have never been implemented due to infrastructure and transportation limitations and financial constraints, so there are many regions in Poland with schools where there are still only a few registered pupils.

The Polish research and policy literature does not clearly define the term *small school*. One of the first definitions of a small school was adopted by the Ministry of National Education in 2000 (Uryga, 2013). It was related to the ministerial program addressed to rural communities, which were encouraged to associate in NGOs and take control over local small schools. In this program small schools were defined as "a group of primary public schools, operating in a rural area, with up to 30 students, with a certain degree of organization (Grades 0–III), which were in danger of being closed by the decision of the municipal authority" (Uryga, 2013, p. 11). In practical terms then, the term small school referred to the "incomplete" rural school that did not carry out a full education program at the primary level. However, this interpretation does not persist in government records or in journalistic or scientific discourse.

A second definition of small schools arises where schools are taken over by local communities and organizations. Here the small school started to be understood as a reopened school, which had been closed by local authorities and reopened by community groups or organizations. This particular interpretation of a term small school is a curiosity and does not address the number of attending students (Uryga, 2013).

In 2009, there was a further development in the definition of small schools. Due to massive school closure in rural areas and the rising interest of NGOs in the taking over of schools from local authorities the new law stated that the number of students in a dispossessed school should not exceed 70. This administratively determined threshold seems to be the main factor in the classification of small schools today. Using this definition, in 2012, there were 3.7 thousand small schools, which was nearly 50% of all the primary schools located in the rural regions.

Rural Schools and Combined Classes Education

Combined classes education, which required a teacher to work at the same time and in the same place with two (or more) different grades, pursuing two different educational programs, was for many years one of the constant features of public education. As in other countries, combined classes' education is found in schools with small numbers of students where it would be impossible or uneconomic to open a new school.

It was especially pertinent to rural areas with scattered settlements and small schools. The proportion of schools with combined classes has been changing with time. By the end of the 1930s the proportion was over 57% of schools; immediately after WWII it increased to 80%, and then dropped in the following years—to 36% in the 1970s and just 14% in the 1990s. According to the 2012 data, the number of primary schools officially permitted to educate in combined classes amounted to a little over 3.1 thousand, approximately 23% of the total (Pęczkowski, 2014). However, these values are inflated as they represent the number of schools that de facto declared their participation in combined class education, but did not necessarily implement it. The number of primary schools that actually taught combined classes (i.e., the ones that have declared their participation and implemented it) amounted to 1,349 in 2012, out of which 1,331 were located in rural areas (98.5%) They amounted to nearly 10% of all the primary schools in Poland. Taking into account the number of rural schools (close to 8.8 thousand) we can assume that in 2012 over 15% of rural schools educated in the combined class system.

Although in 2012, there were some larger schools (one with 115 students) that maintained this type of teaching, it has been mainly implemented at small and very small schools. The average number of students educated in this system is 32 (median value is 30 students). As stated before, over 97% of rural schools with combined classes are considered small schools teaching no more than 70 students. Furthermore, over two thirds of such schools educate fewer than 40 students (see Table 6.2).

Figures 6.5 and 6.6 show how combined class primary schools are unevenly distributed across Poland. They are virtually nonexistent in the

TABLE 6.2 Size Structure of Rural Schools With Combined Classes Teaching Systems in 2012

No. of Pupils in School	No. of Schools With Combined Classes	% of Schools
100 and More	2	0.2
90–99	2	0.2
80–89	7	0.5
70–79	27	2.0
60–69	67	5.0
50–59	122	9.2
40–49	216	16.2
30–39	241	18.1
20–29	231	17.4
10–19	317	23.8
9 and Fewer	99	7.4

Source: Own collaboration based on Polish System of Educational Information.

Figure 6.5 Distribution of rural primary schools with combined classes in Poland in 2012. *Source:* Own elaboration on a basis of Polish Educational Information System.

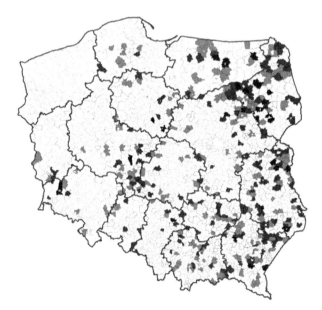

Figure 6.6 Share of primary schools with combined classes (%) in Poland in total number of rural schools in Poland's municipalities in 2012. *Source:* Own elaboration on a basis of Polish Educational Information System.

western and northern parts of the country, but are frequent in the southeastern and eastern parts.

Regional differences are even more apparent when we take into account the number of students attending the combined class schools. High numbers of students and schools are distinctive for southeastern and eastern Poland. However, they occur also in other parts of Poland—in municipalities located on regional borderlines. For this reason the considerable significance of combined class schools within the local school networks may perhaps be treated as an indicator of peripherality (a concept proposed by Kučerová and Kučera in 2009 in a study on the relation between peripherality and education in Czechia).

The arrangement of combined class education in peripheral areas can be linked to one of the principal problems regarding these schools; namely, the stereotypes that have grown around this form of education for many years (Pęczkowski, 2010). It is thought to be an inefficient and costly form of education, with a poor teaching infrastructure and teachers who hold inferior qualifications. However, the same author claims that these accusations do not represent reality, arguing that combined class schools achieve educational results which are above average; the teachers are not inferior to teachers from other schools in terms of qualification, and the high costs of education do not result from the manner of teaching, but principally from the small number of students attending these schools (Pęczkowski, 2010).

In general, the combined class system has never enjoyed great popularity among the educational authorities and this situation is exemplified by a lack of any statutory provision for combined class education (Pęczkowski, 2010). It was treated as an embarrassing necessity or even a negative circumstance, which should be eliminated from the educational system.

SUMMARY

The break with the conservative centralist past during the period of socialism, combined with high social expectations, led the national government in the mid-1990s to transfer the running of schools from the lowest level of education into the hands of local authorities. These local authorities took on responsibility for shaping the school network, for the appointment of school heads, as well as the financing of education, including the payment of teachers' salaries. This situation became a challenge, especially for rural municipalities.

Due to the demographic decline and migrations to urban areas and abroad (after Poland joined the EU in 2004), many rural municipalities experienced a steep decrease in the numbers of children and young people.

As a consequence, the number of children attending rural schools dropped markedly, dramatically increasing the cost of education per student, especially in small rural schools. A second significant problem for the authorities of small rural municipalities was the implementation of the 1998 educational reforms that required the establishment of lower-secondary schools and, consequently, a reorganization of the primary school network. This, together with very slowly increasing educational subsidies granted to local authorities by central government, resulted in a rise in expenditure for education-related activities. As a result, many municipalities have decided to close the smallest primary schools.

Although the background of the process of mass school closure in rural areas is similar to that of other countries, there is a certain "Polish specificity" here. It involves: (a) total decentralization of education management and financing from national to local government, (b) the dynamic process of school closure after 1989 (by 2012 the number of rural primary schools had dropped by nearly 40%), and (c) an often radical use of the principles of financial efficiency when making decisions on school closure, for example, the transfer of students from closed schools, not to those in the vicinity, but often to ones at risk of closure, even when located in another part of a municipality. Such actions have provoked many local conflicts (Bajerski, 2014c; Pawlak, 2004; Sobotka, 2016).

Closing schools in rural areas after 1989 was most widespread in Eastern Poland, a region characterized by scattered small settlements, which suffered long-lasting and profound depopulation (Bański, 2002; Gawryszewski & Potrykowska, 1988; Wilkin, 2007).

Researchers in various disciplines have dealt with issues of mass school closure after the educational reform of 1998 and the consequences of the decentralization of education and demographic decline. As shown in this chapter, in pedagogical sciences one may observe a kind of a "fight" against negative stereotypes associated with small rural schools. Sociological research suggests that with the transformation of the school system and school networks, the traditional division into rural–urban educational inequalities is less valid than a more appropriate division into peripheral and central areas, characterized by deep differences in the available resources of social, cultural, and financial capital, and real opportunities for school choice (Dolata, 2008; Domalewski, 2015). The division into peripheral and central areas also plays an important role in geographical and economic research on Poland's rural education. Whatever the various local conditions, the geographical location of a municipality strongly influences the shape of its school network, the size of the schools, and the financial situation of the municipality (Herbst, 2012; Herbst et al., 2009; Herczyński & Siwińska-Gorzelak, 2011; Swianiewicz et al., 2008). This chapter has shown that it is the educational subsidy that is the biggest problem for peripheral municipalities with scattered settlements and a rural character, and it is these municipalities which have a high proportion of schools with combined classes and the highest rates of school closure since 1989.

REFERENCES

Åberg-Bengtsson, L. (2009). The smaller the better? A review of research on small rural schools in Sweden. *International Journal of Educational Research, 48*(2), 100–108.
Autti, O., & Hyry-Beihammer, E. K. (2014). School closures in rural Finnish communities. *Journal of Research in Rural Education, 29*(1), 1–17.
Bajerski, A. (2011). *Organizacja przestrzenna i funkcjonowanie usług edukacyjnych w aglomeracji poznańskiej*. Poznań, Poland: Bogucki Wydawnictwo Naukowe.
Bajerski, A. (2014a). Klasyfikacja typologiczna sieci szkół podstawowych w gminach Polski. *Przegląd Geograficzny, 86*(4), 541–566.
Bajerski, A. (2014b). Le rôle de l'administration locale dans l'organisation et la gestion de l'éducation en pologne, (w:) Éducation, formation, recherche. Quelle place pour les collectivités territoriales?, G.R.A.L.E (red.), *Droit et gestion des collectivités territoriales 2014*. Paris, France: Le Moniteur.
Bajerski, A. (2014c). Lokalne konflikty wokół rejonizacji kształcenia na obszarach wiejskich w Polsce. *Studia Regionalne i Lokalne, 58*(4), 125–143.
Bajerski, A., & Błaszczyk, A. (2015). Likwidacja szkół podstawowych na wsi: perspektywa władz lokalnych, nauczycieli, rodziców, uczniów i pozostałych mieszkańców. *Przegląd Badań Edukacyjnych, 21*, 81–105.
Bański, J. (2002). Typy ludnościowych obszarów problemowych. *Studia Obszarów Wiejskich, 2*, 41–53.
Bański, J. (2003). Współczesne i przyszłe zmiany w strukturze przestrzennej obszarów wiejskich–wybrane zagadnienia. *Studia Obszarów Wiejskich, 4*, 11–25.
Bański, J. (2005). *Przestrzenny wymiar współczesnych procesów na wsi*. Warsaw, Poland: Polish Geographical Society.
Bański, J., Kowalski, M., & Śleszyński, P. (2002). *Zarys problemów związanych z uwarunkowaniami zróżnicowań przestrzennych wyników sprawdzianu dla uczniów szkół podstawowych w 2002 r.* Warsaw, Poland: IGiPZ PAN.
Bański, J., Pantylej, W., Janicki, W., & Wesołowska, M. (2014). *Współczesne przekształcenia społeczno-gospodarcze a potencjał ludnościowy wschodniej Polski*. Warsaw, Poland: Instytut Geografii i Przestrzennego Zagospodarowania PAN.
Bauch, P. A. (2001). School-community partnerships in rural schools: Leadership, renewal, and a sense of place. *Peabody Journal of Education, 76*(2), 204–221.
Bell, A. B., & Sigsworth, A. (1987). *The small rural primary school: A matter of quality*. London, England: Routledge.
Bell, A. B., & Sigsworth, A. (1992). *The heart of the community: Rural primary schools and community development*. Norwich, England: Mousehold Press.
CBOS. (2012). *Zaufanie społeczne* [Social trust]. Warsaw, Poland: Fundacja Centrum Badania Opinii Społecznej.

Czapiewski, K., & Janc, K. (2012). Dostępność do edukacji, jakość kształcenia i poziom wykształcenia mieszkańców a struktura funkcjonalna gmin województwa mazowieckiego. *Mazowsze Studia Regionalne, 10*, 33–51.
Czapiewski, K., & Janc, K. (2013). *Edukacja jako czynnik rozwoju Mazowsza*. Warsaw, Poland: Mazowieckie Biuro Planowania Regionalnego.
Długosz, P. (2012). Stare i nowe nierówności edukacyjne wśród młodzieży wiejskiej. *Wieś i Rolnictwo, 154*(1), 132–145.
Długosz, P., & Niezgoda, M. (2010). *Nierówności edukacyjne wśród młodzieży Małopolski i Podkarpacia*. Kraków, Poland: Wydawnictwo UJ.
Dolata, R. (2008). *Szkoła – segregacje – nierówności*. Warsaw, Poland: Wydawnictwa Uniwersytetu Warszaw-skiego.
Domalewski, J. (2002). Typologia gmin wiejskich pod kątem widzenia sytuacji oświatowej. In A. Rosner (Ed.), *Wiejskie obszary kumulacji barier rozwojowych* (pp. 107–132). Warsaw, Poland: IRWiR PAN.
Domalewski, J. (2010). Edukacja a procesy rozwoju obszarów wiejskich. In M. Stanny & M. Drygas (Eds.), *Przestrzenne, społeczno-ekonomiczne zróżnicowanie obszarów wiejskich w Polsce. Problemy i perspektywy rozwoju*. Warsaw, Poland: Instytut Rozwoju Wsi i Rolnictwa PAN.
Domalewski, J. (2015). Zróżnicowanie środowiskowe a wyniki edukacyjne gimnazjów wiejskich: Studia przypadków w ujęciu dynamicznym. *Edukacja, 135*(4), 73–90.
Duś, E. (2002). Infrastruktura społeczna na podstawie wybranych wsi południowej Polski. *Studia Obszarów Wiejskich, 2*, 106–118.
Falski, M. (1925). *Materiały do projektu sieci szkół powszechnych: Na obszarze województw: Warszawskiego, łódzkiego, kieleckiego, lubelskiego i białostockiego oraz m.st*. Warsaw, Poland: Książnica Atlas, Lwów.
Flaga, M., & Wesołowska, M. (2002). Warunki kształcenia dzieci i młodzieży na obszarach wiejskich w województwie lubelskim. *Studia Obszarów Wiejskich, 2*, 83–93.
Gabryelak, E., & Psyk-Piotrowska, E. (2015). Wykorzystanie środków unijnych w obszarach nierówności w edukacji: Na przykładzie działań wybranych trzech gmin wiejskich województwa łódzkiego w latach 2006–2013. *Studia Obszarów Wiejskich, 40*, 95–113.
Gawryszewski, A., & Potrykowska, A. (1988). Rural depopulation areas in Poland. *Geographia Polonica, 54*, 81–99.
Gil, A., & Semczuk, M. (2015a). Dostępność edukacji podstawowej na obszarach wiejskich województwa małopolskiego—studium przypadku powiatu miechowskiego. *Studia Obszarów Wiejskich, 45*, 65–80.
Gil, A., & Semczuk, M. (2015b). Uwarunkowania współczesnych zmian w sieci szkół podstawowych na obszarach wiejskich województwa małopolskiego, przedsiębiorczość. *Edukacja, 11*, 152–164.
Grykień, S., & Tomczak P. (2002). Infrastruktura społeczna obszarów wiejskich województwa dolnośląskiego w okresie transformacji. *Studia Obszarów Wiejskich, 2*, 119–127.
Herbst, M. (2004). Zróżnicowanie jakości kapitału ludzkiego w Polsce: Od czego zależą wyniki edukacyjne? *Studia Regionalne i Lokalne, 17*(3), 89–104.
Herbst, M. (2012). *Edukacja jako czynnik i wynik rozwoju regionalnego: Doświadczenia Polski w perspektywie międzynarodowej*. Warsaw, Poland: Wydawnictwo Naukowe Scholar.

Herbst, M., Levitas, A., & Herczyński, J. (2009). *Finansowanie oświaty w Polsce—diagnoza, dylematy, możliwości*. Warsaw, Poland: Wydawnictwo Naukowe Scholar.

Herczyński, J., & Siwińska-Gorzelak, J. (2011). *Administracyjna waga wiejska w algorytmie podziału subwencji oświatowej*. Raport dla Ośrodka Rozwoju Edukacji i Ministerstwa Edukacji Narodowej.

Hryniewicz, J. T. (2015). *Polska na tle historycznych podziałów przestrzeni europejskiej oraz współczesnych przemian gospodarczych, społecznych i politycznych*. Warsaw, Poland: Wydawnictwo Naukowe Scholar.

Jezierski, A., & Leszczyńska C. (1994). Okres 1918–1990. In *Historia Polski w liczbach. Ludność. Terytorium, Warszawa*. Warsaw, Poland: GUS.

Jezierski, A., & Leszczyńska, C. (2003). *Historia gospodarcza Polski*. Warsaw, Poland: Wydawnictwo Key Text.

Kloc, K. (2012). Konflikty w procesie racjonalizacji sieci szkół. In A. Levitas (Ed.), *Strategie oświatowe. Biblioteczka Oświaty Samorządowej, 1* (pp. 157–216). Warsaw, Poland: Wydawnictwo ICM.

Kučerová, S., & Kučera, Z. (2009). Vztah periferiality a vzdělávání: Lze definovat periferní oblasti na základě vývoje sítě základních škol? *Acta Geographica Universitatis Comenianae, 53*, 59–73.

Kučerová, S., & Kučera, Z. (2012). Changes in the spatial distribution of elementary schools and their impact on rural communities in Czechia in the second half of the 20th century. *Journal of Research in Rural Education, 27*(11), 1–17.

Kvalsund, R., & Hargreaves, L. (2009). Reviews of research in rural schools and their communities: Analytical perspectives and a new agenda. *International Journal of Educational Research, 48*(2), 140–149.

Kwieciński, Z. (1970). Z badań nad poziomem szkoły wiejskiej w rejonie płockim. *Notatki Płockie, 15*(4), 41–48.

Kwieciński, Z. (1973). *Poziom wiedzy uczniów a środowisko szkoły*. Toruń, Poland: Wydawnictwo Naukowe Uniwersytetu Mikołaja Kopernika.

Levitas, A., & Herczyński, J. (2012). Decentralizacja w Polsce w latach 1990–1999: Tworzenie system. In M. Herbst (Ed.), *Decentralizacja oświaty* (pp. 55–117). Warsaw, Poland: Ośrodek Rozwoju Edukacji.

Lyson, T. A. (2002). What does a school mean to a community? Assessing the social and economic benefits of schools to rural villages in New York. *Journal of Research in Rural Education, 17*(3), 131–137.

Marzec-Holka, K., & Rutkowska, A. (2010). Małe szkoły w środowisku lokalnym regionu kujawsko-pomorskiego—założenia badawcze. In J. Surzykiewicz & M. Kulesza (Eds.), *Ciągłość i zmiana w edukacji szkolnej: Społeczne i wychowawcze obszary napięć* (pp. 241–254). Łódź, Poland: Wydawnictwo Uniwersytetu Łódzkiego.

Niezgoda, M. (1993). *Oświata i procesy rozwoju społecznego: Przypadek Polski*. Kraków, Poland: Wydawnictwo Uniwersytetu Jagiellońskiego.

Niezgoda, M. (2011). Jak patrzeć na zmianę edukacyjną. In W. Polsce, & M. Niezgoda (Eds.), *Społeczne skutki zmiany oświatowej w Polsce* (pp. 19–31). Kraków, Poland: Wydawnictwo UJ.

Oncescu, J., & Giles, A. R. (2012). Changing relationships: The impacts of a school's closure on rural families. *Leisure/Loisir, 36*(2), 107–126.

Ozga, W. (1960). *Organizacja szkolnictwa w Polsce*. Warsaw, Poland: Państwowe Zakłady Wydawnictw Szkolnych.
Ozga, W. (1974). *Rozmieszczenie szkół w Polsce*. Warsaw, Poland: Wydawnictwa Szkolne i Pedagogiczne.
Pawlak, R. (2004). Polska reforma oświaty a europejska polityka edukacyjna. *Studia Europejskie, 3*, 101–121.
Pęczkowski, R. (2010). *Funkcjonowanie klas łączonych w polskim systemie edukacji*. Rzeszów, Poland: Wydawnictwo Uniwersytetu Rzeszowskiego.
Pęczkowski, R. (2014). Małe szkoły w systemie edukacji—konieczność, problem czy szansa. In K. Mayerová (Ed.), *Vzdelávanie a sociálna stratifikácia* (pp. 174–192). Prešov, Slovakia: Prešovská univerzita v Prešove.
Pilch, T. (2009). Pedagogika społeczna wobec kryzysu świata wartości i instytucji. In E. Marynowicz-Hetka (Ed.), *Pedagogika społeczna* (vol. II; pp. 89–108). Warsaw, Poland: Wydawnictwo Naukowe PWN.
Piwowarski, R. (1992). *Sieć szkolna a dostępność kształcenia*. Warsaw, Poland: Wydawnictwo Naukowe PWN.
Piwowarski, R. (2000). *Szkoły na wsi—edukacyjne wyzwanie*. Warsaw, Poland: Instytut Badań Edukacyjnych.
Rutkowski, J. (1946). *Historia gospodarcza Polski, t. I*. Poznań, Poland: Księgarnia Akademicka.
Sawiński, Z. (2008). Zmiany systemowe a nierówności w dostępie do wykształcenia. In H. Domański (Ed.), *Zmiany stratyfikacji społecznej w Polsce* (pp. 89–112). Warsaw, Poland: IFiS PAN.
Śleszyński, P. (2003). *Uwarunkowania zróżnicowań przestrzennych wyników egzaminu gimnazjalnego w 2002 r.* Warsaw, Poland: IGiPZ PAN.
Sobotka, A. (2016). Trudności we wprowadzaniu reformy gimnazjalnej na obszarach wiejskich. *Edukacja, 138*(3), 75–97.
Stańczak, M. (2015). Współpraca środowiska szkolnego i rodzinnego w opinii nauczycieli z małych szkół wiejskich. *Forum Oświatowe, 27*(2), 131–151.
Swianiewicz, P., Herbst, J., Lackowska, M., & Mielczarek, A. (2008). *Szafarze darów europejskich: Kapitał społeczny a realizacja polityki regionalnej w polskich województwach*. Warsaw, Poland: Wydawnictwo Naukowe Scholar.
Szczucka, A., & Jelonek, M. (2011). *Kogo kształcą polskie szkoły?* Warsaw, Poland: PARP.
Sztompka, P. (1996). Trust and emerging democracy: Lessons from Poland. *International Sociology, 11*(1), 37–62.
Szymański, M. (1973). *Środowiskowe uwarunkowania selekcji szkolnej*. Warsaw, Poland: Państwowe Wydawnictwo Naukowe.
Szymański, M. (1978). *Modernizacja systemu szkolnego na wsi*. Warsaw, Poland: Państwowe Wydawnictwo Naukowe.
Trnková, K. (2009). Village schools: Wrinkles for mayors? *European Countryside, 1*(2), 105–112.
Uryga, D. (2013). *Mała szkoła w środowisku wiejskim: Socjopedagogiczne studium obywatelskich inicjatyw*. Warsaw, Poland: Wydawnictwo Akademii Pedagogiki Specjalnej.
Waloszek, D. (2005). Czy szkoła może być miejscem wzajemności porozumienia się nauczycieli—rodziców—uczniów? In M. Nyczaj-Drąg & M. Głażewski (Eds.), *Współprzestrzenie edukacji: Szkoła, rodzina, społeczeństwo, kultura* (pp. 129–141). Kraków, Poland: Impuls.

Wilkin, J. (2007). Obszary wiejskie w warunkach dynamizacji zmian strukturalnych. In *Ekspertyzy do Strategii Rozwoju Społeczno-Gospodarczego Polski Wschodniej do 2020, t. I.* (pp. 593–616). Warsaw, Poland: Ministerstwo Rozwoju Regionalnego.

Zarycki, T. (2008). Polish space in the perspective of the long duration. In P. Jakubowska, A. Kukliński, & P. Żuber (Eds.), *The future of regions in the perspective of global change. Part one* (pp. 247–298). Warsaw, Poland: Ministry for Regional Development of Poland.

CHAPTER 7

RURAL EDUCATION IN SERBIA
Conflict Between Rhetoric and Reality

Ana Pešikan
University of Belgrade

Slobodanka Antić
University of Belgrade

Ivan Ivić
University of Belgrade

In spite of a dearth of research, of reliable and disaggregated education data and the problematic definition of *rural*, some negative trends in rural education in Serbia can be discerned. There are evident conflicts indicated between the declared aspirations in the education laws, the constitution, and reality. The ideal of free, compulsory, universal primary education conflicts with the violation of rural students' rights to education, as shown by the reality of a lower enrollment and a higher dropout rate for students in rural schools, with a lack of compensatory mechanisms for students from remote and poor areas. The ideal of quality education for all conflicts with the reality of the increasing gap between rural and urban schools (e.g., the quality of ambience, resources, equipment, teaching and learning processes, teacher quality, and lower student achievement). The ideal characteristics of the school network conflict with the needs of rural students and the support of rural development. The ideal of enhancing rural development as an economic priority for the country conflicts with the evident neglect of rural education and cultural development. Even the reality of the regional development of Serbia conflicts with the population migration to cities, especially the migration of families with children. Many measures could be recommended and implemented, even in a developing country in the process of transition, as is the case with Serbia.

In the following text we are going to present the Serbian context for rural education and the main problems being faced today: the problem with the definition of rural, the neglect of rural education in strategic and other relevant national documents and in practice, as well as the poor quality of rural education due to that contextual influence. However, even with the modest economies of developing countries differences can be made. We sketch seven assumptions for the improvement of rural education that can be applied generally, not just in the Serbian context.

AN OVERVIEW

General Facts About the Republic of Serbia

The Republic of Serbia was a constitutive part of the former Socialistic Federal Republic of Yugoslavia (SFRY) and has been a sovereign state since 2006. Situated at the crossroads between central and southeast Europe in the central Balkans (and including Kosovo), it is a country covering an area of 88,361 km^2 of which 86% is rural, with a population of about 7.1 million people (Statistical Office of the Republic of Serbia [SORS], 2016). The urban population forms 56.4% of the total population and almost half, 43.6%, live in the rural areas—that is at least two out of every five people (SORS, 2014). The capital of Serbia, Belgrade, with about two million inhabitants, is one of the largest cities in southeast Europe. Serbia is a multiethnic country of 83% Serbs, 4% Hungarians, 2% Roma, 2% Bosnians, and 9% others (SORS, 2011). It is a parliamentary constitutional republic and an official candidate for membership of the European Union. It already belongs to the United Nations, the Council of Europe, the Organization for Security and Cooperation in Europe, the Partnership for Peace program, the Black Sea Economic Cooperation and the Central European Free Trade Agreement, and is a militarily neutral state. It has an upper-middle income economy with the service sector dominating (accounting for 60.3% of GDP), followed by the industrial sector (31.8% of GDP) and agriculture (7.9% of GDP). Agriculture has been declared as one of the economic priorities of the country (Government of the Republic of Serbia [GRS], 2005a, 2005b; Ministry of Agriculture and Environmental Protection of the Republic of Serbia [MAEPS], 2012).

The Context for Rural Education

The development and current status of rural education in Serbia is under the influence of the wider sociocultural and historical context of the country. Unlike other countries previously "behind the Iron Curtain," Yugoslavia had developed specific politics between East and West, and was one of the founder countries of the nonalignment movement.[1] In the SFRY some significant achievements had been realized: considerable progress in human rights (particularly working, education, and social rights) and personal freedoms (e.g., citizens were free to travel without visas almost all around the world); education and health care were free for all citizens; universal compulsory free primary education for all had been provided by the state since 1958; gender equity and respect for women's rights in many areas of life, such as education (e.g., early care and a preschool education system) had been established as part of the state support for women's rights (Pešikan & Ivić, 2016); the parity index in education is about 1.00—much better than that of many developed countries (Index Mundi, 2018). All these democratic achievements by Yugoslavia are alive even now in the documents of Serbia, as the successor of SFRY. However, there is an evident gap between the wishes (the legal level, i.e., the constitution, laws, etc.) and the reality, particularly when bearing in mind rural issues. After the bloody civil war of the 1990s in the territory of ex-Yugoslavia, with its huge numbers of refugees, and the so-called October Democratic Revolution (2000), political changes took place that initiated a transition process (economic, social, and political), setting the scene for the necessary reforms to enable education to perform new roles and support the modernization of the country. Education has been seen as an instrument for reducing poverty and inequality, and for enhancing economic growth in the country (GRS, 2006[2] the original paper having been adopted by the government in 2005, GRS, 2011; 2014). The route is properly laid out, but expectations have not been met (Pešikan & Antić, 2011; Pešikan & Ivić, 2009; Ivić, 2015; Ivić & Pešikan, 2012), as we will show.

Rural areas in Serbia are mostly undeveloped; regional differences in levels of development are among the highest in Europe; the wages are lowest in rural areas in the country; poverty is much more widespread in rural than in urban areas (families with two or more children are particularly affected) and year by year this difference increases (SORS, 2008). Every year more and more people (especially the young and able-bodied) leave the villages (GRS, 2007) causing depopulation and aging in rural areas, when more people are needed to strengthen and generate rural development (Bogdanov, Tomanović, Cvejić, Babović, & Vuković, 2011).

The situation in rural areas in Serbia is concisely depicted in the analysis of prerequisites for the EU accession:

> Regional disparities are high due to geographical conditions (mountainous, hilly, plain agricultural land), demographic trends, economic structures, environmental conditions, transport accessibility, and employment and income possibilities. Services in rural areas are generally in decline and many areas lack access to basic services due to lack of investment in construction or reconstruction of local roads, waste management, and sewage systems. Climate change poses additional risks to agricultural production, supply of water and other natural resources. Depopulation, internal migration, and lack of access to job possibilities in rural areas remain critical issues, and not so far efficiently addressed. Creation of new employment possibilities through diversification of on/off farm economic activities is needed. Overall there is a great need to improve socio-economic living conditions of the rural population, including the development of rural infrastructure. (European Commission, 2014, p. 36)

Today, Serbia is faced with low levels of education and investment in human capital, research, and technological development. Demographic trends are unfavorable, with a low birth rate, an ageing population, and outward migration, causing a brain drain (European Commission, 2014, p. 36) that is reflecting on education, and the lack of a quality workforce (Ivić, 2014, 2015; Pešikan, 2016). Serbia has one of the most ageing populations in the world, with a median age of 41.9 years. The birth rate is insufficient to ensure simple reproduction of the population numbers (SORS, 2016). One third of the population does not have any professional qualification; out of the population aged 15 years and older, 34.4% have primary education or less (International Standard Classification of Education—ISCED Levels 0–2), including 2.7% having no education; 48.9% have secondary or postsecondary, non-tertiary education (ISCED Levels 3–4); and 16.2% have tertiary education (ISCED Levels 5 or 6; SORS, 2011). The Serbian GDP is US$97.5 billion (2015 estimate). Out of modest GDP about 4.0% (Knoema, World Data Atlas, 2017) is allocated annually for education and about 0.3% of GDP for science (GRS, 2010a, p. 3). Over 90% of the funds for education go to salaries, while a small part, insufficient for demand (Pešikan, 2012a, 2015, 2016), remains for investment in development.

In Serbia, the enormous regional disparities between levels of education within the population correspond to urban–rural differences and differences in levels of regional economic development. People living in the countryside have a lower level of education than people in cities. According to the Census (SORS, 2011), the data indicate that there has been an improvement of the educational level in Serbian rural areas, although that of the rural population is still significantly lower than that of the urban population. The proportion of illiteracy in rural areas is approximately 1.5 times higher than illiteracy in the population overall. The educational attainment of rural women is unfavorable in relation to that of the rural male population. One in five Serbian rural women is illiterate, and 75% of illiterate women live in the countryside (SORS, 2011). This is an important finding because the level of a mother's education is a variable strongly correlated with the academic achievement of her child. In urban areas, 23% of persons have higher education as compared to only 6% in nonurban areas. The ratio is the opposite in the share of persons with primary education and lower—this rate is about 23% in urban areas and as high as 51% in nonurban areas (GRS, 2014, p. 136).

The gap between the urban and rural areas is evident from all perspectives, although in some areas, like ICT usage, there has been a decrease over the years. For example, in ICT usage (73.5% in urban; 60.7% in nonurban) the gap has decreased since 2016 when the rise in the number of computers in urban areas was 0.2%, and 6.7% in nonurban areas (SORS, 2017, p. 13). As a comparison, in the European Union (in the EU-27), the difference since 2012 in the standard broadband connection between rural and total households is no longer significant—99.4% compared with 96.1% (European Commission, 2013, p. 269).

This context influenced rural education in various ways (financing, access, enrollment, equity, equality, completion rate, and quality), which were, unfortunately, mostly negative, and thus jeopardized the quality of education and the right to the education of rural children. Serbia needs to develop the quality of its education system to support economic growth through human capital development (European Commission, 2014, p. 33). Generally speaking, the situation of rural education in Serbia fits into the picture of the previous findings on the state of rural primary education in Europe:

1. the large proportion of small rural schools in Europe that are disadvantaged and lack a voice in national educational policy formation;
2. the need to establish professional support for rural teachers;
3. a tendency for rural schools to be staffed by unqualified or inexperienced teachers;
4. continued rural depopulation, subsequent school closures, and in some cases intercommunity animosity;

5. the lack of research targeted specifically at rural school issues despite the high proportion of such schools;
6. official indifference to the plight of rural schools; and
7. the implementation of educational strategies that lack adequate research evidence as to their educational efficacy (Hargreaves, 1997, p. 4).

Rural or Non-Urban? Problems With the Definition

The problem of defining rural is neither new nor specific to Serbia. One way that is often used is to define rural by determining what it is not. Until 1981, the Statistical Office of the Republic of Serbia used the divisions of rural, urban, and mixed areas, classifying them by economic activity and the size of settlements. However, nowadays SORS classifies divisions as *city*, and *the rest*, which quite blurs the notion of what rural is (e.g., rural is mixed with weekend-settlements, suburbs, etc.). At the same time, researchers of rural issues in the country usually use the OECD (Organisation for Economic Cooperation and Development) definition in which regions have been classified as *predominantly rural, intermediately,* and *predominantly urban,* based on the percentage of population living in local rural units (OECD, 2013, p. 50).[3]

In spite of the lack of a good official definition of rural, there is no problem in defining rural education by location of schools. Nevertheless, the problem arises in the use of official national education statistics for the analyses of the system. The data sources for rural areas are not adequately disaggregated, nor sufficiently valid, mainly due to the inadequate definition of rural (Pešikan, 2012a, 2012b; Ivić & Pešikan, 2013). The adopted strategic documents (GRS, 2010a), predict new solutions, starting from the point of view that rural areas are distinguished by unique economic and social characteristics, specifically reflecting the existence of certain traditional activities. The extent to which the strategy of Serbia 2020 will be applicable in the rural sector of the economy is determined by the adopted priorities for rural development (GRS, 2010b).

RURAL DOES MATTER

Losing Sight of Relevance of the Rural Development and Rural Education in Serbia

The concept of rural development can be found in economic theory and economic practice in recent decades and nowadays is usually present in researches and political documents. The concept was created as a response to problems related to *intra* and *inter* regional disparities in economic development, and serves as a (suitable) complex analysis of the developmental potential of rural areas (Grujic & Roljevic, 2014). The rural development is in the focus of several national strategic documents: *National Sustainable Development Strategy, Strategy on Agricultural Development of Serbia, National Strategy on Economic Development of the Republic of Serbia for period 2006–2012*, and *National Rural Development Programme 2011–2013*. All these documents emphasize the relevance of rural development and consider the measures to enhance it, but not one of them considers education as a parameter that influences rural development significantly (e.g., see Atchoarena & Gasperini, 2003, pp. 55–68), that is, that the education of the rural population is one of the prerequisites for rural development. For example, if one of the aims is to "create appropriate social and economic conditions in rural areas and ensure their contribution to the economic growth of the country" (GRS, 2007, p. 134) the role of rural education is easy to recognize.

Beside it, there is a "parallelism" in development thinking and practice between rural development and education showing similar intervention principles, such as: recognizing the potential of indigenous knowledge, promoting the use of participatory approaches, emphasizing community involvement, adopting an holistic view of the development of the rural space, preparing rural people for off-farm employment by building knowledge and skills capacity, understanding the complementarity of urban/rural linkages, developing partnerships with NGOs and the civil society, and focusing on gender issues (Atchoarena & Gasperini, 2003, pp. 52–53). These two spheres, rural development and education, are closely connected and have much to learn one from another. Rural children and rural education are not at all on the radar of the system. In the *National Report on Social Inclusion and Poverty Reduction in the Republic of Serbia* (GRS, 2014), Roma and children with disabilities are mentioned while there is no word about rural children (not even Roma children or children with disabilities who live in the countryside being important because of multiplying risk factors).

Not only do the national strategies overlook the importance of rural education, but also the EU analysis on the country's accession process. Rural education is simply not considered at all in the document. Bearing in mind the high and increasing urban–rural disparities, the depopulation of rural areas and the inflow of people to major cities, it is quite clear that the economic development plan of the country has to take into account mechanisms for supporting rural development, with education in first place. Therefore, it was surprising that in the EU analysis on the occasion of Serbia's EU accession[4] this angle was completely lacking. It is evident in the analysis devoted to the accession process (European Commission,

2014) which has to direct reforms in Serbia that should be in line with EU countries. In the part on education (European Commission, 2014, pp. 33–35), rural children are not mentioned at all, even in the list of vulnerable groups. Further, in the discussion on agriculture and rural development (European Commission, 2014, p. 36) the link between education and rural development is not recognized. This is a double problem. Firstly, two of the five headline targets of the "Europe 2020 strategy for smart, sustainable, and inclusive growth" are aimed at raising employment and education levels. With the recent enlargements of the EU the rural population has considerably increased from 75 million to 116 million (European Commission, 2011, p. 9). In that sense, rural areas deserve special attention because of, in general, lower rates of higher education and higher rates of school dropout. Secondly, accession to the EU is a powerful tool for moving country development forward. Overlooking the importance of education of rural people of all ages, not just children and youth, decreases the chances for a balanced territorial development in rural areas, for diversification of economic activities, and for investments in rural infrastructure in the country.

The link between rural education and rural development, the position of rural children, and the quality of education in rural areas are elaborated only in the "Strategy on Education Development in Serbia up to 2020" (Ministry of Education, Science, and Technological Development of the Republic of Serbia [MESTDS], 2012). But, although rural education is taken into account in the strategic document, and, as previously said, nearly half of the Serbian population lives in rural regions, in practice there is neither a sector nor a person appointed to work on these issues in the Ministry of Education, Science, and Technological Development.

A similar situation exists in the field of research. SORS (which accounts for more than 80% of all statistical activities within the system of the official statistics of the Republic of Serbia) regularly collects various data, but the picture of the situation in the rural areas is obscured, due to the definition of rural as non-urban. The main sources of data on rural education are different kinds of reports for the Serbian Government or for international agencies (e.g., reports on the strategy for poverty reduction in Serbia, living standard measures, education for all, Millennium development goals, Serbian multiple indicator cluster surveys, policy impact analyses, etc.). Rural education is a rare and rather marginalized topic in research. The authors of this chapter, with some sociologists and cultural researchers, are the only small group of educators who are interested in rural education and in trying to draw the attention of relevant institutions to address this question (Bogdanov & Cvejić, 2011; Cvejić, Babović, Petrović, Bogdanov, &Vuković, 2010; Đukić-Dojčinović, 1998; Ivić, Pešikan, & Antić, 2010; Pešikan & Antić, 2012; Pešikan & Ivić, 2009; Pešikan & Ivić, 2016; See Note 5.) It seems Serbia shares this problem of an underdeveloped research field with other EU countries (Arnold, Newman, Gaddy & Dean, 2005; Hargreaves, Kvalsund, & Galton, 2009). The situation is better in rural development research. In Serbia, there are 19 institutions dealing with rural issues, providing most of the research related to economic and agricultural production. However, there is a lack of many relevant investigations, such as qualitative research (e.g., Bogdanov et al., 2011) and action research (e.g., Ivić, Pešikan, & Antić, 2010), although those methodological approaches can add valuable insights about rural education.

The European Commision (2008) report, *Poverty and Social Exclusion in Rural Areas*, identifies four problematic categories that characterize rural areas and determine the risk of poverty and social exclusion: demography (the migrations of residents and the ageing population), remoteness (such as lack of infrastructure and basic services), education (e.g., lack of quality preschool education and difficulties of access to primary and secondary schools), and labor markets (lower employment rates, persistent long-term unemployment, and a greater number of seasonal workers). The most vulnerable groups are children, young people, women, older workers, lower skilled workers and the unemployed. Rural children are one of the most vulnerable social groups in Serbia. In the first decade of the 21st century, the economic status of children up to 14 years, and youth from 15–19 years, has regressed (Bogdanov et al., 2011), which is evident from the data in Table 7.1.

TABLE 7.1 The Economic Status of Children and Youth in Rural Areas of Serbia

Economic Factor	Rural Statistics
The urban vs. rural population	56.4% vs. 43.6% of the total population
Deprivation	Every second child (45.1%)
Most vulnerable population for poverty	Children under 14 years
Unsatisfactory diversification of food	25.2% rural families with children
Untimely vaccination	10.6%
No availability of other health or medical treatment	23%
No Availability of Regular Financing For:	
New clothes	30.9%
School material	22.7%
School excursions	39.5%
Extra curricular activities and informal education	36.1%
Attending tertiary level of education	1.0%

Source: Bogdanov et al., 2011

State of Affairs in Rural Education in Serbia

Pre-School Education

There are significant regional differences in the coverage of children by pre-school education (PSE). The enrollment of rural children (who need the support most) is lower than the enrollment of urban children (see Table 7.2). Enrollment from the socially vulnerable categories is significantly lower than overall preschool enrollment. The same trend of lower enrollment of children from low socioeconomic families occurs in developed countries, but the general enrollment into high-quality preschool education in these countries is significantly higher, between 90%–100% (Barnett, 2008; European Commision, 2012; European Commission/EACEAE/Eurydice/Eurostat, 2014; see Table 7.2).

The network of PSE institutions is underdeveloped in rural areas (MESTDS, 2012). The distance of preschool institutions from family homes in rural areas is twice as high as in the urban ones (in urban—1.1 km, and in rural—2.2 km; SORS and UNICEF, 2010). With regard to the Preparatory Preschool Program (PPP) the percentage of students living more than 2 km distance from PPP facilities in rural areas is 24.8% (10.6% of them travelling there on foot) compared to 12.2% in the urban ones (SORS & UNICEF, 2015, p. 171). In Serbia, the funding of preschool education is under municipality jurisdiction. Many poor municipalities do not have financial resources for the development of a network of preschool institutions and in many the traffic infrastructure cannot provide increased accessibility to such institutions.

Since 2007, a compulsory PPP for children aged 5.5–6.5 years (one year before compulsory primary education) was introduced. This was the policy measure to reduce the gap between different social groups of children and to decrease dropout rates in schools. Unfortunately, the policy impact analysis has shown this measure to have had a limited effect (Pešikan, 2012; Pešikan & Ivić, 2009).

TABLE 7.2 Pre-School Education Coverage of Children in Serbia	
Total enrollment of children by PSE (2014)[a]	62.6%
Enrollment of rural children (2014)[a]	27.3%
Coverage of rural children aged 3–5years (2008)[b]	14% (43% average for that school year)
Coverage of children from the poorest families (2008)[b]	7% (43% average for that school year)
Coverage of children from families with low educational levels (2008)[b]	16% (43% average for that school year)

Sources: [a]SORS and UNICEF, 2015; [b]SORS, 2008

School Network

The educational system in Serbia has a long tradition, and a developed institutional network. In SFRY, a good primary school network had been established. Thanks to that, approximately 60% of settlements with 100 or more inhabitants have 4 years of schooling (ISCED 1; UNESCO Institute for Statistics, 2012), but the school network has not been adapted to the numerous social changes (demographic, industrial and economic, as well as social) which have occurred in the country (MESTDS, 2012). Of the 3,145 rural schools in Serbia, about 750 (23.8%) have fewer than 15 students per teacher (Jelić & Jovanović, 2014); 2,621 (83.3%) have fewer than 300 students; 2,042 (65.9%) have students from the first to the fourth grade only, while 1,024 schools (34.1%) extend to the eighth grade; in 501 of multigrade classes four grades are combined (Ivić, 2012; Nenadić, 1997; see Figure 7.1). The

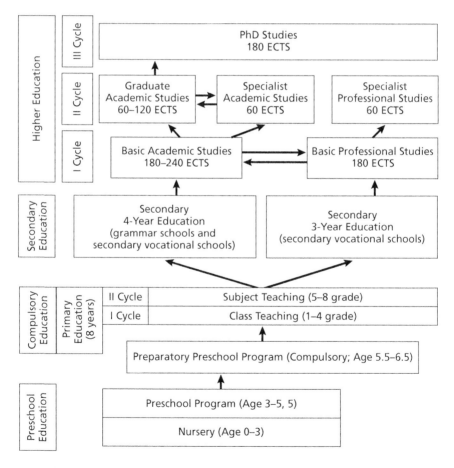

Figure 7.1 Structure of the education system of Serbia.

corrective mechanisms of the school network are poorly developed; there are no specific support measures for children from vulnerable groups to continue with their education, such as scholarships, dormitories, or travel expenses, ensuring conditions for practice and work at school (MESTDS, 2012; Pešikan & Ivić, 2016).

The last decade saw an expansion of educational institutions, mostly in urban areas, so that access to all levels of education are not equally distributed and carry sources of inequity (Jelić & Jovanović, 2014; Pešikan & Ivić, 2016; Stanojević, 2013). In rural areas the education on offer is limited and there is a mismatch between what is available and the needs and demands of local communities. Education is considered the most important social mobility channel for people in all modern societies because it is the main link to the labor market. For several decades there has been a process of migration from villages to cities in the search for jobs and a continuation of schooling. Because of the need for economic efficiency in education, instead of optimization, rationalization of the school network was initiated, which led to the closing of some rural schools. This rationalization may lead to additional threats regarding the fairness of primary education and can adversely affect its already poor pedagogical achievements.

Efficiency of Rural Education

The quality of the learning environment (conditions, equipment, learning resources, students' socio-culture and their economic background, etc.) can have a great impact on achievement. In that sense the rural schools in Serbia are facing many challenges: territorial isolation of villages, inadequate learning conditions in schools, an insufficiently flexible curriculum, financial problems, early dropping out, poor school equipment, teachers who are not properly qualified, no support for teachers' work, and so on.

Primary school enrollment of rural children stands at 77.4% in comparison with the national average of 95.2%; primary school dropout rates are higher in rural than in urban areas (14% and 5%, respectively). The primary school completion rate of rural children is lower than the national average (74.14% compared to 95.2%; MESTDS, 2012). Rural children in Serbia perform significantly lower academically than urban children in national tests—they attained just half of the average achieved by urban children, who reached an average of just 50% (Institute for Quality Evaluation of Education, 2005; 2007). The analysis of PISA (Programme for International Student Assessment) results for the period 2003–2006 shows that

> the variance in performance of children with different SES (socioeconomical status) in Serbia is quite evident. If we compare the student performance of the 10% lowest SES students in relation to the 10% highest SES students, the variance is in the range of 100–110 score points, which is equivalent to approximately 2.5 years of school,

and "the students ranked in the most successful 20%, based on their performance, but who belong in the lowest SES group, have three times fewer opportunities than other students in the most successful group" (Baucal & Pavlović-Babić, 2009, p. 43).

Teaching has to take into account all the specificities of the learning context, and to enrich the educational experience of students who depend on it. In the initial teacher education or in-service teacher training in Serbia there is no specific education or training for work with diverse students in diverse contexts, especially not with children from rural areas (Ivić, Pešikan, & Antić, 2003; Pešikan, 2015). Unlike single-grade (monograde) classes, in multigrade classrooms students from two or more grades are taught by one teacher at the same time. In all countries, multigrade teaching is found mainly in rural areas and arises largely through necessity (Little, 2001, p. 489). This is the case in Serbia. About 3,000 rural schools (95.4%) have multigrade classes in the first four grades, and 500 of them have combinations of four grades in one class (Ivić, 2012). Teachers should be trained to teach multigrade classes and to use cross-age tutoring (Mulryan-Kyne, 2007). But initial teacher education as well as in-service teacher training in Serbia does not support any kind of preparation for this work, and "multigrade teaching remains invisible" (Little, 2001, p. 481). That is not just the case in Serbia. In spite of the fact that a large proportion of teachers throughout the world teach in multigrade classrooms most preservice and in-service teacher training systems prepare teachers to teach in monograded schools. "Multigraded settings are neither acknowledged nor acknowledged within most national policies on education. Teachers are expected to cover curricula and fulfill assessment expectations as if the class was monograded" (Little, 2005, p. 3).

The lower achievement of rural students is in the "melting pot," a result of the combination and accumulation of different negative impacts that face rural education in Serbia: poverty, inadequate teaching/learning conditions, much hard-to-apply school bureaucracy (inflexible curricula, standard day/school cycle instead of local adaptation), unqualified teachers, and so on. However, that does not always have to mean lower showings in rural education, as, for example, Miller's (1991) analyses of 21 quantitative studies on multigrade classrooms in which the students performed academically as well as the single grade class students. Miller's analysis displayed no consistent pattern of findings of cognitive outcomes; findings on noncognitive outcomes were reported in favor of multigrade classes, or reported no difference between them (Little, 2001, p. 486). There are studies that show significant educational gain for children in multigrade classes (Lloyd, 1999; Pavan, 1992) especially for children from disadvantaged social groups, but with alternative teaching approaches (Farrell, 2008).

The research on the efficacy of multigrade classes produced inconsistent effects. It is difficult to separate the effects of multigrade classes because many factors are interfering in this relationship (e.g., rural context, ethnic diversity, SES poorness, school size, school level, minority status, school location; Coladarci, 2006a, 2006b; Little, 2005; Mariano & Kirby, 2009; Sirin, 2005). Examination of these researches shows both mixed evidence regarding the effects of multigrade classrooms on student achievement and that this topic is not on the radar of current research. Many of the reviews and studies were done in the late 1990s (e.g., Burns & Mason, 1998, 2002; Little, 2001; Lloyd, 1999; Mason & Burns, 1996; Russell, Rowe, & Hill, 1998; Veenman, 1995, 1996, 1997). This is one more indicator of the treatment of the rural in contemporary education.

HOW TO MAKE A DIFFERENCE: SEVEN ASSUMPTIONS FOR THE IMPROVEMENT OF RURAL EDUCATION

We strongly subscribe to that sociocultural historical frame of reference (Vygotsky, 1978, 1986) enriched with Bronfenbrenner's ecological model (Bronfenbrenner, 1979). It gives the useful conceptual apparatus for coping with rural education challenges. For example, in the previous parts of this chapter we sketched out the zone of actual development of rural education in Serbia. But the most challenging issue is what that zone of proximal development (ZPD) should look like? ZPDs are neither the same for different students, nor for different rural settings. But the mindset, a general approach to rural education should be changed and can be joint: instead of the "urban deficit model," the model of rural education as an "authentic entity," neither better nor worse, but substantially different.

Undoubtedly, the first step is to change our approach to rural schools and education. The global driving forces emphasize highly educated, diverse, mobile knowledge workers (cognitive capitalism) and rurality is positioned as the antithesis of modernity (Corbett, 2013). Formal education is seen as the main mechanism for mobility out of rural areas: "Education is designed for those who leave" (Corbett, 2009, p. 1). In the perception of rural people, rural schooling is increasingly marginal in a globalized, urban-centric, networked society (Corbett, 2009). On the other hand, economic interests are in conflict with educational aims; some indicators are the closure of small schools, prescriptions for teaching, narrowing of curricula, lack of contextual relevance of prescriptions (Ivić, 2012).

Our suggestion is to affirm an approach in which rural education has a specific model and context, and not the "urban deficit model." Rural schooling has a different, specific quality. We have to have reliable data on rural education in order to have a good and clear picture of conditions, of what is missing, and of what is underdeveloped. There is, so far, little research published on the conditions of rural education in Serbia, and on that basis it is particularly necessary to reveal evidence of rural conditions. However, rural schools do not need to imitate urban schools; their backwardness and shortcomings have to be overcome in relation to what they want to achieve from their students, taking into account all the facts and needs in a specific context. In other words, "'business as usual' and 'more of the same' will not solve the education problem in rural areas. The challenge is to find specific modalities to address the demand and supply issues that education faces in these areas" (Atchoarena, & Gasperini, 2003, p. 24). Therefore, proper visions of development of rural education cannot be created unless we treat rural education as a different "organism" with specificities, authentic characteristics, potentials, and needs. This promotion of rural specificities can solve the "learning to leave" dilemma described by Corbett (2009), while leaving the opportunity for rural youth to decide where they want to live and work. Social and political intervention should emphasize rural specificities and disseminate them to the urban public. Both contexts can benefit from mutual exchanges.

There is a paradox: a one-size-fits-all approach, based on urban models or examples from developed countries and leading economies, in fact limits potential achievement, because of staying blind to diversity and insensitive to context. Economies of scale are looking for room to apply some invention and earn money through occupying new markets. However, this approach uniformalizes countries, wipes out differences, and stays insensitive to a diversity of possible solutions developed in specific sociocultural contexts. So, there is a collision between the global spreading of unique solutions for all, and the need for smart and innovative growth that can only benefit from diversities of small communities and small economies.

The second assumption, which should be changed, is looking at rural education through the lens of traditional teaching/learning processes, that is, the teacher delivers lectures and the students are recipients. Efficient learning in a small rural school must be based on the new philosophy of teaching and learning. Rural teachers must try to "find a path" to rural children in a rural context, which includes improvising (Corbett, 2013). The multi graded classes in rural schools can be models to solve practices dealing with heterogeneity in all schools (Smit, Hyry-Beihammer, & Raggl, 2015). Of course, for that challenge teachers should be given autonomy and professional support. Rural teachers should have the independence to change the school calendar, the organization of time, methods of teaching, ways of using local resources, and so on, in accordance with their local situations. We all need more research in this field, not only on national, but also on a European level. Teachers need more support from research and policy.

The third assumption is the promotion of place-based education—finding learning activities that are aligned both with age, developmental stage, learning needs of students, and with learning goals and outcomes, content and specific rural ambient. The ambient is seen as an advantage rather than an obstacle (Broda, 2007; Bunting, 2006; Hargreaves et al., 2009; Smith, 2002). This approach fosters thematic lesson planning, and makes overcoming the shortcomings of a school's grade–subject–class organization possible. Also, it supports change in the approach to rural schools (see the first assumption).

The fourth assumption is changing the concept of teacher education and training, which must be tailored to the needs of teachers who are working in specifically demanding conditions requiring special knowledge and skills (e.g., work in small, multigrade classes, in rural, undeveloped, poor areas, work with children from socially disadvantaged groups, etc.). As Miller (1991) stressed, the reality of teaching in more than two grades at the same time requires specific training, community understanding, and support. Unfortunately, there is a serious lack of all these requirements in the Serbian context; there is no specific education and training for the student teachers who are very often ignorant and indifferent towards a rural school and its community; and there are many obstacles in acquiring support, from a lack of understanding of the importance of rural schools for the development of local communities, to the lack of resources (financial, professional, and human).

The fifth assumption is that rural education is not only the subject of the education sector, but that it must be supported by several different sectors. More than any other social group, rural people, and especially rural children, are in need of a synergy of economic, educational, medical, social, political, communal, and other help.

The sixth assumption is the promotion of the concept of schools as multifunctional centers of local rural development (Bogojević, Ivić, & Karapandža, 2002). As such, a rural school is a place for various activities needed in the local community (e.g., compensatory education, adult education, vocational training, cultural, administrative, social, and medical activities, etc.). New, profitable agricultural crops can be introduced at the school farm. For the first time in Serbia soybeans and hybrid corn have been planted on the farms of rural schools in Mionica municipality. Meaningful learning, its social relevance, and the durability of knowledge gained can be enhanced through students' work at a school farm, building up the sense of the students' belonging to their school. This can also be an educational advantage for a rural school and is another argument against a deficit in the treatment of these schools. Small rural schools should be preserved wherever possible, because they have an impact on the demographic situation. When a place is left without a school, it is immediately left without a population (MESTDS, 2012).

The seventh assumption is to give support to rural schools and rural communities by a diversification of economic and educational activities, such as the development of a program for rural educational tourism (RET). In order to support rural development UN agencies—United Nations Development Program (UNDP), United Nations Environment Program (UNEP), Food and Agricultural Organization (FAO), United Nations World Tourism Organization (UNWTO), and United Nations International Children's Emergency Fund (UNICEF)—with national partners in Serbia—namely, the Ministry of Economy and Regional Development, Ministry of Agriculture, Forestry and Water Management, and Tourist Organisation of Serbia, as principal partners—have started the joint program, Sustainable Tourism for Rural Development (Puškarica, 2011). In this project, the concept of RET has been developed by the Education Forum (Pešikan & Antić, 2012).

Rural education tourism is the new model of rural tourism which includes rural households (families), rural schools and teachers, students from both rural and urban areas and stakeholders in local communities. Rural education tourism joins several sectors: education, culture, economy, and even regional development (rural development and development of cultural tourism). The focus of the RET is through the development of active learning in out-of-school activities; specific models and programs intended for urban and rural students and their families will be developed. The goals of the RET project are: enhancement of the education of all children (urban and rural) by providing quality out-of-school programs (learning in nature, leisure, and recreation); improvement of the status of rural children; strengthening the role of the rural school as the center of community development; diversification of the rural economy leading to networking and collaboration between key partners in the development of local communities, the revitalization of villages, and consequently, a more balanced regional development in Serbia.

The RET programs are inquiry-based, student-centered, hands-on, and problem oriented. In addition, learning should be adapted to meet the interests and experiences of the students, applied to real-world contexts, and involve communication and collaboration. All activities in the RET programs are educational by their nature, although to students they look like leisure or recreational activities. The programs have to be both educational and entertaining, so they are best described by the term *edutainment*. The RET is going to be created according to local circumstances and resources. It is a kind of socio culturally sensitive model and implies including activities that are, specifically, using cultural, social, and natural local resources. All activities should be associated with particular features, and each locality should have its own recognizable image. Therefore, the RET is not a uniform offer of quality accommodation. In one situation, it will be an educational farm, in another the development of human relationships and healthy lifestyles, in a third it will be a rural art center, or an open museum for children, or research of linguistic, traditional games, and so on. What is a good solution for one local setting may be inapplicable or unsuccessful in another.

RET promotes education in rural areas and empowers schools to be centers of local development. Rural schools and the teachers in them represent an important resource that can be utilized for local development. As a rule, rural schools have available space that can be used for the RET initiatives. When teachers integrate the local environment with knowledge of its community members, the bond between the schools, students, and families grows. In rural schools, in multigrade classes, teachers are positioned to teach students of different ages and grades at a specific time, or throughout the day. We can learn from these teachers by examining how they integrate subject areas and combine age groups and grade levels. Those teachers can also become educators for adults, provided they are given adequate in-service training, creating space to extend roles for rural schools, so that they can become multifunctional centers and agents of local rural growth. In Serbia, several models of RET were developed: an Education Farm, a Rural School-Related Tourism, and a Rural Youth Edutainment Programme (Ivić, Pešikan, & Antić, 2010). The fates of these projects have been different. Some, in the absence of continuous support, stopped developing after the completion of the project; some were developing after completion and are still working today. The ideas behind these projects were the basis for the creation of some new ventures. The experience shows us that changes in rural areas cannot happen quickly, and especially not with one off financed projects (those financed for one year only in particular). It shows us that a systematic multidisciplinary approach is needed in order to to give strength to local communities, so they can develop feelings of ownership over projects and the changes they are expected to bring about, and to fully involve local stakeholders encouraging them to take responsibility for the further realization and development of activities.

CONCLUSION

As Hargreaves and collaborators (Hargreaves et al., 2009) noted, every educational policy has to provide an answer to the question: "Are rural schools a national luxury or local necessity?" In Serbia, there is evident conflict between the declared aspirations in the education laws and the constitution on one side, and reality on the other. There are many indicators of this conflict: free compulsory universal primary education conflicts with a violation of rural students' rights to education, as demonstrated by lower enrollment, a higher dropout rate, and the lack of the compensatory mechanisms for students from remote and poor areas; quality education for all conflicts with the increasing gap between rural and urban schools, for example, the quality of ambience, resources, equipment, teaching/learning processes, teacher quality, and lower student achievement; characteristics of the school network conflict with the needs of rural students; enhancing rural development as an economical priority conflicts with indicators that show long-term neglect of rural education and the development of culture; even the regional development of Serbia conflicts with population migration, especially of families with children, to the cities.

The Strategy on Education Development in Serbia up to 2020 (MESTDS, 2012) suggested necessary interventions that would raise the chances of rural children in Serbia fulfilling their rights to qualitative education. Based on the analysis of conditions, systematic planning of the necessary financial, material, and human resources necessary to provide children with additional support and access to high-quality primary education should be provided. This would raise the quality of work in small, rural schools and in multigrade classes, meaning better educational conditions, such as decent infrastructure, hygienic standards and an appropriate security level, work equipment, didactic tools, assistive technologies, and Internet connections. Planning and administrative activities should be adapted to the specific circumstances. Of course, it is just one more declaration, but unlike others, this document, based on the analysis of the situation in Serbia, sets the scene for a significant change of attitude toward rural education, and offers realistic measures towards achievement. The strategy, supported by rare but important research on the issue of the approach to the rural as a matter of diversity, offers evidence that rural education is neither a luxury nor an unprofitable squandering of money, but a necessary endeavor for a better development of the country.

Postscript: Recent Migration Into Serbia, and a Miracle

There are no systematic data about migrant children in Serbian schools. However, some features can be recognized. The main wave of migrants was in 2017; this is much reduced due to altered routes. There have been some attempts to include migrant children in some form of education in order to have a meaningful time structure (UNICEF and UNHCR, and some local initiatives).

In migrant groups, there are many children. Younger children have been away from their fatherland for a long time (five or six years on the road in some cases), living in camps with no formal schooling. There is a huge need to take these children and youth out of camp environments and help them normalize their lives in one place, even if it is for a short period of time. A first step toward that noble aim is a struggle with negative attitudes towards and prejudice against migrants. As we have already been made aware, prejudice towards others is not just specific to poorly educated and low-income people. An education project that included migrant children in Vojvodina (North-West part of Serbia), in the city of Šid, faced a situation where the educators initiated protests against migrants in their city. In spite of that, the inclusive education project continued owing to the devoted effort of the school psychologist, the director and a small group of teachers. The project achieved excellent results.

In the camp in Šid most migrants are from Syria and Afghanistan, two very different milieus. Syria had a good education system before the war started, but Afghanistan, on the contrary, had a very poor one (64% of men and 90.3% of women never attended school). The majority of the children of this camp could not remember their fatherland. All were hungry for education and were very motivated to attend school. When the action of a small team from the high school of Šid (with the school psychologist, the member of Education Forum) started an education project, the migrant parents had confidence in the school. In the beginning, local children were afraid of and reserved toward the migrant children, and so joined the protests. They felt serious hesitation and fear because of the reaction of local adults toward migrants generally. However, a miracle has happened.

A case study analysis of the effects of migrant children staying in the high school has shown that a great transformation has taken place. The migrant children were obedient, silent, and eager to work on tasks and they initiated a great change in the school. The curriculum has been modified due to this novelty, much new content has been discussed with students (e.g., about common human needs and cultural differences—various ways to satisfy them; about refugee situations and experiences), common new instructional and out-of-instruction and out-of-school activities have been carried out. Local students have developed a better understanding of themselves and others, improved their social competence, openness, and tolerance toward differences, and critical thinking ability. They have studied together and established emotional ties between each other. Generally, the case study of the high school (Gymnasium) in Šid has demonstrated that this type of action has multiple benefits not just for migrant children but also for the children of the host country and for the quality of their education.

NOTES

1. The Non-Aligned Movement (NAM) is a forum of developing world states that are not formally aligned with or against any major power bloc. NAM is dedicated to representing the interests and aspirations of developing countries to ensure the national independence, sovereignty, territorial integrity, and security of nonaligned countries in their struggle against imperialism,

colonialism, neocolonialism, racism, and all forms of foreign aggression occupation, domination, interference, or hegemony. The NAM was started in Belgrade in 1961. It was created by Yugoslavia's president, Josip Broz Tito, India's first prime minister, Jawaharlal Nehru, Egypt's second president, Gamal Abdel Nasser, Ghana's first president Kwame Nkrumah, and Indonesia's first president, Sukarno. The NAM countries represent nearly two-thirds of the United Nations' members containing 55% of the world's population. Membership is particularly concentrated in countries considered to be developing or part of the Third World, though the NAM also has a number of developed nation members.

The NAM supports policies and practices of peaceful multilateral cooperation. The movement accepts the universality of human rights and social justice, but fiercely resists cultural homogenization. The NAM appeals for the protection of cultural diversity, and the tolerance of the religious, sociocultural, and historical particularities that define human rights in a specific region. As of 2012, the movement has 120 members. The last conference, the 17th NAM Summit, was held in Venezuela in 2016.
2. The Poverty Reduction Strategy paper for Serbia was adopted by Serbia's government on 16 October 2003. On 17 February 2005, the Deputy Prime Minister was tasked with the requirement to regularly inform the government on the PRS implementation and coordination process.
3. The OECD regional typology is based on three criteria. The first criterion identifies rural communities according to population density. (A community is defined as rural if its population density is below 150 inhabitants per 2 km.) The second criterion classifies regions according to the percentage of population living in rural communities. Thus, a TL3 region is classified as: *Predominantly rural* (rural or PR), if more than 50% of its population lives in rural communities; *Predominantly urban* (urban or PU), if less than 15% of the population lives in rural communities; *Intermediate* (IN), if the share of population living in rural communities is between 15% and 50%. The third criterion is based on the size of the urban centres. Accordingly, a region that would be classified as rural on the basis of the general rule is classified as intermediate if it has an urban center of more than 200,000 inhabitants representing no less than 25% of the regional population; a region that would be classified as intermediate on the basis of the general rule is classified as predominantly urban if it has an urban center of more than 500,000 inhabitants representing no less than 25% of the regional population. This typology has been refined by introducing a criterion of distance (driving time) to large urban centers. Thus, a predominantly rural region is classified as a predominantly rural remote region (PRR) if a certain percentage of the regional population needs more than a fixed time to reach a large urban center; otherwise, the rural region is classified as predominantly rural close to a city (PRC; OECD, 2013, pp. 153–154).
4. The objective of EU assistance is to support ongoing education and training reforms in order to improve the quality of educational provision at all levels and their relevance to the labor market, to support the reforms of employment and social protection policies and to improve social inclusion of the most vulnerable groups (European Commission, 2014, p. 34).

5. Two conferences have been realized by the group in the Serbian Academy of Science and Art: *Rural education in Serbia and rural development* (Oct. 2009), and *The role of rural education in rural development* (March, 2016).

REFERENCES

Arnold, M. L., Newman, J. H., Gaddy, B. B., & Dean, C. B. (2005). A look at the condition of rural education research: Setting a direction for future research. *Journal of Research in Rural Education, 20*(6), 1–25.

Atchoarena, D., & Gasperini, L. (2003). *Education for rural development: Toward new policy responses.* Joint study by UNESCO and FAO, Rome, Italy. Retrieved from http://files.eric.ed.gov/fulltext/ED499625.pdf

Barnett, W. S. (2008). *Preschool education and its lasting effects: Research and policy implications.* Boulder, CO: Education and the Public Interest Center & Education Policy Research Unit. Retrieved from https://nepc.colorado.edu/sites/default/files/PB-Barnett-EARLY-ED_FINAL.pdf

Baucal, A., & Pavlović-Babić, D. (2009). *Quality and equity of education in Serbia: Educational opportunities of the vulnerable—PISA assessment, 2003 and 2006 data.* Draft paper. Retrieved from https://www.researchgate.net/profile/Aleksandar_Baucal/publication/265528712_QUALITY_AND_EQUITY_OF_EDUCATION_IN_SERBIA_EDUCATIONAL_OPPORTUNITIES_OF_THE_VULNERABLE_PISA_ASSESSMENT_2003_and_2006_data/links/544036320cf21227a11ba77e/QUALITY-AND-EQUITY-OF-EDUCATION-IN-SERBIA-EDUCATIONAL-OPPORTUNITIES-OF-THE-VULNERABLE-PISA-ASSESSMENT-2003-and-2006-data.pdf

Bogdanov, N., & Cvejić, S. (2011). Poverty and social exclusion in rural Serbia: Position of family farms. *Economics of Agriculture, 58,* 3–189.

Bogdanov, N., Tomanović, S., Cvejić, S., Babović, M., & Vuković, O. (2011). *Access for women and children to service in the rural areas of Serbia and proposed measures to improve their situation.* Belgrade, Serbia: UNICEF Serbia.

Bogojević, A., Ivić, I., & Karapandža, R. (2002). *Optimization of the network of schools in Serbia.* Belgrade, Serbia: Education Forum and UNICEF.

Broda, H. W. (2007). *Schoolyard-enhanced learning.* Portland, ME: Stenhouse.

Bronfenbrenner, U. (1979). *The ecology of human development.* Cambridge, MA: Harvard University Press.

Bunting, C. J. (2006). *Interdisciplinary teaching through outdoor education.* Champaign, IL: Human Kinetics.

Burns, R. B., & Mason, D. A. (1998). Class formation and composition in elementary schools. *American Educational Research Journal, 35*(4), 739–772.

Burns, R. B., & Mason, D. A. (2002). Class composition and student achievement in elementary schools. *American Educational Research Journal, 39*(1), 207–233.

Coladarci, T. (2006a). School size, student achievement, and the 'power rating' of poverty: Substantive finding or statistical artifact? *Education Policy Analysis Archives, 14*(28). https://doi.org/10.14507/epaa.v14n28.2006

Coladarci, T. (2006b). Do small schools really reduce the 'power rating' of poverty? *The Rural Educator, 28*(1), 1–8.

Corbett, M. (2009). Rural schooling in mobile modernity: Returning to the places I've been. *Journal of Research in Rural Education, 24*(7), 1–13.
Corbett, M. (2013). Improvisation as a curricular metaphor: Imagining education for a rural creative class. *Journal of Research in Rural Education, 28*(10), 1–11. Retrieved from http://jrre.vmhost.psu.edu/wp-content/uploads/2014/02/28-10.pdf
Cvejić, S., Babović, M., Petrović, M., Bogdanov, N., & Vuković, O. (2010). *Socijalna isključenost u ruralnim oblastima Srbije* [Social exclusion in rural areas in Serbia]. Belgrade, Serbia: UNDP.
Đukić-Dojčinović, V. (1998). *Pravo na razlike, selo-grad* [The right to differences, village-city]. Belgrade, Serbia: Zadužbina Andrejević.
European Commission. (2008). *Poverty and social exclusion in rural areas*. Retrieved from https://ec.europa.eu/social/BlobServlet?docId=2087&langId=en
European Commission—Agriculture and Rural Development. (2011). Rural areas and the Europe 2020 strategy: Education. *EU Agricultural Economic Briefs*. Retrieved from https://ec.europa.eu/agriculture/sites/agriculture/files/rural-area-economics/briefs/pdf/04_en.pdf
European Commision. (2012). *Key data on education in Europe 2012*. Education, Brussels: Audiovisual and Culture Executive Agency-European Commission. http://www.youthmetro.org/uploads/4/7/6/5/47654969/134en.pdf
European Commission. (2013). *Rural development in the EU–Statistical and economic information 2007–2013*. Retrieved from https://ec.europa.eu/agriculture/statistics/rural-development_en
European Commission. (2014). *Indicative strategy paper for Serbia (2014–2020)*. Instrument for pre-accession assistance (IPA II). Adopted on 19/08/2014.
European Commission/EACEAE/Eurydice/Eurostat. (2014). *Key data on early childhood education and care in Europe. 2014 Edition*. Eurydice and Eurostat Report. Luxemburg: Publication Office of the European Union. Retrieved from http://ec.europa.eu/eurostat/documents/3217494/5785249/EC-01-14-484-EN.PDF
Farrell, J. P. (2008). Education in the years to come: What we can learn from alternative education. In P. D. Hershock, M. Mason, & J. N. Hawkins (Eds.), *Changing education—Leadership, innovation and development in a globalising Asia Pacific* (pp. 199–224). Hong Kong: Comparative Education Research Centre.
Government of the Republic of Serbia. (2005a). *National sustainable development strategy*. Retrieved from http://www.gs.gov.rs/english/strategije-vs.html
Government of the Republic of Serbia. (2005b). *Strategy on agricultural development of Serbia*. Retrieved from http://www.gs.gov.rs/english/strategije-vs.html
Government of the Republic of Serbia. (2006). *First progress report on the implementation of the poverty reduction strategy in Serbia*. Retrieved from https://www.imf.org/external/pubs/ft/scr/2006/cr06141.pdf
Government of the Republic of Serbia. (2007). *National strategy on economic development of the Republic of Serbia for the period 2006–2012*. Retrieved from http://www.gs.gov.rs/english/strategije-vs.html
Government of the Republic of Serbia. (2010a). *Srbija 2020–Koncept razvoja Republike Srbije do 2020* [Serbia 2020—Development concept of the Republic of Serbia until

2020]. Retrieved from http://www.srbija.gov.rs/extfile/sr/145381/koncept_razvoja_srbije_do_2020.pdf
Government of the Republic of Serbia. (2010b). *National rural development program 2011–2013*. Retrieved from http://app.seerural.org/wp-content/uploads/2013/08/Sebia-National-Rural-Development-Program-2011-2013-February-2010-ENG.doc
Government of the Republic of Serbia. (2011). *First national report on social inclusion and poverty reduction in the Republic of Serbia: The status of social exclusion and poverty trends in the period 2008–2010 and future priorities.* http://socijalnoukljucivanje.gov.rs/wp-content/uploads/2014/06/First-National-Report-on-Social-Inclusion-and-Poverty-Reduction.pdf
Government of the Republic of Serbia. (2014). *Second national report on social inclusion and poverty reduction in the Republic of Serbia–the status of social exclusion and poverty trends in the period 2011 –2014 and future priorities.* Retrieved from http://socijalnoukljucivanje.gov.rs/wp-content/uploads/2014/11/Second-National-Report-on-Social-Inclusion-and-Poverty-Reduction-final.pdf
Grujic, B., & Roljević, S. (2014). Interdependence of rural development and rural economy local communities in Serbia. In D. Cvijanović, J. Subić, & A. J. Vasile (Eds.), *Sustainable agriculture and rural development in terms of the republic of Serbia strategic goals realization within the Danube region: Rural development and (un)limited resources* (pp. 122–137). MPRA Paper No. 58558, posted 14 September 2014. Retrieved from http://mpra.ub.uni-muenchen.de/58558/
Hargreaves, L., Kvalsund, R., & Galton, M. (2009). Reviews of research on rural schools and their communities in British and Nordic countries: Analytical perspectives and cultural meaning. *International Journal of Educational Research, 48*(2), 80–88.
Hargreaves, L. M. (1997). *Issues in rural primary education in Europe.* A summary of a symposium on issues in rural education at the European Conference on Educational Research (Seville, Spain, September 25–29, 1996).
Index Mundi. (2018). *Serbia country profile.* Retrieved from http://www.indexmundi.com/serbia/gender-parity.html
Institute for Quality Evaluation of Education. (2005). *Nacionalno testiranje učenika III razreda osnovne škole* [National testing of III grade students in primary school]. Belgrade, Serbia: Zavod za vrednovanje kvaliteta obrazovanja i vaspitanja.
Institute for Quality Evaluation of Education. (2007). *Nacionalno testiranje učenika IV razred aosnovne škole* [National testing of IV grade students in primary school]. Belgrade, Serbia: Zavod za vrednovanje kvaliteta obrazovanja i vaspitanja.
Ivić, I. (2012). Osnovna škola [Primary school]. In A. Pešikan (Ed.), *Osnovni resursi u preduniverzitetskom obrazovanju u Srbiji* [Pre-university education in Serbia: the facts and the trends] (pp. 38–76). Belgrade, Serbia: Filozofski fakultet.
Ivić, I. (2014). Obrazovanje i razvojni problem Srbije [Education and development problems of Serbia]. In Č. Ocić (Ed.), *Moguće strategije razvoja Srbije* [Possible development strategies of Serbia] (pp. 131–160). Belgrade, Serbia: Srpska akademija nauka i umetnosti.
Ivić, I. (2015). Obrazovanje kao razvojni resurs: Strateški pogled [Education as a development resource: A strategic view]. In A. Kostić (Ed.), *Obrazovanje kao*

razvojni resurs Srbije [Education as a development resource of Serbia] (pp. 27–55). Belgrade, Serbia: Srpska akademija nauka i umetnosti.

Ivić, I., & Pešikan, A. (2012). Education system reforms in an unstable political situation: The case of Serbia in the first decade of the 21st century. *CEPS Journal, 2*(2), 31–53.

Ivić, I., & Pešikan, A. (2013). *Obrazovna statistika* [Education statistics in Serbia]. Belgrade, Serbia: Ministry of Education, Science and Technological Development of Serbia.

Ivić, I., Pešikan, A., & Antić, S. (2003). *Active learning*. Belgrade, Serbia: UNICEF and Institute of Psychology.

Ivić, I., Pešikan, A., & Antić, S. (2010). *Rural education tourism*. Belgrade, Serbia: Education Forum.

Jelić, S., & Jovanović, T. (2014). Educational potential of rural areas and rural development. In D. Cvijanović, J. Subić, & A. J. Vasile (Eds.), *Sustainable agriculture and rural development in terms of the republic of Serbia strategic goals realisation within the Danube region; Rural development and (un)limited resources* (pp. 888–903). MPRA. Retrieved from https://mpra.ub.uni-muenchen.de/58558/1/MPRA_paper_58558.pdf

Knoema, World Data Atlas. (2017). *Serbia—Public spending on education as a share of GDP*. Retrieved from https://knoema.com/atlas/Serbia/Public-spending-on-education

Little, A. W. (2001). Multigrade teaching: Towards an international research and policy agenda. *International Journal of Educational Development, 21*(6), 481–497.

Little, A. W. (2005). *Learning and teaching in multigrade settings*. Unpublished paper prepared for the UNESCO. Retrieved from http://citeseerx.ist.psu.edu/viewdoc/download?doi=10.1.1.605.7317&rep=rep1&type=pdf

Lloyd, L. (1999). Multi-age classes and high ability students. *Review of Educational Research, 69*(2), 187–212.

Mariano, L. T., & Kirby, S. N. (2009). Achievement of students in multigrade classrooms. *Institute of Education Sciences, RAND Education.* https://www.rand.org/pubs/working_papers/WR685.htm

Mason, D. A., & Burns, R. B. (1996). 'Simply no worse and simply no better' may simply be wrong: A critique of Veenman's conclusion about multigrade classes. *Review of Educational research, 66*(3), 307–322.

Miller, B. A. (1991, March). A review of the qualitative research on multigrade instruction. In *Reaching our potential: Rural education in the 90s*. Conference Proceedings, Rural Education Symposium, Nashville, TN.

Ministry of Agriculture and Environmental Protection of the Republic of Serbia. (2012). *Strategy of agriculture and rural development of Republic of Serbia from 2014 to 2024*. Retrieved from https://www.leader.org.rs/next/en/ipard202/181-the-strategy-of-agriculture-and-rural-development

Ministry of Education, Science and Technological Development of the Republic of Serbia. (2012). *Strategy on education development in Serbia up to 2020*. Retrieved from https://erasmusplus.rs/wp-content/uploads/2015/03/Strategy-for-Education-Development-in-Serbia-2020.pdf

Mulryan-Kyne, C. (2007). The preparation of teachers for multigrade teaching. *Teaching and Teacher Education, 23*(4), 501–514.

Nenadić, M. (1997). *Novi duh obrazovanja* [A new spirit of education]. Belgrade, Serbia: Prosveta.
OECD. (2013). *Regions at a Glance 2013.* http://dx.doi.org/10.1787/reg_glance-2013-en
Pavan, B. N. (1992). The benefits of nongraded schools. *Educational Leadership, 50*(2), 22–25.
Pešikan, A. (Ed.). (2012a). *Osnovni resursi u preduniverzitetskom obrazovanju u Srbiji* [Pre-university education in Serbia: The facts and the trends]. Belgrade, Serbia: Faculty of Philosophy.
Pešikan, A. (Ed.). (2012b). Obrazovna statistika u Srbiji: Metodološki problemi [Educational statistics in Serbia: The methodological problems]. In A. Pešikan (Ed.), *Osnovni resursi u preduniverzitetskom obrazovanju u Srbiji* [Pre-university education in Serbia: the facts and the trends] (pp. 127–145). Belgrade, Serbia: Faculty of Philosophy.
Pešikan, A. (2015). Preduniverzitetsko obrazovanjei vaspitanje u Srbiji: Stanje, izazovii pravci razvoja [Pre-university education in Serbia: State, challenges and developmental trends]. In A. Kostić (Ed.), *Obrazovanje kao razvojni resurs Srbije* [Possible development strategies of Serbia] (pp. 55–107). Belgrade, Serbia: Serbian Academy of Sciences and Arts.
Pešikan, A. (2016). Serbia: An overview. In T. Sprague (Ed.), *Education in non-EU countries in western and southern Europe* (pp. 247–269). London, England: Bloomsbury.
Pešikan, A., & Antić, S. (2011). Analiza karakteristika i problema osnovnog obrazovanja u Srbiji u svetlu budućeg razvoja zemlje [Analysis of primary education in Serbia in the light of future country development]. *Nova srpska politička misao, XIX*(1–2), 69–94.
Pešikan, A., & Antić, S. (2012). Kada se ukrste obrazovanje, kulturni turizam i razvoj sela: Seoski obrazovni turizam [Education, culture tourism and rural development: Rural education tourism]. In M. Nikolić (Ed.), *Zbornik radova Fakulteta dramskih umetnosti: Menadžment kulture i medija u društvu znanja* (pp. 255–275). Belgrade, Serbia: Faculty of Dramatic Arts, Institute of Theatre, Film, Radio and Television.
Pešikan, A., & Ivić, I. (2009). *Obrazovanjem protiv siromaštva–Analiza uticaja uvođenja pripremnog predškolskog programa u Srbiji* [Education against poverty—The analysis of the impact of introducing the preparatory preschool programme in Serbia]. Belgrade, Serbia: Ministarstvo prosvete RS i Tim potpredsednika-Vlade za implementaciju SSS.
Pešikan, A., & Ivić, I. (2016). The sources of inequity in the education system of Serbia and how to combat them. *CEPS Journal, 6*(2), 101–124.
Puškarica, K. (2011). *Sustainable tourism for rural development.* Belgrade, Serbia: National Steering Committee Meeting. Retrieved from http://mdgfund.org/program/sustainabletourismruraldevelopment
Russell, V. J., Rowe, K. J., & Hill, P. W. (1998, November–December). *Effects of multigrade classes on student progress in literacy and numeracy: Quantitative evidence and perceptions of teachers and school leaders.* Paper presented at the 1998 Annual Conference of the Australian Association for Research in Education, Adelaide, Australia.

Sirin, S. R. (2005). Socioeconomic status and academic achievement: A meta-analytic review of research. *Review of Educational Research Fall, 75*(3), 417–453.
Smit, R., Hyry-Beihammer, E. K., & Raggl, A. (2015). Teaching and learning in small, rural schools in four European countries: Introduction and synthesis of mixed/multi-age approaches. *International Journal of Educational Research, 74,* 97–103.
Smith, G. (2002). Place-based education: Learning to be where we are. *Phi Delta Kappan, 83*(8), 584–594.
Stanojević, D. (2013). Međugeneracijska obrazovna pokretljivost u Srbiji u XX veku [Intergenerational educational mobility in Serbia in the 20th century]. In M. Lazić, & S. Cvejić (Ed.), *Promene osnovnih struktura društva Srbije u periodu ubrzane transformacije* [Changes in the basic structures of the Serbian society in the period of accelerated transformation] (pp. 124–127). Belgrade, Serbia: University of Belgrade, Institute for Social Research, Faculty of Philosophy.
Statistical Office of Republic of Serbia. (2008). *Studija o životnom standardu* [Living Standard Survey]. Belgrade, Serbia: Author.
Statistical Office of Republic of Serbia. (2011). *Census of population, households and dwellings in the Republic of Serbia: Population.* Retrieved from http://pod2.stat .gov.rs/ObjavljenePublikacije/Popis2011/Nacionalna%20pripadnost-Ethnicity .pdf
Statistical Office of Republic of Serbia. (2014). *Population projections of the Republic of Serbia 2011–2041.* Retrieved from http://pod2.stat.gov.rs/ObjavljenePublikacije/Popis2011/Projekcije%20stanovnistva%202011-2041.pdf
Statistical Office of Republic of Serbia. (2016). *The statistical yearbook of Serbia 2016.* Retrieved from http://pod2.stat.gov.rs/ObjavljenePublikacije/G2016/pdf/G20162019.pdf
Statistical Office of Republic of Serbia. (2017). *Upotreba informaciono-komunikacionih tehnologija u Republici Srbiji* [The use of ICT in the Republic of Serbia]. Retrieved from http://pod2.stat.gov.rs/ObjavljenePublikacije/G2017/pdf/G20176006.pdf
Statistical Office of Republic of Serbia and UNICEF. (2010). *Serbia multiple indicator cluster surveys* (MICS4). Belgrade, Serbia: Author. Retrieved from http://www.childinfo.org/files/MICS4_Serbia_FinalReport_2010_Eng.pdf
Statistical Office of Republic of Serbia and UNICEF. (2015). *Serbia multiple indicator cluster survey 2014* (MICS5). Belgrade, Serbia: Author. Retrieved from https://www.stat.gov.rs/media/3528/mics5_report_serbia.pdf
UNESCO Institute for Statistics. (2012). *International standard classification of education.* Montreal, Canada: ISCED 2011. Retrieved from http://uis.unesco.org/sites/default/files/documents/international-standard-classification-of-education-isced-2011-en.pdf
Veenman, S. (1995). Cognitive and noncognitive effects of multigrade and multi-age classes: A best-evidence synthesis. *Review of educational research, 65*(4), 319–381.
Veenman, S. (1996). Effects of multigrade and multi-age classes reconsidered. *Review of educational research, 66*(3), 323–340.
Veenman, S. (1997). Combination classrooms revisited. *Educational Research and Evaluation, 3*(3), 262–276.

Vygotsky, L. (1978). *Mind in society*. Cambridge, MA: Harvard University Press.
Vygotsky, L. (1986). *Thought and language* (A. Kozulin, Trans., & Ed.). Cambridge, MA: MIT Press.

CHAPTER 8

DEVELOPMENT AND RESEARCH OF THE RURAL SCHOOL SITUATION IN SPAIN

Begoña Vigo-Arrazola
University of Zaragoza, Spain

Juana Soriano-Bozalongo
University of Zaragoza, Spain

Our purpose in this chapter is to render an account of the meaning of rural schools in the education system in Spain, to explore changes during the last 50 years by the national providers of education, and how these changes have happened. Education, geography, and governmentality are important aspects in a larger historical geography of Spanish education. The current situation of rural schools in Spain is referred to first, followed by an analysis of development and changes made over these years. Finally, this chapter focuses on the interest in rural schools from theoretical, practical, and research viewpoints.

RURAL SCHOOLS IN SPAIN: SOME DEFINITIONS

Spain has an area of 504,645 km2. It is divided into 17 autonomous communities, 50 provinces and 8,112 municipalities with their own local authorities (town councils). According to the Organisation for Economic Co-operation and Development (OECD), there are 15 *predominantly rural* provinces in Spain. These occupy 40.7% of the surface area and are home to 11.3% of the population.

In Spain, the National Statistics Institute (*Instituto Nacional de Estadistica* [INE], 2010) uses a demographic criterion to define extreme rurality as being towns with fewer than 2,000 inhabitants. Although official regulations do not define rural schools, the current education act (Organic Act, 8/2013) identifies them as located in isolated or inaccessible areas, due to their surrounding geography, or with very small population centers. The different kinds of rural schools in Spain include grouped rural schools, one-room schools, incomplete schools, and rural educational innovation schools.

Grouped rural schools are comprised of several incomplete schools organized legally as single schools with classes distributed in different localities. They have one education, administration, and management center and are identified by different terms in the autonomous communities: *Colegios Rurales Agrupados* (CRA, grouped rural schools) in Cantabria, Extremadura, Asturias, Castilla-León, Castilla-La Mancha, Madrid, Murcia, Galicia, Aragon, Navarre, and La Rioja; in Catalonia they are known as *Zonas Educativas Rurales* (ZER, rural educational areas); in the Canary Islands as *Colectivos de Escuelas Rurales* (CER, rural school collectives); in Andalusia as *Colegios Públicos Rurales* (CPR, rural state-funded schools); and in the Basque Country as *Eskola Txikiak* (small schools).

A *one-room school* is a school with only one teacher (Corchón, 2004). An *incomplete school* has more than one class and fewer than six. Its characteristic is that there are classes with one teacher dealing with several grades (Corchón, 2004).

> *Centro Rural de Innovación Educativa* (CRIE, rural educational innovation school): As a result of pupils from different areas and rural schools periodically boarding together, the priority objectives of these schools have been to contribute to improving pupils' personal development and socialisation process in the rural sphere and, at the same time, support the implementation of the school curriculum. (Order 29, 1996)

These schools accept children from different rural schools as boarders several times a year for around fifteen days, so that, besides living together, they can perform educational activities that would be difficult to carry out in their own school (laboratory, languages, etc.). The CRIE action complements the activity the children perform in their respective schools (Roche,

1993). CRIE schools also aim to collaborate in the development of innovative curricular and teacher-training activities. Every CRIE has an educational team comprising five or six teachers, and sometimes a workshop teacher and members of staff that supervise children at break and lunchtimes.

In Spain, the changes in the number of these schools have been conditioned by demographic changes and changes to education policy, structures and systems, in a context marked by negative representations of rural areas. The practical problems of representation and rhetoric will be apparent in the different considerations of space and rural education in what follows.

SPACE AND EDUCATION

Education systems, in general, are organized on the basis of a *metrocentric model* (Green & Letts, 2007). This means that some areas are more privileged than others. Using Bourdieu's (1986) concept of cultural capital to examine schools in rural areas, Spanish schools are mediated by economic and different forms of capital, and are in a twofold-disadvantaged condition. On the one hand, economic investment is lower and employment opportunities fewer than in urban localities, causing population movement from rural to urban areas, and so resulting in school closures. On the other hand, the school cultural capital is representative of a dominant population group that is different from those with lower educational levels of achievement and less economic and social capital (Ball, 1993). Consequently, rural schools are often described as problematic places for learning, for the economy and for attracting market investment (Corchón, Raso, & Hinojo, 2013; Vázquez, 2016), and as suffering from less attention and research than urban schools (Hargreaves, Kvalsund, & Galton, 2009). In this context, a school's tendency towards the values of the dominant culture is evident when, firstly, the school's habitus and field, and then the habitus of families with those same values is observed. This provokes a situation in which a section of the population whose values may differ misses information and fails to benefit from the opportunities this information may present, thus running the risk of exclusion from schooling and hence from developing social capital. The exclusion observed in these rural areas seems to support this theory (Bourdieu, 1986).

As described by Bourdieu and Passeron (1970) in the book *La Reproduction*, the spaces and the people who live there are ideologically devalued. As both Corbett (2015) and Massey (2011) suggest there is a broad degradation of many rural spaces and people and this situation, together with the more recent ways that global social and economic conditions work within the discursive context, creates difficulties of identity (Green & Letts, 2007).

In Spain, rural areas have been bombarded for decades by representations of their history as "troubled" and "poor," and the people in them as in need of special help (Hernandez, 2000). Nevertheless, as Massey (2011) points out, it is space and not time that makes differences, hiding consequences and possibilities from us; it is in relation to space that teachers, families, and pupils together develop and reveal strategies for working in this context. It is a process of ongoing construction in each particular context that reflects the development of different discourses (Corbett, 2015).

CHARACTERISTICS OF THE SPANISH ELEMENTARY SCHOOL SYSTEM

In Spain schooling is mandatory for 10 years: six primary and four secondary. Children begin primary school at the age of six. Generally, early childhood education, that is, for children aged three, four and five, also takes place in primary schools. Secondary education is taught in separate schools when there is state-funded teaching, but in the same buildings in the case of state-subsidized private schools.

Primary school characteristics are considered in relation to their size, funding, and ownership. As far as size is concerned, in 2016–2017, 9.4% of schools in Spain had fewer than 25 pupils and 23.6% fewer than 100 (see Table 8.1). In 2016–2017, schools with fewer than six classrooms represented 13.4% of all primary schools in Spain (see Table 8.2).

The majority of primary schools in Spain are state-funded, the forecast for the 2017–2018 academic year being 74.6 % (see Table 8.3). The remainder are privately funded whilst some are subsidized by the state.

TABLE 8.1 Percentage of Primary Schools Based on the Number of Pupils in the 2016–2017 School Year

Number of Pupils	% Primary Schools
< 25	9.4
26–100	23.6
101–200	15.9
201–300	11.8
301–500	21.8
501–700	9.5
701–1,000	5.5
> 1,000	2.5

Source: Based on data from the Ministry of Education, Culture, and Sport (2019)

TABLE 8.2 Percentage Distribution of Primary Schools Based on the Number of Classrooms in the Academic Year 2016–2017

Number of Classrooms	% Primary Schools
1	1.8
2–3	6.2
4–5	5.4
6–11	34.7
12–17	16.0
18–23	26.9
24–29	7.0
30–35	1.5
36–41	0.4
> 42	0.1

Source: Own table based on data from the Ministry of Education, Culture, and Sport (2019).

TABLE 8.3 Forecast for the 2016–2017 Academic Year

Ownership	Numbers (Absolutes)	%
State-Funded Schools	10,335	74.6
State-Subsidized Private Schools and Private Schools	3,528	25.4
Total	13,863	100

Source: Own table based on data from the Ministry of Education, Culture, and Sport (2019)

DEVELOPMENT OF RURAL SCHOOLS IN SPAIN

An analysis of the development of primary schools in Spain by the authors shows that the number of schools has dropped continuously since the late 1960s when there were around 65,000. Based on analysis by Santamaría (2012), 72% were one-room schools in 1967. This high number could be related to the fact that it was customary at that time for classrooms to group children of different ages together. Furthermore, the creation of up to three types of one-room schools had been initiated 10 years earlier in 1957—schools for boys, for girls, and for infants (mixed). This meant there could be up to three schools in one small locality.

Rural School Closures 1960s–1970s

By the end of the 1960s, there was a significant drop in the number of schools (from 60,717 in 1960 to 44,138 in 1969). A national policy promoting the economic and social development of cities and district capitals (Hernández, 2000) had consequences for the educational system. It generated the implementation of a decree (Decree 400/1962) to combine one-room schools situated in close proximity. These amalgamations led to (Jiménez, 1983) the start of a process of concentration, grouping together pupils from different small schools (sometimes from as many as 23). The process was supported by the creation of boarding schools, and also of school lodgings where children from small villages lived during the week.

The reasons given to justify the creation of school concentrations were that the quality of teaching would be improved and costs lowered (Corchón et al., 2013; Vázquez, 2016). However, the quality of the teaching did not improve and standards dropped because the model being applied had been designed for an urban/industrial society (Santamaría, 2012). This was a school model based on business organization and focused on obtaining results and optimizing resources, which proved to be inappropriate in small school situations. Educational space was considered as "a 'container' within which education simply takes its space with varying degrees of effectiveness" (Green & Letts, 2007, p. 1). The argument for lowering costs was questioned by several authors (Carmena & Regidor, 1984; Corchón, 2000, 2005; Grande, 1994; Jiménez, 1983), who point out that the cost of school transport and catering services was higher than the supposed saving on teachers' salaries.

The biggest drop in the number of schools began in the 1970s, ending the decade with 24,832 schools in Spain (Ministerio de Educación, Cultura y Deporte, 2016). This decrease of 40,000 schools, compared with the previous decade, could have several explanations: firstly, economic and technocratic rationality criteria that centered on effectiveness through the combination of a technical reform and Catholic church confessional principles (Berlanga, 2003), and, secondly, the industrial development of the districts and urban environments that led to the dismantling of the rural framework and of smaller population centers. In addition, the 1970 General Education Act adopted technical criteria that led to the creation of national grade schools with classes of 30 pupils of the same age, and to the closure of schools with fewer enrolled pupils (Santamaría, 2012). These criteria meant that thousands of school classes were closed throughout Spain and schools concentrated into groups, with many small ones absorbed into schools with school lodgings in larger towns. The aim was to establish the grade school system as the organizational model for basic general education for all children aged between 6 and 14. In this context, the reduction in the number of schools, as occurred in the 1960s, involved the generalization of an urban school model based on standardization. Consequently, neither the conditions, characteristics, and particular features of the environment, nor the social, cultural, and economic consequences, were considered (Hernández, 2000).

Democracy, Decentralization, and Rural Resilience: 1980s–1990s

In the 1980s, with Spain's transition to democracy, a royal decree on compensatory education contributed to school decentralization and to the reconstruction of rural schools. Nevertheless, the decrease in the number of schools continued and continues to this day. The reasons for this could be related to the decentralization of the autonomous communities, and, again, to the interest in the socioeconomic development of district capitals (Morales, 2012). After the 1978 Spanish Constitution, government was no longer centralized and the responsibility for education was transferred to the authorities of each autonomous community (Grande, 1994). Decentralization began in 1979 when the different Communities (Aragon, Rioja, Andalusia, etc.) were granted autonomy in relation to transport, school lunches, pedagogic conditions, and material aspects (Hernández, 2000).

In this context, and from 1976, social movements, encouraged by consideration of the conditions, characteristics, and particular features of the local environment, arose to defend rural schools. Summer schools, trade unions, and educational authorities, demanding that no child be without a school in the rural environment and that every town should have a quality school, promoted these social movements. They aimed to lessen the social, cultural, and economic consequences of closing schools. One example was the Aragon Summer School.

The Royal Decree of 1983 (Royal Decree 1174/1983, of April 27, for compensatory education) recognized the need to compensate for the disadvantages occurring in depressed geographical areas, by providing school support services and resource centers, incentives for the teaching staff to continue at the same school, and investment in infrastructure and equipment. As a result, in the mid-1980s a new regulation was approved that included the creation of CRAs (grouped rural schools). Furthermore, the CRIEs (rural educational innovation schools) established and added to this experimental framework of educational reform in the rural environment.

However, in the 1990s, a new education act (Organic Act 1/1990) seemed to fail to recognize the rural situation as something specific and different. The rural school was only mentioned in relation to diversity and compensatory education. The drop in the number of rural schools continued, although to a lesser extent than in previous decades. This decrease could essentially relate to the application of the CRA regulation. In the academic year 1990–1991, there were fewer than 20 CRAs (Santamaría, 2012), so the number of incomplete schools was still high. This CRA model became more generalized throughout the decade until the number rose to 456 in 1998. Consequently, schools with eight or more classrooms started to increase and schools with only one teacher to decrease. There was still a very small number of incomplete schools in some autonomous communities (Ministerio de Educación, Cultura y Deporte, 2016).

Criticism of the CRAs began around 1993/1994. It highlighted a lack of information, low participation of the educational communities, the excessive number of classrooms in CRAs, inappropriate groupings and insufficient or inappropriate material and human resources (STECyL, 2012). As a result, the Order dated 29 June 1994 (Order 29, 1994) approved instructions regulating the organization and operation of early childhood education and primary schools. It required a specific section in school timetables for teaching staff coordination and time designated for travelling CRA teachers shared by different schools. However, it was difficult for schools to comply, as they were not provided with the staff needed for curricular timetables and for coordination among the teachers. In 1996, the Ministry of Education and Culture implemented a proposal to improve the working conditions of teachers shared by different schools, which resulted in a considerable improvement in the standard of CRA staff (STECyL, 2012).

Decentralization and Immigration 2000–2019

The birth rate in Spain fell in the 1990s leading to a decrease in the number of pupils. Nevertheless, the number of schools was maintained, due to the establishment of food processing and to tourism companies, which halted the migration of the rural population to cities (STECyL, 2012).

From 2000, the number of schools stabilized. This may have been due to fewer changes to the school model and an increase in the population as a result of migration. Spain became one of the major destinations for international migration flows, particularly from 2000 to 2008. In rural areas, the opportunities in agriculture, tourism, and construction were plentiful, and steady economic growth in these (and other) industries generated a rising demand for flexible international labor. Many new immigrants settled in rural areas and although there was a considerable drop in the immigration flow in 2008 generally, the foreign-born population has increased faster in the provinces since then (Collantes, Pinilla, Sáez, & Silvestre, 2014). Nevertheless, classrooms continued to close (Vázquez, 2016). In 2012, there were 14% of schools with fewer than six classrooms, which reduced to 13.6% by

2016. The apparent reason for this was the global economic recession. The impact of neoliberal policies based on economic criteria seems to have consolidated urban population centers.

The emphasis on decentralization, personal choice, and the creation of competitive markets, on private involvement and consumer responsibility and influence has had uneven effects in several respects (CES, 2018; Escardíbul & Villarroya, 2009). Possibilities of choice proliferate in urban areas; whilst in areas of lower population density further from urban centers there are usually no choices at all (Gurrutxaga & Unceta, 2010).

In the first part of this century, the emphasis is also focusing on minority rights, between other aspects, with convictions that identities are heterogeneous. However, in rural areas the state is the single supplier of education services. In Spain, public schools in rural areas are remaining open with as few as three or four pupils on roll, at least at present. The state has thus not, as is sometimes suggested, surrendered total responsibility for education to market forces alone, recognizing the value of a local school as a significant resource in rural areas (Bagley & Hillyard, 2015).

In this context, new avenues of exploitation are also being found, often by feeding off the back of the new migration, in order to save schools from closure. Newspapers often show offers of houses and work for families with children. Through them small villages try to obtain more stable populations. A recent study (funded by the authorities on Valladolid, in the community of Castilla León, where the rural population is one of the highest in Spain), aimed to evaluate the impact of settling Syrian refugees and sub-Saharan migrants in rural areas. An exhaustive survey was applied to the inhabitants of 200 villages about their attitudes to receiving people from overseas. The study also analyzed the availability of resources such as houses and schools in order to facilitate the lives of the new inhabitants, and it concludes that these populations are agreeing to accept refugees because they consider that the migrant people could resolve the problem of depopulation, and might contribute to reopening previously closed schools. However, they are concerned with the permanence of these families because, in this context, the possibilities for work are restricted (AVUVA, 2017).

Thus, it was argued continually, the outcome of a low quality of education, high rates of failure and low academic results, was that school populations shifted to urban schools, while waiting for educational quality to rise, academic failure to drop, and performance to improve in the rural schools. Ironically, however, as Quílez and Vázquez (2012) and Santamaría (2012) suggest, rural schools in Spain have neither worse results than urban schools, nor do they lack quality. They based this affirmation on the analysis and the interpretation of the better results shown by the official data from the Educational Ministry. Santamaria (2012) highlighted these better results when the administration considered that they related to fewer requirements from rural teachers.

Another aspect to be considered refers to differences in educational costs between the communities, having ramifications for schools located in less populated areas. In autonomous communities with a higher population index (Madrid, Andalusia, Catalonia, and Valencia) the education cost per pupil is lower than in the less populated communities (Castilla-La Mancha, Castilla-León, Aragón, Extremadura, and Galicia). Consequently, the smaller the population the higher the cost of education will be, due to the dispersal of people. In this context, where economic criteria prevail classrooms close, and the pupil to teacher ratio increases. This is particularly noticeable in rural classrooms (Vázquez, 2016).

The pattern of decreasing numbers and the clustering of rural schools seen in this analysis seems to be conditioned by market issues, with a predominant concern for results, profitability, lower costs, and investment. Consequently, rural areas are bombarded by representations of these areas and their history marked as "troubled" and "poor" with the people in them being in need of special help. These representations work through the views and subjectivities of not only stigmatized rural areas but their inhabitants as well. The relationship between socio-spatial location, representation, and the formation of distinctive identities, based upon rural areas' affiliations, seem to remain. Table 8.4 is a synthesis that shows key milestones in the development of the rural school in Spain.

RESEARCH AND DEVELOPMENT OF RURAL SCHOOLS

On reviewing the literature, the subjects receiving the most attention are those perceived to be in situations of disadvantage compared with those of urban schools, because of their inherent characteristics, and, more recently, because of the teaching and learning practices at these rural schools. Several publications and conference papers also show the value some autonomous communities attach to them.

Rural Teachers: Professional Development and Innovation

The development of the rural environment has become a focus of interest for educational renewal movements, university and interuniversity groups, research groups in the autonomous communities, and rural school observatories. *Educational renewal movements* arose in Spain in the mid-1970s with the aim of transforming schooling by providing alternatives to the

TABLE 8.4 Milestones and Arguments in the Development Rural School

	Actions	Reasons
1957	• One-room schools: Schools for boys, girls, and infants (mixed).	
1960s	• Grouping of nearby one-room schools • Beginning of school concentration • Creation of boarding schools and school lodgings	• 1962 decree involved grouping one-room schools • Policy promoting the economic and social development of cities and district capitals • Quality model of an urban/industrial society
1970s	• Creation of national grade schools (classes of 30 pupils of the same age) • Closure of schools with fewer pupils • Creation of school concentrations	• 1970 General Education Act • Technocratic stance of Francoism • Industrial development of the districts and urban environments
1980s	• Development of school concentrations and school lodgings • Creation of CRAs (grouped rural schools) • CRIEs (rural educational innovation schools)	• Decentralization of autonomous communities • Interest in the socioeconomic development of district capitals • Movements to defend rural schools • Decree on Compensatory Education in view of disadvantages in depressed geographical areas • New regulation that included the creation of CRAs
1990s	• Drop in the number of schools, although to a lesser extent than in previous decades	• A new education act (LOGSE, 1990) • Generalization of the CRA model • Decrease in birth rate • Establishment of processing and tourism companies
2000s	• Number of schools stabilized	• No changes in the school model • Increase in migration
	• Closure of classrooms since 2007	• Impact of neoliberal policies focused on quality models • Recession

existing technocratic model. Their ideas were based on the ideas of Freinet (1982), Neill (1963), and Freire (1972), among others. These educational renewal movements were linked to rural schools in various autonomous communities (Gairín, 2004) essentially until the 1990s. At this point, the Education Act (Organic Act 1/1990) recognized many of the educational practices demanded by these groups of educational renewal teachers.

The approach detailed in this law made it possible to react to the conditions of rural schools (Sauras, 2000) and provided for specific teacher training. At the Conference for Educational Renewal Movements in Barcelona in 1983 the taskforce demanded respect for the particular contexts, circumstances, and requirements of rural schools. Following on from this, institutions such as Rosa Sensat (where teachers exchanged, shared experiences, and expanded their learning), summer schools, working parties, and educational conferences have all contributed to this movement, promoting permanent training, analysis of practice, innovation, and the creation of curricular materials.

The objective of groups of teachers working for educational renewal in several autonomous communities was to improve education in the rural environment. Their work addressed problems with the schools, the teaching staff, and the towns. They exchanged experiences, organized training, and the continuing education of teaching staff. They also made proposals to the public authorities and, in some autonomous communities, they organized rural school conferences. Several publications contain the systematized knowledge of these experiences and have become key reference sources in Spain. These include: Salanova (1983) in *The Rural School. Methods and Contents (Mesones de Isuela, an Experience in Freedom*) and Satué (2000) *Caldearenas: A Journey Through the History of Rural Schools and Teaching*, experiences to encourage reading and the organization of libraries at a *grouped rural school* (CRA Juan Pérez Avello, 2004), the coordination of inter-CRAs and collaborative work (Vilela, 2004), the experience of CRIET (rural educational innovation schools in Teruel) in Alcorisa (Berlanga, 2004), experiences with information and communication technologies (Blesa, 2004) and experiences with different groupings (Codina & Felip, 2004).

University and inter-university rural school groups have been a framework for analysis, reflection, and exchange of studies and have conducted joint research on rural schools. Several congresses and conferences have helped structure the study groups, such as: the Andalusian Conferences on the Organisation and Management of Educational Institutions held in Granada in 2001; these conferences tackled the subject of leadership at rural schools. The Rural School Congress was held in Aragon in 2000. Other examples were the annual conferences held by the Catalonian inter-university group.

Several education faculties at Spanish universities, such as Barcelona and Saragossa, offer specific subjects in their teacher education and master's degrees on rural schooling. In other cases, more generic master's degrees also include contents on this subject.

Rural education observatories are present in various autonomous communities and they are committed to new institutional and internal organization designs, based on networking, valuing possibilities, and the creation of employment, and acknowledging local innovative initiatives. By way of example, the objectives of the rural education observatory in Aragon are to consolidate the quality of the education system and to promote research on innovative practices that take place in rural schools, and to disseminate such practices and experiences. They also aim to create a collection of documents, search for rural educational innovation in Europe, promote continuing education, foster the development of educational material and software, boost educational activities and serve as a place of meeting and exchange.

Through official requests for proposals, autonomous community governments have also approved various rural school projects and have recognized innovation implemented by rural teachers. Examples in the autonomous community of Aragon are entitled "Development and Application in the Curriculum Within a New Organisational Framework for Grouped Rural Schools: Methodological Adjustment" (CRA Del Poyo del Cid) in Teruel and "Rural School Organisation Alternative" (CRA Tres Riberas de Maluenda) in Saragossa. In addition, projects submitted jointly by university researchers and schoolteachers have been recognized. One example is "Assessment and Methodology: Basis for Improving Teaching and Learning in Inclusive Rural Schools" (Vigo, Soriano, & Julve, 2010).

On Research About Rural Schools

There has been little general research on rural schools in Spain and it has tended to focus on studying the geographical and demographical conditions of rurality. The disadvantaged socioeconomic and cultural situation in which rural schools find themselves compared with urban schools has been one of the core subjects of interest. Analysis of limitations and shortcomings has been attributed, historically, to families, children, special educational needs, geographical spaces, the environment itself, teachers, resources, and so on (Bello, 1934; Carmena & Regidor, 1984; Fernández & Agulló, 2004; Ortega, 1995; Sauras, 2000). There are also studies on the "negative" effects of globalization compared with the urban school ideal, and these were the focus of research interest up to the end of the 20th century (Arellano & Zamarro, 2007; Escardibul & Villarroya, 2009; Hidalgo, 2005). Later, other studies tried to analyze the potential of rural schools (Boix, 2004; Feu, 2008; Vigo & Soriano, 2014; 2015).

The relationship between the geographical and sociocultural context and educational aspects, in the strict sense of the term, is another of the core themes explained in descriptive research. The presentation of schools located in places with a widely dispersed population highlights those organizational and operational characteristics that differentiate them from urban areas; for example, schools are smaller (Corchón, 2004; Martín-Moreno Cerrillo, 2002) and pupils are divided into multigrade or multilevel groups (Bustos, 2014). Research also shows teaching teams are smaller and often change (Vigo et al., 2006), and that staff are satisfied with collaboration among professionals (Palomares, 2000). Another feature of rural schools that appears in research is that collaborations between schools and town councils, other social institutions, the inspectorate, teacher training centers, INEM (Spanish Department of Employment), and with adult education centers appears to be less in demand (Corchón, 2005). Teachers in rural schools have been found to be satisfied with a well-established family collaboration (Palomares, 2000; Vigo & Soriano, 2014) and with the relationships that form in the community. Research also shows that the inclusion of information and communication technologies in educational practice in rural schools has been significant (Blesa, 2004; Del Moral & Villalustre, 2011; Raso, Hinojo, & Sola, 2015).

In the research we reviewed, we also noted attention paid to classroom management and curricular development. Ortega (1994) argues that individualized instruction in rural schools seems to be based on better knowledge of pupils and context. Classroom management based on the incorporation of contents from the surrounding area, active educational strategies, flexibility in time and space, development of curricular materials, inclusion of technologies for collaborative work, and ongoing assessment are all highlighted (Bustos, 2014; Vigo et al., 2006). Concerning pupils' achievements, various studies (Quílez & Vázquez, 2012; Santamaría, 2012) provide evidence of rural school pupils achieving similar results to urban school pupils. Other more recent studies highlight the innovation in rural schools related to the commitment of the teachers (Álvarez-Álvarez &Vejo-Sainz, 2017; García, Vilches, & García, 2017).

Recent Ethnographic Research: A Progressive, Community-Focused Rural Pedagogy

So far, there have been few in-depth studies, except Ortega (1995), providing an account of how rural schools operate. Nevertheless, those conducted by Barba (2011), Domingo and Boix (2015), Vigo and Soriano (2014), and Vigo-Arrazola and Beach (2018) have analyzed the operation of several rural schools. Domingo and Boix (2015) conducted work within the framework of an interpretative model, combining quantitative and qualitative techniques.

Recognizing the Space, Families, and Children as a Value
The analysis of three case studies shows how teachers use participative and active didactic strategies, considering the organization of time and space, materials, and methods of evaluation. Vigo and Soriano (2014) present a 3-year ethnographic study of three small schools, which considers teaching practices and teachers' perceptions of diversity before and during a collaborative action that reinforces and develops creative teaching

practices. The data in this study have provided some useful insights, but one specific empirical-analytical category seems to be very important and consistent. It is that rural teachers present their schools highlighting the importance of the kind of teaching practices that they carry out in this space, rather than the limitations of rural schools. In this context, teachers reinforce the spatial conditions by adapting their practices, depending on the people in it (Massey, 2011), in an interactive way. This means that whilst aspects of "poor rural schools" cover the literature on the subject of rural education, there are other issues more significant to them. One teacher commented: "I cannot understand how this school would work otherwise. This is normal. You cannot work only with the textbook. It is different in a classroom where groups are made up of pupils of the same age" (Teacher).

It helps to question why the rural schools are disadvantaged as a result of their location and uniform characteristics. Through words and actions in different schools, the authors have identified a shared way of dealing with these situations. A collective consciousness and even commitments toward collective action (Vigo & Soriano, 2014, 2015) can be glimpsed.

Teachers in these rural schools recognized the values of children and their families who wanted to be with them, in order to be involved. A teacher of a small rural school explained how experience shows the need to encourage shy families who find it difficult to participate:

> You cannot have a situation in which the families come and some participate and others are just spectators... I have to feel comfortable, otherwise I have a bad time when I see that they've come and are feeling left out. (Teacher)

The research highlights how teachers incorporated strategies such as recognition of the potential of the pupils' families, expression and communication, into creative teaching practices. These strategies emerged in contexts in which pupils' interests outside of school are addressed, thus incorporating the voices of their families (Woods & Jeffrey, 1996). Heeding the voices of children and parents and reinforcing a listening environment in teaching practices makes it possible to recognize potential and considers how best to express and exchange experiences with parents, and vice versa. An example was in one school where meetings between the family and the school were encouraged through institutionalized or spontaneous activities to help identify the strengths of each family. Producing a cookbook, conducting a workshop on Chinese, and participating in local celebrations allowed teachers to find out more about the lives of the pupils and their families, strengthen their relationships with them, and help families integrate into both the school and the community. Both types of activities were linked to the curriculum. Teachers performed activities to facilitate attention to the individuality of each person. The interest of teachers in developing a sense of community, and the sustainability of the latter, was clearly manifest.

This pedagogy therefore departs from a position of reflected normalization of the class-cultural conditions, and the values of children and families. It means that teachers try to consider knowledge from the home community (when outside of the home), in the pedagogical context, and valorize it. Teachers in these rural schools reinforced the environment and emphasized their students' learning processes.

Using ethnographic methods of participant observation, informal conversations, and document analysis, Vigo and Soriano (2015) focused on family involvement practices in two small rural schools in Aragon that were using creative teaching practices as a way to encourage parental participation. The findings show that teachers promote parental involvement using strategies such as acceptance, expression, and communication in school. These strategies seem to be negotiated in each situation based on the values teachers prioritize as a result of their interaction within the context in which they find themselves. Factors such as family mobility, dispersed homes, and sociocultural status appear to condition these. It is a critical ethnographic study that recognizes the value, the sense, and the meanings of teaching and learning practices linked to the particular context of each school and emphasizes the development that takes place during the research process. This research highlights interest in conducting studies that overcome the limitations of the kind of research that tries to generalize results for all rural schools (Coladarci, 2007; Corbett, 2015).

Interacting With the Particular Contexts

The results of theoretical reflection on teaching practices in these rural schools suggest that they consolidate existing good practices in creative teaching and learning, as outlined in the literature nowadays. According to the quality of education, listening to children and family voices in schools is a subject recognized in our own and others' research by national policy, teachers, and school leaders in order to facilitate the inclusion of all. Thus, it is possible to see the way that teachers in rural schools seem to do things: considering the values of children and the family background. However, based on the ethnographic data analyzed, it appears that, when developing strategies to encourage children and family participation in the school, the local context is critical and that it is essential to consider the relationship between the school and the community, not only in terms of an abstract notion of rurality that serves only to distinguish it from what is broadly accepted as the norm of urban life, but also in respect of the individual historical, cultural, and economic context of the rural spaces in question. Here this study shows that the complexity and the contradictions of the situation are responding to the needs in rural schools, previously forced to accept being second class, and then stigmatized.

There are obvious contradictions when the rural school is rated with respect to the advantages of successful learning. Nevertheless, when we analyze detailed ethnographic data, it is possible to see how some rural schools are working.

Also using ethnographic methods, Vigo-Arrazola and Dieste-Gracia (2018) carried out a study in three schools—rural, urban, and suburban. It highlights firstly how school strategies and priorities relate to family participation practices through social media and, secondly, to further the knowledge of the basic aspects involved. The study shows that material class conditions and wider power relations were usually present in the virtual parental participation promoted by the rural school.

In the rural school, the teachers were acutely aware of the importance of addressing families' situations and tried to show the families how to use the Internet so they could access the school websites and find out what their children were doing at school. Teachers appear to create an environment for virtual participation to improve parents' social capital through contact with other parents, other groups, and teachers, which also further influences some students to improve their learning. This kind of description was not forthcoming for the urban school. Facilitating these spaces was less clearly identified and participation seemed to be far more restricted to communicating information to parents rather than involving them. This level of participation was "reserved" for so-called "motivated families" that shared the school's culture.

Constructive relationships between families and school were important and necessary in this rural school, and teachers tried to facilitate family involvement in the interests of the school and the learning that can take place there. As discussed by Massey (2011) and Corbett (2015), we might say living everyday social spaces and interaction with virtual parental participation is an ongoing construction. It can be viewed as the school's institutional initiative to emphasize links clearly with families, their members, and the local community, and to promote the potential of educational services for all. Teachers considered that parents' social capital may also improve through contact with the school, and this then would further influence students to improve their learning.

Reinforcing Positive Expectations

This research shows how some rural schools may be able to challenge the arbitrary value inscriptions and may help actants to recognize and exercise the kind of agency needed in order to challenge cultural reproductions of this kind.

In relation to space, rural schools develop and reveal innovations and interactive possibilities to each other and others (Beach, From, Johansson, & Öhrn, 2018; Corbett, 2016) in a rural context where time did not change the conditions and representations of the place (Green & Letts, 2007). People in rural communities are often committed to their task and are very creative. They are not highlighting the negative representations but instead they are noting the actions and their meaning that they are carrying out. There is no evidence that the pupils cannot learn or do not want to, and few, if any, of the problems of rural schools and the learning in them seem to pertain to the learning difficulties, motivation or intellectual abilities of the pupils, or the lack of commitment toward and interest in their education from other family members and their teachers. These commitments are simply overlooked or missed, it seems, in official accounts, or anticipated as absent because of the peculiarities of ideology (Åberg-Bengtsson, 2009; Beach et al., 2018; Corbett, 2016). The outcomes suggest that what is mainly lacking in mainstream understanding of rural schools is the simple acceptance that people from stigmatized domains like poor rural areas are far more creative than they are portrayed and far more willing, committed, and capable of making a contribution to schools and their learning practices. Material class conditions and wider power relations are not formally politically deconstructed and challenged in and through everyday interactions in schools in terms of how they operate.

Representations seem to operate by creating certain images of inhabitants without thinking of the site of the "other" (Green & Letts, 2007), reproducing the classifications of bourgeois forms of consciousness as knowledge in the school. According to Bourdieu, Darbel, Rivet, and Seibel (1963) any interpretation of a place like the rural school, the behavior in it, or opinions about it, can only be fully grasped when manifest actions and their motivations have been acquired and the link that joins them has become comprehensible under the aspect of meaning.

CONCLUSION

In Spain, the quality model of an urban/industrial school in the 1960s and the impact of neoliberal policies thereafter resulted in a continuous drop in the number of rural schools and a negative representation of them. In this context of falling numbers small rural schools have received the same consideration as standard grade schools in urban areas. As a consequence, the characteristics of the school context, the population and the environment have been systematically omitted and ignored in both educational legislation and school management. The ramifications in the development of teaching practices that are totally at odds with the school population's experiences and life have not gone unnoticed and have sometimes affected academic results. Similarly, the effects have been negative on the communities around schools and have slowed down development.

Recognition of the importance of educational contexts in teaching and learning processes began in the 1990s. This involved paying attention to the needs of rural schools and, consequently, their reform, with the creation of educational centers that group various rural schools together. However, there is still a lack of consideration for the particular context stemming from the economic, social, and cultural experiences of these schools and rural areas at different times in the last 50 years.

In keeping with the situation of rural schools, research up to the 1980s consolidated the analysis of the disadvantages and limitations of rural schools compared with urban ones. Later, research recognized the educational value and the potential of rural schools linked to the community. At the present time, studies that further our knowledge of how rural schools operate are valued. However, these studies show the contradictions between educational quality present in some rural schools and the negative representation of them and could be of interest for the development of research, of research subjects and educational policies in rural and urban schools. Comparative studies, meta-analyses of several research projects, and multi-sited studies could provide more solid knowledge of these schools.

Schools can make a difference in the lives of local agents, and in relation to their understanding of future possibilities and life chances, and in connection to their backgrounds (Corbett & Forsey, 2017; Corbett & Helmer, 2017). The analysis presented shows an important resource for rethinking stigmatized spaces and schools. They are very clear about how people in those rural areas that were researched were far more creative and involved than they were objectively portrayed in educational political discourse, the media, and formal school statistics.

REFERENCES

Åberg-Bengtsson, L. (2009). The smaller the better? A review of research on small rural schools in Sweden. *International Journal of Educational Research, 48*(2), 100–108.

Álvarez-Álvarez, C., & Vejo-Sainz, R. (2017). How do Spanish schools of rural contexts face innovation? An exploratory study through interviews. *Aula Abierta, 45*, 25–32.

Arellano, M., & Zamarro, G. (2007). *The choice between public and private schools with or without subsidies in Spain*. Preliminary and incomplete preprint. Retrieved from http://www.cemfi.es/~arellano/schoolchoice-tr-26Sep2007.pdf

Asociación de Voluntariado de la Universidad de Valladolid. (2017). *Despoblación rural y acogida de refugiados y migrantes en la provincia de Valladolid* [Rural depopulation and reception of refugees and migrants in the province of Valladolid]. Valladolid, Spain: Asociación de Voluntariado de la Universidad de Valladolid.

Bagley, C., & Hillyard, S. (2015). School choice in an English village: Living, loyalty and leaving. *Ethnography and Education, 10*(3), 278–292.

Ball, S. (1993). What is policy? Texts, trajectories and toolboxes. Discourse studies in the *Cultural Politics of Education, 13*(2), 10–17.

Barba, M. (2011). *El desarrollo profesional de un maestro novel en la escuela rural desde una perspectiva crítica* [Professional career of a beginner teacher in a rural school from a critical perspective] (Doctoral thesis). Universidad de Valladolid, Escuela Universitaria de Magisterio, Spain. Retrieved from http://uvadoc.uva.es/handle/10324/822

Beach, D., From, T., Johansson, M., & Öhrn, E. (2018). Educational and spatial justice in rural and urban areas in three Nordic countries: A meta-ethnographic analysis. *Education Inquiry, 9*(1), 4–21.

Bello, L. (1934). La vida rural y la escuela [Rural life and school]. *Revista de Pedagogía, 145*, 1–5.

Berlanga, S. (2004). Los centros rurales de innovación educativa (CRIE) [Rural educational innovation school]. In R. Boix (Eds.), *La escuela rural: Funcionamiento y necesidades* [Rural school: Working and needs] (pp. 81–102). Madrid, Spain: Praxis.

Blesa, J. A. (2004). Aulas autosuficientes y pupitres digitales en una comunidad de aprendizaje [Self-sufficient classrooms and digital desks in a learning community]. In R. Boix (Coord.), *La escuela rural: funcionamiento y necesidades* [Rural school: Working and needs] (pp. 121–154). Madrid, Spain: Praxis.

Boix, R. (Coord.). (2004). *La escuela rural: funcionamiento y necesidades* [Rural school: Working and needs]. Madrid, Spain: Praxis.

Bourdieu, P. (1986). La force du droit. Eléments pour une sociologie du champ juridique [The force of law: Toward a sociology of the juridical field]. *Actes de la recherche en sciences sociales, 64*(1), 3–19.

Bourdieu, P., Darbel, A., Rivet, J.-P., & Seibel, C. (1963). *Travail et travailleurs en Algérie*. Paris, France: Mouton.

Bourdieu, P., & Passeron, J.-C. (1970). *La Reproduction. Éléments pour une théorie du système d'enseignement*. Paris, France: Sens Commun. Les Éditions de Minuit.

Bustos, A. (2014). La didáctica multigrado y las aulas rurales: perspectivas y datos para su análisis [Multigrade teaching and rural classrooms: Perspective and data for analysis]. *Innovación Educativa, 24*, 119–131.

Carmena, G., & Regidor, J. G. (1984). *La escuela en el medio rural* [The school in rural áreas]. Madrid, Spain: Servicio de Publicaciones del MEC.

CES. (2018). *Informe. El medio rural y su vertebración social territorial* [Report. The rural environment and its territorial social vertebration]. Madrid, Spain: Consejo económico y social de España.

Codina, R. E., & Felip, A. M. (2004). Una escuela rural que intenta crecer sin perder su identidad [A rural school that tries to grow without losing its identity]. In R. Boix (Ed.), *La escuela rural: funcionamiento y necesidades* [Rural school: working and needs] (pp. 25–51). Madrid, Spain: Praxis.

Coladarci, T. (2007). Improving the yield of rural education research: An editor's swan song. *Journal of Research in rural Education, 22*(3), 1–9.

Collantes, F., Pinilla, P., Sáez, L. A., & Silvestre, J. (2014). Reducing depopulation in rural Spain: The impact of immigration. *Population, Space and Place, 20*(7), 606–621.

Corbett, M. (2015). Towards a rural sociological imagination: Ethnography and schooling in mobile modernity. *Ethnography and Education, 10*(3), 263–277.

Corbett, M. (2016). Rural futures: Development, aspirations, mobilities, place, and education. *Peabody Journal of Education, 91*(2), 270–282.

Corbett, M., & Forsey, M. (2017). Rural youth out-migration and education: Challenges to aspirations discourse in mobile modernity. *Discourse, 38*(3), 429–444.

Corbett, M., & Helmer, L. (2017). Contested geographies: Competing constructions of community and efficiency in small school debates. *Geographical Research, 55*(1), 47–57.

Corchón, E. (2000). *La escuela rural: Pasado, presente y perspectivas de futuro* [Rural school, past, present and perspectives of future]. Barcelona, Spain: Oikos-Tau.

Corchón, E. (2004). Escuela rural [Rural school]. In F. Salvador, J. J. Rodríguez, & A. Bolívar (Eds.), *Diccionario enciclopédico de Didáctica* (Vol. 1; pp. 641–643). Archidona, Spain: Aljibe.

Corchón, E. (2005). *La escuela en el medio rural: Modelos organizativos* [The school in rural areas: Organizational models]. Barcelona, Spain: Davinci.

Corchón, E., Raso, F., & Hinojo, M. A. (2013). Análisis histórico-legislativo de la escuela rural española en el período 1857–2012 [Historical-legislative analysis of rural Spanish schools' organization from 1857 to 2012]. *Enseñanza & Teaching, 31*(1), 147–179.

CRA. Juan Pérez Avello. (2004). Experiencia de animación a la lectura y de organización y dinamización de bibliotecas central y de aulas en un CRA [Experience of reading animation and organization and dynamization of classroom libraries in a CRA]. In R. Boix (Ed.), *La escuela rural: Funcionamiento y necesidades* [Rural school: Working and needs] (pp. 5–11). Madrid, Spain: Praxis.

Decree 400/1962, February 22. Grouping of schools and management of school groups. *Boletín Oficial del Estado, 59*, 1962 March 9.

Del Moral, M. E., & Villalustre, L. (2011). Digitalización de las escuelas rurales asturianas: Maestros rurales 2.0 y Desarrollo local [Digitisation of the rural schools in Asturias: Rural teachers 2.0 and local development]. *Profesorado. Revista de Curriculum y Formación de Profesorado, 15*(2), 109–123.

Domingo, L., & Boix, R. (2015). What can be learned from Spanish rural schools? Conclusions from an international project. *International Journal of Educational Research, 74*, 114–126.

Escardíbul, J. O., & Villarroya, A. (2009). The inequalities in school choice in Spain in accordance to PISA- data. *Journal of Education Policy, 24*(6), 673–696.

Fernández, J. M., & Agulló, M. C. (2004). *Una escuela rural republicana* [A republican rural school]. Valencia, Spain: Universitat de Valencia.

Feu, J. (2008). La escuela rural desde la atalaya educativa [The rural school from the educational watchtower]. In N. Llevot, & J. Garreta (Eds.), *Escuela y sociedad rural* [School and rural society] (pp. 61–86). Lleida, Spain: Fundación Santamaría/Universitat de Lleida.

Freinet, C. (1982). *Por una escuela del pueblo* [For a people's school]. (Original work published 1969 as *Pour l'école du peuple: Guide pratique pour l'organisation matérielle, technique et pédagogique de l'école.* [For a school of the people: A practical guide for the material, technical, and pedagogical organisation of a popular school]). Barcelona, Spain: Laia.

Freire, P. (1972). *Pedagogy of the oppressed.* Harmondsworth, England: Penguin.

Gairín, J. (2004). Prólogo [Prolog]. In R. Boix (Ed.), *La escuela rural: Funcionamiento y necesidades* [Rural school: Working and needs] (pp. 5–11). Madrid, Spain: Praxis.

García, I., Vilches, A., & García, X. (2017). Innovative teaching strategies in sciences teaching. Case study: Teachers of the Rural Education Foundation of Valencia (1958–1985). *Enseñanza de las ciencias, 35*(2), 2174–6486.

Grande, M. (1994). *La escuela rural en España. De la LGE a la LOGSE. Balance y perspectivas* [The rural school in Spain. From the LGE to the LOGSE. Balance and perspectives]. (Unpublished doctoral thesis). Salamanca, Spain: Universidad de Salamanca.

Green, B., & Letts, W. (2007). *Space, equity and rural education: A 'trialectical' account.* In N. G. Kalervo & C. Symes (Eds.), *Spatial theories of education: Policy and geography matters* (pp. 57–76). London, England: Routledge.

Gurrutxaga, A., & Unceta, A. (2010). La función distributiva de la educación: Un análisis aplicado al País Vasco [The distributive function of education: An analysis applied to the Basque Country]. *Política y sociedad, 47*(2), 103–120.

Hargreaves, L., Kvalsund, R., & Galton, M. (2009). Reviews of research on rural schools and their communities in British and Nordic countries: Analytical perspectives and cultural meaning. *International Journal of Educational Research, 48*(2), 80–88.

Hernández, J. M. (2000). La escuela rural en la España del siglo XX [The rural school in the Spain of the XXI century]. *Revista de educación. Número extraordinario, La educación en España en el siglo, XX,* 113–136.

Hidalgo, I. (2005). *Gasto de las familias en educación básica y elección entre colegio público y privado: Un análisis empírico* [Family expenses on basic education and choice between public and private school: An empirical analysis] (Dissertation). Madrid, Spain: CEMFI 0504.

Instituto Nacional de Estadística. (2010). *Demografía y población* [Demography and population]. Retrieved from http://www.ine.es/nomen2/index.do

Jiménez, J. (1983). *La escuela unitaria* [The one-room school]. Barcelona: Laia.

Martín-Moreno Cerrillo, Q. (2002). Claves para la calidad de los centros educativos rurales [Keys to the quality of rural schools]. In M. Lorenzo & J. A. Ortega. *Liderazgo educativo y escuela rural* [Educational leadership and rural school] (pp. 58–69). Granada, Spain: Grupo Editorial Universitario.

Massey, D. (2011). *Landscape/space/politics: An essay.* Retrieved from https://thefutureoflandscape.wordpress.com/landscapespacepolitics-an-essay/

Ministerio de Educación, Cultura y Deporte. (2016). *Publicaciones de la estadística de la educación en España* [Publications on education statistics in Spain]. Madrid, Spain: Ministerio de Educación, Cultura y Deporte.

Ministry of Education, Culture and Sport. (2019). *Las cifras de la educación en España: Estadísticas e indicadores* [Data on education in Spain: Statistics and indicators]. Madrid, Spain: Ministerio de Educación, Cultura y Deporte.

Morales, N. (2012). La política de concentraciones escolares en el medio rural. Repercusiones desde su implantación hasta la actualidad [School concentrations Policy in rural areas: Repercussions from its establishment to the present time]. *Ager. Revista de Estudios sobre Despoblación y Desarrollo Rural, 11*, 1–43.
Neill, A. S. (1963). *Summerhill. Un punto de vista radical sobre la educación de los niños* [A radical approach to child rearing]. Madrid, Spain: Fondo de Cultura Económica.
Order 29. (1994). June 1994, approving instructions that regulate the organisation and operation of pre-schools and primary schools. *Boletín Oficial del Estado, 160*, 1994 July 6.
Order 29. (1996). April 1996, on the creation and operation of rural educational innovation schools. *Boletín Oficial del Estado, 115*, 1996 May 11.
Organic Act 1/1990, 3 October. (1990). On General organisation of the Educational System (LOGSE). *Boletín Oficial del Estado, 238*, 1990 December 4.
Organic Act 8/2013, 9 December. (2013). On the Improvement of the quality of education (LOMCE). *Boletín Oficial del Estado, 295*, 2013 December 10.
Ortega, M. A. (1994). Escuela rural o escuela en lo rural? Algunas anotaciones sobre una frase hecha [Rural school or school in the rural? Some notes about a phrase]. *Revista de Educación, 303*, 211–243.
Ortega, M. A. (1995). *La parienta pobre. (Significante y significados de la Escuela Rural)* [The poor family: Signified and signifiers of rural schools]. Madrid, Spain: CIDE.
Palomares, M. C. (2000). Variables que condicionan la satisfacción de los profesores que trabajan en Centros Rurales agrupados [Variables that condition the teachers' satisfaction working in grouped rural schools]. *Bordón, 52*(2), 213–227.
Quílez, M., & Vázquez, R. (2012). Aulas multigrado o el mito de la mala calidad de enseñanza en la escuela rural [Multigrade classrooms or the myth of poor teaching quality in rural schools]. *Revista Iberoamericana de Educación/Revista Ibero-americana de Educação, 59*(2), 1–12.
Raso, F., Hinojo, A., & Sola, J. M. (2015). Introduction and teaching use of information and communication technologies (ICT) in Grenadian rural schools (Spain): Descriptive study. *REICE. Revista Iberoamericana sobre Calidad, Eficacia y Cambio en Educación, 13*(1), 139–159.
Roche, P. (1993). *Los Centros Rurales de Innovación Educativa de Teruel (CRIET): respuesta de futuro a la nueva escuela rural* [Rural educational innovation school of Teruel: Future response to the new rural school]. Zaragoza, Spain: Instituto de Ciencias de la Educación, Universidad de Zaragoza.
Royal Decree 1174/1983 April 27. (1983). On compensation in education. *Boletín Oficial del Estado, 112*, 1983 May 11.
Salanova, J. (1983). *La escuela rural: Métodos y contenidos, mesones de Isuela, una experiencia en libertad* [The rural school: Methods and contents, mesones de Isuela, an experience in freedom]. Madrid, Spain: ZERO.
Santamaría, R. (2012). Inspección de educación y escuela rural: Contra el mito del bajo rendimiento de la escuela rural. Visión histórica 1972–2012 [Inspection of education and rural school: Against the myth of the poor performance of the rural school. Historical overview 1972–2012]. *Revista de la Asociación de Inspectores de Educación de España, 17*, 1–29.

Satué, E. (2000). *Caldearenas: Un viaje por la historia de la escuela y el magisterio rural* [Caldearenas: A journey through the history of rural schools and the teaching]. Huesca, Spain: Author.

Sauras, P. (2000). Escuelas rurales [Rural schools]. *Revista de Educación, 322,* 29–44.

STECyL (2012). *Informe STECyL-i. La enseñanza y el mapa escolar en el medio rural de Castilla y León* [Teaching and the school map in the rural environment of Castilla and León]. Recovered from http://www.stes.es/areas/escuela_rural/120708_La_Ensenyanza_y_el_mapa_escolar_en_el_medio_rural_de_Castilla_y_Leon_Informe_STECyL-i.pdf

Vázquez, R. (2016). Las escuelas públicas rurales: entre el bien común y la exclusión [Rural state schools: Between the common good and exclusion]. *Revista Interuniversitaria de Formación del Profesorado, 85,* 67–79.

Vigo-Arrazola, B., & Beach, D. (2018). Significados de la escuela rural desde la investigación. Representaciones compartidas entre España y Suecia en la segunda parte del siglo XX y primeros años del siglo XXI. [Meanings of the rural school from the research. Representations shared between Spain and Sweden in the second part of the 20th century and first years of the 21st century]. In N. Llevot & J. Sanuy (Eds.), *Educació i desenvolupament rural als segles XIX-XX-XXI* [Rural education and rural development in the 19th-20th-21th centuries] (pp. 225–236). Lleida, Spain: Universitat de Lleida.

Vigo-Arrazola, B., & Dieste-Gracia, B. (2018). Building virtual interaction spaces between family and school. *Ethnography and Education, 14*(2), 206–222. Retrieved from https://doi.org/10.1080/17457823.2018.1431950

Vigo, B., & Soriano, J. (2014). Teaching practices and teachers' perceptions of group creative practices in inclusive rural schools. *Ethnography and Education, 9*(3), 253–269.

Vigo, B., & Soriano, J. (2015). Family involvement in creative teaching practices for all in small rural schools. *Ethnography and Education, 10*(3), 325–339.

Vigo, B., Abós, P., Bernal, J. L., Bueno, C., Julve, C., Ramo, R., & Soriano J. (2006). *La atención a la diversidad en los núcleos rurales dispersos de la Comunidad Autónoma de Aragón* [The educational practice of attention to diversity in dispersed population areas of Aragon]. (Research report). Zaragoza, Spain: Centro de Estudios sobre la Despoblación y Desarrollo de Áreas Rurales.

Vigo, B., Soriano, J., & Julve, C. (2010). La evaluación y la metodología: bases para la mejora de la enseñanza y el aprendizaje en una escuela rural inclusive. [Evaluation and methodology: Bases to improve teaching and learning practices in an inclusive rural school]. Retrieved from http://hdl.handle.net/11162/3469

Vilela, P. (2004). La coordinación entre centros rurales agrupados en Galicia: Un modelo de organización [The coordination between rural grouped schools in Galia: A model of management]. In R. Boix (Ed.), *La escuela rural: Funcionamiento y necesidades necesidades* [Rural school: Working and needs] (pp. 5–11). Madrid, Spain: Praxis.

Woods, P., & Jeffrey, B. (1996). *Teachable moments: The art of teaching in primary schools.* Buckingham, England: Open University Press.

CHAPTER 9

SMALL RURAL PRIMARY SCHOOLS IN AUSTRIA

Places of Innovation?

Andrea Raggl
University of Teacher Education Tirol, Austria

Austria has many small rural primary schools, due to topological conditions and a hitherto rather strong political support for small and very small rural schools, especially in the western part of the country. In this chapter, insights into small rural schools are provided, based on the Interreg project Small Schools in Alpine Regions (2012–2015). In this transnational research project, a team of researchers from the Universities of Teacher Education in Vorarlberg (Austria) and the two Swiss cantons Grisons and St. Gallen, investigated the work of head teachers, of teachers in small rural schools, and of teaching and learning practices in mixed age classes (Raggl, 2015; Raggl, Smit, & Kerle, 2015). This project continued previous research from an earlier project, Schools in Alpine Regions (2009–2011) in these regions and, in addition, in the Swiss canton Valais (Müller, Keller, Kerle, Raggl, & Steiner, 2011). Case studies in these two projects showed that small rural schools are portrayed as places of innovation by some of their head teachers (Raggl, 2015). Two of the participating Austrian small rural primary schools have each developed a special profile as a Montessori school. In this chapter the potential and challenges of innovative small schools are discussed along with the consequences of increasing diversity of schooling and the possibilities of choice for those with the necessary economic, social, and cultural capitals (Bourdieu, 1986).

SMALL RURAL PRIMARY SCHOOLS IN AUSTRIA

National Context

Sixty percent of the nationwide primary schools are schools with fewer than 100 pupils; 40% have fewer than 50, and 6% fewer than 20 pupils (Statistik Austria, 2017). Consequently, the international definition of a *small school*, as having fewer than 100 pupils (e.g., Galton, Hargreaves, & Comber, 1998), is not applicable to Austria, as small would mean the standard size of a primary school. Most of these schools are located in western Austria (Statistik Austria, 2017). In spite of the high number of small primary schools, research on these rural schools is rather limited (e.g., Kramer, 1993; Müller et al., 2011).

In Austria, primary education has only four grades, unlike many other countries. This is one of the reasons for the low number of pupils in primary schools compared to those of countries with 6 years of primary education. In educational authority documents small primary schools are defined as having fewer than the four classes (one for each of the grades), where at least two of the classes are organized as mixed age and grade, due to the low number of pupils. According to this categorization, 33% of Austrian primary schools are small (Statistik Austria, 2017). Therefore, mixed age classes are an important characteristic of small rural schools. Very small primary schools with fewer than 20 pupils are one-teacher-schools having one class of all four grades.

Up until the 1960s, most rural primary schools in Austria comprised all eight grades of compulsory schooling (lower primary school from Year 1 to Year 4, and upper primary school from Year 5 to Year 8). A change in legislation in 1962 resulted in a major reduction in the number of pupils in rural primary schools, because most pupils from Year 5 onwards were obliged to go to more centrally located secondary schools. Additional factors led to a wave of school closures throughout rural Austria in the 1960s and 1970s: the extension of road infrastructure (meaning many small hamlets gained better access to the centers of villages); free public transport for pupils; migration of families to the towns; a decline in the birth rate; as well as a harsh critique of small schools by educationalists and decision makers (Kramer, 1993).

The minimum number of pupils for a school is quite different in each of the nine Austrian provinces. Regional politicians are often seen fighting to maintain the existence of small schools. In the research project, Schools in Alpine Regions, a politician of the Vorarlberg province, when interviewed, emphasized this battle: "We try to prevent any school closure as long as possible. There should be at least one primary school in every community." The regional government supports the existence of small schools with additional money, showing that the further existence of these very small schools depends a great deal on (regional) political commitment. This situation differs in the eastern part of Austria where more school closures have taken place in recent years (Kroismayr, 2015) as a result of a community fusion policy. However, more pressure is coming from central government. A recent report of the *Rechnungshof* (2018, Austrian Court of Audit) is putting pressure on Tyrol and Vorarlberg to close more small primary schools.

Currently the development of clusters can also be observed in most provinces in Austria where several small rural primary schools are connected within one regional network. Whereas, previously every primary school had a head teacher, one is now responsible for several schools within a cluster. As a result, this national policy is changing rural education slowly but surely. It is described in official documents as a way to find methods of preventing school closure, and to guarantee high educational standards in remote areas (Bundesministerium für Bildung (BMB), 2018). This national policy corresponds similarly with international policies on building clusters of schools in rural areas, for example in England (Ribchester & Edwards, 1998). Alongside these policy changes, the data of the research project, Schools in Alpine Regions, reveal that small rural schools are inventing their own strategies to secure their existence. One successful strategy was found in two small primary schools that have developed a special profile as Montessori schools.

A Disciplinary Perspective on Rural Education[1]

The issues related to small schools in rural areas and socioeconomic aspects have played an important role in the research project Schools in Alpine Regions (2009–2011) and enabled valuable insights concerning the interconnection of space, work, and the migration of people in rural regions (Müller et al., 2011). In the project Small Schools in Alpine Regions (2012–2015), the researchers mainly investigated the teaching and learning practices in small rural schools with mixed-age classes (Raggl et al., 2015). The two research projects revealed the plurality of small rural schools and showed that it is important to explicate more clearly what is meant by *rural* (Coladarci, 2007). This can be done, for example, by using the distance to the next center and the number of people living in a village. Case studies of 10 Austrian small rural primary schools in the research project Small Schools in Alpine Regions revealed the following typology:

1. very small remote one-teacher schools with fewer than 20 pupils, located approximately 45 minutes driving time to the next small town;
2. small two-teacher schools, of between 20 and 30 pupils, located approximately 30 minutes driving time to the next small town; and
3. small two-teacher schools with a special profile (e.g., a Montessori school) located on the hills surrounding small towns, 15 minutes driving time from the center of town.

These schools face different challenges, depending on their location and distance from the urban centres. The participating very small remote one-teacher schools for example, had to cope with teacher isolation and high staff turnover (Raggl, 2015; Raggl et al., 2015).

This chapter focuses on Type 3 schools, which are small primary schools located on the outskirts of towns that have developed a special profile. Two of the Austrian case studies in the research were Hill School and Green School, both of which have developed a special profile as Montessori schools.

METHODOLOGY

In the transnational research project Small Schools in Alpine Regions the investigations in small rural schools were carried out in Vorarlberg, the most western province in Austria, and in the Swiss cantons, Grisons, and St. Gallen. The mixed methods approach included a questionnaire study with head teachers and teachers, as well as case studies. Case studies (Stake, 1995) involved semi-structured interviews with head teachers and teachers, group interviews with students, participant observation, and documentary analysis (e.g., of the homepages of the schools). The 10 Austrian case studies included 10 interviews with head teachers, 20 interviews with teachers, and 30 group interviews with students from Year 3 and Year 4. Data collection took place during the school year 2013/2014. Interviews with head teachers and teachers lasted around one hour, group interviews with students about half an hour. All interviews were recorded and transcribed. Data analysis was undertaken with the help of the software program Maxqda. This chapter

TABLE 9.1 Case Studies of Small Rural Schools With a Montessori Approach

Hill School		
The school has been a Montessori school for 15 years. It is an inclusive school. Two class teachers (one of them is also the head teacher, David) work with two classes of children from Year 1 to Year 4. The school was renovated and extended a few years ago and is located in a small hamlet (500 inhabitants) on a hill, ten minutes' drive from the center of the town.		
38 pupils (half of them from outside the hamlet)	2 classes with Year 1 to Year 4 for most of the lessons	• 2 class teachers: David (teaching head) and Sandra • 4 part-time teachers: special needs, RE (Religious Education), craft
Green School		
The school became a Montessori school 5 years ago with the new head teacher, Nora, who is also a class teacher. The two class teachers work together with one mixed-age group (Year 1 to Year 4) most of the time. The school is in an old building and is located in a small hamlet (400 inhabitants), 15 minutes' drive from the center of the town.		
20 pupils (a third from outside the hamlet)	One class from Year 1 to Year 4 for most of the lessons	• 2 class teachers: Nora (teaching head) and Theresa • 3 part-time teachers: RE, craft, PE (Physical Education)

mainly focuses on two of the Austrian case studies with a special profile, labeled Montessori Schools (see Table 9.1).

Small Rural Schools as Challenging but Rewarding Places to Work

Small schools differ from their larger counterparts in a number of ways including class size, number of staff members, the use of multigrade class structure, and the role of head teachers (Raggl, 2015; Sigsworth & Solstad, 2001). These characteristics are a source of both educational opportunity and challenge. The findings of the research project Small Schools in Alpine Regions show that many of the participating Austrian head teachers and teachers like to work in their small rural schools; 71% state in the questionnaire study that they are largely content with their work. The case studies reveal that many are very dedicated to their work and experience it as rewarding. In the interviews several of the head teachers and teachers describe their small school as a "special" or "exciting" place and experience their work as challenging though "very diverse" and "never boring." Additionally, student interviews indicate that many pupils like their school and speak very positively about their experiences in a small school setting (Raggl, 2015).

One of the characteristics of small rural primary schools is that they have a teaching head with the dual role of serving both as classroom teacher and head teacher. Several of the participating head teachers indicate in the interviews that they see themselves primarily as classroom teachers: "I'm mainly a teacher. The head teacher role goes next to this." However, some underline that the double role comes along with the freedom to create something: "It's really tiring, but I also like this role because it enables you to act in a very autonomous way (...) for me as a teacher of this school and for the whole staff. (...) I have freedom!" (Head teacher, Hill School).

The freedom goes along with a lot of responsibility that falls to a very small team or even to one person. Teachers explain that they have to be careful not to exploit themselves out of personal dedication to the school. The high responsibility is connected with a rather isolated professional situation especially in very small and remote one-teacher schools. However, case study analysis indicates a strong mutual support in many small schools in spite of small team sizes in general. In addition, several maintain close contacts with other small schools nearby. In Vorarlberg, many teachers are part of a regional network (Arbeitsgemeinschaft Kleinschulen) and meet regularly for informal exchanges and mutual support, or for developing learning materials. In the interviews, several teachers underline the importance of this support network, especially those novice teachers in small schools who feel well supported by it (Raggl, 2015). Many participating head teachers and teachers feel supported by parents and the wider community. Some schools have strong links to the community and can be described as "community active" schools (Sigsworth & Solstad, 2005) that encourage parents and other community members to come into the school and contribute their skills and knowledge. However, in the questionnaire study where 47 head teachers and 85 teachers of small rural schools in Vorarlberg took part, 70% of the head teachers and teachers state that they are not engaged in village activities outside of their work in the school and 65% state that they do not personally live in the village in which they work. In the interviews several of them emphasize that the spatial detachment between work and home is important for them. Nevertheless, several of the head teachers and teachers underline that they feel attached to the place where they are working; many have worked in the same school for more than 10 years. Building on the idea of the community active school of Sigsworth and Solstad (2005), the participating head teachers and teachers can be characterized as "school active" because they are very motivated and "give everything" to the school and the children, but less as community active; they are less willing to engage in activities beyond the school in the wider community. They reject the former expectation of being the main "carrier of culture" (Poglia & Strittmatter, 1983) in a village, and emphasize their professional role by distancing themselves from a total immersion in village life (Raggl, 2015, 2019).

Small Rural Schools as Places for Innovation?

Small schools have been portrayed as places providing unique educational opportunities (Bell & Sigsworth, 1987; Sigsworth & Solstad, 2001; Vulliamy & Webb, 1995). Some historical examples exist which underpin the idea that small rural schools have been inspiring places for educators. One example is that of Helen Parkhurst who worked in a small village school with 40 students in Waterville, Wisconsin (1905–1913) where she developed the Dalton-Plan (Popp, 1999). The idea that the structure of a small primary school makes it easier to implement changes was underlined by several of the participating head teachers and teachers of the project Small Schools in Alpine Regions. Some of them explained in the interviews that they appreciate their freedom and degree of autonomy to create their own profile of the school. Several indicate that the small structure makes it possible to implement new ideas easily:

> It's much easier to do this in a small school when you get along well with each other than in a big one. Too many people join the discussion there...and here you just sit together and decide it...It's not time consuming in the end. I really see this as an advantage. (Head teacher, River School)

A few of the participating head teachers and teachers had deliberately transferred from a larger school to a smaller one because they recognized that it would be possible to realize their educational ideas in a smaller setting. The data reveal that small rural primary schools provide a niche for dedicated teachers where they see better chances of creating their vision for a school.

THE CURRENT HYPE FOR MIXED-AGE CLASSES IN GERMAN SPEAKING COUNTRIES IN CONNECTION WITH THE MONTESSORI PEDAGOGY

Small schools with fewer than 50 pupils have to work with mixed-age classes in order to retain their schools. This tradition of mixed-age classes has spread to larger schools, and has been implemented in many primary schools in Austria, Germany, and Switzerland in recent years. The current boom of mixed-age classes in larger primary schools where there is no organizational necessity could act as an endorsement of the mixed-age teaching and learning approaches of small rural primary schools, based on pedagogical ideals. Educationalists (e.g., Carle & Metzen, 2014) point out the benefits of mixed-age classes, like the cooperation of children of different ages in their learning, or the more flexible grouping of children according to their performance levels and not mainly because of their ages. However, the long standing experiences of teachers in rural schools with mixed-age teaching and learning does not seem to be acknowledged by educationalists very much. There occurs a normative confrontation of innovative mixed-age learning in urban primary schools and old-fashioned mixed-age learning in small rural schools (e.g., Peschel, 2007). The research into small schools in the two transnational projects shows that this is not reflecting the reality in many small rural primary schools, where teachers clearly see the pedagogical benefits of mixed-age teaching and learning, even though they have to have mixed-age classes for reasons of organizational necessity (Raggl, 2012, 2015, 2019).

An analysis of the current literature on mixed-age teaching and learning shows that educationalists often refer to ideas of reform pedagogy, especially those of Maria Montessori (e.g., Laging, 2010). As it is well known, the Italian educationalist Maria Montessori developed her system from working with children with special needs in Rome at the beginning of the last century. The pedagogy included the development of a variety of didactic material, and centers on the individual development of each child (Brehony, 2000).

The steady rise of mixed-age classes since the mid-1990s has been interrelated with an increase in (private) schools with progressive approaches. Many newly founded private primary schools in Austria and Germany are schools with a Montessori approach (for the situation in Germany: Ullrich, 2015). The current popularity of Montessori schools among teachers and parents is striking; the brand Montessori (Oelkers, 2016) seems to work.

Hill School and Green School: Two Small Schools With a Montessori Approach

The Staff: Convinced Mobile Choosers

Hill School and Green School are set up and portrayed on their homepages as Montessori schools. Both were restructured as Montessori schools by their head teachers David and Nora. David moved to Hill School from a larger urban school 15 years ago: "I really wanted to work with mixed-age classes and that was not possible at this large school at that time. So I went to this school" (Head teacher, Hill School).

He gradually altered the rural village school to a Montessori school. Parents from the town nearby took an interest in this newly established small Montessori school within a rural environment and, over the years, it took on more and more children from outside the catchment area.

Nora moved 3 years ago from a larger urban primary school to Green School and altered it to a Montessori school too. Creating schools according to their pedagogical ideas were the dreams of both head teachers, who saw better chances of realizing these in small rural schools with a small team of teachers supportive of the Montessori approach. Nora and David had been committed classroom teachers before they developed their small rural schools and taking on the headship was something with which both struggled, especially David:

> I had to take on the head teacher role to be able to work with a mixed-age class at that time. And it took me many years, perhaps, only now to accept that headship is a part of my work. I'm really a committed teacher but I know I also have to fulfil the role of a head teacher.

Nora experienced being a head teacher as a challenge but found it "really interesting": "I come from a mixed-age class so the change was not so different. However, the new thing is the administration role of being a head teacher. That's a challenge... but I really like it here."

The dual role of being a committed teacher and a head teacher with multiple responsibilities generates certain tensions (Harrison & Busher, 1995). However, the two case studies also show that the role of being a head teacher of a small school endows them with considerable power and authority (Bell & Sigsworth, 1987). Their role enabled David and Nora to realize their own vision for their schools. An important factor was that they had been successful in finding teachers who were trained in Montessori pedagogy in Austria. The data reveal that the teachers really wanted to work in a small rural Montessori school:

> She (the head teacher) said she needed someone and I was really glad. It has always been my dream to work in a small school. I had been in one during my time at Teacher College and I thought: "That's it!" And I thought "I have to take this chance because there are not so many posts in small schools." (Theresa, Teacher, Green School)

To work in a small Montessori school is interpreted by Theresa as a dream that came true, a special opportunity she had to take because such opportunities are so rare. It seemed to her to be a privilege to work there. Both head teachers and teachers felt very connected to their schools and identified completely with them. Sandra, who had been a teacher at Hill School for 10 years, explained: "I'm very committed to this school... I have put a lot of heart blood into it."

Both the head teachers and teachers drive a considerable distance to their small rural schools. They can be described as convinced mobile choosers who live in urban areas and prefer to work in small rural schools. All of them have found their niche where they can realize their pedagogical ideas. They enjoy working in a small team very much, as Nora, the head teacher of Green School described: "I really find it great, the team is functioning really well. It's a small team," while Theresa applauded, "Two teachers in one class is just ideal. I really enjoy this very much now."

The Teaching and Learning Approach

Compared with the other Austrian case studies in the research project Small Schools in Alpine Regions, where teachers often had quite different ideas of teaching and learning within one school, the teaching and learning practices were very consistent at Hill School and Green School, and also between the two schools. Both schools had periods of free work every morning for at least 2 hours, when pupils worked individually on their own tasks with learning materials. They had a morning circle every day and a school parliament that met once a week. Although each school had some differences they both adopted the main concepts of the Montessori approach and relied very much on the reputation and ideas of the famous founder. Both the head teachers and the two teachers were trained in Montessori pedagogy and being a Montessori teacher was an important aspect of their professional identity. The teachers referred often to Montessori when they explained their teaching and learning approaches: "Montessori said..."; "This was also important for Montessori...." The Montessori pedagogy provided a clear orientation. Their strong belief in child-centeredness resulted in distancing themselves from a traditional teaching approach. They saw themselves mainly as assistants of the child's individual learning: "It's nearly only free work. We hardly have any teacher-centered lessons" (David); "I'm mainly observing the children and support them on an individual level" (Sandra); "I'm not a classical teacher who stands in front of the class" (Theresa). The small rural primary school offered them a niche for establishing an alternative teacher role within the state system where they were able to live up to their ideals. They presented a caring ethos of the school—a school that cares individually for each child. Montessori was—next to other educational reformers and modernizers—critical of whole-class teaching and strongly advocated individual instruction (Brehony, 2000). Although the staff firmly believe in the Montessori pedagogy they state that calling the school a Montessori school is also contradictory.

The Ambivalent Label Montessori

Montessori appeared as a label that implied certain contradictions and ambivalences, as the head teacher of Hill School explicates:

> The school defines itself to the outside as a Montessori School with all the advantages and disadvantages this label brings with it. It brings to many people from outside of course an inaccurate picture because they don't have an idea what Montessori pedagogy is.... The most important category for our teaching and learning is individualised learning in the current jargon. That's the centre of our work and where it clearly differs to many other schools because there is only little teacher-centred learning. And the label Montessori pedagogy is still the most appropriate one for me, more significant than "reform school." (David, Head Teacher, Hill School)

The head teacher was very aware of the "advantages and disadvantages" the label Montessori brings along. However, he was intentionally sticking to the label and used it to define the school "to the outside as a Montessori school." Speaking of the label Montessori came close to Oelkers' (2016) term *brand Montessori* indicating the ongoing importance of the famous founder for marketing the school. In his search for a more accurate term the head teacher used the term *reform school* but was not happy with that either: The term "Montessori-pedagogy is still the most appropriate one" for him. Some uneasiness with the label Montessori is connected with the problem of adopting a heavily loaded concept.

The Label Montessori Works: Threat of School Closure and the Importance of Parental Support for Securing the Existence of the School

Hill School and Green School were located on the outskirts of towns. Their existence was not guaranteed; they were highly dependent on the towns' interest in keeping several small schools in its hamlets around the city center. The schools operated in what Taylor (2002) referred to as "a local competitive arena" (p. 199) compared to small village schools in more remote areas whose existence was less questioned. Local governments in towns questioned the existence of these suburban so-called village schools more critically. Showing that they are able to attract parents helps these schools to survive (de Boer, 2014). They have to fend for themselves in a competitive climate (Harrison & Busher, 1995) and are dependent on parental support in this fight. The interviews revealed that the fight to secure their existence has been a major issue for the two schools in recent years. David explained it as the main task of being the head of Hill School: "I mean in recent times it has been, of course, the fight for the...existence of the school. That was the most important and most unpleasant task of the last two years."

Sandra, the Hill School teacher stated: "It has not been easy to keep the school open." A few pupils of Green School referred in the interview to the fear of school closure:

> You know, you are happy for the school, that there are children here again, that it won't be closed. I was the only one (from outside the village) who came in Year 1 and... without me they would have not enough Year 1 children and then the school would have been closed! Then, when I was in Year 2, they said again: "There are not enough children. We have to close," the town said. And then I said: "No!" And we started a petition to support it and nearly the whole town has signed and we got it through. (Amelie, Year 4, Green School)

In order to secure the existence of the schools the two head teachers decided to take on more children from outside than they had done in the past. Now Hill School has half and Green School one third of its pupils from outside their hamlets. The head teacher of Hill School explained that they always had a high proportion of special needs children, but due to the fight for survival this "has been intensified in the last years because more external children have been taken to secure the school."

Montessori Schools for Informed Parents With Their Social and Cultural Capitals

The experience, over time, of David and Sandra of Hill School was that the label Montessori was attracting more parents who were looking for more caring schools for their children. Parents had to ask the regional educational authority for permission to send their children outside the designated catchment area. The caring ethos of these schools also provided hope for parents whose children had already failed in other schools, as the head teacher of Hill School explained:

> And that can be a problem that they have very special ideas about, why they bring their child. If the Bach flowers don't help anymore and the kinesiology, then Montessori must help. There is sometimes the situation that parents are looking for the second or third school because it didn't work... and then they come to us. They have the hope that it could work, because here we respond to each child very individually. (David, Head Teacher, Hill School)

The head teacher indicated that this was creating certain divisions between the parents from the village and the incomers from outside:

> Children from outside, who have above average difficulties, in terms of performance or behaviour... that's something the teacher has to cope with but

also the parents of the village have to tolerate it, that there are coming a lot of children who had difficulties somewhere else. (David)

He reported that some parents would say: "I would prefer a smaller school with one class with only the well behaved children from the village." However, the head teacher of Hill School pointed out:

> Our experience is, of course, that we have, in terms of performance and behaviour, also difficult children from the village. But because of the intake from outside we get more than the average of difficult children—it has intensified. But I don't see it as some parents from the village like to see it: "Here is a safe world, there are the difficult children from the town." (David)

The difficulties of the change from a small village school into a school with a special profile as a Montessori school, which attracts a lot of parents from outside, emerged. Although the two schools are still within the state system it seems that these village schools have changed into "semi-private" Montessori schools. They offer an alternative for informed urban parents to use their social and cultural capital (Bourdieu, 1986) to find ways of opting out of the regulated catchment areas while still using the state system for the education of their children, without having to pay fees.

Students' Perspectives: "I'm Really Lucky—I'm in a Small Mountain School"

Group interviews with Year 4 and Year 5 students revealed that some of the children from outside the village were very aware of their luck at being in a small mountain school:

> It's nice here somehow because I live in the town and I always come by bus and then walk a bit. We always run up the forest path and when we are up here and learn, that's just nice to look out of the window and you don't see for example cars driving along. You just see the hill and you know: "I'm in a, I'm just in a mountain school, in a small one.... I'm really lucky!" That's just a great feeling. (Amelie, Year 4, Green School)

Amelie had constructed a rural idyll when she described her mountain school as walking through the forest with no cars driving along. She mobilized the idealized representation of the green tranquil countryside with freedom from traffic problems, compared to her urban environment, and interpreted being in a mountain school as lucky; she was aware of the privilege of being there and not having to go to the designated school in the town where she lived. Recently her classmates Sabrina and Emma changed to Green School from the designated urban primary school. Being asked what they liked in Green School Emma answered: "It's different from other schools." The following dialogue from the group interviews revealed some of the differences the girls identified:

Interviewer: What do you like in Green School?
Emma: It's different than other schools.
Interviewer: What's different here?
Emma: All the children are in one—Year 1, 2, 3, and 4 are in one room.
Amelie: And it's so nice because the school is so old and small and that there are only so few children... and you don't have to think: "Have I seen her already?" You know all children... That's really nice.
Emma: You get along with all of them and you know them all.
Sabrina: I changed 2 years ago to this school and in my former school we had about 200 children or more.
Emma: Yes, 220! We have been in the same class before.
Sabrina: And now there are 20. That is a very big difference. (Green School)

The smallness of the institution provided familiarity for the girls. The following statement from Sabrina revealed that the Montessori pedagogy was a crucial factor in her family's decision to send her to Green School:

> I decided myself to go away from YY (former school). I live in the town and should actually go to that school but it is not Montessori. And my mum was looking for a really long time for one. Then friends of us... their child goes to Green School and... I just had a look at it and then I changed schools. (Sabrina, Year 4, Green School)

Sabrina presented herself as an independent decision maker: "I decided myself to go away." She knew she would have been obliged to go to the urban school where she lived: "But it is not Montessori." This indicates that the label Montessori marked the difference for the family. Sabrina describes her mother as a committed and skilled chooser (Gewirtz, Ball, & Bowe, 1995) who was looking for a really long time for the right school for her daughter. The mother researched the information, and in the end friends recommended Green School. The importance of social and cultural capital (Bourdieu, 1986), in this situation, comes to the fore: being an informed chooser and knowing the right people. The parents who chose Hill School or Green School were able to provide their children with an urban home *and* a rural education (Valentine, 1997).

DISCUSSION: INNOVATIVE SMALL SCHOOLS IN THE MARKETPLACE OF EDUCATION

The research into small rural schools in Austria showed the plurality of those schools and how much they differ according to their location, their number of pupils or staff or if they have to fight for their existence (Raggl, 2015, 2019). Some of the case studies revealed that the small rural primary school can be a place of innovation and inspiration for educators with a vision, who want to change traditional teaching and learning approaches. The two head teachers of Hill School and Green School deliberately transferred to a small rural primary school from larger urban schools because they saw more chances to realize their educational ideas there and gradually altered the small village school into a Montessori school. They found a niche for their pedagogical ideas, and these schools appear as attractive places to work. The small rural Montessori schools are also attractive for certain parents who are looking for an alternative education for their children. Despite clearly regulated catchment areas in Austria, up to half of the pupils attending the two Montessori schools commuted from the town nearby. The children came to the small rural primary school like travellers to the "rural idyll" (Halfacree, 1996). This appears to be a countermovement for those parents who actually move to the countryside because of their children (Bagley & Hillyard, 2015; Raggl, 2019; Smith & Higley, 2012; Walker & Clark, 2010).

The label Montessori with its emphasis on child-centeredness seems to promise individual support and a caring ethos, it also operates as a modus of distinctiveness, in a Bourdieuian sense—and it sells. Being able to attract urban parents was important for the fight against school closure. However, changing a village school into a semiprivate school with a special profile like Montessori also creates certain tensions (e.g., between villagers and "outsiders"), whereas a private Montessori School deliberately chosen by parents is different. When the local village school has changed into a Montessori school those parents who want to send their child to school locally have to agree with the Montessori approach and with the different clientele of the school. The small Montessori school seems to create differences; this raises the question about whether village schools with special profiles like Hill School and Green School serve an exclusive community. The Montessori pedagogy exemplifies an example of the global in the local. The global brand Montessori seems to be, on one hand, a solution for small rural schools that are fighting for their existence and need to increase the numbers of children by attracting parents from outside their villages. On the other hand this global brand seems to take away something of their uniqueness as local village schools. At the same time the often perceived benefits of small rural schools, such as offering more individual attention to each child (Forward, 1988; Raggl, 2015), seem to be exemplified by the Montessori approach.

NOTE

1. The author has been conducting research into small rural schools in the western part of Austria and in Switzerland for the last few years. Prior to this activity she carried out ethnographic fieldwork in inner city primary schools in England. These inner city schools were populated with up to 1,000 pupils in London and the research in very small schools with 10 to 40 pupils, in the mountains of Austria, is a significant contrast. She also taught in primary schools for 4 years before she started an academic career as an educationalist researcher. Amongst her main research interests are rural schools and teaching and learning practices in mixed-age classes.

REFERENCES

Bagley, C., & Hillyard, S. (2015). School choice in an English village: Living, loyalty and leaving. *Ethnography and Education, 10*(3), 278–292.

Bell, A., & Sigsworth, A. (1987). *The small rural primary school*. London, England: The Falmer Press.

Bundesministerium für Bildung [Ministry of Education]. (2018). Retrieved from https://www.bmb.gv.at/schulen/autonomie/cluster/index.html

Bourdieu, P. (1986). The forms of capital. In J. G. Richardson (Ed.), *Handbook of theory and research for the sociology of education* (pp. 241–258). New York, NY: Greenwood Press.

Brehony, K. (2000). Montessori, individual work and individuality in the elementary school classroom. *History of Education, 29*(2), 115–128.

Carle, U., & Metzen, H. (2014). *Wie wirkt Jahrgangsübergreifendes Lernen? Eine wissenschaftliche Expertise* [What are the effects of mixed-age learning? An academic expertise]. Frankfurt, Germany: Grundschulverband.

Coladarci, T. (2007). Improving the yield of rural education research: An editor's swan song. *Journal of Research in Rural Education, 22*(3), 1–9.

de Boer, H. (2014). Das Neue in Schulentwicklungsprozessen kleiner Grundschulen [The new in school development processes of small primary schools]. In M. Göhlich, A. Schröer, & J. Schwarz (Eds.), *Organisation und das Neue* [Organisation and the New] (pp. 103–114). Wiesbaden, Germany: Springer VS.

Forward, B. (1988). *Teaching in the smaller school*. Cambridge, England: Cambridge University Press.

Galton, M., Hargreaves, L., & Comber, C. (1998). Classroom practice and the national curriculum in small rural primary schools. *British Educational Research Journal, 24*(1), 43–61.

Gewirtz, S., Ball, S. J., & Bowe, R. (1995). *Markets, choice and equity in education*. Buckingham, England: Open University Press.

Halfacree, K. H. (1996). Talking about rurality: Social representation of the rural as expressed by residents of six English parishes. *Journal of Rural Studies, 11*(1), 1–20.

Harrison, D. A., & Busher, H. (1995). Small schools, big ideas: Primary education in rural areas. *British Journal of Educational Studies, 43*(4), 384–397.

Kramer, C. (1993). *Die Entwicklung des Standortnetzes von Grundschulen im ländlichen Raum: Vorarlberg und Baden-Württemberg im Vergleich* [The development of the network of primary schools in rural areas: Vorarlberg and Baden-Württemberg in comparison]. Heidelberg, Germany: Geographisches Institut der Universität.

Kroismayr, S. (2015). Entwicklungstrends von Volksschulen in Österreich zwischen 1990 und 2014 unter besonderer Berücksichtigung von Kleinschulen [Development Trends in Austrian Primary Schools between 1990 and 2014 with special recognition of Small Primary Schools]. *SWS-Rundschau, 55*(1), 115–132.

Laging, R. (2010). Altersmischung—eine pädagogische Chance zur Reform der Schule [Age-mix–a pedagogical chance for reforming school]. In R. Laging (Ed.), *Altersgemischtes Lernen in der Schule* [Age-mixed learning in schools] (3rd ed.; pp. 6–29). Baltmannsweiler, Germany: Schneider Hohengehren.

Müller, R., Keller, A., Kerle, U., Raggl, A., & Steiner, E. (Eds.). (2011). *Schule im alpinen Raum* [Schools in alpine regions]. Innsbruck, Austria: StudienVerlag.

Oelkers, J. (2016). Braucht man zur Schulreform Reformpädagogik? [Do you need the reform pedagogy for the innovation of schools?]. In M. Gronert & A. Schraut (Eds.), *Sicht-Weisen der Reformpädagogik* [Perspectives of reform pedagogy] (pp. 151–163). Würzburg, Germany: Ergon.

Peschel, F. (2007). Vom Abteilungsunterricht zum Offenen Unterricht [From parallel teaching to open learning]. In H. de Boer, K. Burk, & F. Heinzel (Eds.), *Lehren und Lernen in jahrgangsgemischten Klassen* [Teaching and learning in mixed-age classes] (pp. 104–114). Frankfurt, Germany: Der Grundschulverband–Arbeitskreis Grundschule e.V.

Poglia, E., & Strittmatter, A. (1983). *Die Situation der Mehrklassenschulen in der Schweiz* [The situation of multi-grade schools in Switzerland]. Genf, Switzerland: Schweizerische Konferenz der kantonalen Erziehungsdirektoren.

Popp, S. (1999). *Der Daltonplan in Theorie und Praxis* [The Daltonplan in theory and practice] (2nd ed.). Innsbruck, Austria: StudienVerlag.

Raggl, A. (2012). Altersgemischtes Lernen in kleinen Schulen im ländlichen Raum [Age-mixed learning in small schools in rural areas]. *Schweizerische Zeitschrift für Bildungswissenschaften, 34*(2), 285–301.

Raggl, A. (2015). Teaching and learning practices in small rural schools in Austria and Switzerland: Opportunities and challenges from teachers' and students' perspectives. *International Journal of Educational Research, 74*, 127–135.

Raggl, A. (2019). Small rural schools in Austria: Potentials and challenges. In H. Hahnke, C. Kramer, & P. Meusburger (Eds.), *Geographies of Schooling. Knowledge and Space* (pp. 251–263). Heidelberg, Germany: Springer.

Raggl, A., Smit, R., & Kerle, U. (Eds.). (2015). *Kleine Schulen im ländlich-alpinen Raum* [Small schools in the rural-alpine area]. FokusBildungSchule Bd. 8. Innsbruck, Austria: StudienVerlag.

Rechnungshof. (2018). *Bericht des Rechnungshofs. Standorte der allgemein bildenden Pflichtschulen in Tirol und Vorarlberg* [Report of the Austrian Court of Audit. Locations of primary and secondary schools in Tyrol and Vorarlberg]. Vienna, Austria: Author.

Ribchester, C., & Edwards, W. J. (1998). Cooperation in the countryside: Small primary school clusters. *Educational Studies, 24*(3), 281–293.

Sigsworth, A., & Solstad, K. J. (2001). *Making small schools work: A handbook for teachers in small rural schools.* Addis Ababa, Ethiopia: UNESCO.

Sigsworth, A., & Solstad, K. J. (Eds.). (2005). *Small rural schools: A small inquiry.* Cornwall, England: Interskola.

Smith, D. P., & Higley, R. (2012). Circuits of education, rural gentrification, and family migration from the global city. *Journal of Rural Studies, 28*(1), 49–55.

Stake, R. E. (1995). *The art of case study research.* London, England: SAGE.

Statistik Austria. (2017). *Bundesanstalt Statistik Österreich.* Vienna, Austria.

Taylor, C. (2002). *Geography of the 'new' education market: Secondary school choice in England and Wales.* Aldershot, England: Ashgate.

Ullrich, H. (2015). Die nachmoderne Dorfschule. Privatschulgründungen in neuen Nischen [The post-modern village school. Private school foundations in new niches]. In M. Kraul (Ed.), *Private Schulen [Private schools]* (pp. 185–201). Wiesbaden, Germany: Springer.

Valentine, G. (1997). A safe place to grow up? Parenting, perceptions of children's safety and the rural idyll. *Journal of Rural Studies, 13*(2), 137–148.

Vulliamy, G., & Webb, R. (1995). The implementation of the national curriculum in small primary schools. *Educational Review, 47*(1), 25–41.

Walker, M., & Clark, G. (2010). Parental choice and the rural primary school: Lifestyle, locality and loyalty. *Journal of Rural Studies, 26*(3), 241–249.

CHAPTER 10

GLOBALIZING THE LOCAL AND LOCALIZING THE GLOBAL

The Role of the ICT in Isolated Mountain and Island Schools in Italy

Giuseppina Cannella
INDIRE, Italy

In Italy, the isolated mountainous and insular areas represent 70% of the land. The issue of isolation affects 1,400 schools and 900,000 Italian students who live in the mountains and on small islands. In spite of the challenges of the physical terrain, it is extremely important to ensure equal opportunities and services to all, as education is a guaranteed social service. INDIRE (the National Institute for the Documentation, Innovation, and Educational Research) has been observing the teaching practices in some small, isolated mountain and island schools, with the aim of discovering what impact reduced student populations have on the quality of education (http://www.indire.it/area-di-ricerca/miglioramento/).

The National Institute for the Documentation, Innovation, and Educational Research is the Italian Ministry of Education's oldest research organization; it is a public body, scientifically independent, and enjoys statutory, organizational, regulatory, administrative, financial, accounting, and patrimonial autonomy. Since its foundation in 1925, the Institute has worked closely with the Italian school system, investing in training and innovation while supporting processes for improvement in schools and is the benchmark for educational research in Italy. It develops new teaching models, tries out new technology for training courses, fosters innovation in learning and teaching, and has been a leading player in some of the most important e-learning experiences in Europe (http://www.indire.it/en/home/about-us/).

For the last 10 years INDIRE has been investigating distance education strategies, in particular where teaching activities integrate ICT (information and communication technology) into classroom practices as a way to overcome isolation. Information and communication technology can be argued to be an important factor in giving students the opportunity to widen their horizons. However, it is also clear that teaching activities need to be redesigned to accommodate the use of ICT (Biondi, 2007). The process of designing activities for learning with technology in isolated schools means, metaphorically, breaking down the walls of classrooms and transforming geographical isolation into opportunities for whole communities (Cerri, 2010).

Before examining the focus of INDIRE's research, it is important to point out some aspects of the Italian educational background. Children's education is compulsory for the 10 years between the ages of 6 and 16, consisting of 5 years of primary, 3 years of lower secondary, and the first 2 years of upper secondary schooling. After completion of the first 8 years, the final 2 years (from 14 to 16 years of age) can be undertaken at a state upper secondary school (*liceo*, technical institute, or vocational institute), or on a 3 or 4 year vocational education and training course that is within regional jurisdiction. (In Italy secondary education is managed by its regions.) In addition, everyone has a right and a duty (*diritto/dovere*) to receive and pursue education and training for at least 12 years within the education system, or until they have obtained a 3-year vocational qualification by the age of 18. Finally, 15-year-olds can also spend the last year of compulsory education in an apprenticeship, facilitated by a specific arrangement between the regions, the Ministry of Labor, the Ministry of Education, and the trades unions.

There is neither specific legislation nor are there exceptions for those small schools that are based on islands and in mountain areas, although the Italian Ministry of Education has neither an exact definition for nor a database of them. Moreover, there is a centralized policy for the financing of schools based on the *formula funding method* (Eurydice, 2014, p. 25) that sets the number of resources for which each school is eligible, whilst not accounting for the schools' localities.

SETTING THE CONTEXT

Definition of Rural Areas and Schools in Italy

Italy, as well as lacking a definition of small schools, has no clear definition of rural areas either. The term *rural* (widely used at a European level—see Hargreaves, 2009 for a discussion) in Italy generally refers to regions that are mainly devoted to farming activities, to small or offshore islands, and to the inner areas of the country. These regions account for 70% of the Italian land area. The latest data from the Ministry of Education (2017/2018) show that Italy has 1,641 schools in the mountains (with 1,096 of these being in the Lombardia region), and 44 schools on small islands, with a combined total of 900,000 students, so that nearly 4% of all Italian schools are in geographically isolated areas.

Italy's offshore islands experience further difficulties because of being cut off by the sea. There are 36 small island municipalities, each of which offers educational amenities, and here the majority of schools have nongraded, multiage classrooms (in Alicudi, Filicudi, Panarea, Stromboli, Vulcano, Marettimo, Salina, Linosa, Giglio, and Favignana). The largest islands also have separate schools that cover the first 2 years of secondary education (in Lipari, Lampedusa, Ustica, and Pantelleria).

Data produced by the Ministry of Education show those Italian regions that have faced classroom closures during the past 5 years: these include the regions of Molise (a decline of 37%), Lazio (a decline of 25%), Calabria (a decline of 24%), and Campania (a decline of 24%). The closure of schools on small islands shows a decline of 5% over the past 5 years. The Ministry of Education data (for the 2017/2018 school year) for small schools in the mountains and on the small islands shows a student dropout rate of 25% when students transfer to high school.

Education Policy Context in Italy

Before 1923, the Casati Law, passed in 1859, when the country was being unified, governed education in Italy. This law had introduced the term *rural school*, classifying schools as being from either rural or urban areas. The purpose of rural schools during this period was to make as much of the population as possible literate, especially young boys, so that they could serve the Fascist Government (Casiello, n.d). The rural schools had specific characteristics, which gave people a negative view of them. The Casati Law, however, failed to deal with the schooling situation and did not resolve the illiteracy issues that still continued to distress Italian rural areas at the beginning of the 20th century. In spite of the removal in 1942 of the policy that had distinguished between rural and urban schools, rural schools continued to suffer from this reputation of negative disparity, even though the situation had improved in terms of school quality and teachers' salaries (Milani, 1967). The undervaluing of Italian rural schools may well be linked to a more general judgment about rural society that "ends up in disadvantage" (Corbett, 2010).

The Central Government and the Ministry of Education have recently developed a new national Education Strategy, *La Buona Scola* (The Good School Law 107/2015), which has been adapted through the "Italian Inner Areas Strategy" to pay special attention to the interior of the country. The Ministry of Education guidance, *La Buona Scuola per le Aree Interne* (The Good School for the Internal Area), specifically focuses on the needs of rural schools (http://old2018.agenziacoesione.gov.it/it/arint/).

This strategy is based on multilevel governance involving different institutions and agencies working in close contact with local authorities. The main aim is the reorganisation of schooling around [achieving] good balance between [for example] main poles (by which is meant population centres); avoiding excessive teacher mobility and ensuring school networking (http://old2018.agenziacoesione.gov.it/it/arint/). Particular attention is given to teachers, allowing each school to enroll extra staff (according to specific criteria that are included in the school reform) to increase their provision of education. Other actions to overcome isolation listed in the guidance include the opening of the school to extracurricular activities, the development of the technological infrastructure towards the use of ICT for learning activities, and the documentation and dissemination of the best practices within and between the small schools of the area. Also implicit in the strategy is school network consolidation.

Research Literature Context

Internationally, there are several different perspectives on research concerning schools in isolated places, for example, the issue of the role of schools in rural communities. The author agrees with Lyson (2005) who proposes that

> schools in rural communities serve as a symbol of community autonomy, community vitality, community integration, personal control, personal and community tradition, and personal and community identity. Schools are places for sports, theatre, music, and other civic activities... The capacity to maintain a school is a continuing indicator of a community's wellbeing. (p. 49)

In both the mountain regions and small islands of Italy, it can be argued that the presence of a school promotes stability for a population (Cross, 1996) and operates as a defence against social vulnerability. There is very little published work on this issue in Italy.

International literature on rural education also considers the relationship between schools and local territories (Corbett & White, 2014), the organizational aspects dealing with school-size policies (OECD, 2014), access to resources and the issues of curricula and pedagogy in multiage classrooms (Anderson & Pavan, 1993; Hyry-Beihammer & Hascher, 2015; Smit & Engeli, 2015). This chapter covers the final area, so far not fully documented, looking at distance learning and multiage classrooms.

In Italy, the literature regarding small rural schools was written primarily in the 1960s (Pruneri, 2014) with not much published in English. More recent research into historical and contemporary education is beginning to emerge (see, e.g., Pruneri [2018] and Loparco [2017] and publications from INDIRE).

ORGANIZATIONAL STRATEGIES AND OPPORTUNITIES FOR SCHOOLS IN ISOLATED AREAS IN ITALY

Politically, two interconnected major issues emerge when considering rural schools: the efficiency problem and the inequality of educational provision. The economic crisis in the Eurozone led international and national institutions such as the Organization for Economic and Cultural Development (OECD), the Italian Ministry of Education and the National Association of Italian Municipalities (ANCI) to promote the consolidation of schools, involving school closures and amalgamations. To reduce school maintenance costs, and, justified by a reduction in the numbers of students enrolling in rural schools (as a result of a fall in the birth rate), central government embraced a policy of consolidation. In Italy, the Ministry of Education suggests organizational measures to face the issues of small numbers of students per classroom and promotes the creation of multiage classrooms as one of the main features in rural isolated schools.

A similar approach to the reduction in school capacity has been proposed by recent analysis and policy advice from the OECD. In the OECD School Resources Review, (OECD, 2014) there is guidance on how to distribute, utilize, and manage education resources effectively and efficiently. One of the OECD studies (2016) deals with school size and its impact on school quality, and argues, in a broad sense, that there is no "one-size-fits-all" solution (p. 43). Although consolidation may improve school quality and efficiency in some contexts, it could be unfeasible in others, due to their geographical isolation, as is the case on offshore islands. In these cases, where physical interaction with other schools is not viable, the use of ICT to provide opportunities to innovate teaching activities in order to overcome isolation is being considered (see Bertolini, Pisano, Sivini, & Scaramuzzi, 2008).

An additional issue for geographically isolated small schools in Italy is high staff turnover; many teachers choose to stay for no more than 1 year. Poor transport connections, particularly during the winter, lead many families to move to the mainland or to a city.

Non-Gradedness in Classrooms and Schools

Another feature of life in the isolated schools is the grouping of students into "non-graded classrooms," meaning that "a team of teachers generally works with a team of students who are of different ages" (Pavan, 1992). In this scenario, to have nongraded or multiage classes is a way of managing the low numbers of students enrolled. Parents, however, perceive this situation as unsatisfactory, because it represents for them a low quality of instruction compared with that available in urban schools. Nevertheless, multiage classrooms could offer many opportunities for innovation in teaching practices, such as those involving ICT. One example of this kind of innovation was witnessed by the INDIRE research team on the small island of Marettimo where three students studied for 3 years from a distance with a class based in a lower secondary school on the mainland.

Data from the Ministry of Education show that the number of the multiage classrooms in Italy has decreased by about 10% during the last 5 school years (around 8% in mountain villages and 10% on small islands). International debate in current publications is about whether multiage groupings help to increase children's academic skills; so far, the results of the few available studies are inconsistent (Song, Spradlin, & Plucker, 2009).

According to international research, the benefits (perceived and real) of multiage classrooms include the development of students' social, emotional, and verbal skills, and their self-esteem, enabling them to learn at their own pace, building a caring child-centred and project-based learning environment, and improving student attitudes toward school and school work (Cerri, 2010). These benefits require different approaches to teaching that are child rather than curriculum led. Effective teachers based in small schools with multiage classrooms design their own teaching activities, seeing each child on his/her individual continuum of learning within a whole child context: social, emotional, cognitive, and physical (Lyson, 2005). Thus, teaching in a multiage class does not require a teacher to try to fit the child to a predetermined curriculum, but rather to choose a broad-based one to fit individual needs (Corbett, 2010; Gardner, 2005). Although multiage or multigrade groups are regarded as administrative devices to solve the problems of equality in class sizes, small size classrooms as well as small schools have been shown to have several advantages, such as effective physical learning environments and positive influences on students' learning outcomes. Maxwell's (2006) investigation about classroom size in Tennessee, in the project STAR, reports that great improvements in academic performance occur when a class accommodates between 13 and 17 students, or fewer. She registers improvement in students' attitudes and behavior and in their prosocial attributes, such as personal responsibility and cooperation. Furthermore, small class sizes offer the potential for conversation, interactive activities, and a low level of noise. In general, crowding has negative effects such as cognitive fatigue, which can lead to feelings of stress and may elicit aggressive behavior. A small school can achieve Maxwell's results by making the best use of well laid out physical learning spaces. The important thing is that the classroom arrangement should fit the learning activity.

In a recent study carried out by INDIRE published 2020 (https://piccol escuole.indire.it/quaderni/studi), the data gathered reveal that multiage classrooms present some positive features to contribute towards students' learning processes. When interviewed, teachers confirmed that in many cases it is possible to design personalized activities, to involve older students as tutors of the younger ones, and to let all the students take part in their school's daily life. At the same time, some of the respondent teachers referred to their practice of dividing the students of a multiage classroom into groups of the same age in order to organize the curriculum activities. This probably indicates that they do not yet recognize all the innovative opportunities that a multiage classroom can offer (Biondi, Borrie, & Tosi, 2017).

THE NATIONAL INSTITUTE FOR THE DOCUMENTATION, INNOVATION, AND EDUCATIONAL RESEARCH STUDY IN MOUNTAIN AND ISLAND SCHOOLS: RESEARCH APPROACH AND PRELIMINARY RESULTS

One of the dimensions of this study was looking at ways to open the classroom by connecting it to others using twinning activities or videoconferencing. A strategy examined was the use of ICT. The National Institute for the Documentation, Innovation, and Educational Research set up investigations in three networks of small schools: Egadi island network (a small archipelago in the Mediterranean Sea), the Sbilf network (some small schools based in the northeast of Italy near Udine), and a network of schools led by Sassello lower secondary school (near Savona, in the Liguria Region). The researchers identified two main models of teaching with the use of ICT in these small rural classrooms: firstly, *a common learning environment*, where two or more classrooms work together on a project in the same subject using different kinds of technological settings, and secondly, the *shared lesson*, based on everyday distance learning activities. For example, two classrooms with students at different levels in different schools use a videoconferencing system on a daily basis to share the same lesson. In these cases technology is essential; teaching cannot take the form of the usual face-to-face lesson.

The research group, composed of six members, used two different research tools: an observation visit and an online questionnaire (Mantovani, 1998). The questionnaire focused around three main topics: the purpose of each network of schools, the teachers' activities, and the school's profile. Each questionnaire was organized into four key dimensions/indicators: teacher activities, the professional development of teachers, the management of small and multiage classrooms, and the documentation of teaching activities. The respondents were 436 teachers, 61% from primary schools, 32% from lower secondary and 3% from secondary schools. (Four percent of the teachers did not complete the questionnaire.) The teachers' responses showed what these kinds of schools face in terms of the turnover in teaching staff, and drew a picture of their experiences. All who were questioned had at least 10 years of professional employment, although they may have only been working in that particular school for 1 year.

The teachers' perceptions of their schools were positive in terms of organization; they described their own qualities (accrediting the different issues they had had to face) as competent and multi-purpose. As for teacher training, it is usual for them to participate in the national training proposed by the central Ministry, although, at the same time, they (62%) prefer peer-training activities that take place in informal ways during the school year, working towards personalization and interdisciplinary activities for a vertical curriculum.

Analysis of the Results of the Study: Seven Dimensions and Four Principles

From the analysis of data collected through the questionnaire seven key dimensions emerged: ICT usage, the turnover of teachers, multiage classrooms, curricula, schools and local areas, schools and local authorities, and the role of the local network. From these findings four principles were developed to inform effective education in nongraded schools: technology infrastructure, school organization, teachers' training, and innovative teaching activities.

These seven dimensions and four principles have been used as the framework to advance training and curriculum development programs for teachers working in isolated schools. In these new developments, the seven key dimensions have been regarded as horizons, because they represent activities for future progress designed to engender and encourage dialogues with national, social, and political stakeholders, in order to modify the administrative conditions of these schools. The four principles have been regarded as "principles of effective non-gradedness" (Pavan, 1992) in distance education, identified by Anderson and Pavan following their extensive studies between 1968 and 1991 (Anderson & Pavan, 1993). The four principles were evident in all the schools of the three networks but showed different ranges of effectiveness. They will be described more fully in the paragraphs below, since they are the foundation for future improvements in organization and teaching activities for distance education.

The Four Principles of Effective Distance Education for Non-Gradedness in Schools

Distance education is intended as a process to focus attention on the use of a computer network in order to present or distribute some educational content and to provide two-way communication so that students may benefit from interaction with other students and teachers (Paulsen, 2003). Distance education that integrates teaching activities into the classroom's daily routines (Thorpe, 1998), gives students the opportunity to meet school friends from different towns; it also offers occasions for further training for their teachers. The role of ICT is to facilitate links between students and teachers working together on projects while based in different classrooms (Parmigiani, 2010). Due to the organization of Italian schools, distance education is only provided as a supplementary activity to the standard curriculum in compulsory schools. The distance education model that is used is one of a collaborative community of learner models (Scardamalia & Bereiter, 1994).

We are reminded that research to date has not shown significant benefits to pupil learning when using technology; for example, Bernard et al. (2004) and Clark (2003) confirm that "technology itself does not produce learning gains, rather it is the pedagogy that matters" (Clark, 2003, p. 84). Higgins, Xiao, and Katsipataki (2012) in their comprehensive review of the evidence again conclude that there is no clear benefit to learning with the use of ICT.

Finger and Trinidad (2002) have identified four levels in the development of ICT usage in schools, describing a preliminary stage, which is defined as a *threshold level* where practitioner teachers neither know about nor are committed to the use of digital technologies in their classrooms. From this stage they progress towards *investigation* where the school and teachers accept the possibilities of such technologies but have reservations about them and are unsure about the impact they could have on their teaching.

The next progression is *application* where there is greater confidence that the technology will contribute to teaching and learning, but where there is still uncertainty regarding the ways in which it might change classroom practices. The final progression is to their ability to use a videoconferencing system as the *critical border*, where significant change takes place. At this level, where the technology is integrated into the teachers' practices, the result is a transformation in which the combined affordances of the IWB, VC, and other connection software act as a catalyst to support all learners and allow enhanced collaboration, extended community engagement, and "new ways of teaching and learning" (Finger & Trinidad, 2002). Observation of activities within the network of schools showed that most teachers use technology with confidence for connecting with other schools in other regions; they could be said to be in the *application* phase. In this INDIRE project, the classroom observations found some positive aspects of ICT usage in schools, provided that the four principles were in place; appropriate technology infrastructure, good school organization, well-trained teachers, and appropriate curriculum content and organization. All these four factors have a central role to play in enhancing the effectiveness of distance education, including in rural schools (Hannum, Irvin, Banks, & Farmer, 2009), and have been addressed in the teacher training program developed as a result of the research.

Technological Infrastructure

A typology of how well schools are equipped in terms of technological devices emerged. For example, 75% of schools have interactive whiteboards (IWB), although these are used in a traditional way. In a number of cases (47%) teachers used ICT for collaborative learning or group work, but only as a supplement to their activity or as part of a lecture.

As far as the technological infrastructure is concerned, all the school buildings were equipped with a dedicated wireless network in order to support the VC system and/or audio/video connections. However, not all schools had IWBs, which are essential if students need to connect in real time with students in another classroom to work on the same task at the same time, as is the case when sharing a lesson (Hunter & Beveridge, 2008; Jonassen & Carr, 2000) The whiteboard can be replaced with an interactive projector and a Skype connection (Lawson, Comber, Gage, Cullum-Hanshaw, & Allen, 2004). As Tong and Trinidad (2005) pointed out in their study of the adoption of innovative pedagogies using technology with teachers and students in Hong Kong, "despite the huge investments and zealous efforts on introducing ICT into education across the world, there are many examples showing traditional curricula, and teaching methods have remained dominant, and as teaching tools, computers are still marginal" (p. 1). Similarly, Italian small schools' teachers who are unfamiliar with these technologies typically lack confidence about using them.

The researchers observed that if schools do not have the technological requirements that support a VC system many will use a virtual learning environment and repository to produce and share collaborative material between students. In these cases the interaction between those in different classrooms is planned through the tasks assigned to the different groups and guided by the use of tools.

School Organization

In order to plan daily activities with other classrooms at a distance it is necessary that participating institutions subscribe to a network agreement. The National Institute for the Documentation, Innovation, and Educational Research is promoting a design for schools and regional governments. This is needed in order to help teachers of both institutions to work as a team using tools and arranging curricular activities.

The network agreement has clear aims to

- improve teachers' digital competences while launching training activities inside the schools belonging to the network;
- design a technological infrastructure that is the same for all the schools within the network;
- design an effective virtual learning environment that enables two classrooms to share knowledge;
- promote the teaching by competence practices; and
- face practical problems that small rural schools often have to solve: the frequent absence of teachers due to high turnover, poor travel connections and weak social interaction with children in same age groups.

All of the above aims have been observed in the network of schools supported by INDIRE during the past 5 years, but individual schools do not always take all the listed opportunities offered by the agreement. More frequently, a network of schools chooses to use the agreement as an administrative tool to enable them to participate in projects held by their local authorities. In some cases, the key person is the School Head who creates a network of relations between the school, local companies (who are providing financial support) or the local administration. In other cases, the person in charge of the network is a teacher appointed by the School Head as the reference contact. In these situations, the agreement is used to design and propose common training sessions for the teachers of the network at the beginning of or during the school year. The aim is to improve teachers' digital and methodological competences and initiate the distance learning and teaching activities.

Innovative Teaching Activity and Curricula

Rural isolated schools have small classrooms and tend to be nongraded so have students of different ages learning together. In small schools only a few teachers are assigned to the school to cover the curriculum. Mother tongue, mathematics, and foreign language teaching are guaranteed while teachers with tutor roles in distance learning cover the other curricular subjects. The main objective is to have a teacher who designs learning activities to work both in his/her presence and at a distance with technology. Therefore, the distance teacher is not just the expert who gives a lesson, but also a guide who leads the students to build connections within their knowledge (Lave & Wenger, 1991). The teacher who is present in the class, in association with the distance tutors, organizes the group of students and gives them tasks to carry out. These tasks include group work and individualized personalized activities within the curriculum. In some of the observed schools (for example in the network based in Liguria) the teacher in the class was using a micro-learning (Hug, 2007) unit for his/her specific context of teaching. This micro unit of learning is defined as a "situated learning episode" (Rivoltella, 2014), a key element of which is the personal experience of the students.

Teachers' Training

The research project pointed out that the issue that has an immediate concrete impact on distance teaching progress is the teachers' training. Teachers need to be able to manage technological tools and to introduce innovative methodological teaching approaches that help students of each class maintain a high level of attention despite the distance from the other classroom and the technological setting.

The National Institute for the Documentation, Innovation, and Educational Research developed a training model for teachers on e-learning methodology that has been used for all including those in isolated schools. The program includes a basic training (first phase) on digital competences, the ability to use online learning environments to share and collaborate, and to produce digital contents to be delivered from cloud storage and other web applications designed to enable students' work to be collected online. The second phase focuses on methodological aspects of teaching. Particular attention is paid to the vocational skills a teacher should acquire, and the epistemological aspect of the subject. Pedagogically, the analysis of educational practice is conducted using the narrative approach, which places great emphasis on the teachers' experiences and epistemic beliefs, involving paper documentation of their teaching activities during training (Day & Laneve, 2011).

DISTANCE EDUCATION FOR ISOLATED SCHOOLS: TWO TEACHING STRATEGIES AND DEVELOPMENTS FOLLOWING THE RESEARCH PROJECT

Most of the schools observed in this research project set up a kind of activity that is described as the Common Learning Environment scenario. Here, two or more classrooms work together on a common project-based lesson using different kinds of technological settings. The link between the physical place (classroom) and the distance classroom is a virtual learning environment that teachers use for collaboration between students, or for sharing digital contents (Hooper & Rieber, 1995). Teachers would create a project through a narrative approach, as a learning story. After its production the teacher would fit the scenario to his/her teaching subject, to the curriculum, to the students' ages and to the social context.

The second kind of scenario is the shared lesson, where two multiage classrooms work together using a videoconferencing system. The pedagogical approach is informed by social constructivism (Lave & Wenger, 1991) with a problem based learning approach and situated learning. In the shared lesson scenario two multiage classrooms composed of small sized groups of students at the same level, usually primary or lower secondary, work together using a videoconferencing system on a daily basis, each group sharing the same lesson with students of another school in a different town. In these cases, the technological infrastructure is essential. In fact, one of the main requirements for a school to set up distance learning activities is to have Wi-Fi and broadband within the school (and this is still a problem for a small minority of schools).

Videoconferencing for schools has been comprehensively explored and researched (Gage, 2003; Gage, Nickson, & Beardon, 2002; Hunter & Beveridge, 2008; Lawson et al., 2004; Passey, Forrest, Hutchinson, Scott, & Williams, 1997), showing how this model could give students, assisted by a tutor or a teacher, the opportunity to experience educational activities while living in rural areas. Passey et al. (1997) piloted other uses of the video to improve student communication in some subjects. The pilots addressed 10–11 year olds and students with disabilities. Finally, a relevant study described students' improvement in communicative competences and motivation (Austin, Abbott, Mulkeen, & Metcalfe, 2003; Comber, Lawson, Gage, Cullum-Hanshaw, & Allen, 2004; Gage, 2003).

In the case of the distance education model of the shared lesson, the researchers observed that it did not allow teachers to proceed at a suitable pace to complete the curriculum because of the constraints of the technological infrastructure, which, for example, reduces time to devote attention to students. To face these difficulties, the teachers' team designed a special curriculum based on the development of skills interrelated with the subjects of the standard school curriculum.

Informed by this research, INDIRE has designed a framework for distance activities that includes both approaches to teaching and the integration of ICT. The framework, designed within the European iTEC project (innovative technologies for engaging classrooms), proposes a methodological toolkit that leads the teacher step-by-step into the design of a lesson to include group work, the use of different kinds of technological devices, and the development of innovative teaching projects that combine different learning activities. The framework has been adapted for the needs of small schools, identifying activities as effective tools and actions to fit different classroom contexts and to include ICT, focusing not only on technologies but on teaching practices as well, to drive innovative educational processes. More information about the iTEC project can be found at http://itec.eun.org/web/guest;jsessionid=682266AD21481FFC5ECE836FB97E2036

A MANIFESTO FOR SMALL SCHOOLS

A principal outcome of INDIRE's research with small and isolated schools, is the publication of a *Manifesto for Small Schools*, or *Manifesto delle Piccole Scuole* (INDIRE, 2018). This concise document recognizes the 77% of Italy that consists of islands, mountains and hills, and expresses the case for "a different paradigm for this educational reality, which puts at the centre the possibility of creating learning environments adapted to the development of inclusive pedagogical and educational objectives." The manifesto is designed to support INDIRE's enduring aim "to guarantee educational quality in every part of its territory" ensuring therefore that "even small schools must be quality schools." Hence, INDIRE's work to "promote the permanence of schools in isolated territories, in order to maintain an educational and cultural presence and to fight the phenomenon of depopulation." It capitalizes, therefore, on the research findings described above, and the often undervalued resources of the schools themselves. These include (a) the social and cognitive benefits of collaborative learning in multiage classes, implemented by teachers trained to adapt their practices to optimize this approach and (b) the historical and cultural hinterland in which these small rural schools are located. The Manifesto portrays these resources in three key points:

- Communities of memory and quality of learning:
    - Small schools traditionally reinforce and preserve their distinctive cultural and historical traits, becoming great communities of memory. Their relationship with the natural, social, and cultural

environment [is] a resource with strong innovative potential, enhancing it in respect of territorial vocations.
  – Small numbers of students [offer an] "advantage" for curricular innovations that allow a more flexible organization.
- Technologies and social inclusion:
  – The experimentation educational activities in collaboration with other scholastic realities of different territories can represent a real opportunity to overcome the limits of isolation and limited size of territories and social environments.
- The experience of pluri-classes, as a resource, not a limitation:
  – The enhancement of differences, learning while respecting rhythms and characteristics of each student, the promotion of flexible organizational methods through forms of peer learning that promote collaboration and inclusion.

The Manifesto was launched at the national Fiera Didacta Italia in Florence in 2018, and its implementation has already attracted people to move into the local area of the small school (Cannella & Chipa, 2019).

CONCLUSION

This chapter has offered a snapshot view of an INDIRE investigation that took place between 2011 and 2016 in the field of rural schooling. The main aim of the research was to identify the conditions of teaching and possible lesson models to overcome isolation. The observation visits and online questionnaires produced some results in terms of the identification of the stakeholders to be involved in the potential innovation processes of the schools and the emergence of the minimum requirements that a small rural school or a network of small schools needs to implement in order to set up distance education activities. Finally, the observation of teaching practices has shown which models of lesson organization can be integrated with ICT. Two models of lessons emerged: the shared lesson and the common learning environment scenario. Both models offered us the opportunity to reflect on the real quality of small rural schools, where their geographical isolation would otherwise limit social interaction between students. Both lesson models offer the students opportunities to practice soft skills and to let other students understand their cultural context, using ICT as a globalization tool. Both models require a high performance of ICT infrastructure and technological competence by teachers, representing a challenge for schools that could otherwise face the annual risk of closure if they do not maintain their reach to the minimum number of enrolled students. The National Institute for the Documentation, Innovation, and Educational

Researchers' experience and observation activities have shown that schools can work with local authorities and with other small rural schools in order to create a national network to include those on mountains and small islands. If a community of schools with similar features can work together, they will be able to offer a rich learning environment to the students living in those isolated parts of the country.

REFERENCES

Anderson, R. H., & Pavan, B. (1993). *Nongradedness.* Lancaster, PA: Technomic.
Austin, R., Abbott, L., Mulkeen, A., & Metcalfe, N. (2003). Dissolving boundaries: Cross-national co-operation through technology in education. *The Curriculum Journal, 14*(1), 55–84.
Bernard, R. M., Abrami, P. C., Lou, Y., Borokhovski, E., Wade, A., & Wozney, L. (2004). How does distance education compare with classroom instruction? A meta-analysis of the empirical literature. *Review of Educational Research, 74*(3), 379–439.
Bertolini, P., Pisano, E., Sivini, S., & Scaramuzzi, S. (2008). *Poverty and social exclusion in rural areas.* Final Report. Annex 1. Country Studies, Italy. European Commission.
Biondi, G. (2007). *La scuola dopo le nuove tecnologie.* Milan, Italy: Apogeo Editore.
Biondi, G., Borrie, S., & Tosi, L. (Eds.). (2017). *From the classroom to the learning environment.* Florence, Italy: INDIRE.
Cannella, G., & Chipa, S. (2019, September). *A small school in rural area: A challenge for the local community.* Presentation in Network 14, European Conference on Educational Research, Hamburg.
Casiello, A. M. (n.d.). *Gli ordinamenti della scuola elementare nella legislazione scolastica del regno d'Italia 1861–1946.* http://www.forumscuolestorichenapoletane.it/app/download/15280519/Casiello+A.M+Gli+ordinamenti+della+scuola+elementare+nelle+legislazione+scolastica+del+regno+d%27Italia.pdf
Cerri, R. (Ed.). (2010). *Quando il territorio fa scuola.* Milan, Italy: FrancoAngeli.
Clark, R. E. (2003). Research on web-based instruction: A half-full glass. In R. Bruning, C. Horn, & L. Pytlikzillig (Eds.), *Web-based learning: What do we know? Where do we go?* (pp. 1–22). Greenwich, CT: Information Age.
Comber, C., Lawson, T., Gage, J., Cullum-Hanshaw, A., & Allen, T. (2004). *Evaluation for the DfES videoconferencing in the classroom project.* Coventry: Becta. Retrieved from https://www.slideshare.net/Videoguy/evaluation-for-the-dfes-video-conferencing-in-the-classroom
Corbett, M. (2010). Wharf talk, home talk, and school talk: The politics of language in a coastal community. In K. A. Schafft & A. Youngblood Jackson (Eds.), *Rural education and community in twenty-first century* (pp. 115–130). Philadelphia, PA: Pennsylvania State University Press.
Corbett, M., & White, S. (2014). Why put the rural in research? In S. White & M. Corbett (Eds.), *Doing educational research in rural settings: Methodological*

issues, international perspectives and practical solutions (pp. 1–4). New York, NY: Routledge.
Cross, M. D. (1996). Service availability and development among Ireland's island communities: The implications for population stability. *Irish Geography, 29*(1), 13–26.
Day, C., & Laneve, C. (2011). *Analysis of educational practices: A comparison of research models.* Brescia, Italy: La Scuola.
Eurydice. (2014). Il finanziamento delle scuole in europa: meccanismi, metodi e criteri nei finanziamenti pubblici [Financing schools in Europe: Mechanisms, methods, and criteria in public funding]. Retrieved from http://eurydice.indire.it/pubblicazioni/il-finanziamento-delle-scuole-in-europa-meccanismi-metodi-e-criteri-nei-finanziamenti-pubblici/
Finger, G., & Trinidad, S. (2002). ICTs for learning: An overview of systemic initiatives in the Australian States and Territories. *Australian Educational Computing, 17*(2), 3–14.
Gage, J. (2003). *Videoconferencing in the mathematics lesson.* Coventry, England: BECTA.
Gage, J., Nickson, M., & Beardon, T. (2002, September). *Can videoconferencing contribute to teaching and learning? The experience of the Motivate Project.* Paper presented at the Annual Conference of the British Educational Research Association, University of Exeter, England. Retrieved from http://www.leeds.ac.uk/educol/documents/00002264.htm
Gardner, H. (2005). *Educazione e sviluppo della mente. Intelligenze multiple e apprendimento.* [Education and Development of the Mind]. Trento, Italy: Erickson.
Hannum, W. H., Irvin, M. J., Banks, J. B., & Farmer, T. W. (2009). Distance education use in rural schools. *Journal of Research in Rural Education, 24*(3), 1–15.
Hargreaves, L. M. (2009). Respect and responsibility: Review of research on small rural schools in England. *International Journal of Educational Research, 48*(2), 117–128.
Higgins, S., Xiao, Z., & Katsipataki, M. (2012). The impact of digital technology on learning: A summary for the Education Endowment Foundation. *Digital Technology Review.* Retrieved from https://pdfs.semanticscholar.org/d26b/b59f2536107b57f242b8289b1eb6f51d8765.pdf
Hooper, S., & Rieber, L. P. (1995). Teaching with technology. In A. C. Ornstein (Ed.), *Teaching: Theory into practice* (pp. 154–170). Needham Heights, MA: Allyn and Bacon.
Hug, T. (2007). *Didactics of microlearning.* New York, NY: Waxmann.
Hunter, J., & Beveridge, S. (2008). Connected classrooms creating learning communities using video conferencing technology and quality teaching. *Scan, 27*(4), 4–7.
Hyry-Beihammer, E. K., & Hascher, T. (2015). Multi-grade teaching practices in Austrian and Finnish primary schools. *International Journal of Educational Research, 74,* 104–113.
INDIRE. (2018). *Manifesto delle Piccole Scuole* [A manifesto for small schools]. Retrieved from http://piccolescuole.indire.it/en/the-movement-what-it-is/the-manifesto/

Jonassen, D., & Carr, C. (2000). Mindtools: Affording multiple knowledge representations for learning. In S. P. Lajoie (Ed.), *Computers as cognitive tools, Volume 2: No more walls* (pp. 165–195). Mahwah, NJ: Earlbaum.
Lave, J., & Wenger, E. (1991). *Situated learning: Legitimate peripheral participation.* Cambridge, England: Cambridge University Press.
Lawson, T., Comber, C., Gage, J. A., Cullum-Hanshaw, A., & Allen, T. (2004). *Videoconferencing: A literature review.* DfES Research Report, UK.
Loparco, F. (2017). Former teachers' and pupils' autobiographical accounts of punishment in Italian rural primary schools during Fascism. *History of Education, 46*(5), 618–630.
Lyson, T. (2005). The importance of school to rural community viability. In M. S. Waters (Ed.), *A mathematics educator's introduction to rural policy issues.* Appalachian Collaborative Center for Learning, Assessment and Instruction in Mathematics (ACCLAIM) Ohio University.
Mantovani, S. (Ed.). (1998). *La ricerca sul campo in educazione: i metodi qualitative.* Milan, Italy: Mondadori Bruno.
Maxwell, L. (2006). Crowding class size and school size. In H. Frumkin, R. Geller, I. L. Rubin, & J. Nodvine (Eds.), *Safe and healthy school environments* (pp. 13–19). Oxford, England: Oxford University Press.
Milani, L. (1967). *Lettera a una professoressa.* Florence, Italy: Libreria Editrice Fiorentina.
OECD. (2014). *School resources review: Education at a glance.* Retrieved from http://www.oecd.org/edu/school/schoolresourcesreviewbackground.htm
OECD. (2016). *Digital asset management.* Retrieved from http://www.keepeek.com/Digital-Asset-Management/oecd/education/school-size-policies_5jxt472ddkjl-en#page1
Parmigiani, D. (2010). *Le comunità di collaborazione tra la classe e la rete.* In R. Cerri (Ed.), *Quando il territorio fa scuola* (pp. 110–146). Milan, Italy: FrancoAngeli.
Passey, D., Forrest, K., Hutchinson, D., Scott, A., & Williams, D. (1997). *Education departments' superhighways initiative (EDSI): Evaluation of group D: Home-school links: Final report.* Coventry, Engalnd: National Council for Educational Technology.
Paulsen, M. (2003). *Introduction to web-based education.* Berlin, Germany: Springer.
Pavan, B. (1992, April). *School effectiveness and nongraded schools.* Paper presented at the Annual Meeting of the American Educational Research Association, San Francisco, CA.
Pruneri, F. (2014). L'aula scolastica tra Otto e Novecento. *Rivista di storia dell'educazione, 1*(1), 63–72.
Pruneri, F. (2018). Pluriclassi, scuole rurali, scuole a ciclo unico dall'Unità d'Italia al 1948. *Diacronie. Studi di Storia Contemporanea, 34*(2), 1–25.
Rivoltella, P. (2014). *Fare didattica con gli EAS.* Brescia, Italy: La Scuola.
Scardamalia, M., & Bereiter, C. (1994). Computer support for knowledge-building communities. *Journal of the Learning Sciences, 3*(3), 265–283.
Smit, R., & Engeli, E. (2015). An empirical model of mixed-age teaching. *International Journal of Educational Research, 74,* 136–144.

Song, R., Spradlin, T. E., & Plucker, J. A. (2009). The advantages and disadvantages of multi-age classrooms in the era of NCLB accountability in education policy. *Education Policy Brief, 7*(1). Available from ERIC database. (ED504569)

Thorpe, R. (1998). The use of personal video conferencing with special needs pupils from three schools serving rural areas: A case of successful adoption of new technology. *Journal of Information Technology for Teacher Education, 7*(3), 395–412.

Tong, K. P., & Trinidad, S. G. (2005). Conditions and constraints of sustainable innovative pedagogical practices using technology. *International Electronic Journal for Leadership in Learning, 9*(3), 1–27.

CHAPTER 11

THE ROLE OF SCHOOL BOARDS AND SCHOOL LEADERSHIP IN SMALL SCHOOLS IN THE NETHERLANDS

Marjolein Deunk
University of Groningen, the Netherlands

Ralf Maslowski
University of Groningen, the Netherlands

Primary schools in rural areas often have to deal with small, declining student populations. This is also the case in a relatively dense country like the Netherlands. The leading opinion within Dutch educational policy is that small schools (schools with fewer than 100 students) are to be avoided because they are costly and because they form a risk for the cognitive and social–emotional development of students. The fear is that educational quality could be at risk due to multigrade classrooms, and to small teaching teams with, consequently, less diversity in skill sets, and with less specialism of teachers. Furthermore, there is a fear that the shortage of same-age, same-sex peers impacts on students' social–emotional development (Education Council, 2013). Empirical international evidence for these alleged risks is limited (Åberg-Bengtsson, 2009; Deunk & Doolaard, 2014), nor is there information on the pivotal number of 100 students per school. However, a small and declining student population does require schools and boards to take action. Based on a Dutch interview study with school principals from 26 small primary schools with fewer than 100 students, and their boards, actions being taken at classroom, school management, and board level have been analyzed, and preconditions for maintaining educational quality are described. The study reveals the key role of the board in supporting the principals in their task to ensure educational quality in small rural schools.

RURAL EDUCATION IN THE NETHERLANDS

In this chapter we will start by providing some background information on the Dutch educational system and explain the meaning of rurality in a small and dense country like the Netherlands—such contextualization is essential since rurality is socially constructed rather than a universal concept (Bæck, 2016). We will continue with a description of Dutch policy initiatives aiming at reducing the number of small schools, which are based on empirically unfounded claims of a negative relationship between school size and educational quality. The specific characteristics of small schools in rural areas in the Netherlands are illustrated by recounting our study on the role of school boards and school principals in governing small schools, within the context of change due to declining student population. We will end the chapter with a recommendation for school boards on how to provide appropriate support to school principals and with an emphasis on the opportunities a context of change due to declining student population may bring.

PRIMARY EDUCATION AND GOVERNANCE

Organization of Primary Education

Dutch primary education caters for children from 4 to 12 years of age. Although compulsory education starts at age 5, practically all parents send their children to primary school at age 4. Students go to secondary schools at age 12, where they are assigned to classrooms based on their general cognitive ability. During the first year or two of secondary education, a mitigated form of tracking may be used, in which students of adjacent educational levels are grouped together in one classroom, but in the higher years, students are grouped based on general cognitive ability. Consequently, secondary classrooms in the Netherlands are more homogeneous than primary classrooms. Children for whom mainstream education is ineffective due to developmental problems or disorders are referred to special primary education. As of August 2014, a law aimed at school inclusion was implemented in order to enroll more children deemed to have special educational needs (SEN) in regular primary schools (*State Journal of the Netherland*s, 2012). The practical application of this policy change has proven to be very complex and is still in development (Ledoux, 2017; Ledoux & Waslander, 2020).

Due to the country's religious diversity, the Dutch education system is characterized by a relatively large share—about two thirds—of privately governed schools. These are based on religious or ideological views and both public and privately governed schools may work with specific pedagogical concepts like Montessori or Dalton. The Dutch constitution alleges that privately governed schools are entitled to be publicly funded on the same terms as publically governed schools. Many of the privately governed primary schools make use of this regulation. School boards receive a lump sum from the government for every school they govern, which consists of three parts: an amount for personnel, an amount for material matters, and an amount for realizing prespecified plans. The maintenance of school buildings should also be paid from the lump sum, but the annexation or construction of a new building is the responsibility of the municipality. With a few exceptions, parents do not have to pay for primary education, at either publicly or privately governed schools, although there is a voluntary parental fee for trips and extras. Furthermore, it is nationally ordained that parents should have access to a school of their preferred denomination within reasonable traveling distance. This has led to a situation where most Dutch villages and settlements have multiple primary schools, one publicly, and one or more privately governed.

Governing of Primary Schools

In the past, municipalities governed the public schools. During the 1990s the maintenance of school buildings and the policies for combating educational disadvantages were devolved to these municipalities. Due to potential conflicts of interest, independent boards were established by them to govern the public schools within their borders. Traditionally private schools were governed by a board of volunteers, consisting of parents or representatives from the church or local community. Although schools can still choose to self-govern by installing a board consisting of the principal and volunteer parents, due to the complexity of national educational regulations, the lack of expertise and spare time of the volunteer parents, as well as the additional workload for the principal (Maslowski, Deunk, van Kuijk, & Bijlsma, 2015), many schools decided to establish or join a professional multi-school board. The number of single school boards therefore gradually dropped, from 566 in 2009 to 434 in 2017 (Primary Education Council, 2010, 2018). Consequently, most Dutch primary schools are now governed by professional multi-school boards. A vast majority of these boards consists of one or two remunerated board members who supervise about 10 to 30 schools (Turkenburg, 2008). The amount of autonomy individual school principals have differs between boards. The positions in multi-school boards are regular job vacancies, meaning they are neither reserved for parents or municipal officials, nor are they limited by a term of office. Parents can influence school policy through the participation council. Staff members who have specific tasks in their portfolios, like educational quality or public relations, often facilitate the members of multi-school boards. Some boards decide to appoint (certain of) their school principals to governing tasks on a part-time basis, in order to close the gap between the board and the work floor and to reduce personnel costs.

The multi-school board system is a form of clustering (Galton & Hargreaves, 1995), which ensures small schools in rural areas, and other schools, have a supportive and supervisory context, and, to a degree, decreased professional isolation. The personnel of a school are employed by the board, and not by the school. As a result, boards can reassign teachers, principals, and other staff to other schools within the board. Because permanent positions are not related to a specific school, boards may decide, for example, to fill a vacancy in an expanding school with supernumerary staff from a school with a declining student population, instead of hiring someone new.

SMALL RURAL SCHOOLS

Defining Smallness

There is no official definition of what constitutes a rural school in the Netherlands; only what constitutes a small school. The Dutch Inspectorate of Education considers primary schools with fewer than 100 students *small* and fewer than 50 students *very small*. The nationally defined minimum number of students in a school depends on the area in which the school is located: in the most rural areas of the Netherlands the minimum is 23, in other areas this minimum is higher—up to 200 students in dense areas. If enrollments are lower than the nationally defined minimum for 3 years in a row, a school loses its public funding, which means in practice the school will be closed. In 2016, the Netherlands had approximately 6,780 primary schools, of which about 16% consisted of 51–100 students and 4% of 50 students or fewer (Duo, 2017). Due to a scaling up policy in the 1990s, most small schools in urban areas closed or merged (Vogels, 2006); as a result, many of the current small and very small schools are located in rural areas.

The Rural Context in the Netherlands

Many rural areas in the Netherlands are experiencing population decrease. This is explained by labor migration to urban areas (Batenburg, Wiegers, Ruizendaal, Verheij, & de Bakker, 2015), and a decrease in school-aged children in particular (Haartsen & van Wissen, 2012), among other reasons. Certain areas even face a decline in school-aged children of 20% to 30% in the period from 2016 to 2024 (Ministry of Education, 2018), despite the increasing numbers of primary school children from immigrant and refugee families in specific rural areas (Huisman, Nicolaas, & Ooijevaar, 2018). Children residing in the Netherlands less than 4 years are mostly Syrian; immigrant children residing in the Netherlands for more than 4 years are mostly Polish, followed by Somalian (Inspectorate of Education, 2018) Thus, even with immigrant and refugee families settling in rural areas, many schools in rural areas have not only to deal with a small student population, but also with a declining population. This problem is intensified by the fact that many villages have both a publically and a privately governed school, each competing for the few students left.

Historically, schools in the Netherlands were located within walking distance of a student's home. In 2003, for example, only 1% of the school-aged children lived 3 kilometers or more from the nearest primary school (Bunschoten, 2008). Consequently, small rural schools are often located relatively close to other (small rural) schools. Within the three northern provinces of Groningen, Friesland, and Drenthe, regions that are dealing with excessive population decline, the closest primary school is, on average, located within 800 to 900 meters of a student's home, and, within a range of 5 kilometers there are 10 to 14 different primary schools to choose from (CBS Statistics Netherlands, 2018, situation 2016). However, as provinces consist of areas with different degrees of urbanization, the availability of primary education is less in some areas. Furthermore, these numbers are skewed because parents do not always send their children to the nearest school. There are no regulated catchment areas that limit the options, so other considerations, like the school's religious identity, may play an important role in school choice.

Rural is a relative and socially constructed concept (Bæck, 2016). The Netherlands is a small country of about 41,500 km^2 (CIA, 2016) and over 17 million people (CBS, 2016), and areas that are considered to be rural are generally well within driving distance of more urbanized areas. Nationally, municipalities with fewer than 1,000 households per square meter are defined as rural (CBS Statistics Netherlands, n.d.). Although the rurality of the Netherlands is thus of a different kind from that of many other countries, and although there are no really remote areas, except perhaps the Wadden Islands, there is still a perceived difference between *urban* and *rural*, and many schools in small settlements in rural areas have specific features and (alleged) problems, related to their small size.

Alleged Negative Features of Small Rural Schools

Generally, in research and policy, small rural schools seem to be viewed as less desirable. Kvalsund and Hargreaves (2009) note that often "the small rural school is judged in terms of how well it overcomes its deficiencies and weaknesses, as defined by the norms of larger urban schools" (p. 141). The main educational concerns about small schools raised by policy makers in the Netherlands and abroad focus on three topics: the difficulty of teaching multigrade classrooms, a shortage of same-age, same-sex peers, and small teaching teams with consequently less variation in expertise. There is a fear that these specific features of small schools negatively influence the cognitive and social–emotional development of children (Education Council, 2013). However, there is a lack of empirical evidence supporting this fear, as will be described further below.

Suggestions that small schools may have specific features that are beneficial, such as increased social cohesion; flexibility and opportunity to be innovative (e.g., Baker & Ambrose, 1985; Inspectorate of Education, 2012a; Nevalainen & Kimonen, 2013; Raggl, 2015; Vulliamy & Webb, 1995; Zoda, Combs, & Slate, 2011) are poorly received in Dutch policy. These specific characteristics of small rural schools can facilitate the inclusion of children with special educational needs (e.g., Deunk, Maslowski, van Kuijk, & Doolaard, 2015; Walker, 2010). Likewise, they could be particularly beneficial for immigrant and refugee students. However, whether this is indeed the case remains unclear. The sparse research available suggests that small rural schools may be dealing with multilingualism and cultural diversity in suboptimal ways (e.g., Ashbaker & Wilder, 2006; Lee & Hawkins, 2015). In Sweden, education for immigrant and refugee children is organized very well (Hajer, Kootstra, & van Popta, 2018); but possible differences between urban and rural schools are not reported. The Dutch inspectorate of education (2018) signals a lack of expertise in regular primary education in general on how to effectively educate the group of immigrant and refugee children, but whether and how these children are approached differently in small rural schools remains unclear.

Although the arguments used for increasing minimum school size focus on educational quality, financial issues seem to play a major role. Smaller schools are relatively more expensive than larger schools because they have similar overhead costs, and teachers teach classes with fewer students. As explained above, all schools are publicly funded, based on numbers of students. Small schools receive an additional amount to compensate for higher costs, causing them to be more expensive for the government (National Government, 2016).

Evidence on the Effects of Small Schools

A difficulty in interpreting research on the effects of small schools, is that the operationalization of "small size" varies widely in different studies, sometimes even up to 500 students (Deunk & Doolaard, 2014). Dutch primary schools consist of, on average, 227 students (Education in Numbers, 2019), so studies that consider schools with over 200 students small are irrelevant in this context.

Several recent international review studies show no convincing evidence for a negative relation between small school size and student performance and social–emotional development (Åberg-Bengtsson, 2009; Deunk & Doolaard, 2014; Luyten, Hendriks, & Scheerens, 2013; Zoda et al., 2011). Nevertheless, in line with the Education Council, the Dutch Inspectorate of Education inferred a causal relationship between school size and educational quality by stating that small schools more often provide poor quality education (Inspectorate of Education, 2012b, 2013), although they admit there is no direct relationship, and there are many small schools with a good or excellent educational quality (Inspectorate of Education, 2012a, 2013). In more recent annual reports by the Inspectorate, small school size is no longer explicitly linked to poor quality (Inspectorate of Education, 2015, 2016, 2017), perhaps because there has been a general decrease in the schools that are considered to deliver poor value, from about 4% in 2011 and 2012 to less than 2% in the more recent years (Inspectorate of Education, 2016, 2017). However, in the latest annual report a causal relationship between small school size and poor quality is insinuated again (Inspectorate of Education, 2018, 2019).

Proposals for Increased Minimum School Size

While many schools in rural areas have become smaller, the Education Council of the Netherlands has proposed an increase in the minimum permitted school size in these areas from 23 to 100 students (Education

Council, 2013), with the argumentation that 100 students per school to be the absolute minimum (Education Council, 2013, p. 28) to ensure educational quality. The Education Council of the Netherlands is an independent advisory body which advises the government, both on request and unsolicited, on educational policy and legislation. Its members are independent professionals whose appointments are based on their expertise and who originate from different sections of society. Although not binding, advice from the Council is considered important.

The proposal for drastically increasing minimum school size has been dismissed for the time being, owing to lack of support from several political parties. Likewise, pressures to reduce or cancel additional financial resources for small schools in rural areas have not been accepted. Furthermore, claims by the Inspectorate of Education about the poor quality of these schools are somewhat mitigated in recent annual reports. Nevertheless, the concerns raised did fuel the discussion about the future of small rural schools in the Netherlands. The Ministry of Education has stimulated school boards to respond to the declining populations of their schools, for example by clustering or merging schools. The Ministry has also implemented some policies aimed specifically at small schools (e.g., Ministry of Education, 2012, 2014). Indeed, professional multi-school boards are now taking action in order to ensure the quality of all their schools and to stay within their budgets for the coming years, especially in anticipation of prospective further population declines (Deunk et al., 2015; Maslowski et al., 2015), a topic which is definitely on the agenda.

A STUDY OF SMALL SCHOOLS IN THE NORTH OF THE NETHERLANDS

Research Aim

Because a considerable proportion of primary schools in the Netherlands are small, and because further decline of the student population is expected, with far-reaching consequences in some rural areas, it is important to enrich the public discourse about education with empirical facts about the features of small schools, the alleged risks related to small size, and the way they ensure educational quality.

To get more insight into the educational quality of small schools in rural areas, we studied and analyzed the characteristics of those in the North of the Netherlands. The data originate from a larger interview study on how school principals and boards ensured educational quality in different—sometimes interrelated—contexts of change; namely, (a) declining student population and small school size, (b) quality issues and improvement trajectories, and (c) strive for excellence and innovation (Deunk et al., 2015; Maslowski et al., 2015). In this chapter, we reproduce and elaborate on the findings regarding small school size described in the Dutch report written by Deunk et al. (2015).

Method and Data

Thirteen school boards in the North of the Netherlands, of which seven are publicly and six privately governed, agreed to take part in the larger study. Each board selected two to four schools that were going through a process of change, or had been through such a process recently. This procedure led to the participation of 40 principals who described leadership practices at 46 schools, 26 of which had 100 students or fewer and were considered to be small. Open-ended interviews lasting 60 to 75 minutes each were used to get a detailed picture of the issues the schools were dealing with in relation to their changing context. Specific topics addressed in the interviews with principals of small schools, aside from how they responded to a small and declining student population, were what ideas they had about minimum school size and multigrade classrooms. The interviewers prepared themselves by reading relevant school policy documents and reports from the Inspectorate. The interviews were transcribed in detail, verified by the respondents, and thematically analyzed.

Findings: Responding to Small School Size

The policy resolution of the Education Council to increase minimum school size to 100 students does not reflect current practice in the field. Three quarters of the boards (nine) set guidelines for the minimum size of their schools, varying from 80 to 50 students per school. Boards report approaching these guidelines thoughtfully and taking the context of the school into account, especially the educational quality of the school and the presence of other schools of the same denomination in the nearby environment. In other words, boards do not close small schools just because they are small.

Nevertheless, small and declining school size is an involuntary context of change and requires a reaction. A decreasing student population as well as a (national) scaling-up policy are threats to the financial situations of schools and force them and their boards to adapt to the changing circumstances. The actions that the Dutch principals and board members describe can be categorized at three levels: the classroom level, the school management level, and the board level. At classroom level, multigrade classrooms or alternative ways of grouping are implemented. At school management level, the role of full-time principals is shifted towards becoming teaching heads or multi-school principals. At board level, possibilities for cooperation or mergers are explored, as well as school closure.

Actions at Classroom Level

Multigrade Classroom

When multigrade classrooms are mentioned as being a risk factor for small schools, what is being described are classrooms with three or more grades. Multigrade classrooms in which two consecutive grades are combined are common in the Netherlands and abroad (Little, 2001), and are not considered particularly difficult or risky, although the Inspectorate of Education observed lower instructional quality and student engagement in multigrade classrooms compared to single grade classrooms (Inspectorate of Education, 2018). Whether a multigrade classroom with three or more grades is created by *choice*, due to pedagogical views, or out of *necessity*, due to a small student population, will be likely to influence people's attitudes towards it. In the context of small schools, multigrade classrooms are always a necessity. This situation induces some small schools (three in total in this study) to adopt pedagogical structures which are based on a wider age range within a classroom, advocated by educationalists like Peter Petersen (1884–1952), or which focus heavily on individualized learning trajectories, using tablets and other digitized methods, thus proactively responding to the need to form classrooms with three or more grades. For effectively teaching multigrade classrooms, parallel teaching, thus trying to run a multigrade classroom with three grades as if it were three single grade classrooms, should be avoided. Approaching the heterogeneity in small, rural multigrade classrooms from more general perspectives on differentiation and inclusive education seems more promising (Smit, Hyry-Beihammer, & Raggl, 2015).

Twenty-six of the interviewed principals discussed the practice of combining three or more grades in one classroom, and their responses were mixed. About one third (nine) thought it was too difficult and, if possible, creating such multigrade classrooms should be avoided. Almost one quarter (six) stated that these classrooms were managed well by their highly qualified staff. The others (11) were doubtful and thought that although it was possible to manage these classrooms well, it was very hard. Respondents emphasized it was important to avoid parallel teaching, because this would result in being pressed for time, a finding also reported by Raggl (2015).

Alternative Ways of Grouping

There are other solutions to a declining student population at classroom level than creating multigrade classrooms, as was also described by

Nevalainen and Kimonen (2013). Nine of the Dutch school principals reported their experiments with alternative ways of grouping within, or even across, schools. Students were, for example, taught in larger groups for some part of the day, in order to free time for instruction in smaller age groups; or a mathematics and reading room was created, in which students of all grades could work independently and be able to ask questions to a subject specialist teacher. Another solution was to combine students from two schools for some periods during the week in order to temporarily create multigrade classrooms of two grades instead of three.

These alternative solutions may require a small-school principal with a certain attitude. Seven of the principals in our study could be characterized as "entrepreneurs," based on the way they talked about their approach to their team, the board, and the Inspectorate. These principals were proactive, negotiated with their boards, and were not afraid to bend the rules. These factors were likely to incite innovative solutions for dealing with small group size.

The Need for High Quality Teachers

Even though two thirds of the respondents considered multigrade classrooms of three or more grades (sort of) doable, and some schools may have had enough entrepreneurship to implement alternative ways of grouping, the key factor was having qualified and experienced personnel. Annual changes in personnel, and annual changes in the organization of classrooms within a school prevented a team tuning in to the specifics of teaching multigrade classes with three or more grades or other types of grouping.

Principals reported a lack of influence on the personnel they can hire or keep, which is a serious threat to educational quality. Teachers are officially employed not by the school but by the board. In a context of declining student populations, the board may assign fewer teaching staff to a school, or may reassign teachers from other schools within the board, and may generally be reluctant to grant permanent positions. These factors make it difficult for the principal to build a stable team. Annual changes in how grades are organized in multigrade classrooms are often unavoidable in small schools where there are declining student populations, but principals stress that they need to have influence over the personnel they can appoint to the different classrooms in order to ensure educational quality.

Actions at School Management Level

Because schools are for a large part financed on the number of students on the school roll, it is too expensive to assign a full time principal to a small school. Most school boards have a policy on how to arrange the management of small schools, and choose either a policy of appointing teaching heads, or a policy of appointing multi-school principals. Although the interviews with the principals revealed large personal differences in preference for being either a teaching head or a multi-school principal, the goodness-of-fit between the principal and the type of job seemed to be taken into account only marginally by the school board.

Teaching Head

In a review of international research on small schools (Deunk & Doolaard, 2014) one third of the selected studies focused on the role of the school principal. In these studies the principal was often a teaching head, who combined leadership with teaching. These studies showed that the combined tasks of a teaching head are considered demanding—although the independence of this role can be experienced as something positive (Raggl, 2015)—and that teaching heads experience a lack of time for educational leadership. This poses a risk for ensuring educational quality, as educational leadership is the key aspect of a principal's job (Leithwood, Harris, & Hopkins, 2008).

Of the participants in our interview study, 11 were teaching heads. Interestingly, the response to this role was mixed. Some teaching heads considered their combined tasks stressful and admitted that their teaching was not optimal due to a lack of preparation time. However, other teaching heads saw teaching as an enrichment. These were the principals that longed for a strong connection with the students and for "getting their sleeves rolled up," as one respondent put it. Some principals reported they even begged their boards to be allowed to teach.

Multi-School Principal

Combining leadership tasks with teaching is not the only solution for principals of small schools. Sixteen of the respondents in the interview study were multi-school principals: they are part-time principals of two, sometimes three schools simultaneously. The additional advantage of this approach is that it facilitates cooperation between the teams of the different schools. Cooperation between schools, and clustering, are often used as ways for small schools to overcome professional isolation and lack of expertise and materials (Deunk & Doolaard, 2014). The Dutch system of boards governing groups of schools is a form of clustering. Within this context, appointing a multi-school principal can lead to well-coordinated, more intense sub-clustering. It is also used as a way to smoothly work towards a merger. However, lack of time for educational leadership was mentioned as a serious drawback.

Furthermore, multi-school principals are by definition not at *their* school all the time, and will consequently have less contact with students, teachers, and parents, which some of the respondents considered a great loss. In order to be able to manage multiple schools, multi-school principals need to distance themselves from the work floor. It is "a completely different job" from being a teaching head, according to one of the respondents, which suits some principals very well, but others not at all.

Actions at Board Level

A third response to declining student population was to link schools, varying from simply sharing a building with another school (two cases in our study), to (working towards) a merger (nine cases), either with a school from the same or from another board. Although the public debate on the justification of small schools centers around arguments of educational quality (e.g., Education Council, 2013) and the social impact of schools on communities (e.g., Egelund & Laustsen, 2006; Walker, 2010), actual decisions to close or merge schools are mainly based on financial arguments. The budgets school boards receive from the government are primarily based on the number of pupils at school. The boards are generally receptive to other arguments than financial ones in their decision to close a school; nevertheless, budgetary constraints frequently force them to take action.

Inter-Board Cooperation

Due to the Dutch constitution that laid down that both privately and publicly governed schools are publicly funded on the same terms, many villages have two small schools. Sometimes municipalities decide that both schools should be housed in one new building, with, for example, a shared sports hall. Especially when this building is a multifunctional community center with facilities like a library and day care, the hope is that the schools will attract more students from surrounding areas and therefore both schools will stay viable. This solution is only possible when the schools have not already become too small.

Due to the small size of the Netherlands, boards may also decide to each close a school in one village and keep a school in a neighboring one, so both run one larger school instead of competing with each other for students. At a school board level, this may be a sensible solution, at a school level however, principals, staff, and parents may feel they are being "sold out." Principals report spending a lot of time on communication with parents and the local community when there are plans to close a school or merge it with another in a neighboring town. This need for intensive communication is even higher when schools of different boards are about to merge.

Special Merger

Publicly and privately governing boards may decide to create one combined school. This is a special kind of merger, which the Ministry of

Education only allows in certain cases, although lately rules have been loosened (Ministry of Education, 2012). Apart from the legal complexities of creating such a combined school at a board level, it is not an easy merger at the school level either. The stories of the respondents who had experience with this situation showed that school identity is a very emotional topic. Parents as well as teachers fear that their religious or secular views will get lost in the merger. When plans for a merger are made sensitive and frequent communication with parents and teachers is required.

Principals report that working groups responsible for the practical preparation phase for a merger have a particular focus on identity, and less on general educational issues. In light of ensuring educational quality however, the principals emphasize it is important to spend enough time on sharing and fine tuning the merger of the curriculum, pedagogical content knowledge, and didactics.

Keeping the Principal in the Loop

The interviews showed that boards varied in how close they keep the concerning school principal informed or involved in the decision-making process. The build up towards a merger may take years, but board members reported preferring to announce the final decision relatively late in order to avoid turmoil and premature enrollment decline.

This puts principals in a difficult position. They know the board is considering a move, merger, or closure, but do not know whether or when this will take place, and therefore have trouble responding to questions and concerns from teachers and parents. When the news of a potential move, merger, or closure spreads, principals are often confronted with an emotional response from the parents and the local community. Boards differ in how much back up they provide to the principal in these cases, for example, by attending an important town meeting. Generally, school principals value the board's keeping them well informed and showing involvement.

DISCUSSION AND CONCLUSION

Due to demographic changes, with decreasing enrollment rates, the position of small rural schools in the Netherlands has regained attention from practitioners and policy makers over the past few years. The policy debate on rural schools is dominated by an implicit, and empirically unfounded, belief that a declining student population will negatively affect the quality of education. Although recently it has been acknowledged that there is no convincing evidence to support a relationship between small schools and low student achievement, the policy still tends to be oriented towards scaling up school sizes. Opponents to the scaling up of schools, often parents and other stakeholders in the local community, argue that the presence of the school contributes to the social cohesion and quality of life in their village, and closure will mean its death. Although there is evidence there is no such causal relation (Barakat, 2015; Egelund & Laustsen, 2006; Slee & Miller, 2015), the fear of losing the village when losing the school leads a debate largely fueled by emotions.

The Relation Between the Multi-School Board and the Principal

Regardless of the lack of empirical evidence on the effects of small school size, small schools do share some vulnerability and are forced to respond to a small and declining student population (Deunk & Doolaard, 2014). Our interview study shows that in all the reactions towards declining student population—at classroom, management, and board level—the board plays a crucial role (Deunk et al., 2015). Decisions at board level influence the staff composition of the school, the job-specifics of the principal, and levels of cooperation with other schools. Multi-school boards take decisions at macro level, which could be efficient, and aim to relieve the principals from task overload. Indeed, principals of self-governing schools that are not part of a multi-school board report difficulties keeping up with governmental rules and regulations, and with conducting tasks related to human resources and administration, in combination with their educational leadership (Maslowski et al., 2015). Transferring some governing tasks to a multi-school board may thus be helpful.

However, it is important that boards maintain a close relationship with principals, and take into account the specifics of individual schools. Boards can support their principals by giving them a voice in the choice of personnel, by helping them to create time for educational leadership, by having an eye for the goodness-of-fit between principal and tasks, and by keeping them well informed on, or involved in, decisions on cooperation or mergers.

Because multi-school boards take into account all the schools under their authority when making decisions, the specifics of individual schools are in danger of being overlooked. Principals indicate that they are in need of board decisions that are tailored to their schools—either by appointing teachers who have the competencies to deal with multigrade classes, or by using innovative schooling arrangements. Boards, however, are not always sensitive to these needs, or not inclined to provide certain facilities to small schools in rural areas. Consequently, the risks these schools face, instead of being tackled, may result in a self-fulfilling prophecy.

Communication About Mergers or Closures

Declining student population, especially in the absence of prospects of prompt stabilization, may lead boards to plan closing or merging schools. These processes usually take years before a final decision is taken and the process is seldom made transparent to the school team, parents, and other local stakeholders. This is often done deliberately, as the announcement of a closure or merger may cause parents to decide not to enroll their child at the school, which would increase the financial problems, and may create a lot of uncertainty and demotivation among school staff. However, involving the school leader in the process from an early stage onwards might be a better strategy. This could empower the school leader to deal with rumors and questions from the community and personnel more effectively. Furthermore, it could avoid the time pressure to make all the necessary arrangements that announcing a merger or closure at short notice brings.

Opportunities of Student Decline

Population decline requires schools and boards to take action. This creates opportunities as well. Rearranging multigrade classrooms or preparing for mergers is an opportunity for reflection on pedagogy, didactics, and curricula. Furthermore, there are examples of proactive principals who are not afraid to bend some rules and to have a difference of opinion with the board—the principals we called "entrepreneurs" (Deunk et al., 2015)—who have creative solutions for their small schools. These local innovations could inspire other schools, and therefore should be shared within the board, in order to reshape the problem of population decline into an opportunity. The Primary Education Council shares solutions for declining student population as well (De Argumentenfabriek, 2012), but these are inevitably more general and may therefore be of lower applicability.

Postscript

Although the Netherlands is a small country without any really remote areas, there are many rural areas that are suffering from population decline. Small schools in these areas share specific features and are forced to undertake action in response to their size. Rural education in the Netherlands is less about the distance to the next school, but more about dealing with its small size and about the connection with the local community. The fact that rurality is socially constructed implies that rural education is too, which makes international comparisons of rural education challenging

(Bæck, 2016). However, a small student population is a common challenge for many rural schools. Therefore, this study on the role of the boards and principals in maintaining educational quality in Dutch small rural schools may be relevant for small schools in rural areas of other countries as well.

REFERENCES

Åberg-Bengtsson, L. (2009). The smaller the better? A review of research on small rural schools in Sweden. *International Journal of Educational Research, 48*(2), 100–108. https://doi.org/10.1016/j.ijer.2009.02.007

Ashbaker, B. Y., & Wilder, K. K. (2006). Responding to multicultural challenges in rural special education. *Multicultural Learning and Teaching, 1*(1), 31–44. https://doi.org/10.2202/2161-2412.1003

Bæck, U. K. (2016). Rural location and academic success: Remarks on research, contextualisation and methodology. *Scandinavian Journal of Educational Research, 60*(4), 435–448. http://dx.doi.org/10.1080/00313831.2015.1024163

Baker, R., & Ambrose, B. (1985). The small rural school and in-service provision in science. *Research in Rural Education, 3*(1), 31–34.

Barakat, B. (2015). A 'recipe for depopulation'? School closures and local population decline in Saxony. *Population, Space and Place, 21*(8), 735–753. http://doi.org/10.1002/psp.1853

Batenburg, R., Wiegers, T., Ruizendaal, W., Verheij, R., & de Bakker, D. (2015). *De NIVEL Zorgmonitor Krimpgebieden: Resultaten van een quick scan en conceptueel monitorontwerp.* [NIVEL monitor of areas with population decline: Results of a quick scan and conceptual monitoring design]. Utrecht, The Netherlands: NIVEL.

Bunschoten, B. (2008). Hoe ver woon ik van... [How far do I live from...]. *Bevolkingstrends, 2e kwartaal,* 19–22.

CBS Statistics Netherlands. (n.d.). *Definitions: Rural area.* Retrieved from https://www.cbs.nl/en-gb/our-services/methods/definitions?tab=r#id=rural-area

CBS Statistics Netherlands. (2016). *Population counter.* Retrieved from https://www.cbs.nl/en-gb/visualisaties/population-counter

CBS Statistics Netherlands. (2018). *StatLine: Nabijheid voorzieningen; afstand locatie, regionale cijfers* [Proximity facilities, distance location, regional data]. Retrieved from https://opendata.cbs.nl/statline/#/CBS/nl/dataset/80305ned/table?ts=1516697360072

CIA. (2016). *The world factbook: Europe: Netherlands.* Washington, DC: Central Intelligence Agency. Retrieved from https://www.cia.gov/library/publications/the-world-factbook/geos/nl.html

De Argumentenfabriek. (2012). *Denkhulp krimp voor schoolbesturen* [Thinking aid for school boards]. Utrecht, The Netherlands: Primary Education Council.

Deunk, M. I., & Doolaard, S. (2014). *Onderwijs op kleine scholen: Een systematische review naar de effecten van kleine scholen op leerlingen, leerkrachten, de school en de lokale omgeving.* [Education in small schools: A systematic review study on the effects of small schools on students, teachers, the school and the local environment]. Groningen, The Netherlands: GION.

Deunk, M. I., Maslowski, R., van Kuijk, M. F., & Doolaard, S. (2015). *Scholen in verandering* [Schools in change]. Groningen, The Netherlands: GION.

Duo. (2017). 01. *Leerlingen po per onderwijssoort, cluster en leeftijd.* [Students primary education per type of education, cluster and age]. Retrieved from https://duo.nl/open_onderwijsdata/databestanden/po/leerlingen-po/po-totaal/bo-gewicht-leeftijd.jsp

Education Council. (2013). *Grenzen aan kleine scholen: Sterk en pluriform onderwijs in tijden van krimp.* [Boundaries to small schools: Strong and diverse education in an era of population decline]. The Hague, The Netherlands: Education Council.

Education in Numbers. (2019). *Omvang van scholen in het primair onderwijs* [Size of schools in primary education]. Retrieved from https://www.onderwijsincijfers.nl/kengetallen/po/instellingen/omvang-instellingen-po

Egelund, N., & Laustsen, H. (2006). School closure: What are the consequences for the local society? *Scandinavian Journal of Educational Research, 50*(4), 429–439. https://doi.org/10.1080/00313830600823787

Galton, M., & Hargreaves, L. (1995). Clustering: A survival mechanism for rural schools in the United Kingdom. *Journal of Research in Rural Education, 11*(3), 173–181.

Haartsen, T., & van Wissen, L. (2012). Causes and consequences of regional population decline for primary schools. *Tijdschrift Voor Economische En Sociale Geografie, 103*(4), 487–496. https://doi.org/10.1111/j.1467-9663.2012.00736.x

Hajer, M., Kootstra, G. J., & van Popta, M. (2018). *Ruimte en richting in professionalisering voor onderwijs aan nieuwkomers: Een verkenning van opleiding en scholing voor leraren in basis- en voortgezet onderwijs in Vlaanderen en Zweden* [Space and direction in professionalization for education to newcomers: An exploration of education for teachers in primary and secondary schools in Flanders and Sweden]. Utrecht, The Netherlands: Hogeschool Utrecht.

Huisman, C., Nicolaas, H., & Ooijevaar, J. (2018). Demografie [Demographics]. In J. Dagevos, W. Huijnk, M. Maliepaard, & E. Miltenburg (Eds.), *Syriërs in Nederland* [Syrians in the Netherlands] (pp. 39–52). The Hague, The Netherlands: SCP.

Inspectorate of Education. (2012a). *Krimpbestendige onderwijskwaliteit. Regio-onderzoek in Zuid-Nederland naar de gevolgen van krimp* [Decline-proof educational quality: Regional study in the South of the Netherlands on the effects of population decline]. Utrecht, The Netherlands: Inspectorate of Education.

Inspectorate of Education. (2012b). *De staat van het onderwijs* [The state of education]. Onderwijsverslag 2010/2011 [Educational report 2010/2011]. Utrecht, The Netherlands: Inspectorate of Education.

Inspectorate of Education. (2013). *De staat van het onderwijs* [The state of education]. Onderwijsverslag 2011/2012 [Educational report 2011/2012]. Utrecht, The Netherlands: Inspectorate of Education.

Inspectorate of Education. (2015). *De staat van het onderwijs* [The state of education]. Onderwijsverslag 2013/2014 [Educational report 2013/2014]. Utrecht, The Netherlands: Inspectorate of Education.

Inspectorate of Education. (2016). *De Staat van het onderwijs* [The state of education]. Onderwijsverslag 2014/2015 [Educational report 2014/2015]. Utrecht, The Netherlands: Inspectorate of Education.

Inspectorate of Education. (2017). *De Staat van het onderwijs* [The state of education]. Onderwijsverslag 2015/2016 [Educational report 2015/2016]. Utrecht, The Netherlands: Inspectorate of Education.

Inspectorate of Education. (2018). *De Staat van het onderwijs* [The state of education]. Onderwijsverslag 2016/2017 [Educational report 2016/2017]. Utrecht, The Netherlands: Inspectorate of Education.

Inspectorate of Education. (2019). *De Staat van het onderwijs* [The state of education]. Onderwijsverslag 2017/2018 [Educational report 2017/2018]. Utrecht, The Netherlands: Inspectorate of Education.

Kvalsund, R., & Hargreaves, L. (2009). Reviews of research in rural schools and their communities: Analytical perspectives and a new agenda. *International Journal of Educational Research, 48*(2), 140–149. https://doi.org/10.1016/j.ijer.2009.02.002

Ledoux, G. (2017). *Stand van zaken, deel 3: Wat betekent passend onderwijs tot nu toe voor leraren en ouders* [State of affairs, part 3: What does inclusive education mean for teachers and parents so far]. Amsterdam, The Netherlands: Kohnstamm Instituut.

Ledoux, G., & Waslander, S. (2020). *Evaluatie passend onderwijs. Eindrapport* [Evaluation inclusive education. Final report]. Amsterdam: Kohnstamm Institute.

Lee, S. J., & Hawkins, M. R. (2015). Policy, context and schooling: The education of English learners in rural new destinations. *Global Education Review, 2*(4), 40–59.

Leithwood, K., Harris, A., & Hopkins, D. (2008). Seven strong claims about successful school leadership. *School Leadership and Management, 28*(1), 27–42. https://doi.org/10.1080/13632430701800060

Little, A. W. (2001). Multigrade teaching: Towards an international research and policy agenda. *International Journal of Educational Development, 21*(6), 481–497. https://doi.org/10.1016/S0738-0593(01)00011-6

Luyten, H., Hendriks, M., & Scheerens, J. (2013). *School size effects revisited*. Enschede, The Netherlands: Twente University.

Maslowski, R., Deunk, M. I., van Kuijk, M. F., & Bijlsma, H. (2015). *Adaptief onderwijsbeleid: een veldstudie onder besturen en scholen in Noord-Nederland naar de mogelijkheden voor het voeren van een adaptief onderwijsbeleid* [Adaptive educational policy: A field study with boards and schools in the North of the Netherlands on the opportunities for pursuing adaptive educational policy]. Groningen, The Netherlands: GION, Rijksuniversiteit Groningen.

Ministry of Education. (2012). *Kamerbrief: Opbrengst project sleutelexperimenten* [Letter to the chambers: Results project key experiments]. The Hague, The Netherlands: Ministry of Education.

Ministry of Education. (2014). *Kamerbrief: Stand van zaken voornemen wijziging regelgeving samenwerkingsscholen* [Letter to the chambers: update prospective adaption regulation mergers of schools with different denominations]. The Hague, the Netherlands: Author.

Ministry of Education. (2018). *Gevolgen leerlingendaling* [Effects declining student population]. Retrieved from https://www.rijksoverheid.nl/onderwerpen/leerlingendaling/gevolgen-leerlingendaling

National Government. (2016). *Besluit bekostiging WPO. Artikel 24 aanvullende bekostiging voor kleine basisscholen* [Decision funding act primary education: Article 24 additional funding for small primary schools]. Retrieved from http://wetten.overheid.nl/BWBR0003862/2016-08-01#HoofdstukIIIa

Nevalainen, R., & Kimonen, E. (2013). The teacher as an implementer of curriculum change: A case-study analysis of small schools in Finland. In E. Kimonen & R. Nevalainen (Eds.), *Transforming teachers' work globally: In search of a better way for schools and their communities* (pp. 111–147). Rotterdam, The Netherlands: Sense.

Primary Education Council. (2010). *Eenpitters. Praktijkervaringen en oplossingen voor knelpunten* [Single school boards: Experiences from the field and solutions for problems]. Utrecht, The Netherlands: Primary Education Council.

Primary Education Council. (2018). *Het primair onderwijs in cijfers* [Primary education in numbers]. Retrieved from https://www.primaironderwijsincijfers.nl/dashboard

Raggl, A. (2015). Teaching and learning in small rural primary schools in Austria and Switzerland: Opportunities and challenges from teachers' and students' perspectives. *International Journal of Educational Research, 74*, 127–135. https://doi.org/10.1016/j.ijer.2015.09.007

Slee, B., & Miller, D. (2015). School closures as a driver of rural decline in Scotland: A problem in pursuit of some evidence? *Scottish Geographical Journal, 131*(2), 78–97. http://dx.doi.org/10.1080/14702541.2014.988288

Smit, R., Hyry-Beihammer, E. K., & Raggl, A. (2015). Teaching and learning in small, rural schools in four European countries: Introduction and synthesis of mixed-/multi-age approaches. *International Journal of Educational Research, 74*, 97–103. https://doi.org/10.1016/j.ijer.2015.04.007

State Journal of the Netherlands. (2012). Wet van 11 oktober 2012 tot wijziging van enkele onderwijswetten in verband met een herziening van de organisatie en financiering van de ondersteuning van leerlingen in het basisonderwijs, speciaal en voortgezet speciaal onderwijs, voortgezet onderwijs en beroepsonderwijs [Law of 11 October 2012 amending some education laws in connection with a revision of the organisation and financing of the support of pupils in primary education, special and secondary special education, secondary education and vocational education]. *State Journal of the Netherlands, 533*. Retrieved from https://zoek.officielebekendmakingen.nl/stb-2012-533.html

Turkenburg, M. (2008). *De school bestuurd: Schoolbesturen over goed bestuur en de maatschappelijke opdracht van de school* [Governance of schools: School boards on good governance and the social function of the school]. The Hague, The Netherlands: SCP.

Vogels, R. (2006). Onderwijs [Education]. In A. Steenbekkers, C. Simon, & V. Veldheer (Eds.), *Thuis op het platteland* [At home in the countryside] (pp. 121–148). The Hague, The Netherlands: SCP.

Vulliamy, G., & Webb, R. (1995). The implementation of the national curriculum in small primary schools. *Educational Review, 47*(1), 25–41. https://doi.org/10.1080/0013191950470103

Walker, M. (2010). Choice, cost and community: The hidden complexities of the rural primary school market. *Educational Management Administration & Leadership, 38*(6), 712–727. https://doi.org/10.1177/1741143210379059

Zoda, P., Combs, J. P., & Slate, J. R. (2011). Elementary school size and student performance: A conceptual analysis. *International Journal of Educational Leadership Preparation, 6*(4), 1–20.

CHAPTER 12

INCLUSIVE AND COLLABORATIVE SCHOOL NETWORK PLANNING IN FINLAND

A Critical Process for Rural Schools

Sami Tantarimäki
University of Turku, Finland

Anni Törhönen
University of Turku, Finland

This chapter looks at the schooling and school system in Finland, focusing on the present state of the school network and its planning, and the challenges of future planning, based on a series of school network studies. Developments in school network planning have critical significance for small rural schools whose futures frequently hang in the balance. Hence this chapter's special relevance for rural educational provision, as Finnish school network planning shifts towards a more democratic and collaborative process.

THE IMPORTANCE OF COLLABORATIVE SCHOOL NETWORK PLANNING

Changes in Finnish school networks have been directed particularly towards small rural schools, threatened, as they have been, after a long period of time, by earlier changes in Finnish society. A declining birth rate, and structural changes in the countryside, including increasing out-migration with urbanization and advances in rural infrastructure, saw school closures beginning in the late 1960s (Autti & Hyry-Beihammer, 2014; Tantarimäki, 2010). By the 2000s, these longer, nationwide "waves" or variables have changed to several smaller, local, and more municipality-led adaptations, sometimes affected by "extra flavors" like chance, simultaneousness, and short-sightedness (Tantarimäki & Törhönen, 2017; see Table 12.1). We shall return to the changes in the 2000s in more detail later in this chapter.

Democratic school network planning is a crucial matter for the future of rural schools. The importance of recognizing local knowledge of place is easily demonstrated by looking back over decades of dispute and hostility in network planning decisions. Without the establishment of openness and participatory or deliberative democratic methods, local place-based needs and know-how cannot be attained and used in the changing situations of the municipal school network. This chapter focuses on an alternative approach involving collaborative planning with local people integral to the development of school networks and the future of small rural schools. This way of working is being adopted in some of the 311 Finnish municipalities, and willingness and readiness for change are found in several others. We shall refer to this process as *collaborative school network planning*. This next section of the chapter will focus on the importance of the place-based know-how and needs in school network discussions and planning in the municipalities from the perspective of regional development. But first, a brief introduction to the rural characteristics of Finland, to schooling in the country, and to the key words in this chapter.

A BRIEF INTRODUCTION TO THE RURAL CHARACTERISTICS OF FINLAND

Finland is one of the most sparsely inhabited and rural countries of the European Union. Rural areas cover 95% of Finland and are home to 29% of the population (Eurostat, 2017; Rural Policy Committee, 2014). The population is concentrated in the southern part of the country (see Figure 12.1).

Finland is divided into 311 municipalities (107 of them have city or town status), which again are divided into 18 regions on the mainland and the autonomous province of the Åland Islands. As Solstad and Granlund show

TABLE 12.1	Waves of School Closure From 1960s to 2000s	
	Key Changes in Society	Effects on the School Network
1960s 1960: 6,939 1965: 6,384 primary schools	Decrease in the birth rate, structural changes of agriculture and countryside, industrialization, urbanization, rural depopulation.	Decrease in the enrollment, mass closings of small countryside schools, building of new schools for the growth centers.
1970s 1969/70: 5,221 primary schools 1975: 4,861 comprehensive schools (primary + secondary)	The new comprehensive school system, concentrating regional politics, rise of economic-political thinking.	Situation slow down towards the end of the decade, individual closings of small countryside schools.
1980s 1980: 4,877 1985: 4,874 comprehensive schools	Time of the economic growth, state subsidy to the small schools, rise of individualism, the decision-making powers of municipalities is increased.	Decade of less change, even though the individualism and independence of schools see their own solutions beginning to be noticed in schools as well as in school network planning.
1990s 1990: 4,869 1995: 4,474 comprehensive schools	Economic recession, savings policy, decision-making powers of the municipalities increased EU membership, public–private–people partnership.	The closing of schools accelerates in a similar way to the beginning of the 1970s, which is again seen primarily in the countryside.
2000–2015 2000: 3,726 2015: 2,397 comprehensive schools 2019: 2,187	The state subsidy for small schools ends, the economic recession is repeated, municipalities debt increases, the renewal of municipality and service structure is carried out, the popularity of big school units increases, the problem of the poor condition of school buildings increases, the new curriculum of the comprehensive school, province reform, and the reform of public social and a health care services.	The closings of schools continue, the administrative connecting of schools and establishment of bigger units increases, school choices have effect, increasing risks of differentiation and inequality in education are real.

Sources: Autti & Hyry-Beihammer, 2014; Tantarimäki, 2010; Tantarimäki & Törhönen, 2016a; Majamaa, 2008; Statistics Finland, 2020; Suomen Tilastollinen Vuosikirja, 1961, 1966, 1971, 1977, 1982, 1987, 1992, 1996

in Chapter 3 of this volume, they vary enormously in size and population (from a good 90 inhabitants in Sottunga, Åland Islands, to over 640,000 in the capital city of Helsinki; Local Finland, 2017a, 2017b; Suomen Kuntaliitto, 2018; Statistics Finland, 2017).

In 2013, Finland completed a new urban–rural classification based on spatial data sets. The classification identifies seven different regional

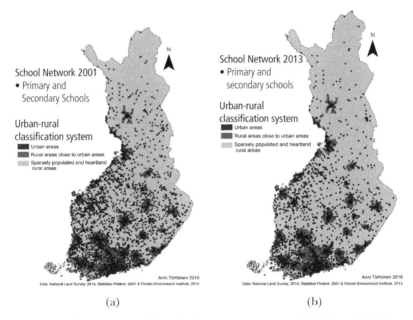

Figure 12.1 Changes to the Finnish school network from 2001(a) to 2013(b).

classes: inner urban areas, outer urban areas, peri-urban areas, local centers in rural areas, rural areas close to urban areas, rural heartland areas, and sparsely populated rural areas (a simplification appears in Figure 12.1). One municipality may consist of several different types of area, as well as featuring country landscapes and ways of rural living, which may vary from one municipality to another (Finland's Environmental Administration, 2017; Rural Policy Committee, 2014).

The vitality of the rural village has also an important role to play. In rural Finland there are over 4,000 villages, of which over 3,000 have registered village development associations. Village development associations are nonprofit, nonpolitical, open to all from the bottom up, and beneficial for the whole community, both socially and economically (Village Action Association of Finland, 2017).

A BRIEF INTRODUCTION TO SCHOOLING IN FINLAND

The essential aim of basic Finnish education is to provide all citizens with equal opportunities regardless of geographic residence or socioeconomic background (Autti & Hyry-Beihammer, 2014). The Basic Education Law regulates principles, and the teaching is guided by the national core curriculum. The Finnish National Agency for Education is the office for developing and providing expertise, with the Ministry of Education and Culture determining the guidelines and strategic definitions of the education policy (Finnish National Agency for Education, 2017a, 2017b).

Basic education caters for all those between the ages of 7 and 16 years; first to attend primary school up to age 12, followed by secondary school. In Finland, a *comprehensive school* means, in the first place, a common nonselective school offering basic education to everybody. In daily usage it is also a term for a bigger school unit that includes the whole school, primary and secondary (Finnish National Agency for Education, 2017a; Ministry of Education and Culture, 2017; Suomen yhtenäiskouluverkosto, 2017). In this chapter a comprehensive school unit describes a particular type of school.

The Swedish and Finnish languages hold equal status under Finnish law, so bilingualism is an essential factor affecting school networks that maintain separate, parallel school systems in some municipalities. A municipality must accommodate bilingualism if at least 8% of the inhabitants speak either Finnish or Swedish, or if the minority consists of at least 3,000 inhabitants. Furthermore, teaching in Sami, a minority language has been supported in Lapland since 2013 (Finlex, 2017).

Municipalities in Finland are obliged to arrange early childhood and basic education. However, ultimately, they can decide how to run their own schools and school networks. Every municipality has an education department, with an elected education board and budget. All education providers receive computational state subsidies (Kupiainen et al., 2009). All children under school age have a subjective right to early childhood education and care (Finnish National Agency for Education, 2017b). These services are organized by the municipality itself, or bought in from other municipalities, federations of municipalities, or from the private sector. Preschool and basic education can be arranged either by the municipality itself, together with other municipalities, or by other organizations who have permission, as defined by the law (Karjalainen et al., 2016).

Key Concepts

Certain words or concepts hold key positions in this chapter, and are defined below.

Antunes and Peeters (2000) define a *School Network* as a set of schools through which education is provided to a given community. In general school discussions, the school network is also referred to as a data network in schools (or between schools). When thinking of the future, an interesting question is how the physical school network and the digital school network (with its virtual environments) will overlap to serve rural needs.

School network planning is a process that gives information about where and when new schools should be built, what their size should be, which schools should be kept open and which closed. A *school network discussion* is understood here as a public discussion about the changes. It is important to note also a "new language" of euphemistic expressions that was used to identify schools at risk, such as "school consolidation" and "program relocation" (Basu, 2007, p. 118), along with terms like "rechecking" or "reorganizing" school networks, instead of "school closure." Additional terms to understand the school system in a wider societal context are "service network" and "service network planning." Service networks cover public sector services in a municipal locality, including school buildings and functions. Public service network planning is carried out by municipalities and is connected to "regional planning" structures and systems.

Unlearning the Old Ways of Doing Things

There has been much research about local reactions to school closures and the effects on their communities (e.g., Egelund & Laustsen, 2007; Haartsen & Wissen, 2012; Izadi, 2015; Kvalsund 2009; Onescu & Giles, 2012; Witten, McCreanor, Kearns, & Ramasubramanian, 2001). Additionally, costs, including unintended and hidden costs, have received some attention (e.g., Svendsen, 2018; Tantarimäki, 2011; Zheteyeva et al., 2017), as have the geographical differences and risks of socioeconomic inequity (e.g., Bernelius & Vaattovaara, 2016; Lee & Lubienski, 2017; Paulgaard, 2016). Instead it is more difficult to find studies showing how the school closure processes can be transformed into collaborative planning processes, beyond those of Andres (2013), Irwin and Seasons (2012), Müller (2008), Basu (2007), and Antunes and Peeters (2000). This collaborative process matters for schools anywhere, but especially in rural areas. In many villages the school can be the last public service that can be used to attract new social capital to the villages. Furthermore, services and functions support each other, and this is more critical in declining areas than in growth areas. One cannot think only in terms of black and white, that the only possibility is to close the service. Instead, it must be possible to discuss redeveloping, revitalizing, and/or reorganizing alternatives too.

The main issue in school network planning is very much the same as in general public service network planning: to satisfy as many people as possible. Understanding of the full potential for stakeholders is challenging for planners. Parties involved in school network discussions (primarily parents, community inhabitants, local authorities, decision-makers, civil servants, teachers, and children) engage with difficult questions, such as what is the optimal time to open or close an education facility (Müller, 2008). In a bigger picture, these are questions of economy as well as of education, and about children and teaching, as well as questions of municipal communality, vitality, and local needs in regional development.

Participatory or collaborative planning has developed since the launching of public–private partnership models in the EU in the 1990s, and the later public–private–people partnership models (e.g., Healey, 1999; Majamaa, 2008). Naturally, numerous other democracy models have been developed, as well as more strategic terms, such as "big society," "participatory budgeting," or "public participation spectrum" (International Association for Public Participation, 2018; MacMillan, 2013; Participatory Budgeting Project, 2018). Despite all this, progress and adoption of collaborative planning have been slow. Even less progress has been made in the planning of school networks (Tantarimäki, 2011, 2014), which has focused primarily on reducing them through a system of "threat and crisis." Challenges to school network planning usually arise when a report, plan or draft proposal concerning the schools is first brought for public discussion by municipal authorities (e.g., Tantarimäki, 2010, 2011). This is a critical stage as public participation will be much more crucial to the real-world planning process than school network planning models (Antunes & Peeters, 2000).

The history and frequency of the school closure situations, specifically in Finland, say much more about a series of independent closure projects instead of about evaluated, developed process continua. The formula has been the same even though experience has shown what kind of reactions and questions (e.g., of benefits and/or savings) lie in wait (e.g., Tantarimäki, 2011). Rather than being a learning process, this unsystematic planning, systematic non-planning, closeness, and narrowness has usually caused a counter reaction from the school community, not interaction with them.

Running-in of New Ways of Working

During the last few years, however, there have been positive developments in participative public consultations in Finland's municipalities. The municipality law, introduced in 2015, has naturally had its effect, giving the inhabitants of the municipality and users of the services a right to participate in the operation of the municipality. Participation and influence can be promoted in several ways: by arranging discussions, hearings, inhabitant panels, and other opportunities to participate, by asking inhabitants' opinions before decisions are made, by choosing the representatives of the users for municipality organs (councils), and by supporting inhabitants, organizations, and others to plan spontaneously (Finlex, 2015).

This change can be seen also in Finnish school network planning or discussions of closure situations: methods that include initiatives, complaints, demands for rectification, public writings, addresses or appeals, participation in association activities (such as in parent or village/inhabitant associations) and social media have had an increasing role. Approaching the 2020s, it is very encouraging to see that "doing otherwise" is really possible in municipalities, that planning is more open, and that there are places where far-reaching, instead of short-term, decisions are being made. The City of Oulu offered one example: as a responsible authority, the education department made preparations to set up a web inquiry for the inhabitants. It arranged public panels and council seminars, drew up the preliminary alternatives, evaluated effects on children, anticipated possible effects in general, collected all the material to be displayed on the municipality home pages, and finally presented a report and proposal for the decision-making process (Tantarimäki & Törhönen, 2017, p. 43).

Although progress has been exemplary in some cases, these are in a minority. School network planning in the majority does not yet seem to be influenced by evaluations of earlier school network solutions. The fact is that school network discussions have still continued, more or less, "in an old way," even in forward-looking municipalities (Tantarimäki & Törhönen, 2017, p. 43). There have been similar experiences of using the new methods in Ontario, Canada (Andres, 2013; Basu, 2007). This may show the contradiction between individuality and communality, and especially how challenging the running-in of new ways of working are, and how hard it is to unlearn the old ways of doing things.

All in all, when municipalities consider their future, they can choose what kind of school network they want, and what role the school networks will play. This, of course, requires that there are several schools still left in the municipality. For example, in Finland, there are already 60 municipalities (out of 311) in which only one school operates (Tilastokeskus – Statistics Finland, 2018). What next? That is why the school planning process will become more and more crucial (see Figure 12.2).

Our early studies about the need and structure of inclusive and collaborative school network planning processes reveal the importance of a phased approach with stages like pre-evaluation, introduction, preparation, decision, implementation, and after-evaluation. We will come back to these below, but, generally speaking, the lessons of our research have much in common with the processes introduced in the deliberative mapping approach: plan, monitor, and evaluate; learn and empower; research and analyze; communicate and analyze; and finally facilitate (Participation Research Cluster, 2018). And it should be thus because, after all, the high level aim in municipalities should be to have a cross sectional way to work collaboratively in any possible decision-making situation.

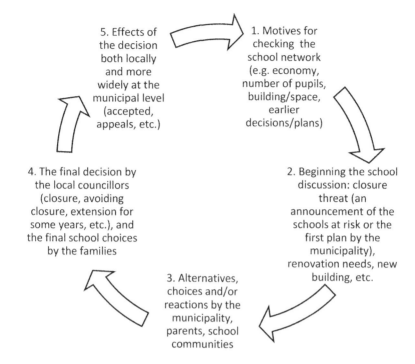

Figure 12.2 Typical phases in the school discussion and the school network planning process. It is described here as a circle because of its (partly self-fulfilling) repetitiveness. *Source:* Based on Tantarimäki, 2014; Tantarimäki & Törhönen, 2017).

Increasing Risks of Differentiation and Inequality in Education and Daily Life

With the structural changes taking place in Finland, there is an increased risk of unequal development. The division of the geography of education into fortunate and unfortunate areas (in a technical sense) could again have an influence on the equity of educational provision (Bernelius & Vaattovaara, 2016; Trade Union of Education, 2016). PISA (Programme for International Student Assessment) results, although they have some faults, already show signs of this growing inequality. Recent results show regional differences bigger than ever before, with metropolitan areas doing better than other areas of Finland. At the national level, the differences between metropolitan schools and countryside schools are small; they are, however, significant (Helsingin Sanomat, 2016; Vettenranta et al., 2016).

In daily life, in these changing situations, pupils and parents are confronted with a series of choices. After a closure announcement parents weigh up whether they should remain loyal to their own nearby school or move on to ensure a place at a school with a seemingly more secure future, or which is otherwise appropriate. It is a question of how well the school alternatives offered by the municipality meet the wishes or reactions of families (Tantarimäki, 2014, pp. 46–47; Witten et al., 2001, p. 311).

Although school choice might be less relevant in rural areas the phenomenon does exist. Research on the operation of school choice in rural Finland identifies distance as the strongest influence, with the other main reasons being threats of closure, teaching quality, and factors to do with fitting in with family life (Tantarimäki, 2014; Tantarimäki & Törhönen, 2016b). These findings correspond to and support the results of other studies. It has also been noticed that essential priorities for choice are school profile, size, the authority responsible, personal connections, children's needs, family needs, transportation, familiarity, and safety (de la Torre et al., 2015; Müller, 2008). According to Müller (2008) school choice leads to two problems for school network planning. Firstly, attractive, popular schools become overcrowded, and secondly, choice is limited to those schools available to students. This is directly linked to, and is a result of, school network planning.

In other words, traditionally, schools have been seen as promoters of vitality in areas helping to make places attractive to live in; the school building itself has been and still is an "actant" (Corbett, Williamson, Gardner, & Nickerson, 2016), an active part of, or an institution in, its community (Kearns, Lewis, McCreanor, & Witten, 2009), but this kind of thinking is no longer shared by all. Abandoning the community-based school as the "heart of the village," thinking changes the way school networks are discussed, planned, offered, and delivered (Tantarimäki, 2014).

This observation supports, and gets support from, Massey's (1994) thoughts on change in "sense of place." According to her, a place may have a character of its own, but it is not a single sense of place that everyone shares. People have multiple identities, and such multiple identities can either be a source of richness or a source of conflict, or both. Change in attitudes towards the "heart of the village" may describe or be symptomatic of this balancing with identities or prioritizations. Massey (1994) also highlighted how a progressive concept of place might be developed. Firstly, place is not static but more like a process. Secondly, boundaries are not necessary for a conceptualization of place itself. Thirdly, as regards the multiple identities mentioned above, places do not have single, unique identities. And fourthly, none of this denies place or the importance of the uniqueness of place. A number of sources from history to social relations, networks of everyday lives, and globalization continually reproduce the specificity of place. And because of the continuous reproduction of place Kearns et al. (2009, p. 131) have stated aptly that "status quo is not an option" for rural schools (or their communities) anymore. According to them it is a paradox of everyday life that schools are often taken-for-granted elements of social infrastructure until they are placed under threat.

In previous (and still, in some cases) school network planning such issues have not really been considered because, most typically, public consultation was used only *after* the decision or the plan had already been made (Basu, 2007, p. 113; Tantarimäki, 2011; Tantarimäki & Törhönen, 2017).

In the following sections three Finnish studies will be presented as key material to illustrate the challenges of, and drivers behind the school network changes. The connection between a municipal school network and service network will be explained, and finally the reality of school network planning in Finland is described.

SERIES OF SCHOOL NETWORK STUDIES

Three studies by Tantarimäki and Törhönen (2016a; 2016b; 2017) were designed to examine the impact of changes resulting from past and future municipal reforms on municipalities and municipal residents (Local Finland, 2017b). The first two studies were part of the ARTTU2 research program (2014–2018) of The Association of Finnish Local and Regional Authorities. This program included 40 target municipalities, selected by location, size, and language relation. The first was an audit of school network changes in Finland in the 2000s. The second examined the mutual relationship between school networks, other public service networks, and everyday life (in a municipality). Both studies focused on the first year of four different council seasons: 2001, 2005, 2009, and 2013 (local councils are elected for 4 years). Both studies used data from Statistics Finland, including publicly available reports, programs, and strategies connected to the school network or service network of the 40 target municipalities. The data were analyzed using GIS software to show changes in school networks in these municipalities, and to identify possible rural–urban differences in network changes (as classified by the Finland's Environmental Administration, 2017).

The third study examined the present state of school network planning in Finland (Tantarimäki & Törhönen, 2017). It focused on school network plans, planners, and planning practices, in all 297 municipalities of Mainland Finland during the council season from 2013 to Spring 2016 and was financed by the Kunnallisalan Kehittämissäätiö (The Foundation for Municipal Development). Data were collected through public media discussions about school networks, along with school network plans, reports, and municipal strategies available publicly online. Three groups of municipality school network planning systems were identified: firstly, municipalities with no public school discussion; secondly, municipalities with public discussion ($N = 172$);

TABLE 12.2 Prompt Phrases Used in the Survey

Preparation = Thoroughness of the preparation of the school network plan.

Participation in the preparation of the plan = Opportunities to participate in the planning process.

Openness = Progress and supply of information during the preparation.

Inhabitant participation = Opportunities for the inhabitants and parents to contribute to preparation of the plan.

Interaction = Opportunities for and ease of communication in the discussion during preparation.

School network alternatives = Opportunities to think about alternative solutions.

Administrative sector cooperation = Cooperation between the sectors responsible for the municipal services.

Municipal cooperation = Cross-border cooperation between municipalities.

New service solutions = Opportunities to discuss a school (building) network as a resource to collect, coordinate, and offer local services.

Evaluation = Evaluation of the school network planning process and decision-making with a view to informing future planning.

After treatment = Taking care of the welfare of the school community(ies) after the final school network plan was agreed.

and thirdly, municipalities that have produced a plan or report during the examination period ($N = 86$ of 172). An online survey was sent to the heads of the education departments, municipality education policy makers, and to representatives of parents in schools in all 20 municipalities that had recently (2015–2016) made some kind of school or service network. Altogether 376 inquiries were sent, with 89 answers obtained (23.6 % response rate), principally from the officials and the parents. Using prompts drawn from earlier research (Tantarimäki, 2010, 2011, 2014; Tantarimäki & Törhönen, 2016a), and public discussions of the schools' network planning (see Table 12.2), the respondents were asked to evaluate the school network planning systems they had used to estimate how successfully the municipality had performed in the latest planning process. The final question asked the respondents to list and prioritize things that would improve the process in the future. These studies' findings underpin the remainder of this chapter.

RESEARCHING CHANGES TO SCHOOLING IN FINLAND

Changes in the School Network in 2000s and Effects on Other Public Service Networks

Changes which took place in the 2000s are characterized by a series of significant individual events described in Table 12.1. The most crucial

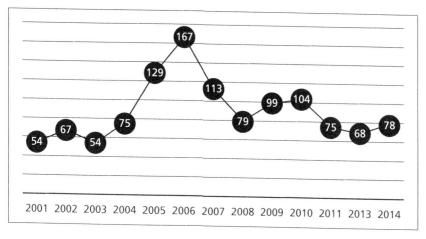

Figure 12.3 "Closure spikes" of the comprehensive schools between years 2001–2014.

phase was experienced when the Finnish state ended additional funding for small schools in 2006. This led to the closing of local schools to solve the financial problems of municipalities (Autti & Hyry-Beihammer, 2014; Tantarimäki & Törhönen, 2016a; see Figure 12.3).

The most recent education reform affecting Finnish schooling includes the new national core curriculum for basic education in 2016 (Finnish National Agency for Education, 2017c). For school networks the next big question would have been the planned reform of regional administration and the reform of public social and health care services. However, this goal, set by the previous government (2015–2019), was not achieved. If it had been realized education services would have been primary functions for municipalities (Ministry of Social Affairs and Health & Ministry of Finance, 2017; Suomen Kuntaliitto, 2017). These new functions, planned as "educational municipalities," did not actually happen, but the "concept" remained in use when describing investment in education.

The changes in Finnish school networks over the last 10 years have been seen primarily as reducing the number of schools and increasing school sizes. The general pattern is a concentration of schools into central and densely populated areas (Figure 12.1). Table 12.3 shows the change in the sizes of schools in Finland during the last decade. The number of elementary schools with fewer than 50 pupils has decreased by over 60% from 1,000 to 364 whilst the number of the larger schools has multiplied (see Table 12.3).

In an urban context the development of bigger comprehensive school units (for ages 7 to 16) has been seen as an alternative, whereas in small rural municipalities this development is viewed in a less positive way, more

TABLE 12.3 The Change in the Size of the Schools in Finland Between 2005–2016 (Statistics Finland 2017)

Size (pupils)	1–19	20–49	50–99	100–299	300–499	500–999	1,000–	Total
2005								
Comprehensive Schools								
Primary school unit (from age 7 to 12)	105	895	579	758	290	33	0	2,660
Secondary school (from age 13 to 16)	0	3	23	204	192	50	0	472
Comprehensive school unit (from age 7 to 16)	4	9	8	71	68	54	1	215
2016								
Comprehensive Schools								
Primary school	30	334	368	614	251	53	1	1,884
Secondary school	0	1	15	109	118	37	0	325
Comprehensive school	8	10	23	124	100	135	7	366

like a last possible choice. The justification for these developments is made on the basis of teaching quality, resources, and economic efficiency.

School networks are linked to wider public service networks in municipalities through the use of the school buildings and mutual relationships. For example, the formation of bigger school units will reduce the size of the school networks, and thus reduce the wider public service networks that use the school buildings for services, facilities, and locally organized activities. However, school consolidations may offer opportunities for new collaborations and combinations of public utilities, with school buildings becoming multipurpose (Tantarimäki & Törhönen, 2016b). Tantarimäki and Törhönen (2016b) also found that 10 of the 40 target municipalities had made school network planning reports part of more comprehensive service reports of municipal services (encompassing day care, early childhood education, child welfare clinics, libraries, youth clubs, and/or upper secondary education). These wider service reviews were done in the bigger municipalities, those with over 50,000 inhabitants.

These observations show that it is possible to explore the connection between services associated more widely with school network planning, and that new collaborations and combinations of public utilities already exist. Besides interesting observations in the research (Tantarimäki & Törhönen, 2016b) were that the synergy between municipalities and citizens that can be found when designing new schools and services, mainly in the cities, is more difficult to develop in rural villages where the services associated with old (village) schools were almost always organized by the local people.

Naturally an "empty table" is easier to fill with possibilities, but possibilities and wishes are included in both situations, and both can be going on at the same time in the same municipality.

In the context of this chapter, the aim of seeking creative alternatives, compositions, and sharing of responsibilities is to promote the continuance of the rural services (Tantarimäki & Törhönen, 2016b). In a wider sense it is a question of combining resources (Lees, Salvesen, & Shay, 2008), decreasing waste of resources (Abrahamsson, 2004, quoted by Andres, 2013), and seeing resources as valuable, renewable, and combinable (Hargreaves, 2007).

FUTURE PLANNING CHALLENGES IN FINLAND

This section looks at the school network discussion, plans, and the planners, and what the future of the planning looks like from the perspective of the key stakeholders of the discussion.

School Network Plans and the Planners in the Finnish Context

School network discussions have taken place in over half (172 of 297) of the mainland municipalities (Figure 12.4). Fifty-two percent of these are based on economic factors, or reasons such as declining pupil numbers and the poor state of school buildings.

Altogether 86 of the 172 municipalities had made a school network plan or report, and from these reports it is possible to identify the kinds of people involved in the school network planning process. While some referred to "external consultants," or "steering groups," others included the composition of their planning teams. These included 51 different job titles or roles, of which 13 were mentioned at least three times, signifying their importance to the process (see Table 12.4). These data show that those responsible for Finnish school network planning are still principally the education managers, including those from the municipal education departments, the local boards of education, head teachers, and (elected) representatives of local councils. Significantly, parents were mentioned only four times as members of a planning team, revealing that the most typical school network planning and preparation is still carried on narrow shoulders.

Closer examination of the reports, municipality by municipality, gives a better idea of the more diverse realities of the planning processes. Sixteen of the 30 planning teams had at least five different stakeholders sharing preparations (such as education departments, local boards of education, heads of municipalities, local government/councils, technical departments, head

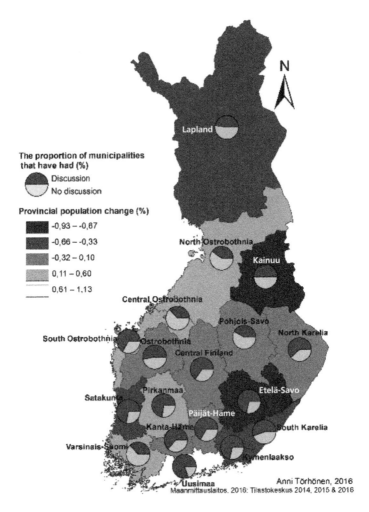

Figure 12.4 The proportion of municipalities of the Provinces of Finland that have/have not had school network discussions during the years 2013–2017.

teachers, early childhood education), while the widest coalition in one municipality included, at some stage, 22 additional parties such as welfare services, teachers, student counseling, catering, youth work, and parents. Only three municipalities (with 12, 13, and 22 parties) had taken on board the idea of wide-ranging, collaborative planning. At the other end, 12 municipalities had only one implementer, generally the head or a member of the municipality educational management. It becomes obvious that nearly 40% of these reports indicate that the responsibility for school network planning lies with one person.

TABLE 12.4 Members of the School Network Planning Teams Named at Least Three Times in the Reports 2013–2017

	Title	# of Mentions
1	Head of Education	25
2	Education Board (formed by the persons elected to a position of trust)	20
3	Representative of the Municipal Council	17
4	Head Teacher of the School	10
5	Education Department	9
6	Management of the Premises	9
7	Management of the Economy	8
8	Representative of the Municipal Government	8
9	Head of the Municipality	7
10	Head of Early Childhood Education	7
11	Head of the Technical Unit	5
12	Parent Association	4
13	Teachers	4
14	Administrative Manager	3
15	Representative of the Staff (no sectors identified)	3
16	Technical and/or Environmental Unit	3
17	Structural Engineer	3
18	Trade Organization	3

What Does This Research Say About Future School Network Planning?

Study 3 included an evaluation of the school network planning process and a consideration of what school network planning might look like in the future. The respondents were generally satisfied with both the preparation and the opportunity to participate in preparing the planning process (see Figure 12.5). New service solutions (such as multipurpose buildings), active participation, and cooperation of stakeholders in the preparation of planning was seen as positive by council members, education board members, officials, and parents. However, there was general dissatisfaction with the municipality cooperation over the evaluation of the planning process, with after-treatment and with inhabitant participation. The numbers of "cannot say" responses may suggest a lack of awareness of these "newer" approaches to planning processes.

In general the parents' associations were the most critical group regarding the realization of participatory school network planning. Their greatest dissatisfaction was often based on that first impression of the process, that the decision to close schools had already been made and everything following was more like a formal, or "one way" information session (Roberts, 2004). Further, work still needs to be done on the role and significance of parents in planning.

With regard to future planning of school network discussions, the respondents were also asked to put the given alternatives in order of importance (see Figure 12.6). Participation in the preparation, and openness, were seen as the most important elements of future school network planning. On the other hand, results shown in the bottom right-hand corner of responses may again suggest a lack of awareness. Inhabitant participation in the process and in preparation was also important, especially in the big municipalities. People in small municipalities saw cooperation between different departments as valuable; interaction with the participants mattered to people in medium-sized municipalities. Participation generally was seen as vital, primarily with regard to local inhabitant participation, but the data also suggest a wider call for better participation by all the different parties in the preparation of school network plans. It has also been noticed elsewhere that even though collaboration is accepted as a common goal, working across institutional boundaries may be challenging (Lees et al., 2008, p. 598). There are "silos" and "barriers" to break.

Based on the research results we draw up one proposal both as a collaborative school network planning model to be adapted, and/or as the opening of the discussion to find the most fluent model to function collaboratively in these tricky situations (see Figure 12.7).

	1	2	3	4	5	6	7	8	9	10	11	12	Average
Preparation	19	10	4	4	14	8	2	4	7	2	6	9	5,48
Participation in the Preparation	9	13	15	17	2	6	4	3	4	7	7	2	5,09
Openness	12	10	15	6	4	7	3	4	5	12	5	6	5,71
Inhabitant Participation	7	9	7	16	8	7	11	9	4	5	2	4	5,58
Interaction	4	10	13	8	17	6	9	10	7	3	1	1	5,34
School Network Alternatives	3	4	4	3	13	20	16	9	6	7	3	1	6,44
Administrative Sector Cooperation	2	6	8	5	5	17	12	9	10	6	5	4	6,67
Municipal Cooperation	3	8	4	3	7	1	8	13	8	11	14	9	7,73
New Service Solutions	8	6	3	11	10	6	12	7	14	6	5	1	6,2
Evaluation	4	2	8	9	3	6	5	9	13	19	8	3	7,38
After-Treatment	3	8	6	3	3	5	5	9	10	10	26	1	7,74
Total	77	86	87	86	88	89	87	86	88	88	82	46	

Figure 12.6 Matters considered important to future school network planning. The most important ones are shown in the upper corner with the less important ones in the lower corner.

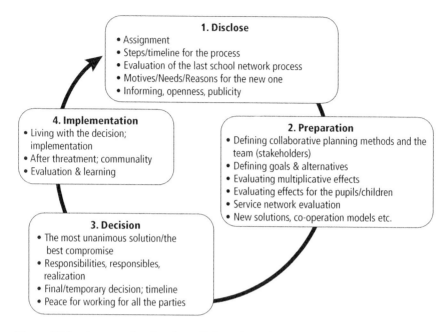

Figure 12.7 A suggestion for the collaborative school network planning model with its central steps and stages.

CONCLUSION

It is no longer sufficient to put the changes in the Finnish school network down to "the big issues" such as a decrease in the birth rate, migration, or the economy. The situation is more complex, more ambiguous. The changes to the school network in Finland are now perhaps more likely to be associated with chance contingencies and an impatience with planning regulations and processes.

It has become important to understand the significance of the multiplicative effects of school changes and closures to local communities and contexts. School network planning is always part of a bigger question about wider municipal service networks, attraction, vitality, and communality in a municipality. Pictured more widely, school network planning is not just about the teaching, the buildings, or the children. It must look to meeting the challenges of equality, differentiation, and specialization in education and in geography.

Changes in society require both the rearrangement of public services and new ways to plan, produce, and organize them; school network planning needs to be part of this discussion. This requires new thinking, new smart and place-based solutions, and new co-working cultures inside individual municipalities, from rural to urban environments, from local to national levels. It also requires learning from the past; the planning process must be a learning process itself, especially when the planning of the schools and teaching is in question; also therefore, a common theme should be found more easily in the wider sense.

REFERENCES

Andres, S. J. (2013). *Connecting school closure and community planning. Understanding the policy and process of accommodation review in Southwest Ontario through a planning lens*. (Master's thesis). University of Waterloo, Canada. Retrieved from https://uwspace.uwaterloo.ca/handle/10012/7458

Antunes, A., & Peeters, D. (2000). A dynamic optimization model for school network planning. *Socio-Economic Planning Sciences, 34*(2), 101–120. Retrieved from http://www.researchgate.net/publication/222695642_A_dynamic_optimization_model_for_school_network_planning

Autti, O., & Hyry-Beihammer, E. K. (2014). School closures in rural Finnish communities. *Journal of Research in Rural Education, 29*(1), 1–17. Retrieved from http://jrre.vmhost.psu.edu/wp-content/uploads/2014/03/29-1.pdf

Basu, R. (2007). Negotiation acts of citizenship in an era of neoliberal reform: The game of school closures. *International Journal of Urban and Regional Research, 31*(1), 109–127. Retrieved from http://onlinelibrary.wiley.com/doi/10.1111/j.1468-2427.2007.00709.x/abstract

Bernelius, V., & Vaattovaara, M. (2016). Choice and segregation in the 'most egalitarian' schools: Cumulative decline in urban schools and neighbourhoods of Helsinki, Finland. *Urban Studies, 53*(15), 3155–3171. Retrieved from http://journals.sagepub.com/doi/abs/10.1177/0042098015621441

Corbett, M., Williamson, J., Gardner, C., & Nickerson, L. (2016, August). *Structural and cultural issues affecting educational access in rural Tasmania*. Presentation in ECER 2016, Schooling in Rural Settings SES 14. Dublin, Ireland.

de la Torre, M., Gordon, M. F., Moore, P., Cowhy, J., Jagesic, S., & Huynh, M. H. (2015). *School closings in Chicago: Understanding families' choices and constraints for new school enrolment*. Consortium on Chicago School Research (CSSR) Research Report, University of Chicago. Retrieved from https://consortium.uchicago.edu/publications/school-closings-chicago-understanding-families-choices-and-constraints-new-school

Egelund, N., & Laustsen, H. (2006). School closure: What are the consequences for the local society? *Scandinavian Journal of Educational Research, 50*(4), 429–439.

Eurostat. (2017). *7 out of 10 city dwellers aged 20 to 64 are employed*. Retrieved from http://ec.europa.eu/eurostat/documents/2995521/7411586/1-30052016-AP-EN.pdf/15823330-b9c3-4813-a8e4-706accc967b3

Finland's Environmental Administration. (2017). *Urban-rural classification*. Retrieved from http://www.ymparisto.fi/en-US/Living_environment_and_planning/

Community_structure/Information_about_the_community_structure/ Urbanrural_classification
Finlex. (2015). *Kuntalaki* [Local Government Act]. Retrieved from https://www.finlex.fi/fi/laki/alkup/2015/20150410
Finlex. (2017). *Kielilaki* [language act 6.6.2003/423]. Retrieved from http://www.finlex.fi/fi/laki/ajantasa/2003/20030423
Finnish National Agency for Education. (2017a). *Basic education.* Retrieved from http://www.oph.fi/english/education_system/basic_education
Finnish National Agency for Education. (2017b). *Early childhood education and care.* Retrieved from http://www.oph.fi/english/education_system/early_childhood_education
Finnish National Agency for Education. (2017c). *The new curricula in a nutshell.* Retrieved from http://www.oph.fi/english/curricula_and_qualifications/basic_education/curricula_2014
Haartsen, T., & Van Wissen, L. (2012). Causes and consequences of regional population decline for primary school. *Tijdschift voor Economische en Sociale Geografie, 103*(4), 487–496.
Hargreaves, A. (2007). Sustainable leadership and development in education: Creating the future, conserving the past. *European Journal of Education, 42*(2), 223–233.
Healey, P. (1999). Institutionalist analysis, communicative planning, and shaping places. *Journal of Planning Education and Research, 19*(2), 111–121. Retrieved from http://journals.sagepub.com/doi/pdf/10.1177/0739456X9901900201
Helsingin Sanomat. (2016). Alueiden eriarvoisuus uhkaa lisääntyä [Regional inequality threatens to increase]. *Helsingin Sanomat* 8.12.2016, Helsinki, Finland.
International Association for Public Participation. (2018). Retrieved from https://www.iap2.org/
Irwin, B., & Seasons, M. (2012). School closure decision making process: Problems and prospects. *Canadian Journal of Urban Research, 21*(2), 45–67.
Izadi, R. (2015). *The impact of school closures on student achievement – evidence from rural Finland.* VATT Working Papers 63, VATT Institute for Economic Research. Retrieved from https://helda.helsinki.fi/handle/10138/153754
Karjalainen, T., Korhonen, K., Kytölä, T., Vikberg, T., Alila, K., & Vuorinen, L. (2016). Kasvatus- ja koulutuspalvelut [Parenting and education services]. *Valtiovarainministeriön julkaisu, 9,* 14–30. Retrieved from http://vm.fi/documents/10623/2326012/Peruspalvelujen+tila+-raportti+2016+osa+2.pdf/9996a87d-0fcf-410d-a8ee-042be89e978c?version=1.0
Kearns, R. A., Lewis, N., McCreanor, T., & Witten, K. (2009). 'Status quo is not an option': Community impacts of school closure in South Taranaki, New Zealand. *Journal of Rural Studies, 25*(1), 131–140.
Kupiainen, S., Hautamäki, J., & Karjalainen, T. (2009). *The Finnish education system and PISA.* Ministry of Education Publications 2009:46. http://julkaisut.valtioneuvosto.fi/discover
Kvalsund, R. (2009). Centralized decentralization or decentralized centralization? A review of newer Norwegian research on schools and their communities. *International of Educational Research, 48*(2), 89–99.

Lee, J., & Lubienski, C. (2017). The impact of school closures on equity of access in Chicago. *Education and Urban Society, 49*(1), 53–80. Retrieved from http://journals.sagepub.com/doi/pdf/10.1177/0013124516630601

Lees, E., Salvesen, D., & Shay, E. (2008). Collaborative school planning and active school: A case study of Lee County, Florida. *Journal of Health Politics, Policy and Law, 33*(3), 595–615. Retrieved from http://jhppl.dukejournals.org/content/33/3/595.abstract

Local Finland. (2017a). *Finnish municipalities and regions.* Retrieved from https://www.localfinland.fi/expert-services/finnish-municipalities-and-regions-0

Local Finland. (2017b). *ARTTU2 research programme.* Retrieved from https://www.localfinland.fi/arttu2-research-programme

MacMillan, R. (2013). *Making sense of the big society: Perspectives from the third sector.* Retrieved from http://epapers.bham.ac.uk/1787/

Majamaa, W. (2008). *The 4th P–people–in urban development based on public-private-people partnership.* TKK Structural Engineering and Building Technology Dissertations: 2 TKK-R-VK2. Espoo 2008. Helsinki University of Technology, Helsinki, Finland.

Massey, D. (1994) A global sense of place. In *Space, place, and gender* (pp. 146–157). Minneapolis: University of Minnesota Press.

Ministry of Education and Culture. (2017). *Basic education.* Retrieved from http://minedu.fi/en/basic-education

Ministry of Social Affairs and Health & Ministry of Finance. (2017). *Health, social services and regional government reform to enter into force on 1 January 2020.* Retrieved from http://alueuudistus.fi/en/frontpage

Müller, S. (2008). *Dynamic school network planning in urban areas: A multi-period, cost-minimizing location planning approach with respect to flexible substitution patterns of facilities.* Berlin, Germany: LIT Verlag Münster.

Onescu, J., & Giles, A. R. (2012). Changing relationships: The impacts of a school's closure on rural families. *Leisure/Loisir, 36*(2), 107–126.

Participation Research Cluster. (2018). *Participation methods.* Retrieved from http://www.participatorymethods.org/aggregator/sources/1

Participatory Budgeting Project. (2018). *Participatory budgeting project.* Retrieved from https://www.participatorybudgeting.org/

Paulgaard, C. (2016). Geographies of inequalities in an area of opportunities: Ambiguous experiences among young men in the Norwegian High North. *Geographical Research, 55*(1), 38–46. Retrieved from https://onlinelibrary.wiley.com/doi/pdf/10.1111/1745-5871.12198

Roberts, N. (2004). Public deliberation in an age of direct citizen participation. *The American Review of Public Administration, 34*(4), 315–353. Retrieved from https://hubert.hhh.umn.edu/Stuck/Asset5PublicDeliberationInAgeOfDirectCitizenParticipation.pdf

Rural Policy Committee. (2014). *Finnish rural policy in a nutshell.* Rural Policy Committee, Ministry of Economic Affairs and Employment. Retrieved from https://tem.fi/documents/1410877/2937056/Finnish+Rural+Policy+in+a+Nutshell

Statistics Finland. (2017). *Statistical grouping of municipalities 2015.* Retrieved from http://www.stat.fi/meta/luokitukset/kuntaryhmitys/001-2015/index_en.html

Statistics Finland. (2020). *Peruskoulujen määrä jatkoi laskuaan, oppilaitokset aiempaa isompia* [The number of primary schools continued to decline, schools larger than before]. Retrieved from http://www.tilastokeskus.fi/til/kjarj/2019/kjarj_2019_2020-02-12_tie_001_fi.html

Suomen Kuntaliitto. (2017). *Tulevaisuuden kunta* [The the municipality of the future]. Retrieved from https://www.kuntaliitto.fi/julkaisut/2017/1812-tulevaisuuden-kunta-acta-nro-264

Suomen Kuntaliitto. (2018). *Kaupunkien ja kuntien lukumäärät* [Number of cities and municipalities]. Retrieved from https://www.kuntaliitto.fi/tilastot-ja-julkaisut/kaupunkien-ja-kuntien-lukumaarat-ja-vaestotiedot

Suomen yhteinäiskouluverkosto [Finnish comprehensive school network]. (2017). Retrieved from http://www.t-tiimi.com/syve/historiaa.htm

Svendsen, G. (2018). The consequences of closures of small primary, public schools in rural areas: The problem of 'hidden costs'. *Keynote Speech, Nordic Conference for Rural Research*, 14.-16.5.2018, Vingsted, Denmark.

Tantarimäki, S. (2010). Kouluverkkosuunnittelun haasteet [Challenges of school network planning]. *Maaseudun Uusi Aika, 2*(18), 32–43.

Tantarimäki, S. (2011). *Mitä lakkautuksesta opimme? Kyläkoulun lakkauttamisen perusteet, prosessi, säästöt ja vaikutukset viimeaikaisessa keskustelussa* [What do we learn from closures? Criteria, process, savings and effects of village school closure]. Turun yliopiston koulutus- ja kehittämiskeskus Brahean julkaisuja B:2 [Publications of the Training and Development Center Brahea at the University of Turku B:2]. Turku, Finland.

Tantarimäki, S. (2014). Kyläkoulukeskustelun muuttuva sisältö—Kohdekuntien sivistysjohdon näkemyksiä ja kansainvälisiä ja kotimaisia havaintoja [The changing content of the village school debate—Domestic and international perspectives.]. In S. Tantarimäki, S. Komulainen, M. Rantanen, & E. Heikkilä. (Eds.), *Vastavirtaan ja valtavirtaan—avauksia kyläkoulukeskusteluun*. Siirtolaisuusinstituutin tutkimuksia A 52, 34–60. Turku, Finland.

Tantarimäki, S., & Törhönen, A. (2016a). Kouluverkkomuutos ARTTU2-kunnissa 2000-luvulla [School network changes in ARTTU2 municipalities in the 2000s]. *ARTTU2-tutkimusohjelman julkaisusarja* Nro 2/2016 [Publication Series of the ARTTU2 Research Program Nro 2/2016]. Suomen Kuntaliitto. Retrieved from http://shop.kunnat.net/product_details.php?p=3208

Tantarimäki, S., & Törhönen, A. (2016b). Kouluverkon, palveluverkon ja arjen suhde ARTTU2-kunnissa [Mutual Relationship of a Municipal School Network, Service Network and Everyday Life of Families]. *ARTTU2-tutkimusohjelman julkaisusarja* Nro 11/2016 [Publication Series of the ARTTU2 Research Program]. Suomen Kuntaliitto. Retrieved from http://shop.kunnat.net/product_details.php?p=3282

Tantarimäki, S., & Törhönen, A. (2017). *Kouluverkko muuttuu—entä kouluverkkosuunnittelu?* [School network changes—What about the planning of it?] Tutkimusjulkaisu-sarjan julkaisu nro 105 [Research Publication Series Publication No. 105]. Helsinki, Finland: Kunnallisalan Kehittämissäätiö.

Tilastokeskus – Statistics Finland. (2018). *Koululaitoksen oppilaitokset 2017*. Retrieved from http://pxnet2.stat.fi/PXWeb/pxweb/fi/StatFin/

Trade Union of Education in Finland. (2016). *Tasa-arvon tiekartta. OAJ:n esitykset koulutuksen tasa-arvon edistämiseksi* [Equality roadmap. OAJ's proposals to promote equality in education]. Helsinki, Finland: Author.

Vettenranta, J., Välijärvi, J., Ahonen, A., Hautamäki, J., Hiltunen, J., Leino, K.,...Vainikainen, M.-P. (2016). *PISA ensituloksia. Huipulla pudotuksesta huolimatta* [PISA—first results. At the top despite of the drop]. Opetus- ja kulttuuriministeriön julkaisuja 2016:41 [Publications of the Ministry of Education and Culture 2016: 41]. Retrieved from https://converis.jyu.fi/converis/portal/detail/Publication/26361802?auxfun=&lang=fi_FI

Village Action Association of Finland. (2017). *The village action association of Finland in brief.* Retrieved from http://www.kylatoiminta.fi/en/home.html

Witten, K., McCreanor, T., Kearns, R., & Ramasubramanian, L. (2001). The impacts of a school closure on neighbourhood social cohesion: Narratives from Invercargill, New Zealand. *Health & Place, 7*(4), 307–317.

Zheteyeva, Y., Rainey, J., Gao, H., Jacobson, E., Adhikari, B., Shi, J.,...Uzicanin, A. (2017). Unintended costs and consequences of school closures implemented in preparation for Hurricane Isaac in Harrison County School District, Mississippi, August–September 2012. *PLoS One, 12*(11). e0184326. Retrieved from https://www.ncbi.nlm.nih.gov/pmc/articles/PMC5665504/

PART III

DEVELOPING AND DEEPENING
THEORETICAL ENGAGEMENT

CHAPTER 13

THE RURAL PRIMARY SCHOOL HEAD TEACHER IN THE FIELD

Carl Bagley
Queen's University Belfast, NI

Sam Hillyard
University of Lincoln, England

The research focuses on the complexities associated with contemporary rural primary school leadership. The chapter draws on in-depth ethnographic research undertaken in one English rural primary school and its surrounding community over a period of 3 years, with data derived from over eight hours of interview with the school's head teacher. The chapter is conceptually informed by the work of Bourdieu (1984) and his work around *field, habitus,* and *capital* as a means of understanding *practice*. The chapter contends that as the neoliberal economic field increasingly contaminates the field of education, so a contextual understanding of the complex and shifting social space which the head teacher occupies, including their habitus and the capital they deploy, is of central importance to understanding practice. The chapter aims to show the ways in which a Bourdieusian conceptual approach, combined with an illuminative ethnographic narrative, can offer a particular critically insightful engagement with rural primary school leadership.

In presenting our work on rural primary school leadership, we wish to echo the sentiment of Eacott (2010) that there is "a complex socio-cultural politics to school leadership that is context specific and multi-layered" (p. 226). In this sense school leadership needs first and foremost to be acknowledged as a "social practice that transcends the domain of being an individual's activity and can only be understood by getting up close to the culture of schooling and the social positioning of school leaders." Our research, drawing theoretically and conceptually on the work of Bourdieu (1984), supports the creation of what has been termed an *enunciative space*, "an opportunity to articulate what it means to be an educational leader, to tangle with the social, cultural, political, and historical issues beyond the technicalities of managing an organization" (Eacott, 2010, p. 226). Subsequently, we focus on school leadership practice in one rural primary school in England to ethnographically uncover and portray the ways in which the head teacher struggles "to enact a vision of education in their school and the relational aspects of this to wider social discourse" (Eacott, 2010, p. 226).

In the English Designation of Rural Primary Schools (Department for Children, Schools and Families, 2008), schools are described as urban or rural depending on whether the majority of the population falls inside a population settlement of 10,000 or more. The overall classification is based on a settlement approach and builds upon the identification of rural towns, villages, and scattered dwellings within a grid framework of cell size of one hectare (100 x100 metre squares). The common features of this arbitrary and normative conceptualization of what constitutes the rural can be categorized as fundamentally materialist and geospatial, determined by population size, and mapped in relative terms against the urban (Bell, 2007). As such, approximately 31% of primary schools in England (5,165) may be designated as rural, attended by 17.3% (735,165) of primary school pupils (Church of England, 2014).

In policy terms, rural schools have found themselves responding to education reforms since the mid-1970s that are the product of an English education system conceived and conceptualized largely in urban terms (Bell & Sigsworth, 1987). Moreover, neoliberal government welfare reforms, including those in education, have targeted "systems of provision, the forms of organisational control and direction, and the relations between 'leaders,' 'staff,' and 'customers' involved in the production and delivery of welfare" (Clarke, Gewirtz, & McLaughlin, 2000, p. 1) with an ever increasing move towards the marketization and privatization of services. As a result, educational reform—including that in rural areas—has witnessed, on one level, the ever diminishing power of local authorities (organizations of elected officials responsible for governance and funding of public services) and the increasing autonomy of schools in terms of local management, whereby they control a budget largely determined by pupil numbers, and schools competing for parents to choose their school. On another level—and simultaneously—schools are being constrained and controlled by a centralized regulatory framework based around standardized notions of inspection, testing, attainment, and performance. In this climate and under the auspices of what has been termed New Public Management (NPM; Hall & Gunter, 2016), the role of head teacher as school manager, along with the act of managing and management, have been discursively reformulated, recalibrated, and repositioned. Hall & Gunter (2016, pp. 25–27) signal the following key NPM developments impacting upon *all* English schools including those in rural areas:

- competition between schools reinforced as a new logic of educational activity;
- Ofsted (Office for Standards in Education, Children's Services, and Skills) inspects and grades schools according to their performance;
- school managers, as head teachers, afforded responsibility for managing schools in line with performance indicators;
- national tests established as key indicators of pupil, teacher, and school performance;
- standards of attainment in relation to national testing are further reinforced as the benchmarks against which pupil, teacher, and institutional performance are judged;
- school league tables, critical to local and national perceptions of school performance;
- schools forced to close through national level intervention where performance falls below benchmarked levels;
- head teachers made responsible for school performance and accountable to Ofsted during periodic inspections; and
- head teachers sacked and replaced by super heads when they fail to deliver improvements in performance.

Hall and Gunter (2016, p. 22) speak of a process of continual multilayering of educational NPM reform over the last 30 years, resulting in a system that "can be characterized as one of complexity, even chaos," and cite the subsequent creation in the English education system of "at least seventy types of schools." It is in the midst of these policy changes and with its focus on the rural that the chapter seeks to explore in depth how one primary school head teacher interprets the complex multilayered socioeconomic, cultural, and political contexts in which her school is situated and how professional knowledge and understanding is translated into specific strategies for leadership and community engagement. Our contention is that research must view "leadership theory critically and contextually" (Addison, 2009, p. 327) if the complexities and contestations associated with contemporary rural primary headship are to be understood. To this end we turn to the work of Bourdieu (1984).

ENGAGING BOURDIEU

The notion of *practice* we use in this study is theoretically informed by the work of Bourdieu, who in his text, *Distinction: A Social Critique of the Judgement of Taste*, presents the following equation to explain his conceptualization: *[(habitus) (capital)] + field = practice* (Bourdieu, 1984, p. 101). Practice is thus determined by the habitus of actors, the capital they possess, and the ways in which they participate in a particular field. In this chapter the concepts of field, habitus, and capital are adopted as a theoretical means of examining the social spaces encountered and occupied by head teachers and the ways in which they assess and respond to these social spaces in their professional lives or practice.

Field

In considering each of these concepts in turn, we are taking field in this sense to be those social and institutional arenas constituted by networks, structures, or relations at micro and macro level, which "produce and authorise certain discourses and activities" (Webb, Schirato, & Danaher, 2002, pp. 21–22). According to Bourdieu (1989, pp. 40–41) a field is: a structural social space, a field of forces, a force field. It contains people who dominate and people who are dominated. Constant, permanent relationships of inequality operate inside this space, which at the same time becomes a space in which the various actors struggle for the transformation or preservation of the field. All the individuals in this universe bring to the competition all the (relative) power at their disposal. It is that power that defines their position in the field and, as a result, their strategies (Bourdieu, 1989, pp. 40–41).

Furthermore, a field is not fixed, but is temporal and dynamic, under constant production and reproduction (Thompson, 1999). For Bourdieu (1996) there are numerous different fields including the economic, the literary, the scientific as well as the educational, each with their own permeable boundaries.

In line with what we have already alluded to at the beginning of this chapter, Bourdieu (1996) identifies the boundaries around the field of education as increasingly breached by the field of the economy, as discourses around marketization and managerialism come to dominate (Addison, 2009). As such, an awareness of these fields and an appreciation of the ways in which cross-boundary contamination and influence might impact upon different fields are of increasing importance in uncovering and understanding the leadership practice of head teachers.

Habitus

The concept of habitus is used by Bourdieu (1977) to methodologically engage and address the dualisms of agency-structure; the concept is used to signify, as Reay (2004) observes, "Not only is the body in the social world but...the social world is in the body" (p. 432). Habitus is thus neither wholly the result of free agency nor determined simply by structures but rather the interplay between agency and structure created through a social process, which, as well as being long lasting and transferable between contexts, "is not fixed or permanent, and can be changed under unexpected situations or over a long historical period" (Navarro, 2006, p. 16).

While in terms of habitus an individual is equipped with agency, individuals are likely to lean towards or be (pre)disposed to particular ways of behaving, inextricably bound up with cultural/structural changes (Reay, 2004). As Bourdieu (2000) states:

> I developed the concept of "habitus" to incorporate the objective structures of society and the subjective role of agents within it. The habitus is a set of dispositions, reflexes and forms of behaviour people acquire through acting in society. It reflects the different positions people have in society, for example, whether they are brought up in a middle-class environment or in a working-class suburb. It is part of how society produces itself. (Bourdieu, 2000, p. 19)

As Reay (1996) points out, habitus influences the relationship individuals have with "localised issues of history and geography" (p. 581). Habitus creates a "sense of one's place," an understanding and awareness of those things individuals consider as being something for, or not for, them (Swartz, 1997, p. 106), excluding the individual from engaging in certain practices, particularly those "unfamiliar to the cultural groupings to which the individual belongs" (Reay, 2004, p. 433). The form of habitus is thus specific to each individual; it is "the way society becomes deposited in persons in the form of lasting dispositions, or trained capacities and structured propensities to think, feel and act in determinant ways, which then guide them" (Wacquant, 2005, p. 316). Conceptually, habitus and field are interrelated:

> On one side, it is a relation of conditioning: the field structures the habitus...On the other side, it is a relation of knowledge or cognitive construc-

tion: habitus contributes to constituting the field as a meaningful world, a world endowed with sense and with value, in which it is worth investing one's energy. (Bourdieu, 1989, p. 44)

Addison (2009) notes the interaction between habitus and field is both predictable and unpredictable and as a consequence the implication for the practice of school headship "is dynamic, fluid and a product of the dominant fields in play at any given time" (p. 334). Habitus thus has a major influence on the ways in which individuals respond to situations and on their understanding and practices temporally shaped and reshaped by the impact of various fields. It thus may have a significant impact on the ways in which individuals such as head teachers perceive the social space in which they are situated and subsequently choose to lead their schools and to react to the situations in which they find themselves (Addison, 2009).

As Lingard, Rawolle, and Taylor (2000) observe, "Habitus is the sedimentation of history, structure and culture in individual dispositions to practice" (p. 36) and directly influenced by the capital they possess (p. 36).

Capital

Capital is a key resource informing habitus, with particular and discernible types defining positions and possibilities of the various actors in any field. Bourdieu (1986) identifies the four types of capital individuals, including head teachers, who bring to practice as economic capital (wealth or money), cultural capital (the ability to navigate the systems of knowledge deemed valid by a society), social capital (networks of relations), and symbolic capital (marks of prestige and honor). For Bourdieu (1986) capital is concerned with an individual's position within an inequitable class-based social structure—the dominant class defining who possesses the most property and wealth, what counts as legitimate knowledge, which social relations are valuable, and what symbols confer prestige and social honor.

In engaging a Bourdieusian analysis to an understanding of rural primary school leadership we are striving to move away from a normative reading of leadership, to one which acknowledges it's temporal, complex, and situated nature, placing the individual actor in local context whilst appreciating the simultaneous interplay of both micro and macro level forces in shaping practice (Eacott, 2010).

THE ETHNOGRAPHIC STUDY

As Bourdieu (1993, p. 271) observes, "One cannot grasp the most profound logic of the social world unless one becomes immersed in the specificity of an empirical reality." In this case the immersion involved a 3-year ethnographic investigation in two contrasting English villages. The research employed participant observation inside the village schools and the village, semi-structured interviews (circa 29 in each setting), with key groups including school staff, parents, the governing bodies, and key members of the local community, and "in-the-field" interviews (circa 40 in each setting) with village residents individually and collectively (long standing and new arrivals) in a host of informal settings including social clubs, public houses, community centers, shops, and personal homes. A detailed use was also made of documentary material including school inspection reports, ordnance survey maps, residents' websites, parish newsletters, and social history records and accounts relating to each village. For the purposes of this chapter the findings are derived, in the main, from eight 1-hour interviews conducted with Mary, the Minbury head teacher. An inductive approach was adopted, with data analyzed thematically through the generation of initial codes, identification of specific themes, thematic review, and report production (Braun & Clarke, 2006).

The data reported in this chapter relate to the "colliery" village of Minbury (not its real name) situated in the North East of England with a population of around 2,500. From the late 19th to late 20th century the village could be classified as a coal mining community. However, as the coal mines were systematically closed by the United Kingdom government in the 1980s, so employment opportunities decreased in the village, with the understanding of those growing up there that they would no longer follow their fathers or grandfathers "down the pit." Rather, they sought to find jobs in the service sector or were unemployed, with the unemployment rate of 12% well above the national UK average. The socioeconomic deprivations within the village were readily apparent in the aged housing stock, diminishing amenities and relatively high levels of poverty.

The first village school was opened in 1804 by a local landholder. This school stood until 1913 when a new local government controlled school was erected near the center of the village; this school was demolished in the 1970s making way for the village's current primary school. The new primary school was a little on the periphery of the village, which is why the head teacher said she had had the school "painted red so that everybody knew where we were." In reality the school was no more than a 5 to 10 minute walk from what was, in effect, the central hub of the village, which had two public houses, a news agent, a bakery, a pharmacy, a hairdresser, a fish and chip shop, and a post office (scheduled for closure). The school had around 164 pupils aged from 4 to 11, with eight teaching staff and two teaching assistants. In formal institutional terms, whereas the role of the church in the village had undoubtedly diminished over time the village school continued to fulfill a key social role as something that was temporally constant, an institution binding successive generations of families together, where lifelong friendships were formed and informal support networks originated (Bagley & Hillyard, 2014).

Research Findings

Observation of the social world of the head teacher at the rural school in Minbury revealed the messy and complex professional role undertaken and encountered by Mary on a daily basis. As head teacher she dealt with, or possibly more accurately, juggled with a myriad of issues and concerns that were pastoral, educational, and political and which involved students, parents, and local bureaucrats. As Mary commented:

> One minute you have a child who has fallen over in the playground and crying, at the same time as the phone rings and the local authority want to know about admissions and a parent in the corridor wanting to speak about her son's performance... and decisions need to be made and documents signed, letters to go out and this is all happening at once. It's definitely getting worse than it was when I first came into teaching. (Mary, Minbury head teacher)

The above statement by Mary, as well as encapsulating the professional complexity of her role, references and reveals the ways in which the field of education is changing and weakening in terms of its boundaries as she responds to requests from the local authority concerning pupil numbers, and a parent on academic performance. As Addison (2009) observes:

> Principals have not operated in an educational vacuum for many years, even given the familiar architecture of their schools. The contemporary organisational space confronting school principals is dominated by a layered interaction of a number of competing fields, most notably the all-encompassing demands of the economic field. The impact of domination of the field of schools by the field of the economy has made the principal leadership of schools complex, layered and increasingly uncertain. (Addison, 2009, p. 331)

Addison (2009) contends it is in understanding the ways in which school principals deal with multiple pressures from different *fields* which is at the heart of present day school leadership. Certainly in our study we found, while Mary sought to deal with a range of educational issues related to pedagogy and the curriculum, the discursive presence of marketization, performativity, and managerialist issues of the kind referred to earlier in relation to new public management (Hall and Gunter, 2016) were found to be ever present and professionally pervasive, an encroachment over time which brought with it specific and heightened concerns for her rural primary school. As she commented:

> Since I came in to teaching 20 years ago, the last five here as head teacher, I have seen an ever increasing pressure placed upon teachers and teaching, it is about performance how well we perform in standardised tests, where we finish in the league tables and as well as Ofsted and the unbelievable stress and pressure inspection places on everyone. But even though my educational priorities might be elsewhere we have to comply and I would be lying if I said we didn't want to do well and who doesn't want to be graded excellent...and of course we have parents being able to choose their school which means school competition and in rural areas numbers are small and you are always conscious of the threat of closure. (Mary, Minbury head teacher)

As Addison (2009) similarly observed so much time of school principals was being given over to issues such as "risk management, governance and enterprise bargaining, their role was just as much corporate as it was educational" (p. 335). Moreover, as Mary stipulates they have very little option in relation to school inspection, school choice, and performance-based league tables other than to comply with the dominant, performative, managerialist rationale, and *doxa* (relations of order and norms) of the fields in play. The need to perform well against targets and the threat of possible closure emanating from the economic field of a new public management culture of interschool competition and school choice was part of the everyday professional reality of schooling for the Minbury head teacher. It informed her habitus and shaped her practice.

Mary's response to the pressures on the field of new public management and its implications for the field of education could, however, be described as accommodating and strategic as she sought to maintain a habitus committed to strong educational values associated with community engagement, whilst ensuring the school's survival in a competitive environment. Mary's habitus had been strongly informed by her own family background.

> I grew up in London in what you might call a disadvantaged working class neighbourhood or if you are being less polite a sink estate, one of those places where people end up when they have very little. The one thing that stayed with me and made me want to become a teacher and what I experienced firsthand is what a good local school and teachers can achieve and what it can mean to kids like me who lived in a community which had nothing or very little. (Mary, Minbury head teacher)

Mary's reasons for becoming a teacher and her formative experiences and disposition or habitus on the value of local schooling went on to shape and inform her professional practice and commitment to have a school with a strong link to the local community.

> I worked in a couple of schools before coming here mainly in the South of England which were inner-city areas not rural and I have always kept to the strong belief as I said of how important a local school is to any community but in a rural one that importance gets magnified as in many ways it is one of the main places for people to meet and come together and that is true over generations. I have grandparents dropping their grandchildren off who tell me how they used to attend the school. But even though it might be different here than in London my desire and belief in the value of bringing the community into the school and taking the school into the community holds true whether I am in the inner-city or here at Minbury. (Mary, Minbury head teacher)

As Mary indicated, her passion for strong school–community relations became further heightened when she moved to a more rural setting and appreciated the ways in which, over time, the local primary school had played a significant role, both material and symbolic, in the life of the village (Bagley & Hillyard, 2011). This understanding of the school's temporal and spatial significance made her determined, despite increasing new public management demands, that they would not prevent her from her mission of establishing a school that was an integral part of the local village community, one open to parents and one which they felt comfortable visiting. She remarked:

> As we get more school inspection, more boxes which have to be ticked, more worries that your school isn't performing as well as the school down the road and you fear parents might start to choose it instead of you, even though you know you are doing a bloody good job in difficult circumstances, it all adds to the stress and pressure and you have to find ways of coping, of not getting distracted from what you think is right, while all the while making sure those boxes are ticked. So whatever the other pressures I wanted us as a school to make the time, find the time, to get parents involved with the school for the benefit of both our students and the wider community. (Mary, Minbury head teacher)

Arguably and interestingly, while Mary sought to strategically defend the field of the school against encroaching new public management pressures emanating from the economic field, so she sought to embrace and accommodate more fully the field of the family into the school. The school had a well-attended and active parent–teacher association, and operated an open door policy providing a regular opportunity for parents to see their child's class in action. Parents were able to use the school to meet and chat with other parents anytime they wished, and to this end the school had a designated room that parents used as a social drop-in for coffee and biscuits. For Mary it wasn't simply about strengthening school–community relations but also about the educational value and benefit she believed resulted from stronger parental involvement in the schooling of children (Henderson & Mapp, 2002; Ho Sui-Chi & Willms, 1996), especially for those children living in relatively poor economically disadvantaged communities such as Minbury, but also inner-city communities like the one in which she had grown up and previously worked (Henderson & Mapp, 2002; Ho Sui-Chi & Willms, 1996). Mary, remarked:

> The community has seen a lot of things close, you only need to drive through the village to see shops closed, houses boarded up, there is very little work, there are very few places for the kids to go or do. Consequently many end up unemployed or simply hanging around on the streets... the school is one of the few constants... and it was important for me to help make sure we keep it for the sake of the village and use it in a way that was more than simply making sure we performed well in Ofsted, it was about giving the kids a better start in life, I suppose a chance to get out and away from the kinds of everyday poverty we have around here. (Mary, Minbury head teacher)

An intriguing tension thus existed within her habitus whereby Mary saw the value and importance of having a strong community-engaged school for the sake of the pupils and the village, whilst success in terms of "giving the kids a better chance in life" might, if realized, mean they leave the village and thus help undermine the village's sustainability, including that of the school.

A more immediate and direct threat to the school's sustainability however, came from the encroaching economic field in the guise of competition and choice. In this regard, the cultural capital Mary brought to her practice as head teacher and which she utilized as a key resource to inform her habitus, informed her strategic understanding of the value of local community engagement and parental involvement, as related to the realpolitik of competition and choice in rural areas (Bagley & Hillyard, 2015). The changing demographic in the village meant the school was attended entirely by long standing working-class residents; middle class newcomers to the village were found to have much less loyalty towards attending the school, these newcomer parents deploying their *economic, social,* and *cultural capital* to choose a different primary school in another village, a choice made not on the grounds of proximity and locale but the perceived academic advantage that attendance at such a school might afford their child (Bagley & Hillyard, 2015). Mary was very much aware of this predicament and, as a consequence, the importance of maintaining the loyalty of the long-standing residents to the school. As she observed:

> I consider myself to have a strong understanding of what needs to be done in order for this school to survive. Yes, number one I want it to be part of the community and for families to feel welcome and see this as their local school but of course I think that in trying to create that I hope it will mean them wanting to choose this school for their children. (Mary, Minbury head teacher)

In effect, as the educational and economic field boundaries interspersed, so Mary utilized her cultural capital to navigate the field in a way in which she could utilize her commitment to the local school and community in a manner which both facilitated a strong bond between them, whilst, at the same time, capitalizing on this relationship to try and safeguard the school's survival—a survival which she perceived as central to the well-being of the community and the village.

Mary's habitus towards the social value of school–community relationships was further evidenced when a neighboring, much smaller, local primary school (Minbury Hill) located about one mile (1.5 km) from Minbury, with around 50 students, encountered the pressures of the economic field in terms of financial viability, and was faced with the possibility of closure by the local authority. Mary commented:

> I didn't want Minbury Hill to close or merge with mine as I think it is important for the parents who live in Minbury Hill to have their own local school. As a deprived working class community Minbury Hill has even greater social problems than around here and I think a local school can make a difference to people's lives. (Mary, Minbury head teacher)

In her response to the fluid and changing nature of the field Mary drew on her cultural and social capital to campaign and lobby alongside local Minbury Hill parents and governors for the school's survival, a campaign which saved the school but ultimately resulted in her agreeing to take over as head teacher of both schools under a federated governance arrangement (made possible by the 2002 Education Act whereby governing bodies can either amalgamate or remain separate under the leadership of a single head teacher). She outlined the situation in the following terms:

> Over the years I have come to know not only the local community but the local government politicians and how politically important communities such as the one in Minbury and in Minbury Hill are as strong Labour voting areas. I knew they didn't want to close a school if it was possible to avoid it and so we spoke and I spoke to the outgoing head teacher and existing governors at Minbury Hill and to my governors and held parents meetings at both schools and from that it was agreed that I would take over headship at both schools. I see it as an opportunity, to try and work with an even larger community, to help address some of the social problems they both face. To take the lessons I have learned from being head teacher here and applying them there. (Mary, Minbury head teacher)

Mary took on the role of federated head teacher at the end of the fieldwork period and in our last interview revealed once again a habitus committed to fostering school–community relations, and the deployment of cultural and social capital within the field to manage the process in two schools. She commented:

> The thing is I know what I want to achieve regards the school and the community and I have a fairly clear idea of how I am going to achieve it, what needs to be done, who needs to be seen, which local councillor I need to get on board and which parents are the activists and have the strongest local voice. I have been at this for quite a while now and you get to know intuitively what is the right thing to do, what to prioritise and what to let go to achieve your goals. I have learnt how to be good at juggling the various pressures when I was the head teacher of one school but now I guess as the head teacher of two schools I am simply going to have to be even better. Look out Cirque du Soleil (laughs). (Mary, Minbury head teacher)

This final quote from Mary referring to her understanding of the field, a habitus in support of fostering strong school–community relations and the deployment of capital to engage the network of stakeholder to achieve her goals, captures nicely, from a Bourdieusian perspective, the ways in which her rural school leadership practice can be conceptualized, not by taking field, habitus, or capital in isolation but as the equation [*(habitus)(capital)*] + *field* = *practice* that Bourdieu (1984, p. 101) suggests, by the interrelationship between them, each one only fully formed and understood when taken in relation to the other (Eacott, 2013).

CONCLUDING OBSERVATIONS

In this study, drawing on the conceptual work of Bourdieu (1984), we have attempted to move away from an historical decontextualized account of school leadership to one which is more strongly problematized and empirically grounded (Eacott, 2013). Thompson (1999) in applying a Bourdieusian analysis to school principals observed:

> Becoming a school principal according to Bourdieu is then a slow and lengthy process of acquiring not only the symbolic and cultural capitals necessary for participation in the field, but also the processes of investing in the game, accepting its doxa and its ways of being, learning the strategies of participation, and acquiring the habitus, that embodied sense of being an administrator. (Thompson, 1999)

We would contend that under a neoliberal political agenda not only has the field of education become contaminated by the economic field but that it has come to be dominated and structured by it with new public management discourses informing and shaping the practices of schools (Hall & Gunter,

2016). As Addison (2009) observes, the economic field "has transformed the workspaces of principal practitioners almost beyond recognition" (p. 333) with school leaders, such as the head teacher in our study, required to deal with the implications for the field of education on a daily basis.

The notion of rural head teacher practice that emerges in the case of Mary is one that is complex, temporal, liquid, and relational to the dominant fields she encounters. In particular, we would contend Mary is engaging and needing to deal professionally with diverse cross paths of multiple fields—most notably, but not exclusively, from the economic field—and has in part developed what Bourdieu (1990) calls a "feel for the game" (p. 11).

> Action, guided by a "feel for the game," has all the appearances of the rational action that an impartial observer, endowed with all the necessary information and capable of mastering it rationally, would deduce. And yet it is not based on reason. You need only to think of the impulsive decision made by the tennis player who runs up to the net, to understand that it has nothing in common with the learned construction that the coach, after analysis, draws up, in order to explain it and deduce communicable lessons from it. (Bourdieu, 1990, p. 11)

We are not suggesting here that Mary does not engage in any calculated and rational action, but rather that it is important to acknowledge how following years of immersion in the field, she is at times able to respond, as she says, intuitively, to the complex array of multiple demands on her time and services as fields cross and collide. Interestingly, as we have revealed, some fields are ones she appears to accept as professionally and administratively inevitable as they relate to the culture of new public management and which she tolerates. Others, especially those which align with her predisposed habitus towards facilitating strong school–community relations and which emanate from the field of the family, she seeks to embrace and accommodate. Further, we would tentatively suggest that Mary's habitus towards school leadership is in part grounded on a commitment to addressing educational and social disadvantage in the local community, and social justice; a discursive positioning in relation to the economic field which could be conceived of as potentially disruptive (Eacott, 2013). Arguably, for head teachers such as Mary, while they understand the rules of the game or dominant doxa of the field, it is not all about making sure they play the existing "game better but challenging the very nature of the game and the formula for success" (Eacott, 2013, p. 175).

For Bourdieu, social transformation in the main occurs according to

> a theory of crisis or hysteresis where the habitus falls out of alignment with the field in which it operates, creating a situation in which belief in the game (illusion) is temporarily suspended and the orthodoxy of practice or doxic

assumptions are raised to the level of discourse, where they can be contested. (Eacott, 2013, p. 175)

Eacott (2013) however, contends that disruption to the game should not simply be limited to moments of crisis. Rather he suggests a conceptual shift in thinking akin to Bourdieu's (2005) classification of a firm as a field in its own right, whereby one conceptualizes the individual school not as a subfield within the field of education but as a field in its own right. Such a reconceptualization, Eacott (2013) claims, enables "scholarship to enter the black box that is the school. In doing so, what we find is not individuals (e.g., principal, teachers, students), but a structure with relative autonomy" (Eacott, 2013, p. 179). The emphasis here is on the importance of acknowledging the relative autonomy of the field rather than other structural limitations placed upon it. As Eacott (2013) continues:

> Just as the strategies that a school adopts are reflective of its position within the larger field of schooling, so too is it reflective of the power positions constitutive of its internal governance or, more specifically, the social dispositions of the players (staff, students, and community) within the field. (Eacott, 2013, p. 179)

In this way key players within a school, such as the head teacher, are able to develop a social disposition or habitus shaped through biography "affected by their field location as well as through relations with time and space" which has the "the skills required to deconstruct and actively challenge the orthodoxy, or doxa of education" (Eacott, 2013, p. 179). A process akin to what Bourdieu (1990) describes as "socio analysis" whereby individuals within a field are able to become reflexively and critically aware of the structures that inhibit or shape their practice (p. 116). As Gunter (2000) states:

> One of the strengths of Bourdieu's concept of habitus lies in its capacity to: keep open intellectual spaces a field member might ask: What intellectual position am I taking in the field? How does that position relate to the position taken by others in the field? How does that position relate to economic, political and cultural structures or fields? (p. 631)

The important point here is that the intellectual spaces for critical reflection and practice which exist for school leaders like Mary, positioned in the relatively autonomous field of the school, allow her to challenge the dominant economically infused doxa of education, to prioritize community engagement and collaboration at a time of individualism and competition, and to take up the position as federated head teacher because she believed in the importance of keeping small rural schools open and utilizing schooling to address social disadvantage. But as we noted previously, the form of habitus and its lasting dispositions is specific to each individual (Wacquant, 2005) and thus an individual head teacher in another rural primary school may well exhibit a completely different disposition towards practice. In many ways this is precisely the point. In drawing on the work of Bourdieu (1984) and applying his conceptualization of practice to a single case we hope to have tentatively signalled an approach capable of engaging critically and contextually with the nuanced complexities of rural primary school leadership.

REFERENCES

Addison, B. (2009). A feel for the game—A Bourdieuian analysis of principal leadership: A study of Queensland secondary school principals. *Journal of Educational Administration and History, 41*(4), 327–341.

Bagley, C., & Hillyard, S. (2011).Village schools in England: At the heart of their community? *Australian Journal of Education, 55*(1), 5–12.

Bagley, C., & Hillyard, S. (2014). Rural schools, social capital and the big society: A theoretical and empirical exposition. *British Educational Research Journal, 40*(1), 63–67.

Bagley, C., & Hillyard, S. (2015). School choice in an English village: Living, loyalty and leaving. *Ethnography and Education, 10*(3), 278–292.

Bell, A., & Sigsworth, A. (1987). *The heart of the community: Rural primary schools and community development*. Norwich, CT: Mousehold Press.

Bell, M. M. (2007). The two-ness of rural life and the ends of rural scholarship. *Journal of Rural Studies, 23*(4), 402–441.

Bourdieu, P. (1977). *Outline of a theory of practice*. Cambridge, England: Cambridge University Press.

Bourdieu, P. (1984). *Distinction: A social critique of the judgement of taste*. London, England: Routledge & Kegan Paul.

Bourdieu, P. (1986). The forms of capital. In J. G. Richardson (Ed.), *Handbook of theory and research for the sociology of education* (pp. 241–258). New York, NY: Greenwood Press.

Bourdieu, P. (1989). Towards a reflexive sociology: A workshop with Pierre Bourdieu. *Sociological Theory, 7*(1), 26–63.

Bourdieu, P. (1990). *In other words: Essays toward a reflexive sociology*. Redwood City, CA: Stanford University Press.

Bourdieu, P. (1993). Concluding remarks: For a sociogenetic understanding of intellectual works. In C. Calhoun, E. LiPuma, & M. Postone (Eds.), *Bourdieu: Critical perspectives* (pp. 236–75). Chicago, IL: University of Chicago Press.

Bourdieu, P. (1996). *Rules of art: Genesis and structure of the literary field*. Stanford, CA: Stanford University Press.

Bourdieu, P. (2000). The politics of protest. An interview by Kevin Ovenden. *Socialist Review 242*, 18–20.

Bourdieu, P. (2005). *The social structures of the economy* (C. Turner, Trans.). Cambridge, England: Polity Press.

Braun, V., & Clarke, V. (2006). Using thematic analysis in psychology. *Qualitative Research in Psychology, 3*(2), 77–101.
Church of England. (2014). *Working together: The future of rural Church of England schools.* London, England: The Church of England's National Education Office.
Clarke, J., Gewirtz, S., & McLaughlin, E. (2000). Reinventing the welfare state. In J. Clarke, S. Gewirtz, & E. McLaughlin (Eds.), *New managerialism new welfare* (pp. 1–26). London, England: SAGE.
Department for Children, Schools and Families. (2008). *Designation order for rural primary schools.* London, England: The Stationery Office. Retrieved from http://www.dcsf.gov.uk/localauthorities/index.cfm?action=content&contentID=15507&letter=D
Eacott, S. (2010). Studying school leadership practice: A methodological discussion. *Issues in Educational Research, 20*(3), 220–233.
Eacott, S. (2013). Towards a theory of school leadership practice: A Bourdieusian perspective. *Journal of Educational Administration and History, 45*(2), 174–188.
Gunter, H. J. (2000). Thinking theory: The field of education management in England and Wales. *British Journal of Sociology of Education, 21*(4), 622–635.
Hall, D., & Gunter, H. M. (2016). Permanent instability in the European educational NPM 'laboratory'. In H. M. Gunter, E. Grimaldi, D. Hall, & R. Serpieri (Eds.), *New public management and the reform of education* (pp. 21–35). London, England: Routledge.
Henderson, A. T., & Mapp, K. L. (2002). *A new wave of evidence: The impact of school, family, and community connections on student achievement.* Austin, TX: Southwest Educational Development Laboratory.
Ho Sui-Chi, E., & Willms, J. D. (1996). Effects of parental involvement on eighth-grade achievement. *Sociology of Education, 69*(2), 126–141.
Lingard, B., Rawolle, S., & Taylor, S. (2000). Globalising policy sociology in education: Working with Bourdieu. *Journal of Education Policy, 20*(6), 759–777.
Navarro, Z. (2006). In search of cultural interpretation of power. *IDS Bulletin, 37*(6), 11–22.
Reay, D. (1996). Contextualising choice: Social power and parental involvement. *British Educational Research Journal, 22*(5), 581–595.
Reay, D. (2004). Education and cultural capital: The implications of changing trends in education policies. *Cultural Trends, 13*(2), 73–86.
Swartz, D. (1997). *Culture and power: The sociology of Pierre Bourdieu.* Chicago, IL: University of Chicago Press.
Thompson, P. (1999, November–December). *Reading the work of school administrators with the help of Bourdieu: Getting a 'feel for the game.'* Australian Association for Research in Education and New Zealand Association for Research in Education Joint Conference. Melbourne, Australia. Retrieved from http://www.aare.edu.au/data/publications/1999/tho99060.pdf
Wacquant, L. (2005). Habitus. In J. Becket & Z. Milan (Eds.), *International Encyclopedia of Economic Sociology.* London, England: Routledge.
Webb, J., Shirato, T., & Danaher, G. (2002). *Understanding Bourdieu.* London, England: SAGE.

CHAPTER 14

PUTTING LEFEBVRE TO WORK ON "THE RURAL"

Cath Gristy
University of Plymouth, England

Social and cultural studies over the past 20 years have been witnessing a "spatial turn," an intellectual engagement with place and space, as a response to a longstanding ontological and epistemological bias that has privileged time over space (Soja, 2008). This is part of a wider theoretical project that grapples with the "unremitting materiality of the world" (Thrift, 2006, p. 139). It appears to offer promise to those looking for acknowledgement that in education place and space matters, in particular in its spatiality of inequalities and injustices (Gulson & Symes, 2007). This chapter uses the work of theorist Henri Lefebvre as a starting point for a spatial engagement with education in rural places. Lefebvre offers a set of ideas to use in developing understanding of the issues observed, connecting these into wider conversations about education, particularly those concerned with equity and justice.

Lefebvre's work requires us to understand space in relation to the practices that produce it (Christie, 2013); for Lefebvre, space is socially produced. He asks us to analyze space in terms of social relations rather than the "things" within it. Lefebvre envisages all space as social space; hyper-complex, overlapping, intertwined, flowing, moving, interfering, and interrupting in a multiplicity of ways (Christie, 2013). In this chapter, Lefebvre's ideas about space, particularly his triad of spatial practice, are put to work on a case study of a rural community and its schools. Christie (2013) argues that Lefebvre's triad can enable fine-grained analysis of the different activities of spatial production, particularly the mapping of the historical assembly of enduring social patterns of inequality. This chapter considers the possibilities of Lefebvre's work for those using rural contexts and practices looking to counter or interrupt normative, metro-centric hegemonic discourse and practice.

THE IMPORTANCE OF THEORY

Kvalsund and Hargreaves carried out a research review on rural schools and education across Nordic countries and the United Kingdom (Hargreaves, Kvalsund, & Galton, 2009) and identified two substantive issues. The first is that much of the research reviewed was dated, being over 10 years old at the time of their study. Secondly, an "external system perspective" dominated most of the research about rural places (Kvalsund & Hargreaves, 2009), in which the researchers looked in from the outside through the lenses of global or national policies, but did not "look out" towards communities and environments. This external system perspective begins with national policy and practice, because this is what dominates the lives and thoughts of education leaders, policy makers, and practitioners. Kvalsund and Hargreaves (2009) call for a new agenda to include independent research, to start from and focus on aspects of education, with schools and communities being seen together as learning environments. They ask researchers to begin from the lived experiences of learners in rural places, but also to improve the rigor of research to include, amongst other things, development and an analytical use of theory (Kvalsund & Hargreaves, 2009, p. 147). They argue for case studies that move beyond description, with theoretical rather than policy-based foundations.

Fine grained case studies that attend to the sites and practices of the lived experiences of education abound in rural education literature, but, as Corbett (2015) suggests, there are risks associated with these kinds of studies. These stories, he argues, can trap or become entrapped in static narratives of deficit, when labeled as "rural education," they have limited access to, and exposure in other bodies of education literature. This entrapment also limits the reach of this body of educational research.

The potential reach of much of the research work on education in rural places is limited by the absence of appropriate theorizing (Kvalsund &

Hargreaves, 2009). Engaging with theory is part of the research *footprint* (White et al., 2012). A research footprint can be thought of as not only the disturbance created by the researchers and their instruments, but also the lasting ripples and repercussions of the researcher-community and of inter-community relationships (Kvalsund & Hargreaves, 2014, p. 43) and their legacies (in the form of relationships), material changes to the locality, and publications about the place and about the research. These research footprints may be beneficial, raising awareness of social injustice, inequalities and environmental issues, but for the same reason, can also be risky and result in damage to people and their places, as well as to the wider reputation of ideas of the rural and of education. Great care must be taken with theory, ethics, and methodology in the conduct of research in any place, but particularly in small rural communities (Gristy, 2014) to counter negative effects of research or "damage" of any kind.

Putting theory to work on case studies, specific sites or incidents, could be a way to optimize the beneficial aspects of the footprints of research, and to extend reach, making it possible to do work in wider spaces of educational enquiry. In a recently translated essay, Lefebvre (1956/2016) suggests:

> Beginning with description but soon confronted with problems that exceed simple descriptions, what is required is another tool of investigation distinct from empiricism. By delving deeply into the problem of rural sociology in order to grasp its laws, the process is confronted as simultaneously historical, economical, and social. In order to know the objective process, a theory is needed. (p. 72)

It can be argued that rural issues have no place or space in global or national drives (Tieken, 2014); work in and of the rural is seen to be of limited value in the business of modernity. However, putting theory to work in educational research within rural context and/or focus can make significant contributions, for example, to the growing body of literature investigating education from different social, political, and geographical situations.

Kvalsund and Hargreaves (2009) argue that some theoretical frameworks are more suitable for studies that go on in rural spaces and places where theory needs to be sensitive to the scale of investigation.

Kvalsund and Hargreaves (2014, p. 45) argue that *specific explanatory theories* such as life course theory (see, e.g., Elder, Kirkpatrick Johnson, & Crosnoe, 2003) or Bourdieu's theories of social and cultural capital (see Bourdieu & Wacquant, 1992) take account of the scale of the study, so may be more appropriate for rural studies than *general descriptive theory*. These theories are context sensitive and also trouble or scrutinize the position of the researcher. Other theories here might include those informed by indigenous knowledge, or the post-human work of Deleuze and Guattari on the molecular scale of life (1984), or vital materialists and Actor Network

Theorists (e.g., Latour, 2005) on the agency of all things human and nonhuman. There is also the work of Lefebvre, the focus of this chapter.

Henri Lefebvre, a spatial theorist, whose work can be applied as being of both specific and general explanatory theory. As Christie (2013) argues, Lefebvre offers ways of thinking that embrace both the local and the national-global at the same time, "the local never disappears into regional or national or global spaces, but continues to exist" (Christie, 2013, p. 777). So with Lefebvre, work from and in rural contexts can engage on different scales and concurrently.

GEOGRAPHY MATTERS AND THE "SPATIAL TURN"

Space has long ceased to be seen as a passive geographic or empty geometric media. For Lefebvre (1991), space is an "encounter, assembly, simultaneity...[of] everything that there is in space, everything that is produced either by nature or by society, either through their co-operation or through their conflicts. Everything: living beings, things, objects, works, signs and symbols" (p. 101).

Reflections on the social production of space that are proving useful, particularly in education, can be found in social and cultural studies and in the writings of geographers: Doreen Massey, Henri Lefebvre, David Harvey, and Edward Soja. In the context of rural education, contemporary work on space can be found in the writings of, amongst others, Bill Green and Joanna Reid, Phil Roberts, Michael Corbett, Keith Halfacree, and Pam Christie.

INTRODUCTION TO THE WORK OF HENRI LEFEBVRE

Henri Lefebvre (1901–1991) was a French philosopher who inhabited the limits of Western Marxism and historical materialism (Elden, 2004, p. 193). Although he was a prolific writer much of his work has not yet been translated into English. His ideas are underpinned by his interest in everyday life. A recent translation of an essay, *The theory of ground rent and rural sociology* (Elden & Morton, 2016), shows Lefebvre's early interests were in rural questions. However, Lefebvre is better known in the Anglophone world as a theorist who focused on the urban because of the significant impact of his major work *La Production de l'Espace* (1974) that was translated into English and published as *The Production of Space* in 1991. Lefebvre's published work was produced rapidly, with brilliant projects; yet these were rarely completed (Merrifield, 2006). This stuttering (Deleuze & Guattari, 1986) rate of the production of ideas and of publications, results in meanings which are unsettling and troubling, yet also make the work experimental and approachable; you can enter it and write your own chapter (Merrifield, 2006). It is in the current "third wave" (Goonewardena, Kipfer, Milgrom, & Schmid, 2008) of interpretation of Lefebvre's writing where his work is being considered as a point of departure, resulting in its use in a wider range of disciplinary and interdisciplinary contexts, such as education (Kipfer, Goonewardena, Schmid, & Milgrom, 2008). Recent studies on the production of space and the spatial distribution of resources, systems, structures, policies, and so on in education, include those of, for example, Middleton (2014), Loxley, O'Leary, and Minton, (2011), and Thompson, Russell, and Simmons, (2014).

Lefebvre's primary arguments in *The Production of Space* center on how the production of social relationships and space has become part of the reproduction of the capitalist system; space, he argues, is *produced* through social practices and so becomes the ultimate locus and medium of struggle (Elden, 2004, p. 183). For Lefebvre (1976), "there is a politics of space because space is political" (p. 33).

KEY IDEAS OF LEFEBVRE THAT HAVE RESONANCE IN WORK ON EDUCATION, RURALITY, AND SOCIAL JUSTICE

Lefebvre Had an Interest in Everyday Life

Lefebvre's theories seem appropriate for researchers in rural education spaces and places, as he had a constant interest in and focus on everyday life (see, e.g., Lefebvre, 1987, 2000). Lefebvre's ideas are suitable for use at the molecular level (Deleuze & Guattari, 1987) engaging with the smallest and seemingly the least significant details of the everyday life of education places and spaces.

Space Can be Seen as Sites of and for Change

Lefebvre's work also appears to lend itself to those looking to develop an understanding of the geographies of injustices. For Lefebvre, the work of social change involved developing critical knowledge of the actual process of the production of space. The notion that space is actively produced, with social and material relations, or that social relations actively produce spatial relations, offers, Christie (2013) argues, an opportunity for theory and possible counter action in order to attend to "ways in which spatial practices can be interrupted, countered, and disrupted" (p. 778).

Space Can be Considered at a Micro and Macro Level, at The Same Time

Lefebvre (1991) envisages space as hypercomplex: "We are confronted not by one social space but by many—indeed by an unlimited multiplicity or uncountable set of social spaces" (p. 86) that are multilayered with layers "embracing...individual entities and peculiarities, relatively fixed points, movements and waves—some interpenetrating, others in conflict and so on" (p. 88). This hypercomplex view of space means that social space includes both local places and global ones and that "the local never disappears into regional or national or global spaces but continues to exist" (Christie, 2013, p. 777).

Lefebvre's ideas of space provide a frame for exploring local practices (*and* global practices, simultaneously). However, this is not a straightforward thing to do. As Christie (2013) lays out, the challenges to researchers include being aware of, acknowledging, and analyzing the multiple and complex social relationships inherent in the production of space as a continuous encounter. These "relationships include historical forms, present practices, things as well as humans. The sounds and the silences, intimate rhythms of the self and those of the state political, imaginary, material, the everyday global" (Christie, 2013, p. 777). The task, "to render intelligible qualities of space that are both perceptible and imperceptible to the senses, is a tough challenge and is a task that necessitates both empirical and theoretical investigation" (Merrifield, 2006, p. 108).

Lefebvre works through the complexity of space by arguing it needs to be understood, not in the usual two ways, as the *conceived*, abstract thought of space, or of the *perceived*, concrete reality of space, but in three ways, with the addition of space as *lived* (Elden, 2004, p. 187). He calls this heuristic a "spatial triad."

LEFEBVRE'S SPATIAL TRIAD

As a conscious move to transcend binary thinking and the establishment of oppositions, Lefebvre, among others, developed thinking triads or trialectics (see also, e.g., Deleuze & Guattari, 1994). Lefebvre's (1991) triad of perceived–conceived–lived space is articulated in *The Production of Space*. The triad is not described in much detail but it is clear that it is not a mechanical framework or a typology, but more of an "orientation" (Lefebvre, 1991, p. 423). Lefebvre referred to the three elements of the triad as *l'espace perçu* (perceived space), *l'espace conçu* (conceived space), and *l'espace vécu* (lived space). These three are referred to as *spatial practices, representations of space*, and *spaces of representation*. The three elements are fluid and alive and blur into each other (Merrifield, 2006).

Spatial Practices, *L'espace Perçu*, Perceived Space

This is physical, real, concrete space, space that is generated and used (Elden, 2004, p. 190). Concrete space is the space of gestures and journeys, of the body and memory, of symbols and sense-making (Elden, 2004, p. 189). Spatial practices have close affinity to people's perception of the world: perceived space. "Spatial practices structure lived reality; routes, networks, patterns and interactions" (Merrifield, 2006, p. 110) which develop continuity and cohesion: "In terms of social space, and of each member of a given society's relationship to that space, this cohesion implies a guaranteed level of competence and a specific level of performance" (Lefebvre, 1991, p. 33). Spatial practices "embrace production and reproduction, conception and execution, the conceived as well as the lived" (Lefebvre, 1991, p. 33). Everyday spatial practices make the local seem absolutely local; on the other hand, they make the global seem absolutely global. Spatial practices thus pivot around the "thing" world of everyday life (Merrifield, 2006, p. 134).

Representations of Space, *L'espace Conçu*, Conceived Space

For Lefebvre (1991), conceived space "is the space of scientists, planners, urbanist, technocratic sub-dividers and social engineers, as of a certain type of artist with a scientific bent—all of whom identify what is lived and what is perceived with what is conceived" (p. 38). This is the space of *savoir* (knowledge) and logic, of maps, mathematics as the instrumental space of social engineers, navigators, and explorers (Elden, 2004, p. 190). Here, space is a mental construct—imagined space. It is the dominant space of any society and "tied to the relations of production and to the 'order' which those relations impose, and hence to knowledge, to signs, to codes, and to 'frontal' relations" (Lefebvre, 1991, p. 33). This is the space of capital; and the state and ideology, power and knowledge lurk in the representations (Merrifield, 2006, p. 109).

Representations of space play a substantial role and specifically influence the production of space. Representation implies the world of abstraction—what is in the head rather than what is in the body. The calculation and measurement result in approximations that begin at the level of abstraction, a level away from the lived. As the representations of space are so powerful, there is a risk of "slippage," with these representations of space becoming a hyperreality or a simulation (Baudrillard, 1983). Representations of space can become mythical (Barthes, 1972)—the map precedes the territory. In order to make this mythic representation believable, the performance of the place has to accord with the image being promoted. The place and the people become the myth. This is often seen in work in, around, and of, rural places.

Merrifield (2006) argues that there has been a universal capitulation towards the conceived over the lived; abstract space has papered over the whole world and argues for a need to counter the power of abstractions and reclaim our society as lived projects (Merrifield, 2006). These arguments resonate with those of Kvalsund and Hargreaves in their call for rural research to begin, not with national or global scale policy or systems, the realm of conceived space, but with lived experiences, lived space.

Spaces of Representation, *L'espace Vécu*, Lived Space

Spaces of representation are the spaces of everyday experience lived directly

> through its associated images and symbols and hence the space of "inhabitants" and "users" and the lived spaces overlay physical space making symbolic use of its objects. Thus representational spaces may be said, though again with certain exceptions, to tend towards more or less coherent systems of nonverbal symbols and signs. (Lefebvre, 1991, p. 39)

These are the lived experiences that emerge because of the dialectical relation between spatial practice and representations of spaces. Here the space is produced and modified over time and through its use. Here spaces are infested with symbolism and meaning; they are felt more than thought. This space is of *connaissance,* of less formal or more local forms of knowledge (Elden, 2004) and is real-and-imagined. Space of representation is *alive* (Merrifield, 2006):

> It speaks. It has an affective kernel or centre: Ego, bed, dwelling house; or, square, church, graveyard. It embraces the loci of passion, of action and of lived situations and thus immediately implies time. Consequently, it may be qualified in various ways: maybe directional, situational or relational because it is essentially qualitative, fluid and dynamic. (Lefebvre, 1991, p. 42)

As we think about education research in rural places we must also attend to Lefebvre's (1991) warning that space as directly lived is also the space "of some artists and perhaps of those, such as a few writers and philosophers, who describe and aspire to do no more than describe" (p. 39). There is a risk that we might only produce descriptive work if we focus solely on lived experiences in our research work. However, as Merrifield (2006) argues, Lefebvre also sees lived experience as a space for development and change and, if he were here, would perhaps argue that a focus on lived experience of education and schooling in rural places would be more effective than a focus on the abstract base of systems and structures. Working with lived spaces, with their human and nonhuman actants, offers opportunities to find sites for change.

PUTTING LEFEBVRE'S TRIAD TO WORK

There are limited published examples in English of the use of Lefebvre's ideas in studies in rural contexts or places of education; a few are worth drawing attention to here. Green, Reid, and Corbett have been developing ideas of rural space that draw on Lefebvre's concept of social space (Corbett, 2016; Green & Corbett, 2013; Reid et al., 2010) There are a number of authors, including Pam Christie, who are using Lefebvre to help develop understanding of the geographies of inequity. Other authors have explored Lefebvre's ideas with respect to education policy and practice contexts (Middleton, 2014), and the appropriation of space in schools by pupils (Loxley et al., 2011) and teachers (Smith, 2014). Researchers are also putting Lefebvre to work on the geography of social issues such as those of young people who are not in education or training (Thompson et al., 2014).

There are a few published studies in English on rural communities that use a Lefebvrian analysis. Halfacree uses Lefebvre's ideas in his work (e.g., Halfacree, 2006, 2007) and there is a notable case study on the gentrification of two villages in England by Phillips (2002).

What follows here is a worked example of a piece of Lefebvrian analysis done when returning to a case study completed some years ago (see Gristy, 2014, for more details). It is in some ways an analysis of a place, an interruption in space (Tuan, 1977) but also an analysis of space within that place. The study begins very small, with the local, whilst also connecting with the regional, national, and global.

A Rural Community and Its Schools: A Worked Example

At the beginning, we must consider the impacts of our research footprints (White et al., 2012), and minimize a risk of harm to spaces, places, and people. This is of particular importance in rural or marginalized places where there are heightened risks of research voyeurism, disturbance, or damage (Gristy, 2014).

The author, who lives and works in and around a similar rural place, carried out this case study of a rural community in England, given the name Morton, and the education provision for its children and young people. To maintain anonymity all names and locality markers have been changed or removed; consequently quotes from texts and sources have not been cited or referenced.

The 3-year case study set out to investigate the role school played in the lives of the young people from Morton. Significant amounts of all kinds of data were generated through the study including documentary material such as local history books, a collection of contemporary and old newspaper articles, local council meeting minutes, and village newsletters. There was also quantitative data in the form of school attendance records and socioeconomic statistical information for the locality. A wide range of people were interviewed in Morton, including a youth worker, parish councillor, two parents of school aged children, the primary school head teacher, and a police officer. People interviewed at the secondary school included members of staff, the education welfare officer, and a school governor. In addition to the documentary and interview data the author kept a research diary of recorded reflections and responses on key events and casual meetings with people who were speaking about Morton.

Spatial Practices: Perceived Space, Material, Concrete, Physical

Morton is a large, compact, isolated village in South West England, centered on a crossroads with a few outlying farms, nine miles (approximately 15 km) away from the nearest town, Riversville. It is clearly a "community of place" (Delanty, 2003) set in a rural, high (relative to the surrounding area) moorland location, 510 m above sea level. Owing to its elevation and geographical location it has a wetter and colder climate than the surrounding area. The granite base rock dates back 295 million years and there are signs of habitation going back to 3,500 years BC. Morton is a village in a postindustrial landscape, a place that in the past has seen extensive quarrying and mineral mining among other small-scale industries. There are beef cattle and sheep farms on the open land around. The village, which currently has a population of around 1,500, is a center for walking and outdoor activities. It has a small grocery shop and post office, a gift shop, and a collection of pubs and cafes. The landscape of the village is dominated by large car parks for summer visitors. New, small business starter units have been built as part of a regeneration program. The church is closed but the chapel still has regular services. The library closed recently, but there is a youth club with its own new building, a football pitch, a new, purpose built community center, and a nursing home. Much of the land and many of the buildings are owned by one landowner. Bus services leave from here to go to town four times a day on weekdays and Saturdays, in addition to the school bus that takes students to the secondary school. A distinctive stone built bus shelter sits halfway between the two ends of the village. The village primary school had a role of 68 children in 2015, but only 45 in 2016. The primary school building was erected in 1850, of traditional Victorian design and stone construction. The majority of children attending the primary school walk there. Some live on outlying farms and arrive in Morton by car or minibus. The majority of young people aged 11–18 go to the secondary school in Riversville; most of these travel to school each day by bus. The young people divide themselves into halves—the top and bottom of the village—and travel to school on two separate buses.

A wave of building by the majority landowner in the 1960s led to more housing, but much of this is of poorer quality and is now in need of repair and refurbishment. Significant numbers of new private houses are currently being built as a response to housing shortage demands in all regions of the United Kingdom.

Representations of Space; Conceived Space, Abstract, Symbolic

Representations of the space of, in, and around Morton, of its landscape and of those that live there, offer a different view of the place. Abstract representations of space include measurements, local government reports, historical texts, stories, and contemporary discourses. Morton appears in local tourist brochures and history books of the area. Here are two examples. An extract from a local history text reads:

> Morton is a grim little town some 1,400 feet above sea level, with an abominable climate of fog, snow, wind, and more than 80 inches of cold rain a year. It stands on a cot between two high moorland tors, exposed to the bitter North and East winds, the least suitable place that could ever have been chosen for a town. But the site was dictated by the landowner so as to be near his granite quarries. (1954)

And a contemporary tourism leaflet:

> With the wild and imposing moor as a backdrop, Morton is ideal for exploring the region. There's a range of outdoor sports for adrenaline junkies, including climbing, canoeing and walking. The high moors are a place of myth, history and natural beauty and with many antiquities and natural won-

ders; you can easily access everything that the high moor has to offer from Morton. (2016)

Morton is perceived as being in an area of wild beauty but is also known as a "grim little town" with an unusually cold and wet climate. At the time of the original case study, Morton was undergoing a program of "community regeneration." An audit carried out as part of this program showed Morton to be a deprived community as measured by the index of multiple deprivation (ODPM, 2004), with access to services being a particular problem, along with high levels of unemployment and poor housing. Much of this housing is rented, with rents being paid for by the local authority. A small group of business units were constructed to promote local employment, but most of these units are still empty. The audit also identified lower than average achievement levels of children at the village primary school and poor school attendance at the secondary school by students from Morton. The combination of these two sets of statistics triggered a review of education provision for Morton's children and young people.

Data from the case study identifies intensely negative, labeling, separating discourses of, in, and around the village. The talk about the village was negative and the talk in the village was generally negative too, about such things as housing, the landlord, services, schools, young people, older residents, local businesses, and the weather. Here are a few examples:

> The cops are there most nights in the car park (Marty, a young person from Morton).
>
> The people in it [Morton] aren't exactly good (Jo, a young person from Morton).
>
> The local council have dumped quite a few problem families at Morton. (Jill, a parent from Morton)

There is also a negative discourse about Morton in the local press. Mike, one of the students from Morton reports: "[It] said in the paper that there were like in Morton, like youths up to like three o'clock drunk, disorderly, smashing the buildings and stuff."

In the schools, there was a less explicit but equally detectable negative discourse about Morton: the young people, their families, and the local community. For example, when asked whether a student's home location affected the way a student was perceived in the secondary school, a teaching assistant replied: "It shouldn't do, although you may get the situation, like with the Morton ones, where things are different" (Fran at Riversville College). A former Morton primary school head teacher said: "I compare it [my work at the Morton primary school] to my work in an inner city school." The current acting head teacher of the primary school (which has been deemed by OFSTED [Office for Standards in Education] to be in a state that "requires improvement") is also an executive head for five other small primary schools, following the national development in the United Kingdom for small schools to form federations. She tries to be at the school at least once a week to meet with staff and parents but does not always make it.

If we attend only to the *representations of space*, Morton would be a place of wild romantic beauty, with great history, but a down-at-heel miserable place to live in for its current inhabitants. The abstract version of Morton would paper over the whole (Merrifield, 2006). It is here that the stories of entrapment are immanent, waiting to be written. Moreover, of course, the act of writing of these spaces, however carefully the writing is crafted, is another abstraction from the real and the material. Writing about spaces and places adds another layer of representation.

The power of the abstract, perceived representations of space over the conceived and lived spaces of Morton is evident here. It is here, in these powerful abstract spaces of representation, hyperrealities of this rural community and its schools emerge. The hyperreal map or model of Morton as the grim little town, formed through exposure to representations through media, culture, history, and so on, takes on a life of its own. In the same way, maps or models of rural places like Morton inform and infiltrate thinking about rural places and schools more generally. This hyperreal version sits firmly in the minds of the school staff, as we see in this case study, and on into the minds of regional and national education leaders and policy makers.

Spaces of Representation: Lived Space, Social, Affective

People who took part in the case study said Morton was "such a remote out place" (Jo, student from Morton). John, a Morton resident said:

> People are never meant to have lived here. [In the past Morton was] a place for industry, getting stuff, doing dirty things, not a place for living. So now it is not a good place to live either. There are problems with high rainfall and cold, it gets into the buildings that get wet and stay wet, so are hard to look after. So they get in a bad way, tenants do not look after them, so property all gets bad and looks bad.

One could be consumed by the abstract representations of Morton and the hyperreality created by these. However, listening to the people who contributed to the case study and experiencing being in Morton, attending to the *spaces of representation*, the human and nonhuman actants in the space reveal other ways in which the space is socially and materially constructed. For example, unlikely to be picked up through the engagement of conceived and perceived space in Morton is the importance of the nursing home to the local young people, who sit on the walls outside; it operates as a "safe space." Other spaces of representation include the big visitor car parks that are sites for football matches when the grass is waterlogged in the winter. Without attending to the lived spaces in Morton we may miss the importance to the young people's connections with people who speak languages other than English that international tourists to the village provide.

When spaces of representation are understood as the education provision for the children and young people in Morton, a long-standing series of issues is evident. The primary school sits physically in the center of the village, an archetypal substantial English Victorian building. Children generally walk to school. It would appear to be an institution that is central to life in the village. However, the significance and meaning of this building for the community is understood differently through an analysis that considers it as a space of representation rather than a site of spatial practices or as a representation of a space.

Perceptions of the primary school held by the local education authority and the head teacher of Riversville College suggest that Morton is seen as a troubled place, and, as the audit showed, children's levels of school achievement and attendance are not good. Listening to people who live in Morton and observing in, out, and around the primary school, it is clear that the lived experience of this school and its community is complicated. A Lefebvrian analysis of observations draws attention to sites of potential alienation or exclusion at the school. For example, some parents of children at the primary school talk about meeting together at the school gate as a positive opportunity to see teachers and chat and gossip. Other parents report that this school gate activity is a barrier to them taking their children to school. The village is a small place. "I can't be doing with it, going up to the school and that. Everyone gets to know your business" (Mary, a parent whose son Daryl is not attending school). The gathering of parents at the school gate may be a space that needs managing differently by the school leaders, to change the patterns of social interactions that take place there.

Students who attend the secondary school in Riversville talk of the problems they have on their daily journeys on the school bus that appear to be a key barrier to school attendance. Morton resident Mr. Seccombe said his daughter Megan was not going to school and the reason was that "she hates the bus." In another chance conversation with a Morton parent at a children's football training session, I heard a similar story. The children of this family were being taken to school every day in the car because they hated being on the school bus (Research diary entry).

The bus journey to school and the material, the furniture of these journeys, are key sites and spaces of representation. Listening to the young people talk about the bus stop in the middle of the village, one becomes aware of its symbolic meaning—a site that divides the village in two, top and bottom. The young people from each half of the village travel to the secondary school in different buses. Here in the bus stop shelter, where the two communities meet, there are fights and settlings of scores as well as trysts and secrets. The resulting graffiti are a constant source of battle between the young people and the parish councillors.

Perhaps in the readings depicting the community of Morton as a space for representation, as a place of lived experience, there is again a risk of generating stories of entrapment. However, lived space is alive, always changing and it is here in lived space, Lefebvre argues, that we can find sites of and for change. In Morton, these sites of change might include the school buses, the welcoming entrances at the primary school and dry spaces to play. It is in theorizing work with Lefebvre's' spatial triad, that we can connect the stories from Morton with a global engagement of issues of inclusion, exclusion, and social justice in education.

CONCLUSION

Lefebvre's idea of the lived space, in addition to the conceived and perceived, gives us the opportunity to explore the empirical work done on places such as rural schools; but this is challenging work. The three elements of Lefebvre's triad, spatial practices, representations of space, and spaces of representation overlap and are fluid, so that clear boundaries between the perspectives are difficult to achieve. Through the act of writing, representations of space dominate and are difficult to challenge. Case studies that examine the minutiae of everyday life are important but we hope that working and making sense of them through theorizing means we can attempt to unsettle, destabilize, and shift assumptions (Ball, 2006). For example, we can examine how rural education research might be contributing to the development of hegemonies that are based on conceived, perceived, and perhaps hyperreal versions of reality, which may not convey the reality of lived experiences of educators, learners, and communities in rural places. There is a possibility here for engagement with the long-established hegemony of the rural as deficit, for example. Lefebvre provides a framework for the important struggle for researchers to trouble and engage with social practices and material relations at all levels and not collapse analysis into abstract notions. The triad encourages fine-grained, molecular level analysis of the different activities of spatial production. It encourages an engagement with the historical production of spatial inequalities, everyday experiences, and the mapping of these onto representations of space. The spatial triad approach promotes the idea of the activities of schooling as spatial practices being enacted and experienced at a local level in specific schools and communities whilst also being national–global. Using Lefebvre's triad requires a theoretical engagement of the case rather than just a description. In this way, the use of theory connects the case study with other bodies of work in education that are looking to develop understandings of how spatial, social, material inequalities and injustices might be challenged and disrupted.

REFERENCES

Ball, S. (2006). The necessity and violence of theory. *Discourse: Studies in the Cultural Politics of Education, 27*(1), 3–10.

Barthes, R. (1972). *Mythologies.* London, England: Vintage.

Baudrillard, J. (1983). *The precession of simulacra, simulations* (P. Fross, P. Patton, & P. Beitchman, Trans.). New York, NY: Semiotext(e).

Bourdieu, P., & Wacquant, L. (1992). *An invitation to reflexive sociology.* Chicago, IL: University of Chicago Press.

Christie, P. (2013). Space, place and social justice: Developing a rhythmanalysis of education in South Africa. *Qualitative Inquiry, 19*(10), 775–785.

Corbett, M. (2015). Towards a rural sociological imagination: Ethnography and schooling in mobile modernity. *Ethnography and Education, 10*(3), 263–277. https://doi.org/10.1080/17457823.2015.1050685

Corbett, M. (2016). Reading Lefebvre from the periphery: Thinking globally about the rural. In A. Schulte & B. Walker-Gibbs (Eds.), *Self studies in rural teacher education. Self-study of teacher and teacher education practices* (pp. 141–156). Cham, Switzerland: Springer International.

Delanty, G. (2003). *Community.* London, England: Routledge.

Deleuze, G., & Guattari, F. (1984). *Anti-Oedipus: Capitalism and schizophrenia.* London, England: Athlone.

Deleuze, G., & Guattari, F. (1986). *Kafka: Towards a minor literature.* (D. Polan, Trans.). Minneapolis: University of Minnesota Press.

Deleuze, G., & Guattari, F. (1987). *A thousand plateaus: Capitalism and schizophrenia* (B. Massumi, Trans.). Minneapolis: University of Minnesota Press.

Deleuze, G., & Guattari, F. (1994). *What is philosophy?* (H. Tomlinson & G. Burchell, Trans.). New York, NY: Columbia University Press.

Elden, S. (2004). *Understanding Henri Lefebvre: Theory and the possible.* London, England: Continuum.

Elden, S., & Morton, A. (2016). Thinking past Henri Lefebvre: Introducing 'The theory of ground rent and rural sociology.' *Antipode, 48*(1), 57–66. https://doi.org/10.1111/anti.12171

Elder, G., Kirkpatrick Johnson, M., & Crosnoe, R. (2003). The emergence and development of life course theory. In J. Mortimer, & M. Shanahan (Eds.), *Handbook of the life course* (pp. 3–19). New York, NY: Kluwer Academic.

Goonewardena, K., Kipfer, S., Milgrom, R., & Schmid, C. (Eds.). (2008). *Space, difference, everyday life: Reading Henri Lefebvre.* London, England: Routledge.

Green, B., & Corbett, M. (Eds.). (2013). *Rethinking rural literacies: Transnational perspectives.* New York, NY: Palgrave Macmillan.

Gristy, C. (2014). Researching within and for a rural community: Research journey. In S. White & M. Corbett (Eds.), *Doing educational research in rural settings: Methodological issues, international perspectives and practical solutions* (pp. 104–119). New York, NY: Routledge.

Gulson, K., & Symes, C. (Eds.). (2007). *Spatial theories of education: Policy and geography matters*. Abingdon, England: Routledge.

Halfacree, K. (2006). Rural space: Constructing a three-fold architecture. In P. Cloke, T. Marsden, & P. Mooney (Eds.), *Handbook of rural studies* (pp. 44–62). Thousand Oaks, CA: SAGE.

Halfacree, K. (2007). Trial by space for a 'radical rural': Introducing alternative localities, representations and lives. *Journal of Rural Studies, 23*(2), 125–141.

Hargreaves, L., Kvalsund, R., & Galton, M. (2009). Reviews of research on rural schools and their communities in British and Nordic countries: Analytical perspectives and cultural meaning. *International Journal of Educational Research, 48*(2), 80–88.

Kipfer, S., Goonewardena, C., Schmid, C., & Milgrom, R. (2008). On the production of Henri Lefebvre. In K. Goonwardena, S. Kipfer, R. Milgrom, & C. Schmid (Eds.), *Space, difference, everyday life: Reading Henri Lefebvre* (pp. 1–24). New York, NY: Routledge.

Kvalsund, R., & Hargreaves, L. (2009). Reviews of research on rural schools and their communities: Analytical perspectives and a new agenda. *International Journal of Educational Research, 48*(2), 140–149.

Kvalsund, R., & Hargreaves, L. (2014). Theory as the source of 'research footprint' in rural settings. In S. White & M. Corbett (Eds.), *Doing educational research in rural settings: Methodological issues, international perspectives and practical solutions* (pp. 41–58). New York, NY: Routledge.

Latour, B. (2005). *Reassembling the social: An introduction to actor-network-theory*. Oxford, England: Oxford University Press.

Lefebvre, H. (1976). *The survival of capitalism: Reproduction of the relations of production* (F. Bryant, Trans.). London, England: Allison & Busby.

Lefebvre, H. (1987). The everyday and everydayness. *Yale French Studies, 73*, 7–11.

Lefebvre, H. (1991). *The production of space* (D. Nicolson-Smith, Trans.). Oxford, England: Blackwell.

Lefebvre, H. (2000). *Everyday life in the modern world*. (S. Rabinovitch, Trans.). London: The Athlone Press.

Lefebvre, H. (2016). The theory of ground rent and rural sociology. Contribution to the International Congress of Sociology, Amsterdam, August 1956. *Antipode, 48*(1), 67–73. https://doi.org/10.1111/anti.12172 (Originally published in 1956)

Loxley, A., O'Leary, B., & Minton, S. (2011). Space makers or space cadets? Exploring children's perceptions of space and place in the context of a Dublin primary school. *Educational and Child Psychology, 28*(1), 46–63.

Merrifield, A. (2006). *Henri Lefebvre: A critical introduction*. London, England: Routledge.

Middleton, S. (2014). *Henri Lefebvre and education: Space, history, theory*. Abingdon, England: Routledge.

Office of the Deputy Prime Minister. (2004). *The English indices of deprivation 2004* (revised). London, England: Author.
Phillips, M. (2002). 'The production, symbolization and socialization of gentrification: impressions from two Berkshire villages.' *Transactions of the Institute of British Geographers, 27*(3), 282–308.
Reid, J., Green, B., Cooper, M., Hastings, W., Lock, G., & White, S. (2010). Regenerating rural social space? Teacher education for rural-regional sustainability. *Australian Journal of Education, 54*(3), 262–276.
Smith, C. (2014). *Secondary school staffrooms as perceived, conceived, and lived spaces: An investigation into their importance, decline, and sublation* (Unpublished doctoral thesis). Ontario Institute for Studies in Education, University of Toronto, Canada.
Soja, E. (2008). Taking space personally. In S. Aria & B. Ward (Eds.), *The spatial turn: Interdisciplinary perspectives* (pp. 11–35). London, England: Taylor & Francis.
Thompson, R., Russell, L., & Simmons, R. (2014). Space, place and social exclusion: An ethnographic study of young people outside education and employment. *Journal of Youth Studies, 17*(1), 63–78. https://doi.org/10.1080/13676261.2013.793793
Thrift, N. (2006). Space. *Theory, Culture and Society, 23*(2–3), 139–155.
Tieken, M. (2014). *Why rural schools matter.* Chapel Hill: The University of North Carolina Press.
Tuan, Y. (1977). *Space and place: The perspective of experience.* London, England: Edward Arnold.
White, S., Anderson, M., Kvalsund, R., Gristy, C., Corbett, M., & Hargreaves, L. (2012, September). *Examining the research 'footprint' in rural contexts: An international discussion on methodological issues and possibilities.* Symposium presented in network 14, Communities, families and schooling in educational research, European Conference on Educational Research, Cadiz, Spain.

PART IV

EDUCATIONAL RESEARCH AND SCHOOLING
IN RURAL EUROPE:
CHANGE, INNOVATION, AND HOPE

CHAPTER 15

SCHOOLS AND THEIR COMMUNITIES IN RURAL EUROPE

Patterns of Change

Cath Gristy
Plymouth University, England

Linda Hargreaves
University of Cambridge

Silvie R. Kučerová
J. E. Purkyně University in Ústí nad Labem, Czechia

This book has shared knowledge of the contexts and challenges faced by rural schools and their communities across Europe. The inclusion of the eastern European countries, Czechia, Hungary, Poland, and Serbia, informs us of the major and rapid developments in their rural schooling during the post-socialist period. These chapters are juxtaposed with chapters relating recent rural history, policy, and educational research situated in rural contexts in other European countries (Austria, England, Finland, Italy, the Netherlands, Norway, and Spain). Individual authors have presented authentic accounts of their national rural educational circumstances. They attend to national and European definitions and conceptualizations of "rural" and "schools" and make use of educational and structural statistics in their consideration of the wider social, economic, and geographical contexts.

Our emphasis has been to identify emergent themes, rather than predetermine the critical issues on the basis of the western anglophile rural education literature. Some issues are shared inevitably across the continent, notwithstanding its diverse political complexions, but the differing circumstances, pace, and extremes of change are exposed here. Our analysis and discussion of key issues raised by this collection of work spans the two final chapters. This first focuses on schools and their social, economic, political, and geographical contexts. It also considers the dilemmas of definition which surface through the book.

Before going further, we must refer to the "migrant crisis" that has been affecting Europe and was happening during the writing of this book. We anticipated that it would be a potent issue for several authors. It was surprising, therefore, to find a clear silence in their chapters with very little reference to migrations, possibly because there had been little impact on rural areas at that time. We include a discussion of the key issues for education later in this chapter and have included an overview of the migrant situation across Europe in an appendix written by Libor Jelen, a sociopolitical geographer from Czechia, and expert on European migration.

This chapter has three main sections. The first is a discussion of the patterns of schooling across rural Europe witnessed by our authors, addressed through a series of "axes of change." The second part is a reflection on recent developments as a result of the arrival of migrants into schools and communities in rural areas of Europe. The final part considers the diversity and dilemmas of definitions raised by the authors.

PATTERNS OF CHANGE IN SCHOOLING ACROSS RURAL EUROPE

Declining Numbers and Widening Distribution of Schools

The most obvious change, reported throughout the book, is the reduction in school numbers, especially of small schools in rural areas, since the mid-20th century. Similar enforced declines in school numbers are mirrored globally: in China (Wang & Lewin, 2016), the United States (Showalter, Klein, Johnson, & Hartman, 2017), and Australia (Starr & White,

2008). Educational provision has generally become spatially concentrated away from small settlements to larger centers (Hampl, 2004; Ribchester & Edwards, 1999). Kučerová, Meyer, and Trahorsch examine these patterns of school closure in Europe, in Chapter 2.

Changes to school numbers and structures of school networks in the last 30 years have been particularly dramatic in the post-socialist countries in Eastern Europe. The authors from Hungary, Serbia, Czechia, and Poland all report stories of very rapid social, economic, and political changes in moves toward more democratic, capitalist, neoliberal, market-oriented economic systems. The fast pace of political and economic change has precipitated alteration in education systems and structures. Elsewhere in Europe reductions in rural school numbers have taken place, not only following the ending of totalitarian regimes in Spain and Italy, but also in long established democracies. As shown in Chapter 2, the process of school closures has happened with different levels of intensity, at different periods and especially under different political regimes. Nevertheless, the intended purposes of school closure programs and the arguments used to defend them are similar: economic and operational effectiveness, cost savings, the following of particular pedagogical doctrines, and reactions to population decline or migration flows.

Responses to School Closure Programs: Axes of Change

Kučerová, Meyer, and Trahorsch (Chapter 2) undertook an analysis of the factors identified in the chapters here as influencing elementary education. They classified these under three principal headings: (a) educational policy, (b) political and economic conditions, and (c) physical geographical and sociocultural parameters. The great diversity of such factors across Europe, and the interplay between them in each country results in different national responses and leads us to identify a number of axes of change.

Closure or Cluster?

The poles of this axis are the closure of schools, versus the clustering or rearrangement of them. Several countries, including Norway, Finland, Hungary, and Spain, following periods of regular school closures, have adopted clustering strategies either formed voluntarily or imposed on small schools. Various models of clustering exist, including federation (see, e.g., the model described in The Netherlands), where head teachers and other resources are shared across schools. There is some evidence that federation can "rescue" schools otherwise likely to close (Ireson, 2012). In Hungary, voluntary clustering was initially encouraged through incentives but later made obligatory. The success of this strategy in maintaining school numbers was subsequently diminished in a sweep of "rationalization" by a right wing central government (see Kovács, Chapter 4 for details). In Spain a long tradition of small schools groups working together voluntarily is reported, in Chapter 8, by Vigo and Soriano, but support for these clusters varies in different autonomous regions.

At the other end of this axis are countries where schools were routinely closed without the opportunity to form clusters. In Poland, for example, Bajerski (Chapter 6) refers to the "shock treatment" of political and economic changes after 1989 when a staggering 40% of all rural schools in Poland were closed between 1990 and 2012. A similar pattern of mass closures is recorded in Czechia by Kučerová and Trnková (Chapter 5).

Resistance and Resilience or Submission and Surrender?

Another axis of change connects poles of resilience and resistance to change, with submission. This axis is more subjective and relies on the written reports of school changes by authors in these chapters and elsewhere. The long history of resistance to school closures and changes is well documented by scholars in Finland, Norway, Sweden, Denmark, and the United Kingdom. Here, communities have a history of well-developed strategies for questioning, confronting, resisting, or subverting changes to school networks. Discussion and consultation about school changes that are also happening in Spain are reported by Vigo and Soriano (Chapter 8), where there is a history of engagement with educational renewal. Countries from Eastern Europe, however, have seen the greatest reduction in rural school numbers over the past 30 years with little apparent resistance, possibly as a consequence of years of political compliance with authoritarian governments. Authentic testimonies from Czechia in Kučerová and Trnková's Chapter 5 provide insight into the impact of the centralized school closure decisions on people and communities. Kovács describes a short-lived civic movement that challenged changes to schools in Hungary (Chapter 4).

There is another way to approach what Corbett and Tinkham (2014) call the "wicked problem" of the precarity of small and rural schools. The studies from Poland (Chapter 6) and Finland (Chapter 12) focus on aspects of school network planning, and make the radical suggestion that the rural population needs to "[abandon] the community-based 'heart of the village' thinking, and change the way school networks are discussed, planned, offered and delivered" (Tantarimäki & Törhönen, Chapter 12, p. 268). Such thinking is ingrained and generations old, and arguably fossilized. Instead, and in line with Massey's (1994) vision of a progressive sense of place, a democratic, deliberative planning process including all sections of the school community is very gradually being adopted in Finland. This replaces planning decisions made purely at the political and/or administrative level, sometimes by a single person. It considers educational futures as part of a bigger picture that takes account of how a school closure affects multiple aspects of welfare and daily life. It offers a way out of the government-dominated "iron cage" for the present and future generations for whom digital communication is now second nature. It envisages what Hoogeboome and Ossewaarde (2005) call "reflexive authority." We shall return to this in Chapter 16.

Local Autonomy or Centralized Control?

A third axis of change in this collection involves the locus of control and responsibility for schools and their educational autonomy. At one end of this axis are places where there is tight authoritarian control of state funded schooling by national or local governments; at the other end are education systems that have more autonomy. In the stories from Eastern Europe and England, we hear of tight control of schools by the central government, whereas in Norway and the Netherlands control of schools happens at a more local level. In the Netherlands there is, generally, local control of schools, and here clusters (that include both private and public schools) are overseen by local professional school boards rather than local governments. In Italy, groups of schools have considerable autonomy with regards to teaching, assessment, and curriculum development. There is no clear link seen in this book between the locus of control of schools and patterns of school closure. It would appear that it is not the relative location or scale of governing authorities but the way policies of governing bodies are enacted and implemented that determines how and where schools are closed. For example in Norway, the control of schools was moved from national to municipal government and rather than protect numbers of schools in the municipalities as might be expected, the move to local control resulted in increased school closure rates, on budgetary grounds (Solstad & Karlberg-Granlund, Chapter 3).

Kovács' Chapter 4 provides a detailed account of the impact of swings in the locus of control of schools in the turbulent recent past in Hungary. Here, in the immediate post-Soviet period there was rapid decentralization of control over schools and increased teacher professional autonomy but this was found to be economically unsustainable. Hungary has seen a return to a right wing centralized system on grounds of economic viability, a system which has also been responsible for closing the national borders to refugees, and the internal ghettoization of Roma people in rural areas. This trend is evident in other European countries and is well documented by organizations such as the United Nations High Commission for Refugees (UNHCR) and Human Rights Watch (HRW; UNHCR, 2018; HRW, 2018).

THE ARRIVAL OF CHILDREN WITH MIGRANT BACKGROUNDS INTO SCHOOLS AND COMMUNITIES IN RURAL AREAS OF EUROPE

We expected to hear more about the movement of people within and across Europe in this collection of work, particularly as the book was being written during a period of significant immigration in the region. The absence of specific, detailed accounts of children with migrant backgrounds arriving in communities and schools may be due to a number of factors. These reasons include the waves of immigration from 2015 being considered as, initially, primarily an urban rather than a rural issue (Montero & Baltruks, 2017) and although migrants may well have been removed to reception centers in rural locations on arrival in a country, the settling of migrants into rural areas has happened later in the migration wave sequence. It has also taken time for the integration of children with migrant backgrounds into schools and other social services, their presence being a measure of migrant integration generally (Kordel, Weidinger, & Jelen, 2018).

UNESCO's global education monitoring report of 2019 has global migration as its focus. The familiar patterns of segregation of children with migrant backgrounds into particular schools or slower school tracks that compound their educational disadvantage and exacerbate prejudice (UNESCO, 2018) are evident across Europe. Pan European studies on the integration of children with migrant backgrounds into schooling show different levels of access to and support in education (Koehler & Schneider, 2019). Children with migrant backgrounds are generally registered into schools but the levels of support vary hugely. The challenges of including these children in schools and a lack of preparedness in national and regional authorities are well documented (see, e.g., Tereshchenko, 2014) and it is acknowledged that the situation may be particularly acute for schools in rural areas where there may be less experience of migrant communities, fewer economic resources, and less investment in specialized support services (Koehler & Schneider, 2019). However, we also see in Europe that the "migration crisis" has rekindled arguments about the need for systemic changes in education to make schooling more inclusive, and to strengthen relationships with schools and communities (Ahad & Benton, 2018) through revival and renaissance. These sorts of arguments are expressed in a number of chapters in this book including those focussed on Spain, Serbia, and Finland.

A number of rural areas in Europe have witnessed the challenges and opportunities offered by the arrival and short-term settling of children with migrant backgrounds into schools. It is well documented that in the very far north of Norway and Finland, which share borders with Russia, people traveling the Arctic migration route (see the Appendix for more details of

European migration routes) have arrived in very small, isolated communities above the Arctic Circle. Paulgaard (2019) considers the challenges of refugee integration in Sør-Varanger, a small municipality in Norway's northernmost region, which like similar areas of Finland, as detailed by Tantarimäki and Törhönen in Chapter 12, has experienced significant outmigration over the years. Paulgaard's studies of tiny schools in this region show how the resilience of the rural communities has allowed the reception, inclusion, and settling of young migrants. Paulgaard considers how these new arrivals might present opportunities for challenged communities and their schools, halting population decline and increasing economic activity. Others explore this hopeful theme by considering how immigration in rural Europe may contribute to sustaining local infrastructure such as schools (Kordel, Weidinger, & Jelen, 2018; Woods, 2016). For example the European association for information on local development (AEIDL) reports how refugees in Portugal and Italy are helping to revive rural areas by increasing the populations of small villages and schools.

Before we conclude this section, it is worth considering the language used in discussions about the refugee crisis witnessed in Europe from 2015. The UNHCR defines migrants as those who choose to move not because of direct threat of persecution but mainly to improve their lives by finding work, or in some cases education, family reunion, or other reasons. In this chapter we have used the term *migrant* in a more generic way as used by the European Commission (EC). We also use the term *children with migrant backgrounds* used by the EC in comparison of education policies and systems (Noorani, Baïdak, Krémó, & Riiheläinen, 2019). This term defines children who are newly arrived, first generation, second generation, or returning migrant children and young people.

In media coverage of recent European migrations alarmist, xenophobic language has been used; talk of migration "waves" and "crises." There are also differences in the ways terms are used in different countries. For example, in Germany and Sweden the terms *refugee* or *asylum seeker* are generally used, while the Italian and U.K. press prefer the word "migrant." In Spain, the dominant term is "immigrant." These terms have had an important impact on the tenor of each country's debate (Berry, Garcia-Blanco, & Moore, 2015). Europe's rich linguistic, political, and cultural diversity is evident here in the talk about the migrations in Europe witnessed from 2015. Also evident are attempts by organizations such as the EC to standardize terms and definitions. The next section considers the complexity in defining other key ideas and terms that have appeared in this book.

THE PROBLEM OF DEFINITIONS: QUESTIONS OF RELATIVITY

The words rural and small help to identify the physical location and size of schools in the countries represented here. Their definitions, as relative spatial concepts, are oft debated and frequently conflated (Kučerová, Meyer, & Trahorsch, Chapter 2) a situation reflected in debates published in international literature (Åberg-Bengtsson, 2009; OECD, 2019; Showalter et al., 2017; Shucksmith & Brown, 2016). Many rural schools are small, but as in the Netherlands, many small schools are not rural. The extent, nature, and population of rural territory impacts on the priority given to definitions and their importance in different places. For example, there are big differences in the character of rural spaces in isolated settlements in Scandinavia (see Chapter 12, Finland), and in the fragmented nature of rural areas near settlement units in Czechia (Chapter 5). In Chapter 2, Kučerová and colleagues present a detailed analysis of the spatial definitions encountered in other chapters, and, with fellow geographer Bajerski (Chapter 6), favor the use of relative population density and spatial identifiers such as "peripheral" and "remote," respectively. We will not resolve the definitions debate here, but we can at least summarize some European perspectives.

Defining Rural

The chapters provide several definitions of *rural* ranging from no official definition in the Netherlands, Austria, or Italy; rural as other than city in Serbia (Pešikan, Antić, & Ivić, Chapter 7), to formal national definitions based on population density and inter-settlement distances. In Chapter 4, for example, Kovács defines Hungarian rural schools as "schools run by villages and rural towns smaller than 10,000 inhabitants," a credential she and her colleagues use to extract rural issues from government statistics. England likewise defines rural areas as those that "fall outside of settlements of more than 10,000 resident population" but subdivides these into three rural settlement types (rural town and fringe, villages, hamlets, and isolated dwellings) each classified by its "sparse" or "not sparse" surroundings (GOV.UK, 2017). This results in about 31% of primary schools being defined as rural (Bagley & Hillyard, Chapter 13). In Czechia, Kučerová and Trnková (Chapter 5) use a local definition of rural to mean municipalities with fewer than 3,000 inhabitants. This encompasses about 60% of elementary schools, for children aged 5 to 13. In Spain, Vigo and Soriano (Chapter 8) report national statistics that define extremely rural places as those with fewer than 2,000 inhabitants and small schools as those located in isolated or inaccessible areas. Finland has a comprehensive series of territorial definitions including several pertaining to rural areas (Tantarimäki & Törhönen, Chapter 12).

Defining Small

There is large variation in the definition of a *small* school between and within national boundaries and some countries have no definitions at all. An example of the complexity of defining small schools is amply portrayed in the calculations done by the International Network for Digital Innovation, Research, and Education in Italy to try and determine what is meant by a small school across the country's autonomous regions (see link below in Table 15.1 and a discussion in Chapter 10 for more details). Figure 2.2 (Chapter 2) plots the percentage of schools with fewer than 100 children on roll in six countries and Table 15.1 indicates the scale of *small* and/or *very small* schools for countries included in this book. Unless identified otherwise, the data comes from the relevant chapters and, where necessary, additional sources of information have been cited.

In addition to the array of definitions of school size and types across (and sometimes within) countries, there are differences between definitions used in national and regional education policy and those used in practice. Kučerová, Meyer, and Trahorsch provide a comprehensive and nuanced discussion of the complexities of defining the terms used in studies of schooling in rural contexts, in Chapter 2.

Official Definitions: Is There a Case for International Thresholds?

While some argue that a search for definitions is not helpful, here we suggest agreed definitions of rural as a delimitation of space, and small, with regards to school size, would be useful to scholars and researchers. Also, importantly, geographical delimitations of space are used in and as data for political decision-making, including educational and community resourcing. So definitions (or lack thereof) have implications for the distribution of resources and hence social justice. Centralized definitions of rural and small such as those of the EC appear to be a set of definitions that could be used across Europe (and beyond). An agreed basis for the definitions of key terms across European states would facilitate comparisons of schools and the generation of data to inform policy, resource decisions, and draw attention to issues of rights and social justice for rural areas.

As noted in Chapter 1, the chapter authors have referred to a number of different multinational territory classification systems such as those of

TABLE 15.1 Definitions and Percentage of All Schools Considered "Small" or "Very Small"

Country	Definitions of Small (where available)	100 pupils or less	50 pupils or less	20 pupils or less
Austria	A small school is defined by number of classes and varies between regions.	60%	40%	6% found especially in mountainous Tyrol
Czechia	The minimum depends on the number of classes. A one-class school may have 10 pupils, provided the funding municipality can afford the obligatory expenditure.	43.5%		
England	Researchers tend to use 100 or less (Hargreaves, 2009; National Association for Small Schools, 2019). "Small" was recently defined by government as 210 or less (GOV.UK, 2017).	32% (O'Brien, 2019)	200 or less	
Finland	Small and "village" schools have 50 or less.		50.6%	
Hungary	A school with less than 15 students per grade (eight) is considered too small to be economically viable—125 pupils. Determined by the Education Act of 2007. Act of Parliament 2007 LXXXVII http://www.nefmi.gov.hu/letolt/kozokt/kozokt_tv_modosito_lxxxvii_070823.pdf	Not known		
Italy	Primary school (5 classes) 125 or less Lower secondary school (3 classes) 75 or less Smalls schools are characterized primarily by a number of students that is insufficient to form an entire course (5 or 3 complete classes). http://piccolescuole.indire.it/en/what-we-do/small-schools-in-figures/	Between 2 and 12% depending on the region		
The Netherlands	"Small" is defined by local population density so can range from 23 to 200. 50 or less is "very small" and "incomplete," in that there will be some composite or multi-grade classes.	19.6%		
Norway	Definitions of small school sizes vary with context.	31.1%		
Poland	Small and rural are used concurrently.	64.4%		
Spain	Definitions of small schools vary with locality.	100 or less—37.9%	25 or less—10%	

the Organisation for Economic Co-operation and Development (OECD, 2011), the United Nations Educational, Scientific, and Cultural Organization (UNESCO), and Eurostat (2019; the statistical office of the European Union; see Chapter 1). The OECD definition is the most commonly used in these chapters. The value of a stable, clear definition of rural in the production of longitudinal data sets can be seen in the regular "Why Rural Matters" reports from the United States (e.g., Showalter et al., 2017) which uses definitions and data from the (U.S.) National Center for Education Statistics (2018). Here, trends in student achievement, well-being and so on, can be deduced and compared across and within States.

The idea of a European education area is being developed by the European Commission (2017) and has inclusion and social mobility at its heart. This sort of pan-national project will require, or at least promote, the idea of a pan-European definition of rural in education contexts, in order to monitor the participation of young people from rural areas in the project. Clearly, a high-level definition may be useful for researchers, but could be dangerous in the hands of economists and politicians, making decisions from a distance without recourse to local contexts. Its potential usage demands close attention.

MOVING ON WITH DEFINITIONS

We acknowledge that there is a problem with focusing on definition, to understand the various and plural phenomena and processes in contemporary European rural space (Bell, 2007). It could be argued that it is better to focus on the concept of localities as socially constructed space, which are results of networks, flows, and mobilities (Lefebvre, 1991; Woods, 2011). These ideas are explored by Pesikan et al. in Chapter 7 and at more length by Gristy in Chapter 14 and Bagley and Hillyard in Chapter 13. If we go with this idea, would a more nuanced and critical use of the term rural result? A more positive use of the label rural would certainly help work which aims to achieve a fairer deal for rural schools, communities, and children.

As researchers, we should look beyond simple dichotomies such as rural–urban or core-periphery (Perlín, Kučerová, & Kučera, 2010). There is complexity and difference within what might be called a rural and indeed urban place (Van Dam, Heins, & Elbersen, 2002). Schools in rural, or rather nonurban areas have different levels of access to resources and have pupils with different characteristics and demands, according to the region where they occur. Schools located at the intersection of rurality and peripherality have particular issues, but here too, there is a wide variation in what this circumstance might mean in practice in different contexts. For example, economically successful rural "core" areas may well be considered advantaged compared to peripheral urban areas or socially and economically disadvantaged core urban areas with large but educationally and economically poor schools. While some shared terminology is desirable to facilitate concise accounts, Coladarci's (2007) plea is for researchers to include sufficiently detailed contextual information so that readers can decide for themselves where on the rural–urban spectrum to place the school in question.

In Chapter 1, the results of an OECD study (2013, p. 3) presented in Table 1.1, suggest that in the majority of the mentioned countries "nonurban" and urban schools differ primarily in relation to socioeconomic status and school size. This Program for International Student Assessment based study would suggest that the physical location of a school, whether it is in an urban or rural place for example, does not have a great impact on its school culture, material resources, or the curriculum. The picture is clearly complex.

With urbanization taking place in most European countries, the vast majority of the populations have an urban way of life. It is therefore not surprising that "problems" with rural areas and lives have been defined in urban terms and perception (Cloke & Goodwin, 1992). So, in such an urbanized society is it not better to perhaps dispense with the ideas and labels of rural and urban when considering schools and consider instead small and large schools? Small schools characterized by their human scale (see Raggl, Chapter 9) are associated with rural areas, but this is not always the case. It is quite possible to find large schools in rural locations, with pupils drawn from a wide area (see the extreme example from China, in the opening chapter) and very much part of a mass education system, oriented towards success of individuals in competition. On the other hand, we can find small schools in cities where there are alternative or specialized educational provisions, where there is the respect of pupils' individualities and diversity as would be expected from a small, human scale education provision (Dyson, 2008).

We posit that, in general, the "character" of each rural school, whatever its size and location in Europe, depends on a tripartite series of variable and fluidly contextual factors. These three contextual elements have different levels of influence in particular situations: within and between countries, regions' localities, and individual places. First there is the context that lies externally to the education system in which the school is situated. Here we find international and national economic and political forces at play. The second context is the framework and the institutional factors of the relevant education system. This might be a local system, separate from national governments such as those of the independent schooling networks developing in Austria, or the local nexus of school boards in The Netherlands. Or it might be a national education system such as that described in Norway and Finland, with a devolution of school provision to localities, where local knowledge can influence events previously controlled at national level. The third context is much more local and depends on internal predispositions, connected to the physical locality and the place. We see the effect of this local context particularly in the descriptions of community led school development in Spain.

This chapter has explored key emerging themes from the collection of chapters: patterns of change around school closures, the silence of migrants, and the dilemmas and difficulties associated with the myriad of definitions of key terms and concepts. Through a geography of schooling (Jahnke, Kramer, & Meusburger, 2019) lens, these key themes have been traced through the chapters from individual countries. In the next and final chapter, there is a consideration of the research taking place in education contexts and how this work, together with the innovation happening in rural schools, looks forward to the future.

REFERENCES

Åberg-Bengtsson, L. (2009). The smaller the better? A review of research on small rural schools in Sweden. *International Journal of Educational Research, 48*(2), 100–108.

Ahad, A., & Benton, M. (2018). *Mainstreaming 2.0: How Europe's education system can boost migrant inclusion.* Brussels, Belgium: Migration Policy Institute Europe.

Bell, M. (2007). The two-ness of rural life and the ends of rural scholarship. *Journal of Rural Studies, 23*(4), 402–415.

Berry, M., Garcia-Blanco, I., & Moore, K. (2015). Press coverage of the refugee and migrant crisis in the EU: A content analysis of five European countries. *UNHCR*. Retrieved from http://www.unhcr.org/56bb369c9.html

Cloke, P., & Goodwin, G. (1992). Conceptualizing countryside change: From post-Fordism to rural structured coherence. *Transactions of the Institute of British Geographers, 17*(3), 321–336.

Coladarci, T. (2007). Improving the yield of rural education research: An editor's swan song. *Journal of Research in Rural Education, 22*(3), 1–9.

Corbett, M., & Tinkham, J. (2014). Small schools in a big world: Thinking about a wicked problem. *Alberta Journal of Educational Research, 60*(4), 691–707.

Dyson, A. (2008). Beyond the school gate: Schools, communities and social justice. *Orbis Scholae, 2*(2), 39–54.

European Commission. (2017). *Strengthening European identity through education and culture.* The European Commission's contribution to the leaders' meeting in Gothenburg, 17 November 2017. Report no. 673. Retrieved from https://ec.europa.eu/commission/sites/beta-political/files/communication-strengthening-european-identity-education-culture_en.pdf

EUROSTAT. (2019). *Urban-rural typology.* Retrieved from https://ec.europa.eu/eurostat/web/rural-development/methodology

GOV.UK. (2017). *Defining rural areas.* Retrieved from https://assets.publishing.service.gov.uk/government/uploads/system/uploads/attachment_data/file/597751/Defining_rural_areas__Mar_2017_.pdf

Hampl, M. (2004). Současný vývoj geografické organizace a změny v dojížďce za prací a do škol v Česku [Current development of geographical organisation and changes in commuting to work and schools in Czechia]. *Geografie, 109*(3), 205–222.

Hargreaves, L. M. (2009). Respect and responsibility: Review of research on small rural schools in England. *International Journal of Educational Research, 48*(2), 117–128.

Hoogeboome, M., & Ossewaarde, R. (2005) From iron cage to pigeon house: The birth of reflexive authority. *Organization Studies, 26*(4), 601–619. https://doi.org/10.1177/0170840605051475

Human Rights Watch. (2018). *2018 European Union: Events of 2016*. Retrieved from https://www.hrw.org/world-report/2017/country-chapters/european-union

Ireson, J. (2012). *A study of hard federations of small primary schools: Digital education*. Nottingham, England: National College for School Leadership.

Jahnke, H., Kramer, C., & Meusburger, P. (2019). *Geographies of schooling*. Cham, Switzerland: Springer Nature Switzerland AG.

Koehler, C., & Schneider, J. (2019). Young refugees in education: The particular challenges of school systems in Europe. *Comparative Migration Studies, 7*(28). https://doi.org/10.1186/s40878-019-0129-3

Kordel, S., Weidenger, T., & Jelen, I. (2018). *Processes of immigration in rural Europe*. Cambridge, England: Cambridge Scholars Publishing.

Lefebvre, H. (1991). *The production of space* (D. Nicholson-Smith, Trans.). Oxford, England: Blackwell.

Massey, D. (1994). *Space, place and gender*. Cambridge, England: Polity Press.

Montero A. L., & Baltruks, D. (2017). *The impact of the refugee crisis on local public social services in Europe*. Brighton, England: European Social Network.

National Association for Small Schools. (2019). *NASS charter*. Retrieved from https://www.smallschools.org.uk/charter

National Center for Education Statistics. (2018). *School locale definitions*. Retrieved from https://nces.ed.gov/surveys/ruraled/definitions.asp

Noorani, S., Baïdak, N., Krémó, A., & Riiheläinen, J. (2019). *Integrating students from migrant backgrounds in schools in Europe: Eurydice brief*. Brussels, Belgium: European Commission Audio-Visual and Culture Executive Agency.

O'Brien, N. (2019, July). The decline of small schools and village schools. *Onward Research notes*. Retrieved from https://www.ukonward.com/wp-content/uploads/2019/07/Primary-schools.pdf

OECD. (2011). *Regional typology: Directorate for public governance and territorial development*. Paris, France: Author.

OECD. (2013). *Education at a glance 2013: OECD indicators*. Paris, France: Author. http://dx.doi.org/10.1787/eag-2013-en

OECD. (2019). *Learning in rural schools: Insights from PISA, TALIS and the literature*. Education Working Paper No. 196. Retrieved from http://www.oecd.org/officialdocuments/publicdisplaydocumentpdf/?cote=EDU/WKP(2019)4&docLanguage=En

Paulgaard, G. (2019, September). *Refugee integration and rural resilience?* Conference Paper presented at ECER Network 4, Hamburg Germany.

Perlín, R., Kučerová, S., & Kučera, Z. (2010). Typologie venkovského prostoru česka [A Typology of rural space in Czechia according to its potential for development]. *Geografie, 115*(2), 161–187.

Ribchester, C., & Edwards, B. (1999). The centre and the local: Policy and practice in rural education provision. *Journal of Rural Studies, 15*(1), 49–63.

Showalter, D., Klein, R., Johnson, J., & Hartman, S. (2017). *Why rural matters 2015–2016: Understanding the changing landscape.* A Report by The Rural School and Community Trust. Washington, DC: Rural Schools Community Trust.

Shucksmith, M., & Brown, D. (Eds.). (2016). *Routledge international handbook of rural studies.* Abingdon, England: Routledge.

Starr, K., & White, S. (2008). The small rural school principalship: Key challenges and cross-school responses. *Journal of Research in Rural Education, 23*(5). Retrieved from http://jrre.vmhost.psu.edu/wp-content/uploads/2014/02/23-5.pdf

Tereshchenko, A. (2014). *New migration, new challenges: Eastern European migrant pupils in English schools.* Report British Academy/Kings College London. Retrieved from https://www.naldic.org.uk/Resources/NALDIC/Research%20and%20Information/Documents/Tereshchenko%20%20Archer%20-East EuroPupilsReport2014.pdf

UNESCO. (2018). *Global Education Monitoring Report 2019: Migration, displacement and education: Building bridges, not walls.* Paris, France: Author.

United Nations High Commissioner for Refugees. (2018). *Europe situation.* Retrieved from http://www.unhcr.org/uk/europe-emergency.html

Van Dam, F., Heins, S., & Elbersen, B. (2002). Lay discourses of the rural and stated and revealed preferences for rural living: Some evidence of the existence of a rural idyll in the Netherlands. *Journal of Rural Studies, 18*(4), 461–476.

Wang, L., & Lewin, K. (2016). *Two decades of basic education in rural China: Transitions and challenges for development.* Singapore: Springer.

Woods, M. (2011). *Rural.* London, England: Routledge.

Woods, M. (2016). International migration, agency and regional development in rural Europe. *Documents d'Anàlisi Geogràfica, 62*(3), 569–593.

CHAPTER 16

EDUCATIONAL RESEARCH IN RURAL EUROPE

State, Status, and the Road Ahead

Linda Hargreaves
University of Cambridge

Cath Gristy
Plymouth University, England

Silvie R. Kučerová
J. E. Purkyně University in Ústí nad Labem, Czechia

To conclude this book on research in rural education in 11 European countries, and the patterns of change that it has revealed, we now foreground the forward-looking strategies that have emerged in the preceding chapters. This is not to suggest transplantation of policies or solutions between countries: such schemes frequently fail (Phillips, 2009; Raffe, 2011). Instead, it offers ways of thinking about small, rural, isolated, and peripheral schools' futures. Before that, however, we consider the nature and status of rural educational research in Europe based on the chapters presented here. If rural educational research is to exert an impact on policy, it must achieve greater visibility in the mainstream of educational research.

THE STATE AND STATUS OF EUROPEAN RURAL EDUCATIONAL RESEARCH

European rural educational research practices take many different forms ranging from wide-ranging descriptive surveys to insightful analyses of rich ethnographic data collected in single case studies. A decade ago Kvalsund and Hargreaves (2009) discussed the nature of rural educational research in northwest Europe and identified four factors that required attention to raise its profile within educational research. These are

1. the epistemological stance, of life- or system-world perspectives;
2. the variety of research designs employed;
3. the "voices" of rural research, noting the absence of children, community, and policy-makers; and
4. the role of theory in a field easily dominated by policy-led and pragmatic research.

As Corbett and White (2014), Schafft (2016) and some present authors have noted, rural educational research is a low status area of research outside the mainstream of educational scrutiny. It is a minority, and, largely an insider interest, despite the significant proportions of people served by rural schools. Howley and Howley (2014), who consider direct personal experience of rural living a necessary credential for rural educational researchers, provide four provocative "commitments" for the field: research as transgression, art, communication, and "work at odds with the university" (p. 9). Coladarci (2007), Corbett (2015), and Shucksmith (2016) have also offered advice on improving the status of rural research. That advice includes: avoid unsubstantiated advocacy of the merits of small and/or rural schools, provide better contextual detail (to obviate the angst over dichotomous rural/urban definitions), and increase the criticality, objectivity, and empirical work of the research. These writers broadly concur that rich descriptions of rural deficiency must be replaced with imaginative, constructive ideas and more evidence of community involvement.

The present research histories include a wide variety of examples capable of satisfying demands for more rigorous, well-designed, constructive, and imaginative research. Several chapters here discuss the nature of rural educational research in their countries. In some cases national records dating back well over a century enable researchers to make survey-based comparisons over time. In Serbia, for example, Pešikan, Antić, and Ivić

(Chapter 7) used census data to expose chasms of educational inequality between rural and urban provision including lower school and preschool enrollments, fewer qualified teachers, and high rates of illiteracy especially among women in rural areas.

Naturally, the selections of each nation's research studies will be influenced by the researcher's own academic discipline. Bajerski (Chapter 6), for example, refers to pedagogues, sociologists, geographers, and economists as rural research sources in Poland. Funding, of course, is a critical factor. While in some countries research councils and independent sources of funding can be approached, in others, the only source might be government sponsorship, which is unlikely to support proposals with potential to undermine policy.

THE LIFE-WORLD PERSPECTIVE AND THE RURAL SOCIOLOGICAL IMAGINATION

In contrast to the Nordic and British studies of 2009, the life-world perspective is dominant in the research reported here, as authors draw on their own ethnographic research. Such research foregrounds the voices of those who inhabit the rural schools and communities, thus meeting Kvalsund and Hargreaves' (2009) call for more authentic voices. Vigo and Soriano (Chapter 8), for example, include their own case studies of three rural schools in Spain and contrast the rural teachers' references to their innovative teaching practices with wider extant research that focuses on the disadvantages of "poor rural schools" (Vigo & Soriano, 2015). They highlight the tradition of bringing rural teachers together to share innovative expertise at interschool conferences, established by Catalan teacher, Rosa Sensat (1873–1961). Sensat's vision of the researcher-practitioner was ahead of its time, but is now supported by research partnerships between rural school groups, universities, interschool observatories, and, crucially perhaps, funded by some of the autonomous regional governments.

RURAL RESEARCH IN SPACE AND TIME: QUESTIONS OF DESIGN AND DEMOCRACY

This section employs Kvalsund and Hargreaves' (2009) space and time typology of research designs to classify some of the designs encountered in this book (see also Kvalsund, 2019).

The first quadrant of the typology shows designs set at a single point in time and space, such as a school case study. The single entry is Karlberg-Granlund's (2009) in-depth case study which reveals the destructive stress and strain experienced in a one-teacher school in Finland that had been under threat of closure for several years. In contrast to Kvalsund and Hargreaves' (2009) review, single case study designs were relatively rare in this collection.

The second quadrant includes studies of several points in space but at one time, or in a narrow time frame (Table 16.1). Multiple case studies such as these allow comparison of how similar small and/or rural schools cope with different external circumstances (see Table 16.1).

The third quadrant accommodates the study of change in research conducted in one location but at different times or over an extended period. These designs also permit comparisons, notably analysis of change over time. Kučerová and Kučera's (2012) geographical mixed methods study in Czechia identified associations between an uneven spatial distribution of school closures over time and how this affected the shape of catchment areas and commuting patterns (Chapter 5). Two time referenced case studies of single places in England reveal the insights to be gained by applying appropriate theory to the analysis of the case. Gristy (Chapter 14) exploits Lefebvre's theory of space, while Bagley and Hillyard (Chapter 13) conduct a Bourdieusian analysis of a rural head teacher's accounts of her work, both over a 3-year period. Opportunities and resources for the conduct of long-term studies like this are difficult to obtain, however (see Table 16.2).

Finally, the fourth quadrant, which represents studies based in several points in time and in space, is surprisingly well populated. Table 16.3 shows six studies.

TABLE 16.1 Research Designs Set at One Point in Time but Several Points in Space

Country/Author(s)	Notes on the Research Examples in This Category
Italy: Cannella Chapter 10	Multilevel/non-graded classrooms in three rural schools' networks; pedagogical focus on using ICT for interschool collaboration.
Hungary: Kovacs Chapter 4	Case studies of two rural schools: focusing on teacher attitudes to ethnic diversity and inclusion. One school closed, but where teachers introduced interactive teaching and community participation including Roma families, the school survived
Spain: Vigo & Soriano Chapter 8	Case studies of two small rural schools in one region showing how family involvement has ensured the schools' survival.
Austria: Raggl Chapter 9	Case studies of 10 small rural schools (focus here on two schools) where the Montessori approach is giving very small schools a new lease on life. Interviews with head teachers, teachers, and children.
Netherlands: Deunk & Maslowski Chapter 11	Interview survey of 40 small schools' principals, in 13 school boards, showing leaders' coping strategies as rolls decline, and how these strategies are interpreted at classroom, school, and school board levels.

TABLE 16.2 Research Designs Focused on One Point in Space but Several Points in Time

Country/Author(s)	Note on the Research Examples in This Category
Czechia: Kučerová & Trnková Chapter 5	Mixed methods geographical study of one region; focus on two schools. Combines quantitative data from census, documents, maps; qualitative data from informants from one open and one school closed in the 1970s, revealing uneven spatial distribution of school closures over time and influence on commuting patterns. Using interviews with "period witnesses" in 2009, 2011, and 2013.
England: Gristy Chapter 14	Mixed method geographically focused survey of one small rural town and its school: perceptions, conceptualizations, and experiences of "that space" in a 3 year period, using Lefebvre's tri-partite theory of the social production of space.
England: Bagley & Hillyard Chapter 13	Ethnographic case study of one small rural school and community, focusing on school leadership conducted over 3 years. Analysis of the head teacher's expertise in the Bourdieusian *field* of education to counter arguments from the economic field on small school viability.

TABLE 16.3 Research Designs Using Several Points in Time and Several Points in Space

Country/Author(s)	Note on the Research Studies in This Category
Norway: Solstad & Karlberg-Granlund Chapter 3	The "case" is the school journey, based on multiple examples, comparing the result of surveys conducted in 1990 and 2015 which reveal the considerable extension of children's school journeys as local rural schools have been closed, and the negative effects on their physical and psychological health.
Czechia: Kučerová & Trnková Chapter 5	Trnková's (2012) meta-analysis of Czechian elementary schools' research in seven peer-reviewed journals 1990–2012, updated 2016.
Czechia: Kučerová & Trnková Chapter 5	Cartographic analysis of distribution of school closures, in two regions at specific time points (Kučerová & Kučera, 2012).
Spain: Vigo & Soriano Chapter 8	Case studies of three schools, each over a 3-year time span (Vigo & Soriano, 2014) comparing teaching practices and teachers' perceptions of diversity, before and during a collaborative action to reinforce and develop creative teaching practices (Vigo & Soriano, 2015).
Poland: Bajerski Chapter 6	National surveys of school closures, their geographic distribution, and use of combined classes.
Finland: Tantarimäki & Törhönen Chapter 12	Series of three studies of school networks: documentary analysis at 4 × 4 yearly intervals; analysis of public media discussions, network plans, and online survey.

The Czechian meta-analysis of research on elementary school education included 343 studies, of which 43 have a spatial component, mainly comparing rural and urban locations. Although meta-analysis is not practical empirical research, it is included because it is a strategy that draws on many points both in time and in space that could be used more in rural educational research.

The studies from Finland and Poland exemplify different ways to use the time variable. Tantarimäki and Törhönen (Chapter 12) used a time series of studies conducted in 2009, 2011, and 2013, concerned with what was shown to be the slow progress of a new collaborative approach to school network planning across Finland. Bajerski's Polish study (Chapter 6) uses cartographic evidence and national records over two 5 year periods, from 2003–2008 and 2008–2013, to examine patterns of school closures and their effects on the shape of school networks. These studies have both breadth and depth, and permit a view of the bigger national picture.

To sum up this section, the range of designs seen in the chapters here shows greater diversity than those identified by Kvalsund and Hargreaves in 2009. Possibly a by-product of the authors' varied disciplines, this demonstrates some improvement in rigor and imagination in rural educational research design. That said, there is still a dearth of comparative designs needed to justify judgements of the relative qualities of rural/urban or large/small schools.

WHOSE VOICE IS HEARD IN RURAL EDUCATIONAL RESEARCH?

Kvalsund and Hargreaves (2009) encouraged researchers to access and *listen* to those most closely affected by the life or death of a small and/or rural school, namely children. Despite this, their voice remains underrepresented. Exceptions include Gristy (Chapter 14) and Raggl (Chapter 9). Both include children's words verbatim, which express children's experiences more graphically than any paraphrased report: Children are, as Cutter-Mackenzie, Edwards, Moore, and Boyd (2014) put it, "experts of their own lives" (p. 104). In the same vein, the community voice is still unusual. Incidentally, browsing scholarly databases for rural research and communities reveals few references to schools. Is the implicit message here that rural research, like some rural areas, no longer includes children? Could this situation be changed by the moves towards greater community involvement in rural schools, in Spain, Serbia, Hungary, and in rural school planning in Finland and Poland? Perhaps rural social researchers will begin to notice children's lives, while rural educational researchers might listen more to community voices. Kučerová and Trnková's (Chapter 5) use of "period witnesses" sets an intergenerational example worthy of emulation.

CONNECTING RESEARCH ON EDUCATION IN RURAL CONTEXTS WITH MAINSTREAM EDUCATIONAL RESEARCH

It has been argued that greater engagement with theory could strengthen the quality and raise the status of rural educational research (see Coladarci, 2007; Corbett, 2015; Gulson & Symes, 2007; Kvalsund & Hargreaves, 2014). Schafft (2016) notes the concentration of published research in our field in journals dedicated to rural educational research, thus essentially being sidelined as regards to the mainstream of educational research. To achieve any policy impact, however, publication in mainstream journals with higher impact factors is needed. Only there might we counter persistent stereotyped images of the quality of education in rural schools, and publicize the positive developments, as well as the challenges, presented in the preceding chapters. The word "rural" itself, not to mention semantic alternatives such as "peripheral" or "remote," aggravates the separation from the metro-centric mainstream. High impact educational and social science research journals, however, often favor submissions with a well-calculated theoretical foundation. In Chapter 14 (p. 305) Gristy quotes Lefebvre's plea (2016/1956, p. 72) "that a theory is needed" in rural sociology to deal with the "extremely complicated realities" of rural life (p. 67) that exceed description and empiricism. As an example Lefebvre chose Marx's theory of ground rent to bridge inter-disciplinary boundaries between history, economics, and politics when considering land ownership and use. In a similar way, Gristy shows how Lefebvre's own theory can be applied to a case study to explore the social production of space.

Work with theory to develop and connect ideas from cases, specific sites, or incidents can provide insights that could otherwise go unnoticed, as well as guiding research design. Several authors here have appealed to spatial or sociological theories to frame their research.

Gristy, in Chapter 14, for example, used Lefebvre's theory of the social production of space in her 3-year case study of a rural town, Morton, and its schools. Lefebvre's "spatial triad" of perceived, conceived, and lived space facilitates identification of specific points of conflict or alienation in this anything but an idyllic place. Such points can then be explored and potentially healed. Gristy's research illustrates clearly how theory can guide the research process, and connects with other Lefebvre-based research.

Some authors here have found Massey's theory, as expressed in her seminal 1991 essay "A Global Sense of Place," useful. While retaining the role of landscape or geographical place (Massey, 2005) and respecting human needs for belonging, and rootedness, she defined "place" as "constructed out of a particular constellation of social relations, meeting and weaving together at a particular locus" (Massey, 1991, p. 28). Each place represents the meeting or intersection of all the networks of social relations, movements, and communications going on at any point in time, and moving at different rates in different ways, which involve the social actor. Massey (1991) sought "a sense of place which is extroverted [sic], which includes a consciousness of its links with the wider world, which integrates in a positive way the global and the local" (p. 28). Its borders are open, not closed. The traditional sense of place as stable and constant, is a myth: places are constantly changing, imperceptibly perhaps, whether through the social relations that constitute their histories, or the landscapes, including the slowly moving mountains, that support them (Massey, 2005). The building of a school itself was a change, often seen as an unwelcome form of social control, in rural settlements in the 19th century. Thus, in the context of rural schools, consideration of the future of a school and its so-called community demands openness to connection with other schools and communities for survival.

In this way, Tantarimäki and Törhönen (Chapter 12) used Massey's (1991) global sense of place to help explain the slow progress of new participative network planning, which requires villagers to expand, but not lose, their place identity horizons by collaborating with other places in their municipality. Vigo and Soriano (Chapter 8) also draw on Massey showing how teachers, students, and families from different places come together to develop new strategies for working in small rural schools in Spain. They note how, in so doing, rural people can overcome the ideological devaluation of rural places inherent in Bourdieu's theories of cultural capital and social reproduction.

That is not to reject the strong analytical value of Bourdieusian theory. Bagley and Hillyard's (Chapter 13) analysis of how a rural school head teacher uses her habitus and capital to inform her practice, in countering the increasing "contamination" of the educational field by economic considerations. Like Gristy, Bagley and Hillyard show clearly how theory can be applied to the interpretation of ethnographic data in a rural school context. Raggl (Chapter 9) also found Bourdieu's concept of cultural capital useful to explain urban parents' choices of small Montessori schools in Austria. Kovács (2015) uses Wacquant's (2008) theory to argue that the ghettoization of Roma people in rural Hungary is a more powerful example of "advanced marginality" than Wacquant's original study of Black workers in Chicago.

There remains a case, nevertheless, for straightforward description. In this collection, national rural research is often inaccessible to an international readership because its language of publication is Polish, Hungarian, or Finnish, for example. While national policy-makers might pay attention, wider awareness of national plans and dilemmas can be achieved only through publication in an international language such as English. This was a principal motive for this book.[1]

To conclude this section, putting theory to work in rural educational research can connect to wider bodies of educational knowledge and literature. These might include global issues such as social inequality and injustice, education for climate change, sustainable development and living, as well as educational innovation. Such rural research could be at the forefront of thinking about society, community, and education as we move on from recent neoliberal thinking. The chapters from Spain, Norway, and Finland illustrate how the work of rural educators informs educational discourse and policy whilst maintaining independence from global brands, structures, and systems.

OUT OF THE IRON CAGE? STORIES OF RENAISSANCE AND HOPE

Kvalsund's "Words to the Reader" in the Foreword to this book, warn of the dangers of rural schools finding themselves in Weber's metaphorical "iron cage" as nations pursue economic growth through educational achievement in the global market, and, in consequence, rural schools become "rurbanized." This challenges Bell and Sigsworth's (1987) observation that rural schools share more features across Europe than they do with their national urban counterparts. Have the intervening decades of globalization and the "rurbanization" of rural schools countered this observation?

The present chapters show that rural schools internationally share vulnerabilities, such as closure or "consolidation," limited resources, or negative public and government perceptions. In present times, failing schools in non-rural areas experience similar vulnerabilities to closure or restructuring, while clustering of schools through consolidation, federation, or other strategies, is again familiar in non-rural areas (OECD, 2013).

Despite these familiar threats, this collection includes many stories of renaissance, hope and joy, as ways out of the iron cage. Rural schools can be sites of innovation, at the center of change, resurrected by parent groups, and becoming specialist centers. In Austria (Chapter 9), for example, the Montessori brand is saving threatened small schools, although, ironically, it is alienating some local families.

Another route out of the tyranny of supranational organizations is through increased community involvement in rural schools. In Spain, this encompasses authentic, as opposed to superficial, community inclusion and involvement, achieving what Solstad has called the "community active" school (Chapter 8). In 2009, research on the community–school relationship was unusual except in Finland (Kalaoja & Pietarinen, 2009), where it continues to be an important feature of the small rural school (see Solstad & Karlberg-Granlund, Chapter 3). It has constructive potential in areas where Roma/non-Roma segregation is a challenge, such as Hungary (Chapter 4) where Kovács' example of a school avoiding closure is a "community active" school, inclusive of its Roma inhabitants (see also Flecha & Soler, 2013). The development of community involvement in the school, for example, through inclusive egalitarian dialogue (Flecha, 2015), is a move towards the criteria for Corbett's (2015) rural sociological imagination and Shucksmith's (2016) reimagining of the rural. It represents another way out of the iron cage as communities reclaim their rights to involvement in their children's lives.

The Serbian government (Chapter 7) has been developing Rural Education Tourism (RET) as a strategy to support and strengthen rural schools. As Vignoles (2016) demonstrates, investment in the basic skills of the lowest qualified sections of society, whether children or adults, brings economic benefits. Research case studies of schools and communities before, during, and after development of RET projects could be encouraged.

All these ways of making the school more significant and relevant within a community, increasing community involvement, or reconceptualizing school networks more flexibly, are ways to assert a new more representative democratic authority in rural schools. Schools can be seen as nodes in a network, part of a greater, interconnected, steady, flexible whole, where there are shared values and practices alongside local autonomies. Here, perhaps, there are prospects for sustainable, collective, and collaborative models of education and schooling. Policies and practices proven successful in rural education contexts, which have been "rural proofed" (DETR-MAFF, 2000), could inform the development of schooling models in *all* geographical localities.

A RADICAL ALTERNATIVE: ITALY'S "SMALL SCHOOLS' MANIFESTO"

In Chapter 10, Cannella presents the forward-looking work of the Instituto Nazionale Documentazione Innovazione Ricerca Educativa (INDIRE, 2018), which "for years has been supporting the permanence of schools located in geographically isolated territories, in order to maintain an educational and cultural presence and to fight the phenomenon of depopulation" (p. 1). Instituto Nazionale Documentazione Innovazione Ricerca Educativa has experimented with, and evaluated methods designed to enable very small schools to work together, "to overcome isolation, to link classes with few pupils, and to develop training paths based on the use of technologies and remote collaboration" (p. 1). The radical move is not only to *use* its small schools to fight the challenge of depopulation, given a land that is over 75% islands and mountains, but to recognize those schools and communities in Italy as, "communities of memory, custodians of one heritage of history, art, traditions, and cultures often unique and deep, of environmental treasures of great value" (p. 1). As Cannella explains in Chapter 10, two particular teaching strategies, the "common learning environment" and the "shared lesson" have been developed to capitalize on the affordance of small, multiage classes and new communication technologies. The teachers involved have experienced rapid professional development in learning to use the technologies, and adapting their practice and the curriculum to optimize the learning environments. To conclude, the Small Schools' Manifesto (*Manifesto delle Piccole Scuole*; INDIRE, 2018) proposes three pillars of small or isolated schools' sustainability which capitalize on their strengths as

1. being communities of memory and quality learning
2. having the technologies to support social inclusion
3. using the experience of pluriclasses as a resource, not a limit.

This manifesto has grown out of investment in new technologies and working with teachers, some of them initially reluctant, to bring the schools together but to retain schools in their communities.

DISCUSSION

We see this collection as a contribution to scholarly work being done to develop contemporary narratives that counter historical ones of deficit and despair. It offers what can be seen as a point of departure and contribution to those grappling with the universal challenges of the "Anthropocene," or man's influence on the earth's systems (Smith, Fraser, & Corbett, 2017, p. 1).

Models of education, with their development goals determined by Euro-American standards (Harber, 1996, 2014), can seem globalizing and unifying. However, they can also be seen, as they are here, as multivalent, sometimes in opposition but very diverse, emphasizing plurality, multiculturalism, identity issues, and variety in education (Sadovnik, 2011). The OECD with its six "Schooling for Tomorrow Scenarios" (2011) suggests outlines for possible future developments of educational systems. These models include:

- preservation of the existing status of schools as institutions;
- schools having broadened functions and forms;
- extension of market approaches to education providers; and

- the weakening and decline of formal, organized educational systems in favor of other forms.

While there are stories in this collection that could be aligned with the OECD's six models (2011), these models cannot be blueprints for rural educational development. They must be interrogated, modified, accepted, or rejected by educationists and communities together taking account of their value for each context, culture, and community. Otherwise, as Kvalsund (Foreword, this volume) has warned, they may construct new "iron cages of rationality," driven by the high values currently placed on performance and economic efficiency.

In parallel with this competitive culture, however, this book includes many examples of cooperation between different parties: (a) rural schools and their communities, (b) rural schools and neighboring communities, (c) small isolated schools with other small isolated schools through technology, and between (d) communities trying to find optimal solutions for education and welfare so that each community can retain its place identity but enhance that identity through association with neighboring communities. Each of these partnerships is a step towards the intra- and inter-community cooperation necessary for rural schools to survive and flourish.

Now, imagine the combined power of these cooperative partnerships. Suppose parents and community with firsthand experience of supporting learning at school, join with similarly knowledgeable people from other communities, and come together with educationalists and politicians to discuss their various educational and welfare needs on an egalitarian basis. Such councils would fit Kvalsund's concept of *glocalisation*, built upon Bauman's (2001) concept of *universalism*, wherein "nations, local communities, and persons cooperate in universal dependence," to form "a balanced process of individual agency and collective structures quite unlike what happens in competitive economic or capitalist globalization" (Kvalsund, Foreword, this volume). A key complementary feature here, once achieved, is the power of face-to-face dialogue amongst all sections of the community, including teachers, families, community members, and, ideally, students too. The growth of such fora could offer protection from the decontextualized intrusions into superordinate educational policy authorized by supernational organizations.

Earlier we referred to Hoogeboom and Ossewaarde's (2005) concept of "reflexive authority." They suggest this as a fourth form of authority additional to Weber's traditional, charismatic, and legal-rational forms of authority, the last of these effectively legitimating the psycho-political imprisonment of unsuspecting individuals. Reflexive authority, according to Hoogeboom and Ossewaarde, overrides Giddens's and Beck's arguments that in late modernity Weber's goal-oriented rationality will break down as the bonds between institutions and the individual become unstable, and are replaced by reflexivity, at both institutional level and in individual social action (see e.g., Beck, Giddens, & Lash, 1994). In past eras, the functional relationship between institutions and actors has been bound by belief in traditions or goal-oriented rationality. Subsequently, such beliefs have been eroded, and "in late modern society institutions are engaged in a process of winning and keeping the *trust* of reflexive actors, which by definition is in constant need of maintenance and sustenance" (Hoogeboom & Ossewaarde, 2005, p. 613). Then, stability may be reestablished by reflexive authority, or "the belief in the ability of institutions and actors to negotiate, reconcile and represent arguments, interests, identities and abilities" (Hoogeboom & Ossewaarde, 2005, p. 614).

The participative, deliberative discussions about school networks, being encouraged in Finland, and between schools and communities in Norway, Spain, and Italy could represent the reflexive authority needed to spark Corbett's (2015) call for "rural sociological imagination" and Shucksmith's (2016) for a reimagining of the rural. In theory, at least, this could ease the areas of friction identified using Lefebvrian theory, and capitalize on head teachers' strategic playing of educational values in the economic field of Bourdieusian thinking. Such authority, exercised between communities, could transform what Massey (1991) calls a reactionary, defensive view of place, to a progressive one, which does not deny the uniqueness of place but recognizes the historical layering of different linkages, locally and globally, without being threatened by it (p. 9).

Finally, INDIRE's Small Schools Manifesto, is an inversion of the stereotypical stories of deficit and consequent depopulation to a proclamation of rural schools' potential to counter depopulation, and nurture local cultural associations. Such assertions are not uncommon, hence Coladarci's (2007) concerns mentioned earlier, but the portrayal as a "manifesto," backed by situated research and development, provides teachers, families, and children with three tangible bases (as communities of memory and learning, exploiting new technologies, with the resource of multiage classes) to boost their self-confidence as guardians of the local and participants in the global.

CONCLUSION

This book has presented a range of educational histories, political ruthlessness, and creative developments in its accounts of schooling in rural Europe. It has revealed commonalities in the form and organization of educational systems with positive or negative consequences to small and rural schools. These include first, the extent of centralization, from systems entirely underpinned by state interests to those where decision-making has been delegated to municipal or other local authority structures. Secondly, we have seen educational ideals such as the certainty of schools in every community fall foul of funding shortages. Thirdly, the location of the locus of responsibility for educational provision in rural areas may be at national or state level, when educational systems are more unified with central control over educational processes, but also susceptible to global forces prioritizing narrowly defined academic performance—hence their moves towards creating larger schools, on economic rather than educational grounds (see Solstad and Karlberg-Granlund's discussion of "global forces" in Chapter 3). Although the authority may aim to guarantee equity of opportunities and reduction of inequality, this equalization process can lead to excessive and directive unification of the system. This in turn leads to preference for a normative majority and inevitable restriction or even exclusion of minority interests. We hear this story repeatedly, for example in Hungary, Czechia, and England. Finland alone in this collection has resisted global pressure to seek economies of scale where its educational values and research dictate otherwise (see Chapter 3).

We have, however, heard stories from the mass state education models of a growing confidence and resistance against dominant educational cultures. These include proactive moves towards more democratic models for future planning, positive effects of community involvement and emphasis on strengths, resources, and cooperation between small or isolated schools, using new technologies and adapting teaching to capitalize on the affordances of multiage classes. Here, the ideal of local control of education is more closely attuned to users and their needs.

It is clear that the "stone in Europe's shoe" continues to irritate European governments' intentions and exchequers. The possibility of raising the profile of rural educational research in order to achieve the impact that would lead to investment in rural schools may be a dream. Nevertheless, this book includes examples approaching that dream—in Italy through technology and in Finland through democratic community-based planning, for example. If this book has raised awareness of the diversity, the resource, and potential of rural school contexts in Europe and offered ways in which the stones in some European shoes might be removed, it has achieved one of its aims.

NOTE

1. We are grateful to the European Educational Research Association Network 14 for a grant to support several authors' academic writing in English.

REFERENCES

Bauman, Z. (2001). *The individualized society.* Cambridge, England: Polity Press.

Beck, U., Giddens, A., & Lash, S. (1994). *Reflexive modernization politics, tradition and aesthetics in the modern social order.* Stanford, CA: Stanford University Press.

Bell, A., & Sigsworth, A. (1987). *The small rural primary school: A matter of quality.* London, England: Routledge.

Coladarci, T. (2007). Improving the yield of rural education research: An editor's swan song. *Journal of Research in Rural Education, 22*(3), 1–9.

Corbett, M. (2015). Towards a rural sociological imagination: Ethnography and schooling in mobile modernity. *Ethnography and Education, 10*(3), 263–277.

Corbett, M., & White, S. (2014). Why put the rural in research? In S. White & M. Corbett (Eds.), *Doing educational research in rural settings: Methodological issues, international perspectives and practical solutions* (pp. 1–5). New York, NY: Routledge.

Cutter-Mackenzie, A., Edwards, S., Moore, D., & Boyd, W. (2014). *Young children's play and environmental education in early childhood education.* New York, NY: Springer.

Department of the Environment, Transport and the Regions—Ministry of Agriculture, Fisheries and Food. (2000). *Our countryside: The future: A fair deal for rural England.* (Cm 4909). Norwich, England: The Stationery Office.

Flecha, R. (Ed.). (2015). *Successful educational actions for inclusion and social cohesion in Europe.* London, England: Springer.

Flecha, R., & Soler, M. (2013). Turning difficulties into possibilities: Engaging Roma families and students in school through dialogic learning. *Cambridge Journal of Education, 43*(4), 451–465.

Gulson, K., & Symes, C. (Eds.). (2007). *Spatial theories of education: Policy and geography matters.* Abingdon, England: Routledge.

Harber, C. (1996). *Small schools and democratic practice.* Nottingham, England: Educational Heretics Press.

Harber, C. (2014). *Education and international development: Theory, practice and issues.* Oxford, England: Symposium Books.

Hoogeboom, M., & Ossewaarde, R. (2005). From iron cage to pigeon house: The birth of reflexive authority. *Organization Studies, 26*(4), 601–619. https://doi.org/10.1177/0170840605051475

Howley, C., & Howley, A. (2014). Making sense of rural education research: Art, transgression and other acts of terroir. In S. White & M. Corbett (Eds.), *Doing educational research in rural settings: Methodological issues, international perspectives and practical solutions.* Abingdon, England: Routledge.

INDIRE. (2018). *Manifesto delle piccole scuole* [A manifesto for small schools]. Retrieved from https://piccolescuole.indire.it/wp-content/uploads/2019/08/MANIFESTO-EN.pdf

Kalaoja, E., & Pietarinen, J. (2009). Small rural primary schools in Finland: A pedagogically valuable part of the school network. *International Journal of Educational Research, 48*(2), 109–116.

Karlberg-Granlund, G. (2009). *Att förstå det stora i det lilla: Byskolan som pedagogik, kultur och struktur*. (Doctoral thesis). Åbo, Finland: Åbo Akademi University Press.

Kovács, K. (2015) Advancing marginalisation of Roma and forms of segregation in East Central Europe. *Local Economy, 30*(7), 783–799.

Kučerová, S., & Kučera, Z. (2012). Changes in the spatial distribution of elementary schools and their impact on rural communities in Czechia in the second half of the 20th century. *Journal of Research in Rural Education, 27*(11), 165–184.

Kvalsund, R. (2019). Bigger or better? Research-based reflections on the cultural deconstruction of rural schools in Norway. In H. Jahnke, C. Kramer, & P. Meusburger (Eds.), *Geographies of schooling* (pp. 179–217). London, England: Springer International.

Kvalsund, R., & Hargreaves, L. (2009). Reviews of research on rural schools and their communities: Analytical perspectives and a new agenda. *International Journal of Educational Research, 48*(2), 140–149.

Kvalsund, R., & Hargreaves, L. (2014). Theory as the source of research footprint in rural settings. In S. White & M. Corbett (Eds.), *Doing research in rural settings* (pp. 41–57). London, England: Routledge.

Lefebvre, H. (1956/2016). The theory of ground rent and rural sociology. *Antipode, 48*(1), 67–73.

Massey, D. (1991). A global sense of place. *Marxism Today, 38*, 24–29.

Massey, D. (2005). *For space*. London, England: SAGE.

OECD. (2011). *What schools for the future?* Paris, France: Author.

OECD. (2013). *School governance, assessment OECD (2013): School governance, assessment and accountability*. Paris, France: Author. Retrieved from http://www.oecd.org/pisa/keyfindings/Vol4Ch4.pdf

Phillips, D. (2009). Aspects of educational transfer. In R. Cowen & A. M. Kazamias (Eds.), *Second international handbook of comparative education* (pp. 1061–1077). London, England: Springer.

Raffe, D. (2011). *Policy borrowing or policy learning? How (not) to improve education systems*. Briefing to UK Parliamentary Research Enquiry, No. 57. Retrieved from https://www.ces.ed.ac.uk/old_site/PDF%20Files/Brief057.pdf

Sadovnik, A. R. (Ed.). (2011). *Sociology of education: A critical reader*. New York, NY: Routledge.

Schafft, K. A. (2016). Rural education as rural development: Understanding the rural school–community well-being linkage in a 21st-century policy context. *Peabody Journal of Education, 91*(2), 137–154.

Shucksmith, M. (2016). Re-imagining the rural: From rural idyll to good countryside. *Journal of Rural Studies, 59*, 163–172. https://doi.org/10.1016/j.jrurstud.2016.07.019

Smith, C., Fraser, S., & Corbett, M. (2017). Liquid modernity, emplacement and education for the Anthropocene: Challenges for rural education in Tasmania. *Australian and International Journal of Rural Education, 27*(3), 196–212.

Vignoles, A. (2016). What is the economic value of literacy and numeracy? *IZA World of Labor*. http://dx.doi.org/10.15185/izawol

Vigo, B., & Soriano, J. (2015). Teaching practices for all in small rural schools. *Ethnography and Education, 10*(3), 325–339.
Wacquant, L. (2008) *Urban outcast: A comparative sociology of advanced marginality.* Cambridge, England: Polity Press.

APPENDIX

THE EUROPEAN MIGRATION CRISIS AND THE STATUS OF IMMIGRANT CHILDREN IN EDUCATIONAL SYSTEMS

Libor Jelen
Charles University, Czechia

In 2015, Europe was hit by an "immigration wave." During that year alone, 1.2 million refugees—twice as many as the year before—applied for political asylum from the European Union (EU) member states. The total number of third-country immigrants outside the EU was estimated at 2.4 million, almost 1 million more than in 2014 (Eurostat, 2018). (Third-country immigrants are defined as people in transit through a country to reach another, neither being their country of origin.) The mass media and some politicians subsequently described this situation as a migration or refugee crisis.

OVERVIEW OF MIGRATION TRENDS IN EUROPE

At present, foreign-born people count for roughly 10% of the EU population of whom approximately 4% are non-EU citizens (Eurostat 2018).

European states receiving migrants can be divided into four groups (Dostál & Jelen, 2018). The first group of countries from the Northwest Europe region (the United Kingdom, Germany, France, Benelux, Austria, Denmark, and Sweden) became the immigration destination after World War II in the context of the economic revival of post-war Europe and labor shortages. These countries were welcoming industry workers from their former colonies (France from northern and sub-Saharan Africa, the United Kingdom from India and Pakistan) or were opening their labor markets on the basis of bilateral agreements (receiving immigrants from Spain, Portugal, Italy, and Turkey). The Schengen Treaty (1985) on the free movement of persons within much of the EU has attracted economic migrants from poorer member EU states to more advanced countries, which include those with the longest immigration experience, a high share of foreign-born people in their total population (from 10 to 45%) and a more tolerant approach of their societies to immigrants (Arango, 2012).

The second group consists predominantly of the Southern European countries (Spain, Portugal, Italy, and Greece) along with Finland and Ireland. These countries were predominantly sources of migration during the 20th century, and their migratory balance changed only in the 1980s and the 1990s. It was related to the political changes and the integration of these countries into European structures. Like the previous group, these states and their residents are generally more open to immigration, which can be influenced by their own experience of emigration and re-emigration, as well as experience with foreign cultures from their colonial pasts. The share of foreign-born people is lower in these countries than in the previous group (from five to 15%), but has been increasing for some time.

The third group is represented by the post-communist states of Central and Southeastern Europe: Czechia, Slovakia, Hungary, Poland, Romania, Bulgaria, Slovenia, and Croatia. These countries are linked by their communist past, which isolated them from the political and economic processes in Western Europe. They have become a source of emigration as a result of political repressions by communist regimes and the subsequent economic lag behind the West. After the political changes in these countries at the turn of the 1980s and 1990s, there was a huge emigration wave from the region, caused by the economic recession and the high level of unemployment (Poland, Slovakia, and Romania) and by the war in former Yugoslavia. During the last 20 years about 3.5 million Romanians (nearly 25% of the population) and two million Poles (about 5% of the population) moved to Western and Southern EU countries for economic reasons. In addition, an estimated 2.5–4 million people (more than during the current crisis) escaped in a wave of refugees as a result of the violent break-up of Yugoslavia. Czechia, the only exception in the group, changed from a state of emigration to one of immigration in the 1990s and has recorded a steady, positive migration balance, which has contributed to the country's population growth. Currently about 0.5 million foreign-born people live in Czechia. A typical feature of this group of countries is that their residents have a long experience of emigration, but little or no experience of immigration, and their national/ethnical structure is therefore very homogeneous. Their long-standing isolation as a result of the rule of communism has played an important role here, as most of the population has no knowledge or understanding of foreign cultures (Drbohlav, 2012).

The last, the fourth group of countries (Estonia, Latvia, and Lithuania) are partly similar to the previous group in their historical development. They were a direct part of the Soviet Union until 1991, after which they also suffered from economic difficulties and large-scale emigration. However, their historical context is different as Russians and people from other Soviet nations were moved into their states in large numbers during the period of the Soviet Union as part of a controlled migration program. As a consequence, the share of local nationals fell to 61% in Estonia and to 52% in Latvia (Švec, 2015). A large proportion of foreign-born people (born in the former Soviet Union) includes several tens of thousands without citizenship who continue to live there today (Dostál & Jelen, 2015). Unlike other post-communist countries, the fourth group has a long experience of immigration; however, these influxes carried negative connotations because they seriously jeopardized the existence of local nations (see Figure A.1).

The differences in the historical experience of the migration process among European states provide a basis for understanding the immigration

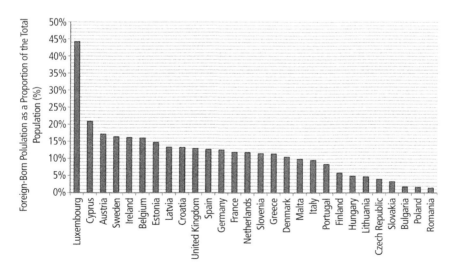

Figure A.1 Foreign born population in the EU member states in 2015. *Source*: Eurostat, 2018.

and integration policies of the individual EU countries, as well as the migration pattern in Europe and the attitudes of the countries concerned during the "refugee crisis" in 2015.

MIGRATION CRISIS, ITS CONTEXT, AND CONSEQUENCES

Parallel conflicts in Afghanistan, Iraq, Syria, and Libya are considered a major cause of the 2015 refugee crisis (Hasman & Lupták, 2016; Jelen, 2016). All of these conflicts are difficult to solve, especially from the aspect of the repatriation of war refugees. The armed conflicts drove an estimated 11 million Syrians (i.e., 50% of the total population), 3.5 million Iraqis, and 6 million Afghans from their homes. Most of the refugees naturally collected in neighboring countries, now among the most exposed areas of the world concerning migration. As a result, people with resources chose one of the very risky ways to obtain political asylum in the safe and wealthy countries of Europe, making Syrians, Afghans, and Iraqis half of all asylum seekers in the EU in 2015 (see Figure A.2).

However, Middle Eastern war refugees are not the only source and component of current migratory movements to Europe. Economic migrants from other parts of Asia and Africa are trying to get a better life and they became part of the refugee wave. Their countries of origin are war-torn, with collapsed states, authoritarian regimes, or are in poverty without much prospect for development, often also affected by natural disasters. Typical examples are mainly sub-Saharan states such as Eritrea and Somalia, or Pakistan and Bangladesh in Asia, amongst others. Migrants from Kosovo and Albania represent a specific phenomenon; they have taken advantage

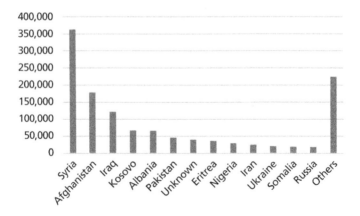

Figure A.2 First-time asylum applicants according to citizenship in 2015. *Source:* Eurostat, 2018.

of the geographical proximity to one of the migratory routes (see below) and joined other refugees. However, their asylum applications have been rejected. The total number of migrants in Europe in 2015 was estimated at 2.4 million, including asylum seekers and other economic migrants.

The uniqueness of the 2015 refugee crisis is a result of the combination of two migration routes; one from the Middle East, the other heading from North Africa. The Frontex agency, which is responsible for protecting the southern borders of the EU, has defined several routes used by migrant gangs for refugees or economic migrants (Frontex, 2018):

1. The western route begins in Morocco and goes either to the Canary Islands or the south of Spain (including the enclaves of Ceuta and Melilla in Morocco).
2. The central route runs from the northern coast of Africa (nowadays mostly from Libya or Tunisia) across the Mediterranean Sea to the south of Italy. These two routes are mainly used by migrants from Sub-Saharan Africa or the Maghreb countries.
3. The eastern, so-called Balkan route runs across Turkey to the Aegean Sea and then to some of the Greek islands, or through a safer, better guarded land route via Greece or Bulgaria. It was the most frequently chosen route during the 2015 refugee crisis for Syrian, Iraqi and Afghan refugees and originally continued further north through Serbia to Hungary, and thence to Austria and Germany. The Balkan Route was stopped in mid-2016 when the EU signed a Refugee Deal with Turkey in exchange for financial compensation and renewed accession talks on Turkey's EU membership. Currently the western and central routes are the busiest with 23,000 migrants in 2018, 18,000 of whom were detained between January and August. Italy and Spain were the countries most exposed to the flow (Frontex, 2018).

There is one other migration route known as the Artic Route that developed in 2015 and operated through 2016; it ran up through Russia and across the border into Norway and later into Finland. Frontex did not monitor the movements across this border so data on how many migrants used this route is not clear, but the numbers were small compared to those using the main routes identified above. Piipponen and Virkkinen (2017) suggest about 7,200 people traveled on this route between 2015 and 2016, people mostly from Syria, Afghanistan, and Somalia.

Three types of motivation can be determined in the migrants' choice of target destinations (Hasman & Lupták, 2016); economic motivation is probably the most important. The second closely related type of motivation is that conditioned by political factors. Besides aspects of security and political freedom, it is the country's migration policy that determines chances for obtaining asylum for refugees or residential and working permits for economic migrants. Furthermore, cultural factors are important in migrants' decision-making; namely, the existence of the ethnic community or, moreover, the presence of family members (in the broadest sense) in the target country. Other cultural factors include cultural (e.g., linguistic) proximity of the home and target country. The relationship between Czechia and Poland as the target countries for economic migrants from Ukraine is a good example and is well documented (Drbohlav, 2012; see Table A.1.)

As Table A.1 illustrates, the countries of Western Europe represent the main destinations of migrants during the refugee crisis; namely, Germany, Austria, Sweden, Italy, and France—states with a long tradition of immigration (see above), economically developed, relatively safe, and with mature social infrastructures and large and often-naturalized immigrant communities. On the other hand, the former post-socialist states have accepted just a few refugees, with the exception of Hungary as the first EU country on the Balkan route, and Poland, which is popular for asylum seekers from Russia and Ukraine. The lack of attractiveness of Eastern and Southeastern Europe for immigrants is thought generally to be due to the economic status as manifest in levels of income or social benefits. Cultural reasons are significant as well, by virtue of the absence of larger ethnic, religious, or family communities from earlier migration flows that could be culturally close to recent migrants.

The refugee crisis has permeated into the political development of the EU and its individual states. The Eurobarometer survey of Spring 2018 clearly shows that immigration is the most important issue at EU macro-regional level for its citizens (38% of respondents claimed this), with Estonia, Czechia, and Hungary with the highest share of the proclamations. Additionally, many people frequently associate immigration with the issue of terrorism from the Middle East (European Commission, 2018). The uniqueness of the contemporary refugee crisis, unlike a similarly strong influx of refugees from the Balkan wars in the 1990s, could be considered from a security perspective. The refugee crisis in Europe, proceeded concurrently with the formation of Islamic State. Militant Islamists, who have subsequently committed several terrorist attacks across Europe, came together with the refugees. Public opinion has been reflected in the results of various recent elections in European countries, where the influence of populist and extreme right-wing political parties has, in the last 5 years, been extremely high. These parties link immigration and security issues and gain relatively strong electoral support, although they have not been government parties yet (with some exceptions such as in Hungary or Italy; Dostál & Jelen, 2018). The impact of immigration on national as well as on international policies is enormous and the attitudes towards it divide

TABLE A.1 Number of First Time Asylum Applicants

Year	2011	2012	2013	2014	2015	2016	2017	Total
EU28	309,040	335,290	431,090	626,960	1322825	1259955	705,705	4,990,865
Germany	53,235	77,485	126,705	202,645	476,510	745,155	222,560	1,904,295
Hungary	1,690	2,155	18,895	42,775	177,135	29,430	3,390	275,470
Sweden	29,650	43,855	54,270	81,180	162,450	28,790	26,325	426,520
Austria	14,420	17,415	17,500	28,035	88,160	42,255	24,715	232,500
Italy	40,315	17,335	26,620	64,625	83,540	122,960	128,850	484,245
France	57,330	61,440	66,265	64,310	76,165	84,270	99,330	509,110
Netherlands	14,590	13,095	13,060	24,495	44,970	20,945	18,210	149,365
UK	26,915	28,800	30,585	32,785	40,160	38,785	33,780	231,810
Finland	2,915	3,095	3,210	3,620	32,345	5,605	4,990	55,780
Norway	8,990	9,675	11,930	11,415	31,110	3,485	3,520	80,115
Spain	3,420	2,565	4,485	5,615	14,780	15,755	31,120	77,740
Poland	6,885	10,750	15,240	8,020	12,190	12,305	5,045	70,435
Czechia	750	740	695	1,145	1,515	1,475	1,445	7,765
Romania	1,720	2,510	1,495	1,545	1,260	1,880	4,815	15,225

Source: Eurostat, 2018

societies. For example, the immigration issue was one of the causes of the vote for Brexit in the United Kingdom (exit of the U.K. from the EU). At the present time, public opinion is forcing politicians to re-evaluate existing conceptions of immigration and integration.

INTEGRATION POLICY AND EDUCATION OF IMMIGRANT CHILDREN

Besides disparities among EU countries in terms of their historical experiences of immigration, there is a great deal of variance between immigration and integration policies. Each immigration policy is the responsibility of each particular EU member state. A key component of their policies is their conception of integration and naturalization, which influences immigrants' rights within society, their chances in the labor market, accessibility to education, opportunities for political participation, or the possibility of gaining citizenship. The nature of the immigration policy is one of the key pull factors in the migrants' choice of a target country. The Migrant Integration Policy Index (MIPEX) is used to measure policies in all EU member states and other countries around the world and can be used to evaluate and compare what governments are doing to promote the integration of migrants (MIPEX, 2015). Based on MIPEX, significant differences in integration policies among individual EU members are visible (see Figure A.3) particularly between "the old" (i.e., the first and the second group) and "the new" (third and fourth group) EU member states.

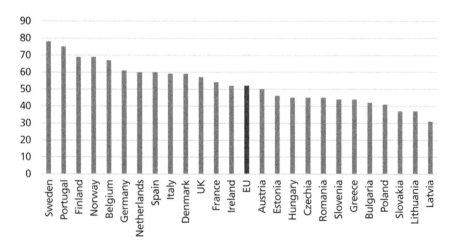

Figure A.3 MIPEX Index: The migrant integration policy index (2015). *Source:* MIPEX, 2015.

More wealthy countries with long histories of receiving migrants have more inclusive social policies, higher levels of security, protection against discrimination, and basic civil rights (MIPEX, 2015), which build mutual trust between immigrants and the majority society. However, there are significant differences even within the countries contained in this group, such as more liberal Sweden compared with rather closed Denmark, or similarly with Germany and Austria. On the other hand, in countries that lack experience of immigration and have a smaller share of foreign-born people, the institutional environment does not provide sufficiently inclusive conditions for the integration of immigrants. Here we see the negative effect of contact theory, which means that the fear of the majority society of unknown cultures leads to xenophobia, to preventing the arrival of others and to an unwillingness to change towards being more inclusive of immigrants (Dostál & Jelen, 2018; see Figure A.3)

Education is an example of a field that should contribute to the inclusion of immigrants. Migrant children account for approximately 4% of the EU population under the age of 15. The definition of a migrant child is not consistent across European countries, resulting in different estimates of their numbers. Generally speaking, migrant children are considered to be those who were born outside of Europe (first generation migrant) or whose parents were born outside of Europe (second generation migrant). Similarly, as in the case of adults, this cohort is geographically distributed according to the traditional Western–Eastern Europe pattern, that is, higher than 5% in the immigrant receiving countries and lower in the post-communist countries (Janta & Harte, 2015). The vast majority of immigrants are concentrated in urban areas in some European cities; migrant children (first and second generation) constitute half of all children in schools (e.g., Vienna, Brussels, Rotterdam, & Birmingham). Migrant children appear in rural schools rather rarely, but where they do, it is as a result of asylum and integration policies of individual states that seek refugees to deploy to regions that are often depopulated, often peripheral and rural, or when there is a refugee crisis caused by a huge inflow of asylum seekers (according to UHNCR, up to one third of them children, some of them traveling alone) directed into asylum centers, often in outlying areas (UNHCR, 2017).

Many studies on immigration in the EU show that migrant children are less successful in education compared to peers from the majority society (but see Tereshchenko, 2014, showing improvement over a 5-year period for Eastern European immigrants in English schools). This also has consequences in their subsequent application to labor markets showing that young migrants generally have a higher rate of unemployment. It also leads to their social exclusion, higher crime rates, and in extreme cases, an ideological radicalization (Agafiței & Ivan, 2016; Harte, Herrera, & Stepanek, 2016). MIPEX identifies differences between European countries in their inclusion of migrant children in education in four key ways: the granting or facilitating of formal education, financial resources, adapting new opportunities from a diverse school population, and incorporating diversity into the school curriculum (MIPEX, 2015). Sweden, Norway, Portugal, and Belgium have the best systems of the countries surveyed; Estonia is similar. Southeast and East European countries (the worst being Hungary and Bulgaria) are reported to have the least successful results for immigrant children in the education system. It is alarming that the situation for migrant students has not improved in the last few years—rather the opposite.

A clear distinction still exists between Western and Northern Europe, where states actively seek to integrate migrant children into the majority society including into education, and South Eastern and Southern Europe, where institutional support for inclusive education policies is lacking (Harte et al., 2016). In practice, the institutional aspects of the integration of migrant children in schools overlap with the approach of the majority society to immigrants; the historical experience of the majority society is the crucial factor.

REFERENCES

Agafiței, M., & Ivan, G. (2016). *First and second-generation immigrants: Obstacles to work*. Eurostat. Retrieved from https://ec.europa.eu/eurostat/statistics-explained/index.php/First_and_second-generation_immigrants_-_obstacles_to_work

Arango, J. (2012). Early starters and latecomers: Comparing countries of immigration and immigration regimes in Europe. In M. Okólski (Ed.), *European immigrations. Trends, structures and policy implications* (pp. 45–63). Amsterdam, The Netherlands: Amsterdam University Press.

Dostál, P., & Jelen, L. (2015). De-Russianisation of the western post-Soviet space: Between the thick and thin nationalising processes. *Geopolitics* 20, 757–792.

Dostál, P., & Jelen, L. (2018). Politicisation and path dependences of the 2015 immigration crisis: Explaining polarised public opinion across the European Union. *Geoforum*. (Manuscript in preparation).

Drbohlav, D. (2012). Patterns of immigration in the Czech Republic, Hungary, and Poland: A comparative perspective. In M. Okólski (Ed.), *European immigrations: Trends, structures, and policy implications* (pp. 179–209). Amsterdam, The Netherlands: Amsterdam University Press.

European Commission. (2018). Standard Eurobarometer, Spring 2018. *Public opinion in the EU*. Retrieved from http://ec.europa.eu/commfrontoffice/publicopinion/index.cfm/Survey/index#p=1&instruments=STANDARD

Eurostat. (2018). *Statistika migrace a migrující populace*. Retreved from https://ec.europa.eu/eurostat/statistics-explained/index.php?title=Migration_and_migrant_population_statistics/cs

Frontex. (2018). *Migratory map*. Retrieved from https://frontex.europa.eu/along-eu-borders/migratory-map/

Harte, E., Herrera, F., & Stepanek, M. (2016). *Education of EU-migrant children in EU Member States* (RR-1715-EC). Cambridge, England: RAND. https://doi.org/10.7249/RR1715

Hasman, J., & Lupták, M. (2016). Faktory ovlivňující volbu cílové země uprchlíků. *Geografické rozhledy, 25*(3), 2–4.

Janta, B., & Harte, E. (2015). *Education of migrant children: Education policy responses for the inclusion of migrant children in Europe* (RR-1655-EC). Cambridge, England: RAND. https://doi.org/10.7249/RR1655

Jelen, L. (2016). Sýrie—hlavní zdrojová země uprchlické krize. *Geografické rozhledy, 25*(3), 5–7.

MIPEX. (2015). *International Key Findings: Changes in context: Can integration policies respond to the needs?* Retrieved from http://www.mipex.eu/key-findings

Piipponen, M., & Virkkinen, J. (2017). Asylum seekers and security at the northern Finnish-Russian border: Analysing the 'Arctic Route episode' of 2015—2016. *RUDN Journal of Economics. 25*(4), 518–533.

Švec, L. (2015). Vztah sovětského centra a (semi)periférie: Závislost a autonomie pobaltských republik v sovětské federaci. In S. Tumis, & H. Nykl (Eds.), *Prekolonialismus, kolonialismus a postkolonialismus: Impéria a ti ostatní ve východní a jihovýchodní Evropě*. Filosofická fakulta Univerzity Karlovy, Praha.

Tereshchenko, A. (2014). *New migration, new challenges: Eastern European migrant pupils in English schools*. London, England: British Academy for the Humanities and Social Sciences. Retrieved from https://www.academia.edu/9816363/New_migration_new_challenges_Eastern_European_migrant_pupils_in_English_schools

UNHCR. (2017). *Refugee and migrant children in Europe: Accompanied, unaccompanied, and separated*. UNHCR, UNICEF, IOM. Retrieved from https://data2.unhcr.org/en/documents/download/6034

ABOUT THE EDITORS

Cath Gristy is a lecturer in the Plymouth Institute of Education at the University of Plymouth, Englad. Cath has a range of research interests in education, schools, and teaching, which include social justice, inclusion, and exclusion. A common thread that runs through her research engagements is a sense of rural place and space. Her research with young people in local isolated, rural communities in the United Kingdom has led to a sustained engagement with research methods and ethics in these places "on the edge." Cath is an active member of a pan-European network of researchers working and writing about education and schooling in rural places.

Linda Hargreaves is Reader Emerita in classroom pedagogy and learning at the University of Cambridge Faculty of Education. She has conducted research in various aspects of primary education, including three nationwide projects on educational provision in English rural schools since the 1980s. In 1996, she convened a symposium on rural schools' research that led to the setting up of Network 14 "Communities, Families, and Schooling in Educational Research," in the European Conference on Educational Research. With Rune Kvalsund, she co-edited a special issue of the *International Journal of Educational Research* on British and Nordic rural schools' research in 2009, and co-authored "Theory as the Source of Research Footprint in Rural Settings" in White and Corbett (Eds.), *Doing Educational Research in Rural Settings* (Routledge, 2013).

Silvie R. Kučerová conducts research and teaches at the Department of Geography in the Faculty of Science of Jan Evangelista Purkyně University in Ústí nad Labem. Her research and teaching interests include the geography of education, geographical education, geocultural aspects of regional development in specific regions (borderland and peripheral areas), and rural geography. From 2014 to 2018 she was a co-president of the Session of Geographical Education of the Czech Geographical Society; she is a convenor of the Network 14 of the European Educational Research Association. Since 2012 she has been responsible for organizing the Geography Olympiad in Czechia.

ABOUT THE CONTRIBUTORS

Slobodanka Antić, is associate professor at the Faculty of Special Education and Rehabilitation, University of Belgrade, Serbia. She is a co-author on the *Active Learning* and *The Critical Thinking Culture* projects. She conducts research on scientific projects in the field of educational psychology. Her research and professional work focus is in the following areas: the development of active learning methodology in education, theoretical and empirical research into interactive and cooperative learning, and theoretical and empirical research into textbooks and instructive materials as mechanisms for improving the quality of the teaching and learning process. She is the director of the Education Forum and a consultant for the Serbian strategy for educational development in 2020 and beyond.

Carl Bagley is professor of educational sociology and head of the School of Social Sciences, Education, and Social Work at Queen's University Belfast in Northern Ireland. He has undertaken research and published extensively in the field of educational ethnography and is deputy editor of the journal *Ethnography and Education.*

Artur Bajerski is currently a lecturer and vice-dean of his faculty at the Institute of Socio-Economic Geography and Spatial Management, Adam Mickiewicz University in Poznań, Poland (AMU). His scientific interests concentrate on the geography of education and the geography of science. He has published many works on school network dynamics, educational inequalities, and school closure in Poland.

372 ▪ About the Contributors

Giuseppina Cannella is a senior researcher at INDIRE. She joined in 2003 after a period of internship at the European Union (European Schoolnet) in Brussels. Her current research is focused on developing distance teaching models and analysis of innovative processes in schools that affect the relationship between space and learning, working specifically with innovative models in small schools or schools with multi age classes.

Marjolein Deunk is assistant professor at the GION Institute for Educational Research at the faculty of Behavioural and Social Sciences of the University of Groningen, The Netherlands. She has a background in developmental and educational psychology and linguistics. Marjolein's work focuses on different topics related to development and education, using both qualitative and quantitative research methods. Among the topics she studies are: teacher–child interactions, differentiation practices in Early Childhood Education and Primary Education, and diversity and inclusion in education. Marjolein is a member of the Comenius network for teaching innovation, of the Royal Netherlands Academy of Arts and Sciences.

Sam Hillyard is professor of sociology at the University of Lincoln, England. She teaches and researches on rural sociology, the sociology of education, and change in the higher education sector. She is editor of the series *Studies in Qualitative Methodology* and has published extensively on qualitative methods, social theory, and rural change, by example, in *Qualitative Sociology Review*.

Ivan Ivić is full professor of developmental psychology within the Department of Psychology at the Faculty of Philosophy, University of Belgrade, Serbia. He is a leading developmental psychologist and educational expert in Serbia and the former Yugoslavia and contributes his expertise to international organizations (OECD expert for education, a high-level expert in CERI/OECD, OMEP, UNICEF, and OSCE). He was the coordinator of the major project on the evaluation of the education system in former Yugoslavia (UNICEF, Belgrade, 2001), has provided the Georgian Ministry of Education with consultancy services (1998–2000), and was involved in the *UNESCO International Peer Group Review in Educational Evaluation* (2005). He was the Minister of Culture in former Yugoslavia (1991). He is a founder member and the president of the Education Forum, a think tank on educational issues, and is a member of the Committee for Education of the Serbian Academy of Science and Art. Ivan Ivić was the coordinator and lead author of the Serbian strategy for educational development in 2020 and beyond.

Libor Jelen is an assistant professor of political geography at the Department of Social Geography and Regional Development of Charles University, Prague, Czechia. He specializes in the research of nationalism, ethnic conflicts, geopolitics, and migration processes with a special focus on the development and spatial aspects of these phenomena in Central and Eastern Europe and in the post-Soviet republics. He taught geography at a grammar school for 10 years and he was the editor-in-chief of *Geograficke rozhledy*, a Czech journal for the popularization of geography.

Gunilla Karlberg-Granlund (PhD) is currently working as a teacher educator at the Faculty of Education and Welfare Studies, Åbo Akademi University, Finland. She has previously worked as a teacher and principal, and been involved in facilitating tailored in-service teacher education in small schools through action research. Her main research interests are facilitation of learning and professional development, and promotion of equity, quality, and sustainability in education. In her doctoral thesis (2009) she explored small rural schools from educational, cultural, and structural perspectives. Her most recent publication is "Exploring the Challenge of Working in a Small School and Community: Uncovering Hidden Tensions" (*Journal of Rural Studies*, 2019).

Katalin Kovács is a rural sociologist, senior research fellow in the Centre for Economic and Regional Studies. This institute and its predecessor have been involved in basic and applied research, usually connected to local and regional development. Studies, part of which included issues of rural school networks, were delivered to various levels of government from district to national level. In the last decade she has dealt with the following themes: rural social and settlement structures, transformation of rural areas with special reference to the role of agricultural restructuring, and rural school networks. She published significant works including an article titled "Rescuing a Small Village School in the Context of Rural Change" in the *Journal of Rural Studies*, 2012, Vol. 28, pp. 108–117, and a book chapter titled "Changing Social Characteristics, Patterns of Inequality and Exclusion," by Bock, Kovács, and Shucksmith (in Copus and de Lima [Eds.] *Territorial Cohesion in Rural Europe: The Relational Turn in Rural Development*, published in London and New York by Routledge).

Rune Kvalsund is professor of education at Volda University College, Norway, Faculty of Social Science and History. His major fields of research are comparative research of rural and urban schooling, focusing on social learning and place-based education, and longitudinal research on vulnerable children and youth/special needs children, transitions, trajectories and life courses, conditions and processes of deviance and normality. He has been researcher, leader, and critical friend of several national and regional research projects on educational provision in Norwegian rural schools since 1989. Together with Linda Hargreaves he has been initiator and convenor of the EERA Network 14 "Communities, Families, and Schooling in Educational Research" for 20 years. They have also coedited a special issue of the *International Journal of Educational Research* on rural schooling in five North European countries, and co-authored the chapter "Theory as the Source of Research Footprint in Rural Settings" published by Routledge in White and Corbett (Eds.), *Doing Educational Research in Rural Settings* (2013). He has also led, conducted research, and published from a longitudinal project following a cohort of special needs pupils for 20 years, studying their adaptations and transitions during and from upper secondary school to and within adult life, tracing the consequences of school experiences and contextual changes for adult life adaptations.

Ralf Maslowski is assistant professor at the Faculty of Behavioural and Social Sciences of the University of Groningen and researcher at the Netherlands Institute for Social Research in The Hague. He received a PhD in educational sciences from the University of Twente on a study into the organizational culture of schools in secondary education. He has published several articles in scientific journals and books on school culture, educational decentralization, internationalization in education, and citizenship education.

Petr Meyer conducts research and teaches at the Department of Geography in the Faculty of Science, Jan Evangelista Purkyně University in Ústí nad Labem, and is also a PhD student at the Department of Social Geography and Regional Development in the Faculty of Science, Charles University, Prague. His research and teaching interests include the geography of education, cartography, and geoinformatics.

Ana Pešikan is a full professor within the Department of Psychology at the Faculty of Philosophy, University of Belgrade, Serbia. Her professional expertise is in educational and developmental psychology. The focus of her work is on theoretical and practical issues around active learning methodology, the construction and analysis of textbooks, teaching and learning history in school, and the analysis of the education system. She is a co-author on the *Active Learning* project. She is a national UNICEF and OSCE expert on education, and has acted as a consultant to the Georgian Ministry of Education (1998–2000). From 2007 to 2008 she was the Serbian minister of science. She is a founder member of the Education Forum, and member of the Committee for Education of the Serbian Academy of Science and Art. Ana Pešikan is one of the co-authors of the Serbian strategy for educational development in 2020 and beyond.

Andrea Raggl, is a professor for educational research at the University of Teacher Education Tirol, Austria. She worked for 8 years at the University of Teacher Education Vorarlberg where, together with colleagues from the Swiss cantons Grisons, St. Gallen and Valais, she carried out research in small rural schools in the two Interreg projects "Schools in Alpine Regions" (2009–2011) and "Small Schools in Alpine Regions" (2012–2015).

Karl Jan Solstad is a senior researcher at Nordland Research Institute. He has taught in small multi-grade schools, teacher education colleges, and universities; he was professor of education at Tromsø University. For 15 years he was director of education in the predominantly rural county of Nordland. His research has focused on rural education issues in Norway, Scotland, and Ethiopia. He has published a number of articles in Norwegian and international journals and several books including *Equity at Risk* (1997); *Making Small Schools Work—A Handbook for Teachers in Small Rural Schools* (2001, with Alan Sigsworth); *Skolen og distrikta—Samspel eller konflikt?* [The School and the Rural Areas—Working together or in Conflict?] (2006, with Annika Andræ Thelin); *Bygdeskolen i velstands-Noreg* [The Rural School in an Affluent Norway] (2009); and *Reaching out—The Place of Small Multi-grade Schools in Developing Countries: The Case of Ethiopia* (2013, with Wanna Leka and Alan Sigsworth).

Juana Soriano-Bozalongo is lecturer in the Faculty of Education at the University of Zaragoza, Spain. She holds a chair in Attention to Diversity. Her research interests and publications are in the field of educational ethnography, teacher education, rural schooling, and attention to diversity.

Sami Tantarimäki, PhD conducts research and development at the Brahea Centre at the University of Turku, Finland. As a geographer his research and development interests include the geography of education and regional development, focusing especially on influences, challenges, and possibilities of municipal school and service network planning. Sami is an active actor in his national field of rural development, research, and policy.

Anni Törhönen, MSc in geography, has worked as a research assistant investigating Finnish school network changes at the Department of Geography and Geology, University of Turku. She is currently studying early childhood education at the University of Helsinki.

Petr Trahorsch conducts research and teaches at the Department of Pre-Primary and Primary Education at the Faculty of Education of Jan Evangelista Purkyně University in Ústí nad Labem. He is also a PhD student in the same department. The main area of his research is geographical education, especially school maps and visual elements in geography textbooks, and the assessment of their usability. He also deals with the didactics of primary science education.

Kateřina Trnková works as an assistant professor at the Department of Educational Sciences, Faculty of Arts, Masaryk University in Brno, Czechia. She has been investigating small rural schools from the perspective of sociology of education and educational policy since the end of 1990s. Besides this, she is involved in other research projects of her university department, with focus on school operation, adult education, and inclusive education.

Begoña Vigo-Arrazola is associate professor in the Faculty of Education at the University of Zaragoza, Spain. She is head of the research group in education and diversity. Her research interests and publications are in the field of educational ethnography, teacher education, rural schooling, and inclusive education.

INDEX

A

Åberg-Bengtsson, L., 25, 30, 131, 192
ability, 92, 166, 226, 228, 238–239, 290, 351
academic, x, xxviii, 3, 15, 58, 63–64, 67, 151, 157, 178–179, 182–183, 193, 214, 222–223, 253, 292, 295, 318, 341, 352
accessibility, 23, 31, 39–40, 134, 150, 156, 364
accountability, 53, 58, 61–62
achievement, 3, 58, 62, 80, 82, 148, 151, 158–161, 165, 168, 177, 250, 314, 316, 333, 347. *See also* assessment; attainment; performance
administration, 41, 43, 80–82, 86, 141, 176, 184, 207, 227, 251, 262, 269, 271, 278, 300
administrative, 24, 26–27, 32, 34, 43, 50–51, 57, 83, 86, 105, 127, 162, 165, 218, 222, 225, 227, 261, 270, 275, 327
advantage, 5, 7, 25, 68, 105, 127, 162, 205, 231, 248, 295, 360
Africa, 318, 358, 360–361
age structure, 23, 26, 36, 39
agency, xv, xviii, 11, 26, 80, 97, 191, 253, 262–263, 271, 289, 306, 350, 361
agenda, 11, 244, 297, 304

ages, 4, 28, 36, 64–65, 150, 154, 156, 164, 178–180, 206, 218, 222, 228–229, 241, 263, 271, 278, 291, 312–313, 330
agreement, 116, 148, 227
agriculture, 85, 149, 154, 163, 168, 182, 261
aim, 2, 12, 22, 49, 103–104, 110, 166, 177, 180, 184, 187, 217, 220, 227, 230–231, 244, 251, 262, 266, 273, 352
Alpine regions, 199, 201–203, 205, 208, 376
amalgamation, 14, 83, 85, 87, 90
amenities, 94, 219, 291
American, 52, 63, 72, 168, 349
Antić, S., 13, 147–164, 330, 340
Arctic, 328–329
arrangement, 139, 223
art, 99, 164, 168, 300, 309, 340, 349, 373, 375
aspirations, 93, 133, 147, 164, 166
assessment, 5–6, 61, 80, 92, 94–96, 99, 158–159, 168, 187–188, 267, 327, 334, 376
asylum seekers, 360–362, 365, 367
attainment, 151, 287
attendance, 28, 81, 97, 108, 295, 312, 314, 316
Austria, xix, 14, 23, 25, 28–29, 31–33, 36, 39, 42–43, 199–214, 324, 330, 334, 342,

346–347, 358, 361–362, 365. *See also* Montessori, M.
authentic, x, 3, 14, 16, 160–161, 324, 326, 341, 347
authoritarian, 41, 326–327, 360
authority, 10, 13, 86–87, 110–111, 115–119, 136, 200, 207, 210, 251, 266, 268, 292, 296, 314, 316, 327, 348, 350–352
autonomy, 10, 14, 24, 80, 86, 95, 119, 161, 181, 205, 218, 220, 240, 287, 299, 327
axes of change, 324–325

B

Bagley, C., 15, 183, 213–214, 285–286, 288, 290, 292, 294–296, 298, 300, 330, 333, 342–343, 346, 371
Bajerski, A., 13, 23, 25, 32, 104, 120, 125–128, 130–136, 138, 140–141, 326, 330, 341, 344, 372
Balkan, 361–362
Barcelona, 185–186
Baudrillard, J., 310, 318
Bauman, Z., xviii, xx, 350
Beach, D., 188, 192
Beck, U., 350–351
Belgium, 7, 335, 366
Belgrade, 147–148, 167–168, 371, 373, 375
belief, 52, 56, 126, 208, 250, 294, 298, 351
Bell, A., 22–23, 25, 41, 114, 116, 120, 131, 205, 207, 286, 333, 347
belonging, xviii, 55, 86, 111–112, 162, 227, 346
benefit, 61, 161, 177, 225, 294
Benelux, 358
birth, 39, 43, 150, 182, 185, 200, 221, 260–261, 277
boarders, 5, 176
border, 106, 110, 226, 270, 361, 367
borderlines, 139
boundaries, 12, 268, 276, 288, 292, 296, 317, 331
Bourdieu, P., xviii, xx, 12, 14–15, 62, 72, 177, 192, 200, 211–212, 214, 285–286, 288–290, 297–300, 305, 318, 346. *See also* capital; doxa; field; game; habitus
Brexit, 364
Britain. *See* United Kingdom
broadband, 54, 151, 229
Bronfenbrenner, U., 14, 16, 160, 168

Brussels, 26, 365, 372
Budapest, 1, 85, 87, 91, 100
budget, 118, 263, 287
Bulgaria, 10, 358, 361, 366
business, xx, 11, 49, 53, 62, 69, 161, 180, 305, 312, 314, 316

C

Canada, xx, 67, 266, 278
Cannella, G., 14, 32, 217–218, 220, 222, 224, 226, 228, 230–232, 348–349, 372
capital, 14–15, 39, 60, 62, 72, 87, 106, 133–134, 140, 148, 150–151, 177, 191, 211–212, 214, 261, 264, 285, 288, 290, 295–297, 300, 305, 309, 346. *See also* Bourdieu, P.
  cultural capital, 15, 133, 177, 200, 210–212, 290, 295–297, 305, 346. *See also* Bourdieu, P.
  economic capital, 62, 290
  social capital, 14, 60, 72, 106, 134, 177, 191, 264, 290, 296–297, 300
capitalism, xvi, xix, 52, 90, 160, 318
catchment, 23, 25, 40, 67, 82, 93, 104, 106, 110–112, 116, 120, 131, 134, 207, 210–211, 213, 241, 342
cause, 61, 97, 252, 360
census, 81, 84, 110, 151, 341, 343
central, xv, xvii–xviii, 10–13, 22, 41, 55, 61, 80, 82, 84, 87, 89–90, 108, 111, 133, 135, 140, 148, 201, 220–221, 224, 226, 253, 271, 277, 285, 291, 296, 316, 326–327, 352, 358, 361, 374
centralization, xii–xiv, xix, 3, 24, 56, 61, 68, 70, 80, 86–87, 95, 99, 108, 351
centre, 8, 80, 85–88, 111–112, 209, 230, 310, 374, 376
CER (Colectivos de Escuelas Rurales), 176
CES (Consejo Económico y Social de España), 108, 111–112, 183
childhood, 72, 178, 182, 263, 272, 274–275, 372, 376
China, 5, 324, 334
choice, xvi, 10, 25, 53–54, 82, 85–86, 91, 93, 104–105, 107, 116, 119–120, 134, 140, 183, 193, 200, 214, 241, 246, 251, 268, 272, 278, 293, 295, 300, 361, 364
church, 34, 85, 91, 107, 114, 180, 239, 245, 286, 291, 310, 312

Catholic, 34, 85, 91, 180
Protestant, 34, 91
CIA (Central Intelligence Agency), 241, 253
citizens, xviii, 3, 149, 262, 272, 353, 357–364
citizenship, 357, 359–364, 375
city, 4, 43, 54, 62, 68, 87, 152, 166–167, 209, 214, 222, 260–261, 266, 278, 294–295, 300, 314, 330
civic, 80, 87, 91, 220, 326
class (school), 26, 30–31, 63–64, 91, 93, 108, 115, 117, 137, 139, 157, 159, 162, 176, 190–192, 200, 203, 206–208, 211–212, 222–223, 228, 289–290, 293–296, 332. *See also* large; size; smaller
   incomplete elementary schools (IES), 108, 111–113, 176, 182, 270
   mixed age, 4, 105, 199–200
   monograde, 159
   multiage, 7, 219, 221–224, 229–231, 349, 351–352
   multigrade, 4, 31, 64, 157, 159–160, 162, 164–165, 187, 203, 222, 237, 242, 245–247, 251–252
   one-room school, 176
   pluriclasses, 349
classification, 8, 41, 92, 97, 136, 150, 192, 261, 286, 299, 331
classroom, xiii–xv, 4, 31, 115, 139, 159–160, 178–179, 182, 184, 188–189, 204, 207, 218–219, 221, 223, 225–226, 228–232, 238–239, 245–246, 251, 342, 369, 373
climate, xv, xx, 6, 10, 53, 55, 150, 209, 287, 312–314, 347
Cloke, P., 334–335
close, xv, 11, 14, 52, 58–60, 63, 67, 71, 96, 115, 117, 120, 137, 140, 167, 180, 182, 184, 201, 204, 209–210, 220, 240–241, 245, 249–251, 262, 264, 276, 286–287, 295–296, 309, 325, 333, 362
closure of schools, 41, 43, 56, 130, 180, 185, 219, 325
cluster, 51, 111, 154, 184, 201, 214, 240, 244, 248, 266, 325, 347
co-operation, 81–82, 176, 232, 277, 306, 333
coalition, 79, 83, 274
coastal, xx, 35–36, 39, 67, 232
cognitive, 159–160, 222–223, 230, 237–239, 242, 289
Coladarci, T., 11, 16, 160, 168, 190, 202, 214, 334–335, 340, 345, 351

collaboration, 64, 96, 129–130, 132, 137, 163, 187–188, 226, 229, 231, 276, 299, 342, 349
collaborative, 186, 188, 225–227, 230, 259–261, 263–267, 269, 271, 273–277, 343–344, 348
collective, xviii, 53, 57, 105, 128, 135, 189, 348, 350
Comber, C., 200, 226, 229
commitment, 55, 95, 188, 192, 201, 293, 296, 298
common core, 28–29, 92
communism, 10, 13, 359
community, xi–xiii, xv, xvii, xix–xx, 4, 13–15, 43, 54–55, 57, 59, 61, 64, 67–71, 81, 93, 104, 107, 117, 131, 136, 141, 153, 162–164, 167, 181, 183, 187–191, 193, 201, 204–205, 213, 220, 225–226, 232, 239, 249–252, 262–265, 268, 270, 278, 285, 288, 291, 293–300, 304–305, 311–318, 326, 331, 335, 340, 342–348, 350, 352, 362, 372
community active schools, 68
comparison, xvi, 4, 29, 31, 88, 108, 151, 158, 329, 342
compensate, 96, 181, 243
competence, 64, 166, 227, 231, 309
competition, xviii, 22, 36, 40, 53, 56, 61–62, 82, 105, 107, 120, 132, 183, 209, 287–288, 293, 295, 299, 334, 350
complexity, 25, 105, 190, 239, 287, 292, 308, 329, 331, 333
compulsory, 25–29, 31, 50–51, 56, 60, 66, 83, 96–97, 108, 127, 147, 149, 156–157, 164, 200, 218, 225, 238
conference, xi, 1, 167, 184–185, 232, 369, 373
conflict, 9, 23, 36, 43, 59, 69, 147–148, 160, 164–165, 268, 308, 345, 376
consolidation, 86, 220–221, 264, 347
constitution, xvii, xx, 147, 149, 164, 181, 239, 249
constraints, 136, 229, 249, 278
constructive, xii, xv, 14, 191, 340, 348
constructivism, 229
cooperation, xiii, xv, 5, 7, 54, 67–68, 71, 81–82, 85, 90, 107, 148, 152, 167, 206, 223, 246, 248–249, 251, 270, 275–276, 350, 352
Corbett, M., xiii–xiv, xx, 11, 16, 60, 67, 106, 160–161, 177–178, 190–193, 220–222, 232, 268, 278, 304, 306, 311, 318, 326,

335, 340, 345, 348–349, 351, 369, 373, 375
cost, 53, 63, 79–80, 127, 140, 180, 184, 325
costs, xiv, 4, 7, 30, 69, 82–83, 86, 119, 135, 139, 180, 184, 221, 240, 243, 264
Council, 81, 85, 148, 238, 240, 242–245, 249, 252–253, 266, 269, 275, 312, 314
countryside, 43, 53, 64, 70, 151, 153, 211, 213, 260–261, 267, 335
Croatia, 4, 358
culture, xiii, xv–xvii, xix, 7, 15, 22–23, 26, 43, 49–50, 52–53, 55, 59, 62, 64–65, 68–71, 95, 104, 114, 117–118, 131, 133, 140, 148, 154, 158, 162–163, 165–167, 177, 181, 187, 190–193, 200, 205, 210–212, 221, 230–231, 242, 263, 278, 286–287, 289–290, 293, 295–299, 303, 305–306, 315, 329, 334, 346, 349–352, 358–362, 365
curriculum, xix, 6, 10, 16, 28–29, 63, 67–68, 92, 126–127, 133, 158, 166, 176, 187, 189, 214, 222–226, 228–230, 232, 250, 261–262, 271, 292, 327, 334, 349, 366
cuts, 95
Czechia, 30, 34, 43, 90, 103–109, 111, 113, 115, 117–120, 343–344, 366, 370, 374

D

Dalton-Plan, 205
database, 27, 105, 109, 218
decentralization, 3, 10, 13, 24, 53, 56, 61, 104, 108, 125–127, 129, 131, 133, 135, 137, 139–141, 181–183, 185, 327, 375
decision-making, 15, 60, 120, 250, 261, 266, 270, 331, 352
decree, 87, 180–181, 185
defence, 59, 93, 181, 185, 221, 294, 325
deficiency, xii–xiii, 340
deficit, 80, 83, 160, 162, 304, 317, 349, 351
define, 3, 7, 13, 29, 32, 106, 108, 110, 126, 136, 152, 167, 176, 200, 209, 225, 228, 240, 242, 263, 330, 332, 334, 346, 352, 357, 361
definition, 7–8, 15, 31–32, 81, 135–136, 147–148, 152, 154, 200, 218–219, 240, 248, 324, 330–331, 333, 351, 365
Deleuze, G., 305–308, 318
deliberative processes, 260, 266, 326, 351
democracy, xvi, 14, 119, 181, 265, 341
demographic, xii, 4, 23, 27, 39, 54, 82, 86, 106, 108, 125–127, 139–140, 150, 155, 157, 162, 176–177, 250, 295
Denmark, 7, 66, 326, 358, 365
density, 7–8, 12, 23, 26–27, 31, 35–36, 39–40, 167, 183, 330, 332
depopulation, xiii, 3, 131, 140, 150–151, 153, 183, 230, 253, 261, 348–349, 351
deprivation, xiv, 155, 314
deregulation, 49, 53, 56, 61
desegregation, 84, 100
design, 11, 14, 160, 180, 218, 222–230, 269, 272, 286, 313
  building, xiii, 11, 92, 108, 153, 162, 201, 203–204, 222, 239, 249, 261, 268, 270, 312–313, 316, 346
  research design, 11, 340–345
  technological, xiii, 150, 154, 220, 224, 226–231
designated, 182, 210–211, 286, 294
destination, 358
Deunk, M., 14–15, 31, 33, 237–238, 240, 242–246, 248, 250–253, 342, 372
developmental, xiii, 41, 118, 153, 162, 239, 372–373, 375
dialogue, 61, 212, 348, 350
didactic, 22, 165, 188, 206
differentiation, 22, 29, 100, 108, 134, 246, 261, 267, 277, 372
diminished, 87, 90, 98, 291, 326
disadvantage, 11, 184, 220, 298–299, 328
discipline, xvi, xviii, 106, 341
discourse, 11, 132, 135–136, 193, 244, 286, 299, 304, 314, 318, 347
discussions, xvi–xix, 7–9, 12–13, 15, 27, 68, 71, 87, 154, 205, 213, 219, 244, 250, 260, 263–266, 269–270, 274, 276, 278, 324, 326, 329, 331, 343, 349, 352
disparity, 220
distance learning and teaching, 218, 221–231
distinction, 86, 288, 300, 366
district, 80, 86, 115, 180–181, 185, 374
diversity, xviii, xx, 3–4, 25, 41, 107, 160–161, 165, 167, 181, 188, 200, 238–239, 242, 324–325, 329, 334, 342–344, 352, 366, 371–372
division, 26, 30, 34, 41, 63, 127, 133–134, 140, 267
doxa, 293, 297–299
dropout, 13, 147, 154, 156, 158, 164, 219

Index ■ 381

E

EACEA (European Commission Education, Audiovisual and Culture Executive Agency) (EACEA), 3, 16, 156
Eacott, S., 286, 290, 297–299
Eastern, xi–xv, xix, 9–10, 12, 53, 55, 111, 128–131, 139–140, 201, 323, 325–327, 360–362, 365–367
economic, x, xvi, xviii, xxxviii, 3–7, 9–10, 12, 15–16, 22–26, 32, 39, 52–54, 59, 62, 64, 66, 69, 79, 85–86, 88, 99, 104, 111, 118, 126, 134–135, 140, 148–155, 157–158, 160, 162–163, 176–177, 180–185, 190, 193, 200, 221, 261, 272–273, 278, 285, 288, 290, 292–299, 324–329, 333–334, 343, 346–348, 350–352, 358–362
economist, 52, 54
economy, 10, 13–14, 53–56, 59, 62, 70, 72, 104, 125–126, 148, 152, 163, 177, 265, 275, 277, 288, 292, 300
education system, 5, 24, 64–65, 80, 87, 91, 127, 135, 149, 151, 157, 166, 175, 186, 218, 239, 286–287, 334–335, 366, 373, 375
educational governance, xix–xx, 72, 100
edutainment, 163–164
effectiveness, 79–80, 180, 225–226, 325
efficiency, 16, 24, 53, 59, 131, 140, 158, 221, 272, 350
Egypt, 167
elementary, 1, 12–13, 21–23, 25–29, 31–35, 37, 39, 41–43, 103–109, 111–114, 117–118, 168, 178, 214, 271, 325, 330, 343–344
emigration, 358–359
empirical, xvii, 22, 27, 52, 106, 189, 232, 238, 242, 244, 251, 291, 300, 308, 317, 340, 344, 371
employment, 54, 126, 150, 153–155, 177, 186, 188, 224, 291, 314
England, x, xix–xx, 1, 10, 12, 15–16, 43, 63, 72, 120, 141, 201, 214, 221, 285–287, 291, 294, 300, 303, 306, 311–312, 316, 318, 323–324, 327, 330, 332, 339, 342–343, 347, 352, 365, 367, 369, 373
enrolment, 24, 278
enterprise, 55, 68, 293
entrapment, xiv–xv, 304, 315, 317

environment, 22, 62, 67, 70, 105, 116, 134, 158, 163–164, 181, 184, 186–187, 189–192, 207, 211, 222–223, 227, 229, 231–232, 245, 289, 293, 349, 365
epistemological, 228, 303, 340
equality, xviii, 59, 100, 151, 223, 277
equipment, 61, 85, 94, 134, 148, 158, 165, 181
equity, xviii, 64, 79–80, 94–95, 99, 149, 151, 168, 214, 267, 303, 352, 372, 376
era, 10, 55, 69, 90, 110, 132, 278
Eritrea, 360
erosion, 82, 86, 120
Espace. *See* Lefebvre, H.
establishment, 9, 23, 51, 104, 140, 182, 185, 260–261, 308
Estonia, 10, 359, 362, 366
ethics, 305
ethnicity, 12, 84, 91, 97
ethnography, 16, 214, 300, 318, 371–372
Euro (EUR), 95, 349
Eurobarometer, 362
europa, 7–8, 16, 278, 335, 366
European Commission (EC), 3, 8, 96, 150–151, 153–154, 156, 168, 329, 333, 362
European Conference on
Educational Research (ECER), xi, 1, 278
European Education Area (EEA), 8, 333
European Educational Research
Association (EERA), xi, xvii, 1, 375
European Union (EU), 4, 7, 9, 43, 83, 96, 127, 148, 151, 260, 333, 357
Eurostat, 4, 7–8, 16, 26–27, 33, 35, 40, 95, 156, 260, 278, 333, 335, 357, 359–360, 363, 366
Eurydice, 3, 16, 26–29, 34, 156, 218
evaluation, 67, 158, 188, 232, 266, 270, 275, 277, 373
evidence, 9, 11, 39, 96, 98, 152, 160–161, 165, 188, 192, 225, 238, 242–243, 250–251, 325, 340, 344
exclusion, 155, 168, 177, 232, 316–317, 352, 365, 369, 373–374
expenditure, 83, 95, 140, 332
experience, xii, xvi, 5, 12–14, 30, 120, 159, 164, 186, 189, 203–204, 210–211, 219, 228–229, 231–232, 248, 250, 265, 310–311, 316–317, 328, 340, 347, 349–350, 358–359, 365–366
expertise, 214, 240, 242, 244, 248, 263, 341, 343, 373, 375
extracurricular, 128, 133, 220

F

facility, 134, 264
family, xii, 54–55, 96, 98, 115, 131, 156, 168, 188–192, 212, 268, 293–294, 298, 316, 329, 342, 362. *See also* intergenerational; involvement; parental choice; participation
   father, 61, 68
   grandparents, xii, 81, 291, 294
   mother, 151, 212, 228
   reunion, 329
farm, 150, 153, 162–164
fascist, 219
fear, xiii, 10, 12, 61, 166, 210, 237–238, 242, 250–251, 294, 365
federation, 325, 347
field, x–xii, xiv, xix–xx, 15–16, 64, 82, 100, 104, 110–111, 154–155, 161, 177, 231, 245, 285, 287–300, 340, 343, 345–346, 351, 365, 371–372, 376
fight, 140, 209–210, 213, 230, 348–349
finance, 127, 271
Finland, xix, xxviii, 6, 9, 13, 15, 25, 28–29, 31–34, 36, 39, 41, 43, 49–56, 59–72, 141, 259–278, 324–326, 328–330, 332, 334, 342–344, 346–348, 351–352, 358, 361, 367
fishing, 53
fjords, xiv, 50, 53
Flecha, R., 348
food, xv, xvii, 95, 155, 163, 182
football, 312, 316
forestry, 53, 163
Foucault, M., xvi, xx
foundation, 218, 225, 269, 345
fragmentation, 81, 111
framework, 23, 25, 82, 95, 180–181, 186–188, 224, 230, 286–287, 308, 317, 334
France, 96, 141, 358, 362–363
Franco, 14
Freinet, C., 14, 185
Freire, P., 14, 16, 185
friendships, xviii, 292
funding, 13, 24, 33, 43, 95–96, 118–119, 125, 127–128, 131, 134–135, 156, 163, 176, 178–179, 183, 218, 239–240, 243, 249, 271, 287, 327, 332, 341, 352

G

Gage, J., 226, 229
Galton, M., 7, 16, 155, 177, 200, 214, 240, 304
game, 11, 15, 50, 278, 297–300
generation, 116, 291, 329, 331, 365–366
Geographic Information Systems (GIS), 27, 106, 269
geography, 3, 27, 50, 104, 106–107, 175–176, 267, 277, 289, 306, 311, 335, 369–370, 372, 374–376
geography of education, 27, 104, 106–107, 267, 370, 372, 374–376
Germany, 7, 106, 205–206, 214, 329, 358, 361–362, 365
ghettoisation, 82
Giddens, A., xvi–xvii, xx, 54, 118, 350–351
girls, xiii, 179, 185, 212
global, xii, xv–xx, 1–2, 12–16, 50, 52, 57, 59, 61–62, 72, 99, 128, 160–161, 177, 183, 213, 217, 219, 221, 223, 225, 227, 229, 231, 304–306, 308–311, 317, 328, 345–347, 351–352
global sense of place, 12, 345–346
globalization, xii, xvi–xviii, xx, 3, 7–9, 12–13, 49–50, 52–56, 58, 61, 66, 68–69, 71–72, 187, 231, 268, 347, 350
glocalisation, 350
governance, xix–xx, 10, 49, 53, 62, 72, 96, 100, 104, 108, 119, 126, 220, 238, 287, 293, 296, 299
government, xiv, xix, 11, 13, 58, 80–83, 85–87, 95, 99, 119, 126–127, 135–136, 139–140, 149, 154, 167, 181, 201, 219–221, 239, 243–244, 249, 271, 273, 275, 286, 291, 296, 313, 326–327, 330, 332, 335, 341, 347–348, 362
grade, 64–65, 83, 92–93, 108, 127, 157, 159, 162, 164, 180, 185, 192, 200, 246, 332, 376
grant, 69, 126, 247, 352
Greece, 358, 361
Green, B., 23, 177, 180, 192, 306, 311
Gristy, C., x, 14–15, 303–306, 308, 310–312, 314, 316, 318, 323–324, 326, 328, 330, 332–334, 339–340, 342, 344–346, 348, 350, 352, 369, 372
Groningen, 237, 241, 372, 375
Gross Domestic Product (GDP), 1, 95, 148–150

Index ■ **383**

grounded, xviii–xix, 297–298
group, xviii–xix, 22–26, 29, 41, 43, 87, 92, 98, 118, 136, 154, 159, 162, 166, 168, 177, 179, 186, 193, 202–203, 211–212, 224, 226, 228–230, 242, 247, 275, 314, 358–359, 364–365, 371, 373
grouped rural schools, 176, 181, 187, e.g., CRA (Colegios Rurales Agrupados); CRIE (Centro Rural de)
grouping, 54, 92, 180, 185, 206, 222, 245–247
growing, xii, xvi, 32, 66, 82–84, 267, 291, 305, 352
growth, xviii, 9, 52, 89, 97, 149, 151, 153–154, 161, 164, 182, 261, 264, 347, 350, 359
Gruenewald, D., xvii, xx
Guattari, F., 305–308, 318
Gunter, H., 287, 292, 297, 299

H

habitus, 15, 177, 285, 288–290, 293, 295–300, 346
Halfacree, K., 213, 306, 311
hamlets, 108, 200, 209–210, 330
Hampl, M., 22–23, 105–106, 325
Harber, C., 32, 349
Hargreaves, L., xi, xiv–xv, xvii, 1–2, 4, 6, 8, 10–12, 14–16, 32, 131, 152, 155, 162, 164, 177, 200, 214, 219, 240, 242, 273, 304–305, 310, 323–324, 326, 328, 330, 332, 334, 339–342, 344–346, 348, 350, 352, 369, 373, 375
Hattie, J., 22, 63
Havas, G., 84, 94, 100
headteacher, 15, 201, 203–205, 207–211, 275, 285–287, 289, 291–300, 312, 314, 316, 342–343, 346
health, xiv, 13, 56, 65–66, 69, 72, 81, 83, 149, 155, 261, 271, 343. *See also* well-being
heart of the village, 268, 326
Helsinki, 51, 261, 278, 376
heritage, 114, 119, 349
Heyerdahl, N., 66
Hillyard, S, 15, 183, 213–214, 285–286, 288, 290, 292, 294–296, 298, 300, 330, 333, 342–343, 346, 373
history, x, xv–xvi, xix, 3, 12–16, 23, 33, 36, 41, 55, 85, 104, 106–107, 110, 149,
160, 167, 175, 178, 184, 186, 190, 205, 214, 221, 230, 265, 268, 286, 289–291, 297, 300, 304–306, 308, 312–313, 315, 317, 323, 326, 345, 349, 351, 359, 364, 366, 374–375
Holloway, S., 24, 40, 104, 106
home, 4, 22–23, 61, 65, 67, 97, 131, 134, 176, 190, 204, 212, 218, 232, 241, 260, 266, 313–315, 362
hope, 3, 16, 210, 249, 295, 300, 317, 321, 347
households, 151, 163, 242
housing, 291, 313–314
Howley, C. & Howley, A., 340
human, xv, xviii, xx, 7, 16, 26–27, 53, 62, 72, 88, 96, 106, 120, 149–151, 162, 164–168, 182, 251, 305–306, 308, 311, 315, 327, 334, 346
  human capital, 62, 150–151
  human resources, 96, 165, 182, 251
  human rights, 149, 167, 327
  human scale, 334
Hungary, xix, 6, 10, 13, 25, 28–33, 36, 41, 79–100, 323–327, 330–348, 352, 358, 361–362, 366, 374
Hyry-Beihammer, E., 36, 41, 43, 59, 72, 107, 131, 141, 161, 221, 246, 260–262, 271, 278

I

ICT (Information and Communications Technology), xvii, 53–54, 151, 217–218, 220, 222–226, 230–231, 342
  computer, 106, 225
  digital, 4, 14, 225, 227–229, 263, 327, 331
  interactive whiteboard (IWB), 226
  Internet, 11, 117, 165, 191
  social media, 191, 266
  videoconferencing, 223–224, 226, 229, 232
  virtual learning environments (VLE), 191, 227, 229, 263
identity, xiii–xiv, xvii, xix–xx, 7, 16, 55, 65, 67–68, 86, 106, 117, 131, 177, 208, 220, 241, 250, 335, 346, 349–350
ideology, 10, 24, 52, 192, 309
illiteracy, 151, 219, 341
image, 115, 132, 163, 310
imagination, 11, 16, 318, 341, 344, 348, 351
immigrant, 241–242, 329, 357–367

immigration, xvii, 43, 182, 328–329, 357–359, 362, 364–366
imperialism, 167
improvement, 148, 151, 160, 163, 182, 218, 223, 229, 244, 315, 344–345, 365
inaccessible, 14, 27, 176, 330, 346
incentives, 80, 83, 95, 181, 325
inclusion, 8, 16, 25, 96, 100, 153, 168, 188, 190, 231, 239, 242, 317, 323, 329, 333, 335, 342, 347, 349, 365–367, 369, 372–373
inclusive, 12–14, 95, 97, 154, 166, 187, 203, 230, 246, 259, 261, 263, 265–267, 269, 271, 273, 275, 277, 328, 348, 365–366, 371, 377
income, xii, 95, 98, 148, 150, 166, 362
incomers, 12, 210
independence, 5, 114, 161, 167, 248, 261, 347
independent, xv, 10, 26, 34, 80, 89, 92, 119, 126, 212, 218, 239, 244, 265, 304, 334, 341
index, 7, 16, 96, 149, 184, 214, 314, 364, 366. *See also* chain development index
Index Mundi, 149
India, 167, 358
indicator, 26, 97, 139, 154, 160, 220
indigenous, 153, 305
INDIRE (Italian National Institute for Documentation, Innovation and Educational Research), 217–218, 221–223, 226–227, 230–232, 332, 348–349, 351, 372
individual, xviii, 54–55, 72, 95, 189, 208–210, 261, 266, 291, 299
industry, 315, 358
inequality, 23, 149, 221, 261, 267, 288, 304, 341, 347, 352, 374
inequity, 158, 264, 311
inflow, 153, 362, 365
informal, xiii, 61, 67, 155, 190, 204, 224, 291–292
injustice, 305, 347
innovation, 96, 100, 176, 181, 184–188, 193, 199, 205, 213, 217–218, 222–223, 227–228, 231–232, 245, 321, 331, 335, 347, 372
innovative, 14, 16, 86, 161, 177, 186, 200, 206, 213, 223–224, 226, 228, 230–231, 242, 247, 251, 341, 372
inspection, 287, 291, 293–294
inspectorate, 188, 240–247
instruction, 31, 166, 188, 208, 222, 232, 247

integrated, xvi, 29, 55, 86, 95–96, 226, 231
integration, xvii, 85, 92, 95, 220, 230, 328–329, 358, 360, 364–367
interaction, xix, 12, 54, 190–191, 222, 225, 227, 231, 265, 270, 276, 290, 292
intercommunity, 151, 305
interdisciplinary, 70, 107, 168, 224, 307
intergenerational, 345
international, xi, xix–xx, 3, 5, 11–13, 15, 27, 31, 43, 49–50, 53, 58, 61–64, 68–69, 72, 80, 107, 120, 126, 131, 141, 150, 154, 158, 163, 182, 193, 200–201, 221–222, 238, 243, 248, 252–253, 265, 267, 278, 316, 318, 330–331, 334–335, 346–347, 362, 367, 369, 373, 375–376
intersection, 70, 333, 346
intervention, 153, 161, 287
investigation, 105, 223, 225, 231, 291, 305, 308, 345
investment, 7, 16, 150, 177, 181, 184, 271, 328, 348–349, 352
invisibility of rural matters, 5, 7, 176
involvement, 65, 153, 183, 190–191, 250, 294–295, 340, 342, 344, 347–348, 352
Iraq, 360–361
Ireland, 278, 358, 371
iron cage of rationality, xix, 327, 347–348. *See also* Weber, M.
Iron Curtain, xii, xix–xx, 9–10, 39, 149
ISCED (International Standard Classification of Education), 29, 150, 157
Islam, 362
island, 14, 51, 63, 66, 68, 100, 217, 219, 222–223
isolation, xvi, 14, 158, 202, 217–218, 220–222, 231, 240, 248, 297, 348, 359
Italy, xi, xix, 6, 14, 23, 25, 28, 31–36, 43, 217–235, 324–332, 348–352, 358, 361–363. *See also* distance learning and teaching; INDIRE (Italian National Institute for Documentation, Innovation and Educational Research); Manifesto delle Piccole Scuole common learning environment, 223, 229, 231, 349
island municipalities, 219
Marettimo, 219, 222
Ivić, I., 13, 43, 147, 149–150, 152–160, 162, 164, 330, 340

Index ■ 385

J

Jackson, A., xiv, xvii, 232
Jelen, L., 324, 328–329, 357–360, 362, 365–367, 374
job, 61, 68, 150, 240, 248–249, 251, 273, 294
Johnson, J., 4, 305, 318, 324
joint, xi, 43, 67, 81–84, 160, 163, 168, 186
journeys, 13, 56, 58, 65–66, 72, 186, 309, 316–317, 343. *See also* travel
    bus, 65–66, 85, 93, 112, 115, 211, 313, 316–317
    car, 115, 312–314, 316
    commute, 13, 22–24, 29, 82, 93, 107, 109–121
    distance (to travel), 11, 65–67, 85, 111–112, 118, 134, 156, 167, 202, 208, 222, 239, 241–242, 252, 268, 330, 333
    transport, 11, 23–24, 26, 39–40, 53–54, 58, 65–66, 69, 72, 93, 108, 111–112, 131, 135–136, 150, 181–182, 201, 222, 268
    walking, 5, 65–66, 115, 211, 241, 291, 312–313, 316
justice, 167, 298, 303, 307, 317–318, 331, 335, 369, 373

K

Kalaoja, E., 43, 57, 64, 348
Karlberg-Granlund, G., 12, 36, 43, 49–52, 54, 56, 58–62, 64, 66, 68, 70, 72, 107, 114, 327, 341, 343, 348, 352, 372
kids, 66, 68, 115–118, 293, 295
Kimonen, E., 242, 247
kindergarten, xiv, 82, 84–85, 95, 127–128
KIR-STAT (Hungarian Ministry of Human Capacities), 88–92, 97–99
Klebelsberg Institution Maintenance Centre (KLIK), 80, 86–87
knowledge, xi–xii, xiv, xvi, xx, 22, 25, 27, 43, 63–64, 67, 71, 104, 107, 153, 160, 162, 164, 186, 188, 190–193, 204, 227–228, 250, 260, 287, 289–290, 305, 307, 309–310, 323, 334, 347, 359
Kosovo, 148, 360
Kovács, K., 13, 23, 32, 79, 84–85, 93, 96, 326–327, 330, 342, 346, 348

Kučera, Z., 13, 23–24, 27, 31–32, 41, 90, 106–109, 113, 140, 333–343
Kučerová, S.R., 12–13, 15, 21–42, 90, 104–117, 120, 133, 323, 325–326, 330–333, 339, 342–343
Kvalsund, R., xi, xiv–xv, xvii, xx, 8–9, 11, 24, 32, 43, 61, 67, 131, 155, 177, 242, 264, 304–305, 310, 340–342, 344–345, 347, 350, 369, 373–374

L

label, 10, 209–210, 212–213, 333
land, 4, 53, 69, 72, 90, 150, 217, 219, 291, 312–314, 349, 361
landscape, 69, 90, 312–313, 346
language, 3, 228, 232, 263–264, 269, 329, 346–347
Lapland, 263
large, xi, 5, 10, 25, 29–32, 36, 39, 43, 51, 58, 66–67, 69, 84–85, 99, 108, 126, 129, 134–135, 151, 159, 167, 207, 239, 247–248, 312, 331, 334, 344, 359, 362
Latvia, 10, 359
LAU (Local Administative Unit), 83, 86
Lave, J., 228–229
laws, 126, 136, 147, 164, 177, 185, 219–220, 239, 262–263, 265, 305
Lawson, T., 226, 229, 232
leadership, 80, 141, 186, 237, 239, 241, 243, 245, 247–249, 251–253, 285–286, 288–290, 292, 296–298, 300, 343
league tables, 62, 287, 293
learning, xii–xvi, xx, 7, 9, 14, 56, 61–63, 65, 67–68, 70–72, 85, 98, 127, 148, 158–159, 161–163, 165, 177, 184, 186–187, 190–193, 199, 201, 204, 206, 208–209, 213, 218, 220–232, 246, 253, 264–265, 277–278, 297, 304, 349–351
leave, Learning to leave, xiii, xvi, 54, 68, 150, 160–161, 295
Lefebvre, H., 12, 14–15, 303–311, 313, 315, 317–318, 333, 342–343, 345
legislation, 32, 56, 59, 69, 71–72, 83, 87, 97, 105, 118, 192, 200, 218, 244
leisure, 55, 65, 115, 163
lesson, 162, 224, 226, 228–231, 349
Letts, W., 23, 177, 180, 192
Levitas, A., 126–127, 135
liberal, xviii, 25, 41, 72, 79, 83, 95, 365

library, 120, 249, 253, 312
Libya, 360–361
life-world perspective, 341
limitations, 41, 81, 96, 111, 136, 187, 189–190, 193, 231, 299
Lingard, B., 52, 290
linguistic, 3, 164, 329, 362
literacy, 60, 62, 219
literary, 3, 288, 300
literature, 4, 52, 68, 96, 104, 107, 136, 184, 189–190, 206, 220–221, 232, 304–305, 318, 324, 330, 347
Lithuania, 10, 359
Little, A., 159–160, 246
locality, 23, 72, 163, 179, 264, 305, 312, 332, 335
locally, 25, 67, 95, 111, 213, 272, 351
located, 22, 104, 110–111, 131, 136–137, 139–140, 176, 184, 187, 200, 202–203, 209, 230, 240–241, 296, 330, 333, 348
location, xv, 5, 9, 11–12, 32, 140, 152, 160, 184, 189, 202, 213, 253, 269, 299, 312, 314, 327, 330, 334, 342, 352
London, 293–294
loss, xix, 11, 41, 55, 69, 80, 86, 131, 248
lowland, 35–36, 41, 50
Lundgren, U., 50, 61
Lyson, T., 131, 220, 222

M

Madrid, 39, 176, 184
mainland, 50, 222, 260, 269, 273
mainstream, xi, 16, 106, 192, 239, 340, 345
maintenance, 30, 80–83, 85–87, 90–92, 120, 131, 221, 239, 351
majority, 24, 32, 50, 61, 80, 83–84, 94–95, 106, 116–117, 130, 166, 178, 219, 240, 266, 286, 313, 334, 352, 365–366
management, xviii, 49, 53, 69, 72, 87, 104–105, 140, 150, 163, 176, 186, 188, 192, 224, 238, 245, 247, 251, 274–275, 287, 289, 292–294, 297–298, 372
managing, 11, 24, 54, 87, 92–93, 104, 110, 119–120, 127, 218, 222, 246, 286–287, 316
Manifesto delle Piccole Scuole, 230, 349
map, 12, 26–27, 40, 89–90, 110, 310, 315, 366

market, xviii, 10, 13, 25, 52, 54, 98, 100, 104–105, 107–108, 119–120, 125–126, 158, 167, 177, 183–184, 325, 347, 350, 364
Marx, K., 306
Maslowski, R., 14–15, 31, 33, 237, 240, 242, 244–245, 251, 342
Massey, D., 12, 15, 177–178, 189, 191, 268, 306, 326, 345–346, 351. *See also* global sense of place
mathematics, 62–63, 228, 247, 309
measure, xix, 41, 53, 56, 60, 69, 80, 87, 95–96, 117, 148, 153–154, 156, 158, 165, 221, 306, 309, 313–314, 328, 364
mechanisation, 53
Mediterranean, 223, 361
merger, 248–250, 252
Merrifield, A., 306–311, 315
MESTDS (Ministry of Education, Science and Technical Development of the Republic of Serbia), 154, 156–158, 162, 165
metropolitan, 85, 267
Meyer, H., xix, 61
Meyer, P., 8, 12, 21, 32, 40
migrant, 9, 15, 165–166, 182–183, 324, 328–329, 335, 357–366
migration, xii–xiv, xvii, xix, 23, 36, 54, 69, 99, 107–108, 127, 148, 150, 158, 165, 182–183, 185, 200–201, 241, 260, 277, 324–325, 328–329, 335, 357–367, 374
milestones, xxviii, 184–185
millennium, 56, 81, 154
minimum, 7, 14, 25, 61, 83, 131, 201, 231, 240, 243–245, 332
mining, 84, 291, 312
minority, 11–12, 16, 23, 85, 106, 160, 183, 229, 263, 266, 340, 352
miracle, 64, 165–166
mobility, xvi, xviii, 8, 158, 160, 190, 220, 333
model, 10, 26, 28–29, 70–72, 92, 110, 160, 163, 177, 180–182, 185, 188, 192, 225, 228–229, 276–278, 315, 325
modernity, xvi–xviii, xx, 16, 54–55, 160, 305, 318, 351
money, 58, 62, 69, 161, 165, 201, 290
Montessori, M., xxviii, 14, 200–203, 205–214, 239, 342, 346–347
Morocco, 361
mountainous, 14, 150, 217
movement, 9, 28, 80, 87, 106, 115, 149, 166–167, 177, 186, 326, 328, 358

Index ■ **387**

multi-school boards, 14–15, 240, 244, 251
multicultural, 107, 253
multifunctional, 83, 86, 89, 162, 164, 249
multipurpose, 272, 275
municipal, 50–51, 56, 58–60, 69, 82–83, 87, 90, 118, 136, 240, 260, 264–265, 269–270, 272–273, 275, 277, 327, 352, 376
municipality, 15, 34, 51, 55, 58–60, 66, 80, 93, 107, 110, 112, 115–120, 131, 140, 156, 162, 239, 260–263, 265–266, 268–270, 273–275, 277, 329, 332, 346
music, 64, 220
myth, 15, 310, 313, 346

N

nature, xv–xvi, 3, 15, 22, 25–26, 52, 55, 62, 79, 83, 87, 93, 111, 125–126, 133, 163, 290, 296, 298, 306, 327, 330, 339–340, 364
neighbourhood, 64, 293
Nekorjak, M., 23, 104, 106
neoliberal, xx, 49, 52–53, 56, 60–61, 69, 79, 104, 183, 185, 192, 278, 285–286, 297, 325, 347
Netherlands, xix, 6, 14, 25, 28–29, 31, 33–36, 39, 43, 72, 237–246, 249–250, 252–253, 324–325, 327, 330, 332, 334, 342, 363, 366, 372, 375
network, xi–xii, xvii, xxviii, 15, 23, 26–27, 39–40, 43, 79–81, 83, 85, 87–91, 93, 95, 97, 99, 104, 107–108, 111, 118–119, 126–130, 134–135, 139–140, 148, 156–158, 165, 168, 201, 204, 220, 223–228, 231–232, 259–278, 297, 305, 326, 331, 343–344, 346, 348, 352, 369–370, 372–376
Network 14 (Communities, Families and Schooling in Educational Research), ix, xi–xii, xvii, 352
network planning, xxviii, 15, 259–261, 263–278, 326, 344, 346, 376
Nevalainen, R., 242, 247
New Public Management (NPM), 49, 53, 62, 69, 287, 292–294, 297–298
non-Roma, 82, 84–85, 93, 96–97, 348
Nordic, xi, 11, 36, 72, 304, 341, 369, 373
Nordland, 49, 376
normative, xiii–xiv, 82, 206, 286, 290, 304, 352

north, xiv, 15, 36, 39, 51, 53, 55, 72, 84–85, 166, 244–245, 291, 313, 328, 361, 375
northern, 41, 49, 53, 84, 90, 139, 241, 358, 361, 366–367, 371
Norway, xiii–xiv, xix–xx, 6, 9, 13, 25, 28–33, 36, 43, 49–72, 324–329, 334, 343, 347, 351, 361, 366
NUTS-2 (Nomenclature of Territorial Units for Statistics (NUTS), 84, 89

O

objective, 22, 62, 135, 167, 186, 228, 289, 305, 345
OFSTED (Office for Standards in Education, England), 287, 293, 295, 314
online, 110, 224, 228, 231, 269–270, 343
Ontario, 266, 278
operational, 86, 88, 96, 187, 325
opportunity, xvi, 12, 100, 134, 161, 203, 207, 218, 225, 229, 231, 242, 252, 275, 286, 294, 296, 307, 316–317, 326
opposition, 131, 349
organization, 5, 7, 10, 12, 22–26, 28, 32–34, 41, 43, 54, 85, 104–105, 111, 125, 132, 134, 136, 141, 148, 152, 161–163, 176, 180, 182, 186–188, 214, 218, 221, 224–227, 231, 238, 247, 275, 286, 333, 351
originate, 292, 314, 346, 357, 360
orography, 23, 36, 39
Ortega, J., 187–188
Oslo, 51, 62
Ossewaarde, 327, 350–351
out-of-school, 14, 118, 163, 166
outdoor, 168, 312–313
outlying, 56, 68, 312–313, 365
outmigration, 85–86, 329
outskirts, 202, 209
ownership, 54, 126, 164, 178–179
Ozga, J., 9, 132, 135–136

P

Pakistan, 358, 360
parental choice, 10, 86, 93, 116
parents, xx, 10, 25, 59, 65, 82, 86, 91, 93, 105, 111, 116–117, 119–120, 190–191,

207, 209–210, 222, 239–240, 250, 266, 275, 292, 294–295, 314, 316, 347
parish, 11, 291, 312, 317
participate, 67, 87, 189, 224, 227, 265, 270, 275, 288
participation, xv, 96–97, 133, 137, 182, 190–191, 240, 245, 265–266, 270, 275–276, 297, 333, 342, 364
partnership, 14, 65, 148, 153, 261, 265, 341, 350
Paulgaard, G., 55, 264, 329
Pavan, B., 159, 221–222, 225, 232
Pawlak, R., 128, 131, 140
pay, 33, 66, 95, 133, 139, 211, 220, 239, 346
Pedagogical Program for Integration, Hungary (PPI), 85, 95–96
pedagogy, 14, 22, 30, 59, 64, 70–71, 85, 95, 100, 105–106, 117, 120, 132, 134–135, 140, 158, 188, 190, 205–209, 212–213, 221, 225, 229–230, 239, 246, 250, 292, 325, 341–342
peer-review, 106, 343
peers, 224, 231, 238, 242
Peeters, D., 263–265
performance, 2–3, 5, 50, 62–63, 67, 80, 94–96, 100, 117, 158–159, 183, 206, 210–211, 223, 231, 243, 287, 292–293, 309–310, 350, 352
period, xi, xvi, 4, 29, 41, 43, 56, 58–59, 79, 88–89, 91, 108, 110–111, 115–116, 125–129, 131, 133, 135, 137, 139, 141, 153, 158, 165, 219, 241, 260, 270, 285, 289, 296, 323, 327–328, 342–343, 345, 359, 365, 372
period witnesses, 110, 343, 345
peripheral, 35–36, 53–54, 63, 84, 111, 132–133, 139–140, 330, 334, 339, 345, 365, 370, 374
permanence, 133, 183, 230, 348
Pesikan, A., 5, 13, 147–150, 152–159, 163–165, 330, 333, 340
phase, 82, 96, 108, 226, 228, 250, 271
physical, 11–13, 15, 22–24, 26, 34, 36, 39, 41, 56, 66, 69–70, 118, 134, 203, 217, 221–223, 229, 263, 309–310, 312, 325, 330, 334–335, 343
Pietarinen, J., 43, 57, 64, 348
PIRLS (Progress in International Reading Literacy Study), 62
PISA (Program for International Student Assessment), xix, 5, 53, 61–64, 72, 80, 92, 94–96, 99, 158, 168, 267

Piwowarski, R., 131, 135
place, xi–xiii, xvi–xx, 2, 4, 9–12, 15, 22, 25, 55, 57, 65, 68, 77, 90, 112, 114–115, 126, 136, 141, 149, 153, 162, 165–166, 178, 186–187, 190–192, 201–202, 204, 213, 224, 226, 229, 231, 250, 253, 260, 263, 267–268, 270, 273, 278, 289, 303, 305, 310–313, 315–318, 325–326, 333–335, 345–346, 350–351, 369, 373–374, 376
    place attachment, 12, 65
    place-based, xi, xiii, xix–xx, 162, 260, 278, 374
plan, xviii, 119, 153, 205, 227, 252, 265–266, 269–270, 273, 277
planning, xix, xxxviii, 11, 15, 41, 43, 58, 61, 64, 69, 97, 105, 162, 165, 259–261, 263–278, 326, 344, 346, 352. *See also* network planning
play, xiv, 11, 15, 36, 54, 115–116, 118, 226, 241, 243, 262, 266, 290, 292–293, 298, 309, 317, 334, 351
plurality, 202, 213, 349
Poland, xviii–xix, 6, 10, 13, 25, 28–29, 31–33, 36–37, 39, 41, 120, 125–141, 241, 323, 325–326, 332, 341, 343–344, 346, 358, 362, 366, 372
policy, xix, 4, 9–11, 13–15, 24–28, 33, 36, 43, 61, 72, 79–80, 82, 86–87, 95–96, 104, 108, 120, 136, 151, 154, 156, 161, 164, 168, 177, 180, 185, 190, 201, 218–221, 237–242, 244–245, 247, 250, 260–263, 270, 278, 286–287, 294, 304, 310–311, 315, 323, 325, 331, 335, 340–341, 345–347, 350, 362, 364, 366–367, 376–377
political, x, xviii, 3–4, 10, 12, 22, 24, 26, 32, 41, 43, 55, 59, 68–69, 81, 90, 93, 104–105, 119–120, 126–127, 149, 153, 161–162, 193, 199, 201, 225, 232, 244, 261, 286–287, 292, 297, 299–300, 305, 307–308, 318, 324–326, 329, 331, 334–335, 350–351, 357–358, 360–362, 364
poor, xvi, 15, 94–97, 99, 132, 139, 147–148, 156, 158, 162, 165–166, 178, 184, 189, 192, 222, 227, 243–244, 261, 273, 295, 314, 334, 341
population, xiii, xix, 4, 7–8, 10, 12, 14, 23, 26–27, 31–32, 35–39, 50–51, 53–55, 66, 69, 81, 84–86, 94, 106, 108, 110, 115, 127, 148, 150–155, 162, 165,

Index ■ **389**

167, 176–177, 180, 182–184, 187, 192, 219–221, 238, 240–241, 244–246, 249–253, 260–261, 286, 291, 312, 325–326, 329–330, 332, 357–360, 365–366
Portugal, 329, 358, 366
positive developments, xviii, 6, 13–15, 62, 99–100, 191, 223–224, 226, 248, 265, 271, 275, 316, 333, 345–346, 351–352, 358
post-communist, 358–359, 365
post-human. *See* Deleuze, G.
post-socialist, 126–146
post-Soviet, 9–10, 327, 366, 374
postmodernity, xvi, xviii, xx
poverty, xvi, 84, 96, 98, 100, 149, 153–155, 159, 167–168, 232, 291, 295, 360
power, xvi, xix–xx, 15, 24, 32–33, 53–55, 60–61, 69, 72, 80, 104, 119, 166, 168, 191–192, 207, 286, 288, 299, 309–310, 315, 350
practice, xix, 64, 148, 152–154, 158, 186, 188, 214, 223, 228, 231, 240, 245–246, 285–286, 288–290, 293, 295, 297–300, 304, 310–311, 331, 333, 346, 349, 366
practitioner-researcher, 341
prejudice, 166, 328
preschool, xiv, 54, 64, 149, 155–157, 168, 263, 341. *See also* kindergarten
preservation, 288, 349
pressure, 15, 56, 63–64, 69, 83, 87, 127, 201, 252, 293–294, 352
prestige, 92, 114–115, 290
principal, xii, 3, 8, 12, 41, 139, 163, 230, 239–240, 247–248, 250–251, 292, 297–300, 325, 347, 372
priority, xix, 126, 148, 165, 176, 330
private, 33–34, 51, 54, 60, 107, 110, 131, 178–179, 183, 193, 206, 211, 213, 239, 261, 263, 265, 313, 327
privilege, 207, 211
production, xiv–xv, xviii, 36, 54, 69, 150, 155, 229, 286, 288, 291, 304, 306–309, 317, 333, 343, 345
professional, 27, 71, 87, 150–151, 157, 161–162, 184, 204–205, 208, 224, 240, 244, 248, 287–288, 292–293, 327, 349, 371–372, 375
profit, 54, 86
programme (program), 5, 27, 61, 63, 80, 85, 95–96, 126–127, 136, 148, 153,

156–158, 163–164, 202, 226, 228, 264, 267, 269, 312, 314, 334, 359
progress, 13, 15, 52–53, 62–63, 92, 149, 225, 228, 265–266, 270, 344, 346
progressive, 12, 125, 188, 206, 268, 326, 351
project, 27, 43, 68, 85, 96, 98, 100, 163–164, 166, 199, 201–203, 205, 208, 222–223, 226, 228–230, 232, 265, 303, 333, 373, 375
proposal, 60, 182, 244, 265–266, 276
protection, 97, 149, 167–168, 350, 365
protests, 59–60, 71, 166
province, 201–202, 260–261
provision, 1–4, 7, 9, 14–16, 23–25, 29, 32–33, 39, 43, 50, 52, 54, 56, 69, 81, 83–84, 108, 111, 118, 120, 139, 167, 220–221, 253, 259, 267, 286, 312, 314, 316, 325, 334, 341, 352, 369, 373, 375
proximity, 11, 40, 96, 118, 134, 180, 253, 295, 361–362
psychology, 3, 371–373, 375
public, 10, 15, 24, 33–34, 36, 39, 49, 53, 56, 60, 66, 68–69, 72, 80, 82–83, 87, 95, 97, 100, 110–111, 115, 119, 131, 136, 161, 168, 183, 186, 193, 200, 218, 239–240, 244, 249, 261, 264–266, 269–272, 277, 287, 291–294, 297–298, 327, 343, 347, 362, 364, 366
publication, 4, 22, 24, 96, 106, 168, 230, 278, 345–347, 372
pupil, 30, 59, 62, 64, 67, 69–70, 184, 225, 273, 287, 292

Q

qualification, xii–xiii, 71, 139, 150, 218
qualified, 5–7, 94, 151, 158–159, 246–247, 264, 341
qualified teachers, 5, 7, 341
quality, xii–xiii, xv–xvii, xix, 2–3, 5, 7, 24, 36, 58–59, 61–64, 66–67, 69, 71, 80, 94, 119–120, 127, 132–135, 141, 147–148, 150–151, 154–156, 158, 160, 163, 165–168, 180–181, 183, 185–186, 190, 192–193, 217, 220–222, 230–231, 237–238, 240, 243–251, 253, 268, 272, 313, 345, 349, 371–372
quarrying, 312
quasi-market, 105, 120

R

racism, 167
Raggl, A., 14, 29, 32, 107, 161, 199–206, 208, 210, 212–214, 242, 246, 248, 334, 344, 346
railway, 54
range, xix–xx, 66, 100, 158, 232, 241, 246, 292, 307, 312–313, 318, 332, 344, 351, 369, 372
reality, xix, 11, 139, 147–149, 162, 164, 206, 230, 269, 291, 293, 308–309, 317
realpolitik, 295
recession, 50, 56, 59, 69, 183, 185, 261, 358
reclaim, 310, 348
recruitment, 62, 127
reduction, 15, 63, 66, 98, 108, 112, 119, 132, 153–154, 167, 180, 200, 221, 324, 326, 352
reflexive authority, 327, 350–351
reform, 126, 140, 180–181, 193, 206, 209, 220, 261, 271, 278, 286–287
refugees, 149, 183, 327, 329, 357–358, 360–362, 365
regeneration, 312, 314
regime, xviii–xix, 14, 24, 80, 104, 106, 110, 118–119, 125–126
regional, xv, xix, 8, 11, 16, 23–24, 34, 36, 39, 49–51, 72, 83, 85, 87–89, 96–97, 104–106, 111, 116, 118–119, 127, 133, 139, 148–151, 153, 156, 163, 165, 167, 201, 204, 210, 218, 227, 253, 260–261, 264–265, 267, 269, 271, 278, 306, 308, 311, 315, 328, 331, 341, 370, 374–376
regions, 219
regulation, 24, 65, 83, 108, 120, 181–182, 185, 239
Reid, J., 306, 311
relationships, xi, xv, 10, 15, 32, 52, 63–64, 66, 68, 133, 160, 184, 187, 190, 221, 230, 238, 243, 250–251, 269, 289, 296, 309, 348, 351, 362, 372
religious, 24, 33, 167, 203, 239, 241, 250, 362
remote, 31, 35, 41, 53, 67, 72, 147, 165, 167, 201–202, 204, 209, 242, 252, 315, 330, 345, 349
renaissance, 328, 347
renewal, 53, 100, 104, 108, 119, 141, 184–186, 261, 326
reopen (schools), 5, 13, 136, 183
repatriation, 360
reproduction, xi, 1, 12, 21, 49, 79, 103, 125, 147, 150, 175, 177, 199, 217, 237, 259, 268, 285, 288, 303, 307, 309, 323, 339, 346, 357, 369, 371
rescue, 14, 325
research, xi–xii, xiv–xx, 1–16, 304–305, 310–311, 315–317, 339–348, 351–352. *See also* design; epistemological; ethics; ethnography; theory; time series
   cartographic, 27, 105, 343–344
   case study, 15, 93, 104, 107, 110, 118–119, 166, 204, 304, 311–312, 314–315, 318, 341–343, 345
   causal relationship, 243, 251
   chain development index, 43–44
   comparative, xii, xv, 11–12, 15, 193, 344, 366, 374
   data, 5, 12, 25–27, 30–31, 33, 41, 43, 57–58, 65–66, 84, 88–93, 95–99, 109–110, 112, 116, 129–130, 137, 147, 150–152, 154–155, 160, 165, 168, 178–179, 183, 189–191, 201–202, 205, 207, 219, 222–224, 244–245, 253, 261, 263, 269, 273, 276, 285, 291, 312, 314, 331, 333, 340–341, 343, 346, 361
   ethnographic, 12, 15, 188, 190–191, 214, 285–286, 290–291, 340–341, 343, 346
   interview, 111, 210, 238, 244, 248, 251, 285, 296, 300, 312, 342
   longitudinal, 11, 68, 333, 374–375
   meta-analysis, 103, 106, 232, 343–344
   method, 24, 111, 218, 245, 343
   methodology, 8, 25, 95, 110, 187, 202, 228, 253, 305, 335, 371, 373, 375
   narrative, 228–229, 286
   observation, 15, 111, 190, 202, 224, 226, 231–232, 268, 291–292, 347
   qualitative, 26, 93, 110–111, 155, 165, 188, 310, 318, 343, 372–373
   quantitative, 26–27, 92, 110, 159, 188, 312, 343, 372
   questionnaire, 5, 110, 202–204, 224
   results (research studies), 94, 133, 166, 223–224, 231, 268, 276, 366
resident, 315–316, 330
resilience, 5, 100, 181, 326, 329
resistance, 13, 60, 87, 326, 352
resolution, 115, 245
resource, 5–6, 68, 70, 164, 181, 183, 193, 231, 270, 290, 295, 331, 349, 351–352

respect, xiii, 3–4, 22, 32, 127, 149, 186, 190–191, 231, 311, 334
restructuring, 51, 126, 347, 374
results (attainment), 15, 64, 80, 94, 96, 134, 139, 158, 183–184, 188, 190, 193, 222–223, 267
revenues, 87, 128
Ribchester, C., 24, 30, 115, 201, 325
rich, xx, 60, 105, 232, 329, 340
right, xii, 63–64, 80, 85, 115, 151, 212, 218, 263, 265, 276, 294, 297, 299, 326–327, 362
right-wing, 80, 362
rise, 9, 14, 54, 70, 82, 126, 140, 151, 183, 206, 261
river, 205
Rogoff, B., xiv–xv
roll, 13–14, 85–86, 183, 247, 331
Roma, 13, 82, 84–85, 91–97, 148, 153, 327, 342, 346, 348
Romania, 10, 95, 358
room, 14, 68, 161, 176, 179–180, 185, 212, 247, 294, 345
route, 149, 328, 347, 361–362, xii
rural education observatory, 186
Rural Education Tourism (RET), 348
rural educational research, 3, 11, 323, 339–340, 344–345, 347, 352
rural idyll, 12, 15, 211, 213
rural school network, 79–81, 83, 85, 87–89, 91, 93, 95, 97, 99
rural sociological imagination, 11, 16, 318, 341, 348, 351
rurality, xiv, xvi, 160, 176, 187, 190, 238, 242, 252, 307, 333
Russia, 328, 359, 361–362. *See also* USSR (Union of Soviet Socialist Republics)

S

Sahlberg, P., 64
Sami, 263
Saragossa, 186–187
Sauras, 185, 187
save, 1, 21, 49, 60–61, 72, 79, 103, 125, 147, 175, 183, 199, 217, 237, 259, 285, 303, 323, 339, 357, 369, 371
scale, xiv, xvi–xvii, 10, 26–27, 36, 39, 69–70, 84, 92–93, 99, 105, 107, 128, 131, 134–135, 161, 305, 310, 312, 327, 331, 334, 352, 359
Scandinavia, 330
scattered, 130, 135–136, 140–141, 286
Schafft, K., xiv, xvii, 232, 340, 345
scheme, 62, 84
Schengen, 358
Schleicher, A., 5
Schmid, C., 307, 318
Schneider, J., 328
scholarship, 299–300, 335
school stories, 110
school-community, 141, 294, 296–298
schoolbooks, 85–86
schooling, x–xi, xiii–xiv, xviii–xx, 1–2, 5, 16, 21–22, 25, 29, 49, 51, 56, 60, 79, 85, 103–108, 110, 119, 125, 127, 147, 157–158, 160, 165, 175, 177–178, 184, 186, 199–200, 217–220, 231, 237, 251, 259–260, 262, 270–271, 278, 285–286, 293–294, 299, 303, 311, 317–318, 321, 323–324, 327–328, 331, 334–335, 339, 348–349, 351, 357, 369, 371–375
Schooling for Tomorrow Scenarios (OECD), 349
Schumacher, E., xvi
science, 3, 62, 94, 96, 150, 154, 168, 253, 345, 369, 372–376
scientific, xix, 63, 104, 136, 288, 309, 333, 371–372, 375
sector, 10, 33, 49, 53–56, 62, 66, 69, 148–149, 152, 154, 162, 263–264, 270, 291, 373
Security, xii, xvi, xviii, 9, 148, 165, 167, 361–362, 365, 367
segregation, 13, 25, 28, 36, 84–85, 91–96, 98–99, 278, 328, 348
selectivity, 91, 93–94
Sensat, Rosa, 186, 341
Serbia, xix, xxviii, 6, 9–10, 13, 23, 25, 28, 31–33, 36–37, 39, 42–43, 147–168, 323, 325, 328, 330, 340, 344, 361
service, xiv, 23, 33, 68, 81, 148, 159, 164, 168, 217, 253, 261, 264, 269–270, 272, 275, 277, 291, 335, 372, 376
setting, 27, 55, 118, 149, 164, 168, 204–205, 219, 228, 291, 294, 369, 373
settlement, xiii, 23, 39, 67, 89–90, 107–108, 111, 118, 134–135, 286, 330, 374
settlement size, 90
settling, 183, 241, 328–329

shared, 11, 55, 87, 182, 186, 189, 191, 224, 229, 231, 249, 252, 268, 323–325, 334, 348–349
shop, 55, 291, 312
shortage, 5–6, 36, 63, 83, 238, 242, 313, 352, 358
Showalter, D., 4, 324, 330, 333
shrinkage, 66, 82, 89–90
Shucksmith, M., 11, 330, 340, 348, 351, 374
Sigsworth, A., xvii, 22–23, 25, 41, 51, 114, 116, 120, 131, 141, 203–205, 207, 214, 286, 300, 347, 376
Singapore, 96
size, xv–xvi, xxviii, 6, 12, 22–26, 29–32, 41, 50–51, 58, 63, 80, 89–90, 111–112, 131–133, 135, 137, 140, 152, 160–161, 167–168, 178, 200, 203, 221, 223, 231, 238, 242–245, 247, 249, 251–252, 261, 264, 268–269, 272, 286, 330–331, 334. *See also* large; smaller; tiny; very small
Slovakia, 10, 84, 96, 358
Slovenia, 358
smaller, xiv, 7, 29, 32, 51, 59, 70, 81–82, 86–87, 89–90, 108, 111, 116, 119, 128, 131, 140–141, 180, 184, 187, 193, 205, 211–212, 214, 240, 243, 247, 253, 260, 296, 307, 330, 335, 365
Smit, R., 107, 161, 199, 221, 246
Sobotka, A., 131, 134, 140
socialisation, 176
socialist, 1, 10, 12, 16, 41, 81–82, 84, 90, 120, 125–127, 129, 131–133, 135, 137, 139, 141, 300, 323, 325, 362
society, xii, xvi–xviii, xx, 22, 52, 61, 70, 72, 94, 104, 141, 153, 160, 180, 185, 220, 244, 260–261, 265, 277–278, 289–290, 300, 306, 309–310, 334, 347–348, 351, 364–366, 370, 374
sociocultural, 12, 21, 23–26, 34, 149, 160–161, 167, 187, 190, 286, 325
socioeconomic, 4–5, 23, 36, 95–97, 133–134, 150, 156, 158, 181, 185, 187, 201, 262, 264, 278, 287, 291, 312
socioeconomic status (SES), 5–6, 118, 334
sociology, xvii–xviii, 3, 27, 72, 214, 300, 305–306, 318, 345, 371, 373, 377
sociology of education, 27, 214, 300, 373, 377
software, 27, 110–111, 187, 202, 226, 269
Soja, E., 303, 306

Solstad, K.J., xiv–xv, xvii, 9, 12–13, 36, 43, 49–52, 54, 56–68, 70, 72, 203–205, 260, 327, 347–348, 352, 376
solution, 164, 213, 221, 247–249, 277
Somalia, 360–361
Soriano-Bozalongo, J., 14, 175, 187–190, 326, 330, 341–343, 346, 372
Soviet, ix, xvi, 9–10, 125, 327, 359
space, xi–xii, xvi–xviii, xx, xxviii, 2, 4, 9, 11–12, 15, 22, 27, 31, 53–54, 71, 77, 105–106, 108, 120, 153, 164, 177–178, 180, 188–189, 192, 201, 253, 285–286, 288, 290, 292, 299, 303–313, 315–318, 331, 333, 341–345, 366, 369, 372–373
Spain, xix, 6, 9, 14, 25, 28–29, 31–33, 36, 38–39, 41, 175–194, 324–335, 341–347, 351, 358, 361. *See also* Sensat, Rosa
  autonomous communities (Spain), 176, 181–187
  CRA (Colegios Rurales Agrupados), 176, 182, 185–187
sparsely populated, xiii–xiv, xvi, 36, 39, 50–54, 57–58, 60, 63, 260, 262
spatial, x, 9, 12–15, 22–27, 30–31, 34, 36, 39, 41, 43, 81, 83, 99, 103, 105–106, 108, 110–111, 115, 118–119, 134, 184, 189, 204, 261, 294, 303–304, 306–310, 312, 316–318, 330, 342–345, 372, 374
spatial distribution, 13, 22, 24, 31, 34, 36, 39, 41, 105, 110–111, 307, 342–343
Special Educational Needs (SEN), 239
specialist, 64, 157, 247, 347
sports, 43, 64, 128, 220, 249, 313
stability, 15, 43, 52, 81, 100, 118, 221, 351
staff, 5, 57, 61, 69, 94, 116, 126, 177, 181–182, 186–187, 202–204, 206, 208, 213, 220, 222, 224, 240, 246–247, 249, 251–252, 275, 286, 291, 299, 312, 315
stage, 27, 86, 98, 112, 162, 225, 252, 265, 274
Stake, R., 71, 80, 202
stakeholders, xvii, 163–164, 225, 231, 251–252, 264, 273–277, 297
standard, 7, 25, 117–118, 150–151, 154, 159, 182, 192, 200, 225, 230, 366
statistical, 4, 6–8, 26–27, 30, 34, 41, 57, 63, 83, 88, 105, 109–110, 129–130, 148, 152, 154, 168, 312, 333
statistics, x, xxviii, 2–3, 7, 16, 26–27, 29–30, 33, 35, 57, 84, 152, 154–155, 157, 176, 193, 241–242, 253, 261, 266, 269, 272, 314, 324, 330, 333, 366
stereotypes, 132, 139–140

Stone in Europe's shoe, 1, 5, 352
strategic, 15, 32, 148, 152–154, 263, 265, 293, 295, 351
strength, xix, 15, 61, 63, 71, 81, 91, 150, 164, 189, 328, 345, 348
structural, x, xiv, 50, 63, 71, 79–80, 91, 94, 99, 260–261, 267, 275, 278, 288–289, 299, 324, 372
structural changes, 63, 71, 79–80, 260, 267, 289
structure, 23, 26, 28–30, 36, 39, 41, 51, 56, 60, 68, 70–71, 81, 89–90, 118–119, 130–133, 135, 137, 157, 165, 186, 203, 205, 261, 266, 289–290, 299–300, 309, 359
struggle, xix, 36, 59, 61, 166–167, 288, 307, 317
subject, 54, 63–64, 71, 105, 107, 157, 162, 164, 186, 189–190, 224, 228–229, 247
subsidy, 127, 134–135, 140, 261
suburbs, 4, 8, 36, 54, 62, 66, 135, 152, 191, 209, 289
success, 54–55, 64, 104, 159, 191, 201, 207, 295, 298, 325, 333–334, 348, 365–366
support, 25, 43, 55–56, 61, 65, 67, 82, 85, 95–96, 110, 118–120, 148–149, 151, 156, 158–159, 161–165, 167, 176–177, 181, 199, 204, 208–210, 213, 226–227, 230, 238, 244, 250–251, 264, 268, 292, 297, 326, 328, 341, 346, 348–349, 352, 362, 366
survey, x, xxviii, 15, 58, 60, 96–97, 110, 183, 270, 291, 340, 342–343, 362, 366
survival, xiii, 3, 53, 110, 210, 293, 296, 342, 346
sustainability, 53, 81, 99, 190, 295, 349, 372
sustainable, xv–xvi, 68, 81, 97, 153–154, 163, 347–348
Switzerland, 206, 214, 318
symbolic, 290, 294, 297, 310, 313, 316
synthesis, 104–105, 107, 184
Syria, 166, 360–361
systematic, 164–165, 253, 265

T

Tantarimäki, S., 15, 25, 32, 36, 54, 59, 64, 259–261, 264–273, 276, 326, 329, 331, 343–346
target, 62, 269, 272, 361–362, 364
Taylor, C., 105, 209, 290
teach, 16, 60, 63, 80, 87, 115, 159, 164, 243, 248
teacher education, 7, 63–64, 69, 71, 73, 76, 159, 162, 171, 186, 199, 235, 318, 320, 371–372, 376
teacher–parent relationships, 189, 210, 294–295
teacher perceptions, 5, 224
teacher qualifications, 134, 151, 159
teacher quality, 148, 165. *See also* expertise
teacher salaries, 86, 127, 135, 139, 150, 180, 220
teacher style, 31, 161, 189, 208–209, 228–230
teaching head, 120, 203–204, 207, 246–249
teams, xvii, xxviii, 64, 120, 166, 177, 187, 199, 204, 207–208, 222, 227, 229, 238, 242, 247–248, 252, 273, 275, 277
technical, 56, 135, 180, 218, 267, 273, 275
technocratic, 180, 185, 309
technology, 14, 52, 218, 224–226, 228, 232, 350, 352
temporal, 288, 290, 294, 298
Tennessee STAR project, 223
territory, 8, 10, 41, 108, 112, 149, 230, 310, 330–331
terrorism, 362
tertiary, 150, 155
testing, xix, 49–50, 61–63, 69, 72, 287
thematic, 162, 291
theory, 11–12, 14–15, 52, 54, 72, 118, 152, 177, 214, 288, 298, 300, 304–307, 318, 340, 342–343, 345–347, 351, 365
Thompson, P., 307, 311
Thompson, R., 288, 297
threat, 14–15, 52, 56–57, 60–61, 71, 82, 85, 113, 116–117, 209, 247, 265, 269, 293, 295, 329, 342
time series, 41, 344
tiny, 68, 329
Tirol, 199, 376
tool, 62, 96, 154, 227, 231, 305, 345
topography, 23
Törhönen, A., 15, 25, 32, 36, 54, 59, 64, 259–261, 266–273, 326, 329, 331, 343–344, 346
totalitarian, xviii, 10, 14, 108, 325
tourism, 14, 163–164, 182, 185, 313, 348
town, 5, 59, 85, 93, 111, 113, 115–117, 176, 181, 188, 202–203, 207, 210–213, 229, 249–250, 260, 312–315, 330, 343, 345
trade, 54, 126, 148, 181, 267, 275

tradition, 39, 52, 63, 157, 205, 220, 326, 341, 362
Trahorsch, P., 8, 12, 21–22, 24, 26, 28, 30, 32, 34, 36, 38, 40, 42, 325, 330–331, 376
Transdanubia, 89–90
transformation, 13, 39, 108, 111, 126–127, 129, 134, 140, 166, 226, 288, 298, 374
transition, xii, xvi, xviii, 29, 148–149, 181
transnational, xix, 9, 199, 202, 206, 318
travel, 15, 65, 149, 158, 185, 213, 227, 239, 313, 316, 328, 361, 365. *See also* journeys
Trinidad, 225–226
Trnková, 13, 24, 31, 36, 104, 106–109, 120, 132, 326, 330, 343, 345
trust, 4, 275, 351, 365
Tunisia, 361
Turkey, 358, 361
Turku, 259, 376
Turnov, 107, 110–116, 118
turnover, 104, 202, 222, 224, 227
typology, 16, 41, 43, 109, 135, 167, 202, 226, 308, 335, 341
Tyrol, 201, 332

U

Ukraine, 10, 362
uncertainty, 61, 115, 226, 252
unemployment, 97–98, 126, 134, 155, 291, 314, 358, 365
United Kingdom, 7, 11, 25, 28, 31, 33–34, 38–39, 43, 291, 304, 313, 315, 326, 358, 364, 369, 373
United Nations Educational, Scientific and Cultural Organisation (UNESCO), 29, 157, 168, 328, 333, 373
United Nations High Commission for Refugees (UNHCR), 165, 327, 329, 335, 365, 367
United Nations International Children's Emergency Fund (UNICEF), 156, 163, 165, 168, 367, 373, 375
United Nations World Toursim Organization (UNWTO, 163
urban, xii–xiii, xvi–xvii, xix–xx, 3, 5–8, 10–16, 23, 25, 31, 53–55, 66, 69, 72, 80, 82, 84, 88–92, 94, 98–99, 106–107, 120–121, 128–129, 132–135, 140–141, 148–156, 158, 160–161, 163, 165, 167, 177, 180–181, 183–185, 187–188, 190–193, 202, 206–208, 211–213, 219–220, 222, 241–242, 261–262, 269, 271, 278, 286, 306, 328, 333–335, 340–341, 344, 346–347, 365, 374
urban deficit model, x, xii–xiii, xix, 5–7, 120, 132–134, 160–161, 180–181, 184–185, 192, 220, 222, 242, 286
Uryga, 131–133, 136
USSR (Union of Soviet Socialist Republics), 10, 359

V

validity, 11, 97
van Zanten, A., 25, 120
variable, 151, 334, 344
very small, xxviii, 14–15, 31, 58, 120, 137, 176, 182, 199–202, 204, 214, 240–241, 311, 329, 331–332, 342, 348
viability, 55, 82, 296, 327, 343
Vigo-Arrazola, B., 14, 175, 187–191, 326, 330, 341–343, 346, 371
village, xvii, 5, 7, 13–15, 59, 69, 71, 81–82, 84–86, 88, 93, 114–117, 202, 204–205, 207, 209–211, 213–214, 249, 251, 262, 266, 268, 272, 291, 294–296, 300, 312–314, 316, 326, 332, 346, 374
visibility, 5, 11, 340
visible, 2, 8, 107–108, 115, 125, 364
vision, 11–12, 15, 205, 207, 213, 286, 326, 341
vocational, 85, 93, 95, 157, 162, 218, 228
voice, 151, 251, 297, 344
voluntary, xi, 81–83, 87, 90, 239, 325
Vorarlberg, 199, 201–202, 204
Vulliamy, G., 205, 242
vulnerability, 221, 251
Vygotsky, L., 160

W

Wacquant, L., xviii, xx, 84–85, 289, 300, 305, 318, 346
Waldorf school, 117
Walker, 213, 242, 249, 318
war, 10, 23, 36, 43, 53, 55, 106, 108, 129, 149, 166, 358, 360

water, 150, 163
Webb, R., 205, 242
Weber, M., xix, 347, 350–351
welfare, xiv, xvi–xvii, 69, 72, 270, 272, 274, 286, 312, 327, 350, 372
well-being, 56, 65–66, 220, 296, 333
Wenger, E., 228–229
white flight, 13, 84, 93
White, S., 106, 221, 305, 311, 324, 340
Why Rural Matters (WRM), 4
wicked problem, 326, 335
winter, 222, 316
wireless, 226
women, 15, 84, 115, 149, 151, 155, 166, 168, 341
woodlands, 50
Wright Mills, C., 11
WWII, 137

X

xenophobia, 329, 365

Y

young, 7, 39, 66, 69–70, 115, 165, 223, 329, 365
   young children, 7, 165, 219, 223
   young people, xiii, 53–55, 85–86, 139, 155, 311–317, 329, 333
youth, xii, xxviii, 43, 55, 72, 154–155, 161, 164–165, 272, 274, 312, 374
Yugoslavia, 10, 43, 148–149, 167, 358, 373

Z

Zaragoza, 175, 371–372
ZER (Zonas Educativas Rurales), 176
Zounek, J., 10, 104, 106
ZPD (Zone of proximal (or potential) development, 160. *See also* Vygotsky, L.

Printed in Great Britain
by Amazon